The Good Government Man

Albert Coates

The Good Government Man

Albert Coates and the Early Years of the Institute of Government

HOWARD E. COVINGTON JR.

University Library
The University of North Carolina at Chapel Hill
Chapel Hill

Designed and typeset in Mailoa by
Kachergis Book Design, Pittsboro, North Carolina

Manufactured in the United States of America

The paper in this book meets the guidelines for permanence and durability of the Committee on Production Guidelines for Book Longevity of the Council on Library Resources.

cloth 10 11 12 13 14 5 4 3 2 1

Distributed by
THE UNIVERSITY OF NORTH CAROLINA PRESS
116 South Boundary St.
Chapel Hill, North Carolina 27514

Additional copies of this publication may be ordered by calling 1-800-848-6224 or from the Press's website, www.uncpress.unc.edu

LIBRARY OF CONGRESS CATALOGING-IN-PUBLICATION DATA

Covington, Howard E.
The good government man : Albert Coates and the early years of the Institute of Government / Howard E. Covington Jr.
Chapel Hill : University of North Carolina at Chapel Hill Library.
p. cm.
Includes bibliographical references and index.
ISBN 978-0-8078-3453-4 (cloth : alk. paper)
1. Coates, Albert, 1896–1989. 2. Institute of Government (Chapel Hill, N.C.)—Presidents—Biography. 3. University of North Carolina at Chapel Hill—Faculty—Biography. 4. Law teachers—North Carolina—Biography. 5. Public administration—Study and teaching (Higher)—North Carolina—Chapel Hill—History.
Coates University leadership series
LD3942.7.C36 C68 2010
378.0092B 22 2010036321

Coates University Leadership Series

Robert G. Anthony, Jr., Series Editor

Contents

Illustrations

between pages 76 and 77

Note: The illustrations are courtesy of the North Carolina Collection (NCC) and the Southern Historical Collection (SHC) at the University of North Carolina Library and the School of Government at the University of North Carolina at Chapel Hill (SOG).

Foreword

"Ay, God, le'me tell you what's so."

And to everybody who would listen, Albert Coates told what was so. For anyone out of earshot, he wrote letters by the thousands and published books and articles by the score.

A man of many words, indeed. But unlike the stereotypical academician whose text could be described as "a rivulet of prose trickling through a meadow of footnotes," Albert Coates crafted his narratives sentence upon sentence, all climaxing in his objective—the reformation of state and local government in his native state.

North Carolina was only gradually recovering from the effects of the Civil War and Reconstruction when Albert Coates was born during an equally dark period—the virtual race war of the 1890s. Raised in a state ruled by a single lily-white political party, the youngster shared the backwardness around him, and if his interest in a better North Carolina had not been sparked as a boy in Johnston County, it was ignited when as a student at the University of North Carolina he came under the spell of its young president, Edward Kidder Graham. From Graham, Coates imbibed the principle that the bounds of the university were coextensive with the borders of the state, and he dedicated his life to extending the influence of the institution to four state lines and the Atlantic Ocean. Only the Harvard University Law School pulled him away from North Carolina, and he returned as quickly as he could.

Within those bounds Albert Coates, in the following half-century, built a monument that does not bear his name, yet would not exist but for his untiring efforts and the assistance of staff members whom he skillfully recruited. The Institute of Government, though different in some ways from what he envisioned, has contributed more to the fairness, effectiveness, and efficiency of state and local government in North Carolina than any other institution devised by man. And Albert Coates was the man. During the middle fifty years of the twentieth century, few names associated with an academic institution were better known across the state's one hundred counties than Albert Coates's. He was a consummate university man to those whom he cultivated. That was the way he wanted to be remembered.

If history does not treat this crusader as favorably as his accomplishments merit, part of the explanation may lie in Coates's conviction that his way was the only route to his goal. His energy appeared endless, and for decades he and his wife, Gladys, sacrificed their domestic comfort—living below the standards of other university professors—by devoting portions of his meager earnings to the institution of his dreams. He was an indefatigable fundraiser who stretched the purchasing power of every dollar. Adjustment to economic reality and acceptance of compromise, however, were not among his strong suits, and his plans sometimes competed or conflicted with those of other academic personalities, departments, and politics. After retiring as director of the Institute, he could no longer count on the intense loyalty to which he had been accustomed from staff members, not all of whom he had hired personally. He also failed to adjust to the changing nature of the university community, an increasing number of whose faculty members exhibited less commitment to the citizens and institutions of the state. By the time he reached age ninety-two, he felt alienated and, instead of taking pride in the great Institute of Government that he and his staff had built, he imposed upon confidants a lengthy, sometimes bitter, critique that saddened his admirers. Equally sad, today's readers of his voluminous and often sermonic writings may yawn without fully realizing that recent progress—the expansion of his Raleigh Road building, the growth of the staff and services, and the designation of the Institute of Government as the School of Government—grew from the foundations laid by Albert Coates.

Inexplicably, not until after Coates's death did the university get around to naming the first Institute building on Franklin Street for the couple who had sacrificed to finance it, and few of the students who attend classes there today know why it bears the Coates name. Albert would, however, appreciate the symbolism of its location—across the street from Edward Kidder Graham's Memorial, the funds for which he helped raise, and up the street from the home of his other favorite professor, Horace Williams.

Although intense and purpose-driven in his professional life, Albert Coates could still exude warmth and charm to those who loved the state and supported his objectives; and, with the rough edges smoothed by the cultured, Virginia-born Gladys, the two were familiar in social circles. They entertained frugally but elegantly, and a measure of their friendship was inclusion on the mailing list for their annual Christmas greeting, which often featured one of Gladys's classic memories. The ultimate acceptance into their inner circle, however, was a visit from Albert's annual peach patrol—his Plymouth loaded with peaches from Clyde Auman's orchards in the Sandhills.

Albert Coates's story has been told in millions of his own words, but it deserves to be told more succinctly by an independent observer. This is it, the first volume in the Coates University Leadership Series. For one who did not know his subject in life, Howard Covington in his narrative comes close to verbally capturing the essence of Albert Coates, North Carolinian. The reaction of readers will depend upon their individual experiences with the man, his work, or his writings. For older readers who shared his sense of mission, Coates was an indefatigable crusader for whom consistency, insistency, and obstinacy were virtues. On the other hand—as is almost inevitable in the case of one whose career was so self-directed—readers may react, as did some of Coates's contemporaries, with less sympathy on the grounds that the path of compromise might have made his and his colleagues' lives less confrontational.

The origin of the Coates University Leadership Series helps explain Albert Coates, who early in his career learned how to enlist others in his cause. As it matured from the seed that he had planted, the Institute of Government appeared to no longer need the founder's intimate involvement. But Albert Coates was always a man with a mission, so he began searching for a new cause. Despite a modest salary, he and Gladys finally designed and paid for a handsome home—a valuable property by the 1980s—within two minutes' walk of the campus. Having no children, his thoughts turned to the disposition of his estate. As a founding member in 1975 of the North Caroliniana Society and as recipient of the Society's annual award for public service in 1980 (with Gladys as the surprise banquet speaker), he threw himself into the organization's objective of promoting increased knowledge and appreciation of North Carolina history. When in the following decade zeal for teaching state history waned both at the university and in the public schools, Albert Coates became deeply concerned. He frequently visited me in the North Carolina Collection in Wilson Library, which displayed a bust of him by William Hipp and a copy of a painting of him and Gladys by Sarah Blakeslee. In addition, our paths repeatedly crossed on South Road, nearly always resulting in mutual commiseration about the status of history and the waning tradition of public service. He began to recognize in the nonprofit North Caroliniana Society a vehicle for continuing his interests—an alternative to the university, which he no longer trusted to carry out his instructions. With each scenario discussed, he became more enthusiastic.

On February 24, 1988, however, despondency over heavy bills from a serious hospitalization led him to write anxiously, "It may mean that all our savings, together with our home, might be absorbed by the cost of health care. If it comes to this our plans for the North Caroliniana Society will die a'borning. 'The best laid schemes of mice and men gang aft a-gley.'" Our conversations continued during visits in his home, culminating in a lengthy and teary visit on December 31, about which I entered in my diary, "He wants Gladys to leave whatever is left of their estate to the Society for studies on the university and its presidents. . . . Albert Coates is one of our state's real treasures." Two days later, he wrote apologetically, "I am sorry my strength gave out when it did; you were getting into things I want to talk about."

That was the last time I heard from Albert Coates, and following his death twenty-six days later, I was dismayed to learn from Gladys that, uncharacteristically, he had not fully disclosed his plans to her. In subsequent discussions, it became clear that she had more faith than her late husband that the university would carry out his wishes. Consequently, in my letter to her during the Christmas holidays in 1991, I wrote: "In envisioning the endowment fund, Mr. Coates had in mind, in addition to the general support for the North Carolina Collection, a specific project: the research for and the writing and publication of biographies of all of the presidents and chancellors of the University of North Carolina" for whom no standard biography existed. I added, "Furthermore, though he never proposed it, I believe that both Mr. Coates and you should be subjects of a biography." Those suggestions were incorporated in her will, and on April 27, 1994, I had the pleasure of speaking during University Librarian Joe A. Hewitt's luncheon recognizing the magnificent bequest contained in Gladys Hall Coates's will. Still, seven more years passed before the university faculty granted an honorary degree to the benefactor, by then ninety-nine years old. She died on September 25, 2002, at the age of one hundred.

In 2004, Robert G. Anthony, Jr., my successor as curator of the North Carolina Collection, inaugurated the Gladys Coates University History Lecture Series, an appropriate annual recognition of Albert Coates's wife and partner, sometimes called a staff member of the Institute of Government "without portfolio." And now, two decades after her husband's death, comes Howard Covington's independent appraisal of Albert Coates, who, if he were here to read it, would find much with which to agree. Nonetheless, as was his wont, he would very probably demand a second opinion—his.

H. G. JONES
Chapel Hill

The Good Government Man

ONE

A Man of Many Words

1896–1914

ALBERT COATES was a man of many words.

He wrote them, spoke them, and piled them on in his arguments in favor of his causes with the sure conviction that sheer volume would ultimately allow him to prevail. He had his own favored subset of the English vocabulary, which generally included bursts of exasperated profanity, but he could easily transition into the profundity of the Bible, the beauty of the poets, and, perhaps the favorite of all, the wisdom of the men of the law. The students in one of his early classes at the University of North Carolina Law School, where he taught for nearly half a century, called him a "phonograph record of Justice [Oliver Wendell] Holmes." A quotation or lengthy passage of verse, once captured by the mind of Albert Coates, was a prisoner forever, to be paroled when he needed it for added emphasis.

In his later years he produced book after book recounting the different dimensions of his inspiration and aspirations for the Institute of Government in Chapel Hill that he organized as the "new University of Public Officials within the old University of North Carolina." The Institute was a masterful creation that continued long past his death in 1989 to assist and improve the service and function of local and state governments. His books about the Institute and civic service all carried distinctive Coatesian passages that first had to pass through the editing of Gladys, his wife and closest companion for more than sixty years. Coates wrote not for the eye, but the ear; his sentences rolled on for line after line with no period in sight. His work carried such a personal hallmark that a former colleague once remarked that if he found an unidentified Coates manuscript discarded on a garbage heap in Guatemala, he would recognize its author immediately.

Coates was a persuader whose carefully crafted verbal expressions advanced his struggles, his vision, his philosophy, and his belief in what citizens could produce if sufficient time and energy were applied in pursuit of a strong and vibrant democracy. He was one of the last of the talented orators to come from the campus at Chapel Hill just as the era of the celebration and development of forensic skills was on the wane. A few years after he graduated in 1918 the modern technology that arose following the Great War changed the way men used "the platform," as Coates called it. His talent for public speaking never failed him, and he could fine-tune a performance to the occasion and the audience, whether he was injecting an earthy anecdote to overcome the doubts of unlettered county sheriffs or presenting a display of erudition and logic that could capture the coveted Ames Prize from the Harvard Law School faculty. Sadly, only two recordings of his public speaking survived the years; neither is an example of the full range of his ability. One is of an address, written and read from the page, that Coates delivered in 1975 at a meeting of the University of North Carolina literary societies. The other is but a snippet and was captured at a 1959 luncheon honoring Thomas Wolfe.[1]

Coates was an old-fashioned patriot who appreciated the endowment of his Anglo-Saxon ancestry and the American legacy of citizen government. He went off to defend the nation in World War I and on returning home was motivated to improve the quality of government out of enthusiasm for what people then called the New South. First and foremost, however, he was a North Carolinian and founded virtually everything he wrote upon the state's historical record, which he knew intimately from the years of Charles II and his Lords Proprietors to the present day. Moreover, he was a proud son of Johnston County, just beyond the rolling hills of the Piedmont southeast of Raleigh, where his father farmed the land and his grandfather presided over the resurrection of local government in the tumultuous years following the Civil War.

Albert McKinley Coates was born on August 25, 1896, two months after William McKinley of Ohio was selected as the Republican Party's presidential nominee at the national convention in St. Louis. He was the grandson of John Rufus Coates, who on the appointment of William Holden, the state's provisional governor appointed by President Andrew Johnson at the end of the Civil War, was one of those responsible for reorganizing local government in Johnston County. The Coates name was well established in the area, and almost common.[2] John Rufus Coates's family had come to the area from Virginia. He served at various times as a county judge, a member of the General Assembly, a justice of the peace, tax assessor, chair of the board of county commissioners, postmaster, and superintendent of schools. He was, in short, a virtual Institute of Government unto himself. Siding as he did with William Holden during the years of Reconstruction, he was a Republican, and his politics was reflected in his grandson's middle name.

Albert's father was Daniel Miller Coates, who was six years old when Confederate troops fired on Fort Sumter. From time to time, young Daniel tagged along with his father, who was too ill to serve on the line and was commissioned to drill recruits and care for the families of men who marched off to fight with Robert E. Lee's army. As an officer of the Home Guard, John Rufus Coates also was charged with apprehending deserters. On one occasion he stood down an AWOL soldier who threatened him with a shotgun. Coates disarmed him and then told him to show up the next day to help train the new soldiers, if he wasn't too scared. John Rufus Coates passed his epaulets, sword, and pistol on to his eldest son, Daniel, who in turn, handed them down to Albert. "Pap won't for secession," Daniel Coates later told Albert's brother, Kenneth, "but when the state joined the Confederacy he sided with the state."[3]

Albert was among Daniel Coates's second crop of children. Three girls—Addie, Callie, and Vickie—were born to and survived his first wife, Mary Ann Byrd, who lost an infant son before her own death. Daniel Coates married again in 1888, and his second wife, Nancy Lassiter, gave birth to ten children. Albert was her fifth born. Her first son, Joseph Reid, died in infancy a year before Albert's birth and was buried in a homemade coffin near his grandfather's farm with a pink geranium folded in his hands.[4] Albert's three older sisters were Bessie, Dora, and Harriet. Four other sisters—Eva, Ethel, Edna, and Elizabeth—and his brother, Kenneth, came after Albert. The youngest, Elizabeth, was born in 1913, a year before Albert headed off to Chapel Hill.

Daniel Coates was a hard-working man, and something of an entrepreneur. John Rufus Coates distributed his own three-thousand-acre farm equally to his ten children, and Daniel worked his portion in the section of Johnston County known as Pleasant Grove, where he raised cotton and cut timber. He was fascinated with machinery and had a steam engine near a big pond that provided power for a sawmill and two cotton gins, as well as a flour and gristmill. A dispute with a neighbor led to a complaint being lodged in the fundamentalist church where the family attended services, so Daniel and Nancy picked up the family in 1901 and moved to an antebellum mansion two miles from the center of Smithfield, the county seat. The home was large enough to accommodate the growing family and it also offered easier access to the only decent school in the county, the Turlington Institute in Smithfield.

The house, a Johnston County landmark, was built in 1850 as the centerpiece of Agrippa Mitchener's cotton plantation. It was two stories tall and had a broad central hallway that allowed summer breezes to flow through open doors on the front and back. Large rooms flanked the hallway on either side. A staircase wound all the way to the attic, where an exit led to a widow's walk from which one could see for miles around. Underneath was a large cellar where the family stored sweet potatoes. There were wide porches on two levels across the front and back of the house, and the overhanging roof was supported by hollow columns that were two feet square and made of heart pine. It was in these columns that the mansion's owner, Mitchener's widow, Frances, managed to hide sixteen bushels of corn, thus keeping it out of the hands of Union foragers when they came through in the closing days of the Civil War. Following the battle at nearby Bentonville, General William Tecumseh Sherman's troops marched through Smithfield in April 1865 on their way to take control of Raleigh. By the time Daniel and Nancy Coates and their growing brood moved into the house on River Road it had lost some of its glamour but none of its historic mystique. At the time, it belonged to James H. Pou, the brother of the district's newly elected congressman, Edward W. Pou. James Pou was a lawyer, not a farmer, and he was in no position to care for the house and land. Soon after the family was settled in, the Coateses held a double wedding for Addie and Callie, Daniel's two oldest girls. There was ample room for both the ceremony and the lavish wedding dinner that followed.

The education of his children weighed heavily in Daniel Coates's decision to move closer to town. Education had long been important in the Coates family. John Rufus Coates had built one of the first schools in Pleasant Grove community on his own land and as county superintendent had helped organize the early public schools. Local and state support was meager, and the one-room schools in the farther reaches of the county were open for no more than four months of the year. The nearest school of any consequence was the Turlington Institute, where Ira Turlington had established a reputation as an excellent educator. Two of his former students were selected as Rhodes Scholars in the early years of the scholarship shortly after the turn of the century. His was a private school with its own military department and was large enough to accommodate 150 students who came from surrounding counties for a term of instruction that lasted from September to May. Classrooms filled a large two-story frame building accented with a distinctive bell tower. Daniel Coates believed his son had exceptional abilities and entered him into the first grade when he was five years old.[5]

Turlington's primary-grade teachers made a distinctive impression on young Albert, who said years later that he learned more than the basics of reading, writing, and arithmetic in their classrooms. "The teachers who meant the most to me in later years were those whose personalities came through the interstices in the subject matter of their teaching and helped me to go beyond the words and read between the lines."[6] In tribute, he brought his teachers magnolia blossoms that he picked from the tree that grew among the boxwoods, huge crape myrtles, and the "largest, oldest oak tree I have ever seen" surrounding the storied old mansion on River Road. Albert walked the two miles from his home to the school on Smithfield's Third Street, accompanied by his older sisters, who coached him on his lessons along the way. Albert's own accomplishments in his class inspired them in return.[7]

He was a precocious child who at a young age produced fearless solitary recitations in front of his class or a room full of adults. He practiced his lines late at night while lying in bed, much to the distraction of his brother. Albert gave speeches at school, but he also performed regularly at the Methodist church in Smithfield where the family attended services. Albert did so well when he first spoke at the Children's Day Exercises that he was asked to repeat year after year. Some in the congregation observed he would make a good preacher; others said he would be a bishop one day. When Albert finally learned that the ministers were promoting his performances because the congregation gave so generously when he spoke, he refused to participate ever again.[8]

Albert took to the religious instruction he received at the Methodist church as readily as to the lessons he learned in Ira Turlington's school. His Sunday School teacher, Mrs. Sadie Spiers, had an avid pupil. One year Albert collected fifty-two brightly colored butterflies for not missing a single Sunday. The Bible, the prophets, and the stories in the Old and New Testaments came alive to Albert in Mrs. Spiers's class. Years later, he would say she was the best teacher he had anywhere—at public school, at the university in Chapel Hill, or at Harvard Law School. "When in later years away from home I heard boys raise the question of whether there was a God," Coates wrote in 1969, "I had no doubt about it, for Mrs. Spiers had shown me his picture on her charts!"[9] His appreciation of the power of religion continued to grow as he spent occasional Sunday evenings visiting a nearby African American church. "I went to see the shouting," he later wrote, but it was more than that. The gospel songs and the powerful message of hope and redemption coming from the pulpit raised the members from their seats and were captured by the absorptive mind of the young man. In the early 1960s, at the height of the civil rights movement in North Carolina, Coates said that he never doubted that the prayers he heard for the removal of the chains of God's people would one day come true.[10]

Daniel Coates was a hard taskmaster when it came to Albert's contribution to the requirements of the farm. The boy had some free time—he bought a baseball glove on time at cousin Tom Hood's store in Smithfield—but mostly he worked when he was not in school. Albert later recalled that he believed his father had the notion that a man could solve his problems by working harder today than the day before. He would impose the same discipline on himself in the years ahead. Albert started as a water boy for the field hands when he was five or six and by the time he was nine or ten he was chopping weeds in the cotton field. He was put behind a plow when he was eleven. On occasion, he drove a team of mules that pulled wagonloads of timber out of the woods to a sawmill on the other side of Smithfield. Being out in the fields and in the woods with his father and the hired men gave him another level of education. There he learned the fine art of swearing and storytelling, and, after taking his first chew of tobacco, the difference between a swallow and a spit. He also came under the firm hand of discipline. His father brooked no foolishness from him or his brother. Idle behavior was handled on the spot, sometimes with a cotton stalk, full of green bolls, pulled from the field, which, Coates recalled, "could satisfy in a Johnston County cotton field all the purposes of the 'cat o'nine tails' in the British Navy."[11]

It was all part of growing up, and Albert grew up fast. One day, he was working with his father sawing lumber when a belt that regulated the flow of steam into the powerful engine flew off. Released from the belt, the engine began turning faster and faster, gaining momentum with each passing second. The rising pressure on the cylinders would have destroyed the engine and seriously injured those nearby if Albert had not jumped from his perch and closed the steam valve, which brought the contraption to a halt. "When the engine stopped, I caught my father's eye again. No word was said. He fixed the belt that put the governor back in operation and went on sawing lumber. I knew, my father knew, and everyone around there knew, that I was no longer a boy doing a man's work. In that moment I felt that my father was proud of his son, and I was proud of that fact."[12]

Albert finished his eleven years of public schooling in 1913, just as Smithfield's new three-story brick schoolhouse opened for students. The town was rising from its lowly status as little more than a country crossroads. By the end of the first decade, Smithfield had its own bank and was home to cotton mills and three warehouses for tobacco sales. The golden leaf was replacing cotton as the crop of choice among area farmers. There were no paved streets, but that didn't prevent the few automobiles in the area from puttering about and throwing such a scare into the horses and mules that the nearby town of Selma attempted to ban them from the streets. The town fathers said the cars were bad for business. There were road connections to Raleigh and Goldsboro, but travel for any distance was far faster by train. Smithfield's location meant rail connections in all directions were easily at hand. The same year, 1913, that Albert delivered the commencement address, Smithfield got a system of electric lights and a public water system. The service didn't extend into the county, however.

In the years just prior to his own graduation from school, Albert's older unmarried sisters, Bessie and Dora, had continued their education at the State Normal and Industrial College in Greensboro (later the University of North Carolina at Greensboro). Hattie left home, too, to begin studies that she hoped would lead to missionary service. At Christmastime, when they returned to spend the holidays at the large house on River Road, Albert would meet them at the train depot with a horse and buggy and carry them home. The family would sit around the table in the warmth of the kitchen, which extended off the back of the main house and was the warmest spot in winter, where all would listen to their stories of life beyond Smithfield. Albert was captivated by what they had to say, and upon his own graduation was ready to enter the university at Chapel Hill. He was well prepared, to be sure, but there was no money available for his education. Instead, he remained in Smithfield where he found a job at the bank.

Clearly Albert's prospects were better off the farm than on it. Daniel Coates had produced enough over the years to provide clothing, food, and shelter for his family, but he had never really prospered, partly because he often shifted from crop to crop without mastering any sufficiently to add to his wealth. Albert never doubted his future was elsewhere. He had learned the classics and much more under Ira Turlington and Adolph Vermont, his successor. Vermont was a Belgian who had been an instructor at the university at Chapel Hill before he succeeded Turlington as superintendent of the local schools. He was a student of the romance languages and knew the life, culture, and religion of many countries. Albert had gained an appreciation for English literature under Vermont, as well as for Latin literature. His course in Virgil was a study of both the writings and the man.[13]

Albert's job at the Bank of Smithfield introduced him to the rudiments of retail and commercial life. He could talk business with his mother's relations who ran small retail outlets, and he also found time to amble over to the Johnston County courthouse when he heard that Ed Abell was summing up a case for the defense. Abell was regarded as the best attorney around, and watching him hold a courtroom in awe was a delicious invitation to follow in his footsteps someday. Albert was being watched, too. He was known in town as a bright young lad, and his year at the bank assured those who ran the institution that he was a good risk. On the word of the bank's president, the Bank of Smithfield gave Albert an open note of $100 a year that he could draw upon as a college man. And with that he began making plans to begin his studies at Chapel Hill.

There was little that Albert had not taken advantage of during his first eighteen years. He had learned about the outside world from teachers who had invested themselves in his future. His parents had taught him the value of strength and resilience and overcoming obstacles large and small as they worked steadily and without complaint. They were serious and sober people whose faith was founded in the church and their own hard work. Businessmen in town had taken a liking to this industrious young man and were willing to put up hard cash to help him secure his future. Over and over again in the years ahead, family, mentors, and friends would become the steam for Albert Coates's engine, which, he would find, would every once in a while shake and rattle and even threaten destruction until some hand reached in to close the valve and restore balance, allowing Albert to proceed on his way.

TWO

"On the Hill"

1914–1918

ALBERT M. COATES arrived in Chapel Hill during the first week of September 1914 to begin his freshman year at the University of North Carolina as eager as any of the other 278 "new men" who had just arrived on the Hill. He didn't know, as he stepped onto the campus for the first time, that he was crossing the threshold into a world that would offer visions and inspiration for a lifetime that would be anchored firmly in the heart of the university.

Coates was not yet one month into his nineteenth year, so he was a few months younger, on average, than the others in the Class of 1918. Altogether, the student body numbered 855 when the university's new president, Edward Kidder Graham, opened the school's 120th year in a ceremony on September 10 under the soaring rafters of Memorial Hall. The total included a hundred more students than the year before, and there was word that the final enrollment could surpass a thousand by the time all the students had been accounted for when registration closed at the end of the week. The boost in enrollment drew a rousing cheer from the men—and a few women—who listened to Graham as the academic year got underway.

Charged with excitement and anticipation, Coates found a community that was a bit smaller and certainly more isolated than what he had known in Smithfield. In 1792, the university trustees, in response to the legislative charter, had chosen a site away from the early county-seat towns. People called Chapel Hill a village and meant it; the annual return of students in the fall nearly doubled the year-round population. The roads to Durham and Raleigh, the nearest cities of any size, were rough, unpaved, and narrow. There was no direct rail connection. The closest train station was a small depot in Carrboro about two miles from the campus. A spur line ran from there to University Station, which was ten miles north on the Southern Railroad main line west of Durham. Freshmen and upper classmen alike stood in line for shuttle services offered by drivers such as C. P. Pendergast—he was called "Colonel," though not because of any official military rank—who hustled passengers to and from Durham for a one-way fare of fifty cents.

Franklin Street was lined with large oaks and maples and constituted the northern boundary of the campus. The one block of wood-frame storefronts was Chapel Hill's center of commerce. Standing side-by-side in ranks facing one another Coates found a bank, a barber shop, a furniture store, two drug stores, a grocery store, Gooch's restaurant, the town's post office, Foister's stationery and Kodak store, and, farther down the street, the University Inn or Pickard's Hotel, a sorrowful excuse for public accommodations. There was a movie house called the Pickwick where admission was five cents. The Franklin street stores provided a living for a small group of merchants, but the university was Chapel Hill's sole reason for being. The university supplied jobs for local workers, and the university-owned utilities provided village residents with a reliable water supply, electric power, and telephone connections to the outside world.

Most of the faculty lived on East Franklin Street and, running parallel one block to the north, East Rosemary Street. Proper housing was a vexing problem for faculty members just arriving on campus. Bachelors usually took up residence in one of a number of rooming houses. Some of the senior faculty were comfortably housed in large homes that sat back from the street under aging trees. Senlac, the home of the venerable former president Kemp Plummer Battle—Class of 1848—was at the eastern edge of the campus. From there, Battle tended to the university's history and traditions and cleared paths through the adjoining woods, where many of the trees bore the carved initials of undergraduates from years gone by. It was a destination for men out strolling with their ladies, as well as a retreat for Sunday walks and soul-searching.

Yet, despite the cozy nature of the village and the generous reception given freshmen by President Graham, Coates found that Chapel Hill's warmth and familiarity extended only so far. One of Smithfield's best-known young men now was simply another new face to the local merchants that he encountered as he tried to get settled. When he went shopping for a table to outfit his rented room, he asked a Franklin Street storekeeper about credit and received a polite, but decided, brush-off. "There are two sorts of accounts I do not accept," Coates was told. "One is where the party is unreliable. The other is where the account is too small. Yours is too small!"[1]

Coates found that the campus he would come to love so dearly was full of curiosities. Some were inspiring, others were not. He saw no beauty in the knee-high rock walls that seemed to be everywhere. Some had been laid nearly a century earlier under the direction of Professor Elisha Mitchell, a transplanted New Englander who knew about such things. For Coates, the walls were a reminder that he had come recently from clearing ground where rocks were the death of plow points and could hobble man and beast. They belonged in a gully. Then there were the grassy lawns in front of the large homes on Franklin Street and the carpet of green in the "noble grove"[2] of maples, oaks, and poplars that shaded the campus from South Building all the way to Franklin Street, where three new dormitories—Battle, Vance, Pettigrew—stood side by side. "I had been brought up to be an enemy of grass—to kill it as I would a snake, to cut it out by the roots," he would later write. "A whipping had been in order when I snagged it and left the roots to sprout again."[3]

While the impressive registration figures announced by President Graham had produced loud cheers, the growing student population meant only more difficulties for the new men like Coates. Seniors had the pick of the dormitory rooms, and by the time the selections opened to freshmen there was little available. At times the sidewalk outside the post office was stacked with the trunks and baggage of homeless students. Many of the local residents took in roomers, and the address Coates supplied for the student directory issued by the Young Men's Christian Association (YMCA) was the home of George Pickard, the university's superintendent of buildings and grounds. Coates lived there with five other freshmen and took his meals on campus at Swain Hall, which was the newest building on campus. A man could eat there for a month on $12.50.

"Taking early impressions all together," Coates later wrote, "I knew I was being introduced into a strange new world, but I was not sure it was the Promised Land." He had done well enough against the competition at Turlington Institute, he observed, but "in Chapel Hill I was meeting boys who came from homes throughout the state and beyond—the best that North Carolina had to offer—and I felt the enlarging power of a new dimension that would expand my horizon and stretch the powers to their limits."[4]

Despite Smithfield's small size and limited resources, the Turlington tradition had given him a foundation in the fundamentals, and as Coates settled into his classes he found teachers like those at home who committed themselves to their students. His first personal contact with a full-blooded faculty member was in the home of Oliver Towles, an associate professor of romance languages who had been assigned as Coates's faculty advisor. It was the first year of such a system. President Graham had introduced it to help freshmen make the transition to university life. As instructed, Coates and a couple of other students found their way to Towles's home, which stood a block off campus at the corner of East Rosemary Street and Hillsborough Street.

Towles put his guests at ease. He was a young man himself, having started his own college career at the University of Virginia only twelve years earlier. He chatted with Coates and his mates and then brought out some wine in the thinnest, most fragile glasses Coates had ever seen. North Carolina was thoroughly dry and Smithfield was parched, and had been for at least five years. Coates's Methodist raising had taught him never to look upon alcohol, much less take a drink. He accepted the offer of a glass, nonetheless. Coates later recalled that when it came time to leave, the students thanked Towles for his hospitality and Towles replied: "Don't mention it." One of Coates's chums responded with a guilty whisper, "We won't."[5]

Proper behavior was expected of everyone on the Hill. Preachments on gentlemanly behavior came in editorials in the *Tar Heel*, the weekly newspaper underwritten by the Athletic Association, and in daily chapel meetings in Gerrard Hall, which enjoyed a full house due to required attendance. Only recently, President Graham had freed the chapel schedule from the "university sermon" delivered by a visiting clergyman to allow more time for student discussion and debate on secular issues and matters of state and national interest. Graham himself often presented the program and infused in students a sense of duty and obligation to the honor and dignity of the university and the part they would play in its life during their time on campus. Graham's advice and counsel became firmly planted in Coates's mind.

"In President Graham's eyes we were not simply students in the University, he greeted us as her sons," Coates later wrote.[6] Graham talked of duty to the state and the nation, as well as the obligation of the men to be true to themselves. They had been given a special opportunity. Graham's own spirituality and Presbyterian upbringing permeated his chapel talks, and he often called upon his minister, the Reverend W. D. Moss, for invocations and God's blessings at special campus events. "Parson Moss," as he was called, wore a high clerical collar and a properly pinched Presbyterian expression that belied a deep warmth and care for the young men whose lives he touched. Coates had been raised in the Methodist church but he would later call on Moss to officiate at his wedding. "He would talk over our problems and perplexities with us by the hour and help us get tangles out of our thinking," Coates wrote.[7]

The overlay of moral rectitude and honor did not preclude lapses into raucous behavior. Gambling and drinking were frowned upon, but they took place nonetheless, along with less serious hijinks. When Coates and his fellow freshmen gathered at Gerrard Hall to elect class officers and get organized for the year, they were assailed by water-filled paper bags tossed from the balcony by the sophomores, who also heaved the hymn books in their direction. The incident brought a rebuke from the *Tar Heel*'s editor, who chided the ambushers and called upon the freshmen to refrain from retaliation.

The center of campus activities and organizations was the YMCA, whose building was just off the quadrangle formed by the Old Well and three of the oldest buildings on the campus, Old East, Old West, and South. The YMCA nurtured the spiritual life of the student body through regular evening discussions and events. On Sundays, teams of students headed into the adjoining countryside to lead Bible studies in rural churches. During one of Coates's years as an undergraduate, the YMCA secretary was an engaging young graduate and history professor-to-be named Frank Graham, who would later succeed his cousin in the university presidency. By the time of Coates's senior year, Coates himself would be the one standing before incoming freshmen to tell them about the spiritual supplement that the YMCA provided for their university life.

If young men followed the weekly regimen suggested by the YMCA and published in the *Tar Heel,* they would lead lives of rectitude. According to the plan, each weekday and Saturday should include nine hours of study or classroom work, eight hours of sleep, an hour and a half for meals, and four hours of free time for exercise, the post office, or reading. An hour and a half of daily "conversation" was recommended. On Sundays, after a half-hour for breakfast, the suggested schedule included Bible class before church with an hour of Bible study after morning services. The afternoons were for strolls, letters, meditation, or work in the rural Sunday schools, with the evenings devoted to supper, another church service, and then two hours for writing letters, conversation, and reading before bed at ten o'clock.

"The *Tar Heel* recommends this schedule to every college student who wishes to make the most out of his year's work,"the paper said.[8] And there is every indication that Coates followed this advice.

Edward Kidder Graham's first year as president was just beginning in the fall of 1914. His lean, youthful appearance and athletic vigor—he excelled in tennis and, as a youth, at baseball—made him a bright, refreshing presence amidst campus elders such as Kemp Battle, "Old Pres," who often turned up for special occasions and announced his arrival with the tap, tap, tap of his cane as he walked into an assembly. Battle, thin and a bit frail, looked for all the world like a leprechaun with his full cheeks and a bushy white beard that began at his temples and followed his jaw line to his chin. He had come to campus as president in 1876, one year after the university reopened following Reconstruction, and it seemed he had remained on Earth in order to hand the school off to a man who would carry it toward greatness in the new century. Graham was that man, everyone seemed to think. He stood a full head taller than his old teacher, and when he reached full stride his long legs would carry him quickly past his companions.

Graham enjoyed a devoted following among both faculty and students. His influence was deep and lasting upon young men who, in the decades ahead, would become North Carolina governors, congressmen, and outstanding leaders in the professions and industry. He inspired his academic family with a pronounced vision of service to the university, and through its good works, to the entire state. Graham was just beginning to launch the university on a program of outreach that would reshape the institution and bring into its universe eager and talented teachers. Coates fully embraced Graham's philosophy as an undergraduate and then would spend his own life in dedication to it.

Graham was a role model for students and teachers alike. He had been an outstanding undergraduate during his years at Chapel Hill in the mid-1890s. "His college record was distinguished for soundness of scholarship, high ideals, and a passion for fair play and square-dealing—a record that was prophetic of the great service he was to render in his later career," wrote Louis R. Wilson, who knew him well.[9] Graham was teaching school in Charlotte when President Edwin A. Alderman brought him back to the campus in 1899 as librarian and an instructor in English. In the succeeding years he was an inspiring teacher of journalism, advanced composition, essays, and oration before he left the campus for about a year to pursue a master's degree in English at Columbia University. On his return in 1907 he was named a full professor and chair of the English department, and two years later he became dean of the college of liberal arts. When a mentally and physically exhausted Francis Venable, Alderman's successor as president, left for a year's rest in Europe in June 1913, Graham was appointed acting president.

At the outset of the new century, Venable had taken on the burden of refitting the university and increasing financial support for what was by all accounts an institution struggling to survive. During his tenure, he weathered sessions with stingy legislators who stubbornly resisted his call to respond to the university's desperate need for capital improvements. Many in Raleigh labored under the notion that higher education was the responsibility of church-supported colleges such as Davidson, Wake Forest, and Trinity and not the state of North Carolina. Some believed the university served only the state's elite families and provided "a place of retirement to develop gentlemen of culture."[10] Venable persevered against this headwind, and during his administration sixteen buildings were occupied, purchased, or built. In addition, modern conveniences such as adequate electric lighting, central heat, and proper sanitation came to the campus.

Further burdening the president was the furor of alumni who were unhappy with the school's athletic program, as well as the aftermath of a hazing incident in September 1912 that resulted in the death of Isaac William Rand. The Smithfield freshman fell from atop a barrel, where students had forced him to sing and dance, and cut his throat on a broken bottle. At commencement in 1913, Venable asked for a leave of absence, and a year later he tendered his resignation. Graham was the first choice of the trustees to replace him.

Graham eagerly accepted the position and set about to move the campus beyond the issues of bricks and mortar. These things were important and he would continue to press the legislature for greater funding, but he was first and foremost a teacher, and by his philosophy it was the state's teachers who would shape the future by producing citizens who would place community above self. Further, he said, "the University was the State's principal instrument for the achievement of its high purposes."[11]

He believed in what he called "everyday patriotism," where enlightened and educated citizens promoted a government that cures diseases, purifies foods, digs canals, and "educates, strengthens, gladdens and beautifies communities in a thousand ways, not in a spirit of alms-giving, but by enlightened public generosity for public development and progress." And it was teachers who were the "guardians of the ideas of the prosperous North Carolinians of the next generation. The wealth of North Carolina must be turned to civic service. It can come only through full acceptance of the primacy of the community idea, and only the teachers of the state can put this idea into the mind of the state."[12]

Graham had first expressed this vision five years earlier in a speech to a gathering of teachers, and by the time of his formal inauguration in April 1915 he had expanded his philosophy to include the university as the principal instrument for extending the state's resources from the isolation of Chapel Hill to the far boundaries of a state that reached from the mountains to the sea. The university, he said, was the "instrument of democracy" for realizing the aspirations of a people and a state.

As the 1914–1915 academic year got underway, Graham's program of outreach was already touching public school students and their teachers, university alumni, and public officials in nearly all of the state's hundred counties. The year before, Graham had created a bureau of extension and put the university's librarian, Louis R. Wilson, in charge of opening the doors of the university to the world beyond the campus. The library offered the loan of books and in its first year responded to seventeen hundred letters of inquiry from people around the state. The university offered more than thirty correspondence courses, and the summer school was expanded with a registration of more than five hundred in 1914. Wilson enlisted faculty members in a speakers' bureau to carry all manner of subjects to town-hall meetings and community centers around the state. A reference service for city, county, and state officials was organized to provide information on comparative legislative material. Wilson launched the *University News Letter* in the fall of 1914 and mailed it to four thousand citizens. The weekly one-page publication included news from the university, debate outlines, and information compiled on individual counties by the newly organized North Carolina Club.

The North Carolina Club was the product of E. C. Branson, a native of North Carolina whom Graham had recruited from Georgia to replicate what he had started there. Branson called his field of study rural-social economics, but by the 1920s it would come under the broader description of sociology after he was joined by Howard W. Odum, who formed an entire department around the subject. Branson recruited students for the club, where they organized themselves according to their home counties. Throughout the year, members gathered data and details about the economic, political, and social conditions back home that were then compiled and organized into the first systematic survey of life on a local level.

"It is a know-your-home-state club," read an enthusiastic description in the 1914 edition of the *Yackety Yack*, the campus yearbook published by the campus fraternities. "Its nucleating belief is that intimate, loving acquaintance with the Mother-State means real education, vital culture, and effective training for competent citizenship." During its first year, club members heard presentations on the diminishing meat supply in North Carolina, the "food-producing and wealth-retaining power of farm communities," and the "inequalities of farmland assessment [for taxation] in North Carolina." The topics weren't the kind to stir orators to full voice, but the presentations offered practical assessments of issues affecting the viability of the state and the communities to which Branson's students would return more fully informed as they set out to build careers and raise families. From the outset, Albert Coates was captivated by Graham's vision of the university as an instrument of service. Branson's plan of promoting interest in one's home county and in building up local government was another seed that was planted deep. Coates began his college career on a mission to fulfill such a responsibility to his community, perhaps as a teacher, a career a number of North Carolina leaders had chosen initially before they distinguished themselves in government, the law, and business. In his freshman, sophomore, and junior years Coates accepted a $60-a-year "loan" to cover the cost of his tuition. The money was made available to students willing to devote at least two years to teaching in North Carolina schools after graduation. Coates also was no stranger to thoughts of running for public office and brought with him to Chapel Hill a latent interest in law and government. In time, he would combine his interest in teaching and in the law and government in ways that even Branson and Graham could not have imagined.

Public affairs seemed to be Coates's deeper ambition. He wasted no time in making himself ready to deliver his first speech, should the occasion arise. In his freshman year, he joined the Philanthropic Literary Society, which along with the Dialectic Literary Society was one of the two organizations whose distinguished histories were as old as the university itself. Their most visible contribution to campus life was the university's library, which had tripled in holdings when the societies combined their private collections and their sixteen thousand books became available to all students. Throughout much of the nineteenth century, society membership was required of all men, with the "Di" gathering its members from the western part of the state, while those from eastern North Carolina, like Coates, joined the "Phi."

By 1914, participation in the societies was no longer compulsory as other activities had begun to intrude on a man's time, but the Phi and the Di remained an important part of campus life. They cultivated the art of debate and offered those willing an opportunity to take part in competitions equal to those a man might find at Harvard, Princeton, or Columbia. Debate retained its status for honor and distinction; an orator was more than a good speaker. He was a person who could take the sum of his learning and organize it in such a way as to persuade others to his point of view. It was a high skill, one practiced by the most accomplished of public men, and Albert set out to expand on the experience he had already gained on a lesser stage in Smithfield.

With membership no longer compulsory, the Phi and the Di became selective. As a result, much of the campus leadership rose from their ranks. Their main purpose was to provide a forum for discussion at weekly meetings, which were held on Saturdays in the societies' carpeted and curtained chambers on the upper floor of New East (Phi) and New West (Di), where portraits of notable graduates from earlier classes hung on the walls. In the spring of 1915, Coates won the freshman debater's medal, and he joined in to assist when 250 high school debaters arrived on campus for the final rounds in a statewide debating union. This competition was another of President Graham's devices to connect the university to local communities. Directly and indirectly, the debating union engaged thousands of young people and their families in discussion about issues of the day, such as the question of women's suffrage or the government ownership of railroads. The competition also was a late manifestation of the role of public speaking in developing leadership among young men.

In the classroom, Coates was most taken with his courses in English, literature, and the classics. He enjoyed Frank Graham's history course, where the class was turned into the United States Senate and students recreated the Hayne-Webster debates.[13] He later described Collier Cobb's geology course that he took in his sophomore year as "the nearest thing to a general science course for popular consumption that the university had ever afforded to the rank and file." Cobb had been to the outer reaches of the world, including the Orinoco jungle in South America. According to Coates, Cobb described the influence of heredity and environment by telling his students, "We are what we are largely because of where we are." Coates said it was more a course in the personality of Professor Cobb than it was about the history and structure of the Earth.[14] If a place shaped a man, Chapel Hill was certainly shaping Albert Coates.

Coates didn't fare as well in physics, where his professor, A. H. Patterson, the dean of the school of applied sciences, wondered why Coates had failed physics while he seemed to succeed in his other courses. (It was a shortcoming that cost him his chance for a Phi Beta Kappa key.) "I told him it was my fault and not his," Coates later wrote, and "that I had put most of my time on courses which I thought would do me the most good in law and government; that I had allowed what I thought was enough time to pass the courses in physics and French, which I was taking for the sole purpose of a college degree; and that I had won the gamble in French and lost the gamble in physics."[15]

Patterson told Coates he was wrong in his strategy for completing his requirements for graduation. There was more to the college experience than winning high grades. He advised that every student should "take one distasteful course, or a course under a distasteful teacher and do his level best to make his highest grade on that course for the sake of the discipline involved," Coates wrote. "I was respectful and appreciative, but not convinced—until I saw the best men in school doing as well on one course as another, whether they liked the course or not and whether they liked the professor or not."[16]

Edward Kidder Graham reinforced Patterson's admonitions. "No student is truly trained," Graham told the men gathered for one chapel meeting in a message that lingered long with Coates, "unless he has learned to do pleasantly, and promptly, with clean-cut accuracy every task he has obligated himself to do." The balance of Graham's instruction was that in addition to discipline, a truly trained student needed curiosity, the qualities of a true gentleman, and a realization that he does not live alone, "but is part of an organic community life that is the source of most of the privileges he enjoys."[17]

Coates enjoyed his lessons in literature and the classics because they comfortably complemented his attraction to debating, where he developed his natural talents as a public speaker. Professor Norman Foerster had Coates in his freshman literature class, where he led him through *Essays for College Men*. Foerster pushed his students to penetrate the essays of Thomas Henry Huxley, William James, Woodrow Wilson, and Matthew Arnold and attempt to discover their essence. "It was not enough to read the lines; we had to read between the lines, get the author's tones and overtones, put them in our own words, and make them our own."[18] Coates received the same treatment in Foerster's Victorian literature course and a semester in advanced composition. The young debater's public presentations likewise penetrated subjects in ways that won him honors.

Coates deepened his understanding of these writers and their ideas under the prodding of Professor Horace Williams, whose course in logic occupied him in his junior year. "It was a course that threw light on all other courses and helped us get into them," Coates wrote, "not a key opening a particular door of learning, but a master key useful in opening all doors."[19] Williams wanted each student to achieve a "Eureka moment" when they could honestly say they had "got it." Each man was pushed to develop his own concept, or "begriff," as Williams called it, that arrived at a conclusion and gave his life purpose.

Coates and Williams already knew one another well before Coates reached the philosopher's classroom. The old professor coached the campus debaters, and over the years Coates often found his way to Williams's house on what was then the edge of Chapel Hill and asked for a review of his debate preparations or his papers. Coates later recalled that "many an evening I heard him say: 'It won't do Mr. Coates, it won't do.' 'What is wrong with it?' I would ask. And he would answer, 'All you've got is a lot of plank nailed together. What you need is a growing tree.'"[20] Coates became as dear to Williams as a son and the professor would inspire his student to consider furthering his education at Harvard, his own alma mater.

Coates easily absorbed and retained the language of the greats from his extensive reading in English literature, Greek drama, Latin, and selections from Professor Edwin Greenlaw's Elizabethan dramatists. He kept passages from the greatest writers of all time, and Frank Graham's lessons in history, in reserve to use on command as the underpinning of his oratory or as seasoning for his polished presentations at the Phi, where he won honors in his sophomore and junior years. In the fall of 1916, largely on his reputation as the best orator in his class, if not the entire campus, Coates was elected junior class president and chosen for other offices with the Phi, the board of campus publications, and the Greater Council, which handled student disciplinary matters and violations of the honor code. At the College Night activities at the YMCA, where he roomed for his junior year, he delivered the gospel to the freshmen on the duty of each student to respect the honor system.

Coates's resume expanded with each passing season. The only segment of campus activities to which he devoted little, if any, time, was athletics, where he limited his participation to that of an enthusiastic spectator. He also seemed to have little time for matters of the heart. For a time, Coates was attracted to the sister of his friend Albert Oettinger, but nothing grew out of that relationship.[21]

His life was certainly full. Throughout his four years he was employed at one campus job or the other, as were many of his classmates in the self-help program in which students worked for the university to offset the cost of their education. In his freshman year, he worked in the office of Charles T. Woollen, the school's business manager. One other year he was the linen steward at Swain Hall. When he was a senior, President Graham assigned him to assist E. C. Branson and the work of the North Carolina Club. The campus jobs, his teacher loans, and the annual advance from the Bank of Smithfield, covered his tuition, room, and board, and kept him clothed in the uniform of the day, a dark suit, white shirt, and stiff collar.

If anything, he may have tried to cram too much of the university life into his days. It wasn't until later, when he arrived at Harvard Law School, that he understood the importance of the advice of Patterson, President Graham, and Edwin Greenlaw, who sat Coates down for a frank talk about his grades three weeks into his senior year. Coates had failed to show up for Greenlaw's classes on Spenser's *Faerie Queen*, and he asked to be allowed to drop the course. Greenlaw insisted he stick with it. "He told me I would get 'discipline' out of it, and he didn't know anybody who needed discipline more than I did. I told him I was looking for literature and not for discipline, and it looked like discipline was all I was going to get." Greenlaw broke into laughter at that point and approved the request.[22]

Coates's first love was "the platform," as he would come to call speaking engagements that would fill his calendar for years to come. He was a regular at the YMCA evening discussions, often with topics that reflected the lessons of President Graham, his role model and personal hero. Two of Coates's presentations covered by the *Tar Heel* dealt with patriotism and citizenship as it related to a man's responsibility to the university. "Mr. Coates contended that not peace, but righteousness should be our aim as citizens of this great community," the *Tar Heel* reported. Coates had said, "We have no written laws by which we are governed; neither have we a Student Council, as policeman, to watch our every action. Our laws are purely and simply those of a gentleman and, as such, supreme. So long as we faithfully obey these laws we execute a moral obligation to the community. But when we violate them, we give not to ourselves a black eye, but we cast discredit upon the community we represent as citizens."[23]

William T. Polk, the *Tar Heel*'s editor, gave generous coverage to appearances by his good friend Albert. Almost weekly reports of his presentations only raised Coates's stature on the campus as he continued to expand his reputation as an orator. Before his junior year was completed, he learned his facility with words and talent for public presentations could improve even his financial situation. In the spring of 1917, he won the Julian S. Carr award by placing first in the junior oratorical contest and went on to compete in the intercollegiate Peace Oratorical contest held in Greensboro in April, where he took home the $75 first-place cash prize.

Coates won the honors with an organized argument that justified America's recent entry into the war in Europe. It was founded in his readings of history and propelled by passion and patriotism. Democracy had grown and flourished in the United States, he said, because it had remained free of foreign entanglements, just as George Washington had argued in his farewell address. But the world was far different in 1917 than it had been more than a century before. The United States was "no hermit nation," and "for any nation to attempt to live unto herself alone is to be untrue to herself and false to the highest interests of the world which is her home." In bold, florid lines, punctuated with patriotic flourishes—but with no acknowledgement of the irony—Coates made a stirring case for peace while arguing for America's entry into the European conflict. "And America, presented with the greatest opportunity the world has yet offered to any nation, with no imperial design, with no material end to blur her vision, but desiring solely to make the right prevail, stands forth today, idealized and immortal, the founder of the league to enforce peace."[24]

President Graham had welcomed the Class of 1918 to Chapel Hill just as the warring nations of Europe were organizing for a conflict that would devastate towns and villages from the Black Sea to the Atlantic Ocean and create human carnage like never before. In Graham's welcome, he had made reference to the billowing war clouds and asked the freshmen to consider how the declarations of war across the sea would eventually hasten the brotherhood of man. Over the coming years the Germans pushed through Belgium and into France, and the combatants became stalemated in trench warfare organized by generals immune to the waste of human life. But the war didn't touch isolated Chapel Hill. The *Tar Heel* carried nothing of consequence about the horrific battles, some of which consumed as many as seven thousand lives an hour. The debate topics at the Phi and Di were focused on domestic issues, such as state ownership of the telegraph, regulation of interstate commerce, and prohibition. One competition did raise the issue of independence for the Philippines. In 1915, when former President William Howard Taft was on the campus for three days to talk about the powers and limitations of being president, there was nothing of note said about the war in Europe.

That changed early in 1917. Students began to take notice of the war after alumni and former students who had served with the National Guard on the Mexican border returned for campus visits. About a hundred students, and ten faculty members, were making preparations to enter military service. In January, even before the March inauguration of President

Woodrow Wilson—the man who had campaigned for reelection on keeping America out of war—President Graham received a petition signed by nearly a third of the students (344 out of 1,137 registered in the fall) asking that a course in military training be organized on the campus.

The roused students in Chapel Hill actually came late to a movement begun on campuses elsewhere. General Leonard Wood had started small training sessions for college students as early as 1913. One of them took place near Asheville. The *Tar Heel's* editor, William Polk, put the paper solidly behind the petition drive and said Chapel Hill men could do no less than students elsewhere who had made themselves ready to serve. Writing on Polk's editorial page, junior George B. Lay of Raleigh observed that Harvard University had sent half of its student body to one of Wood's training sessions in Plattsburg, New York, in the summer of 1916. A few men on campus, including football coach and Harvard graduate T. J. Campbell and Dr. James B. Bullitt of the university's medical school, had been to a session in Plattsburg.

Virtually overnight, the entire campus rallied behind the growing move toward preparation for war. President Graham had long been encouraging Wilson to become engaged in the European conflict and had told Josephus Daniels, a university trustee and Wilson's secretary of the navy, that he planned to resign his position and enlist as a private. Wilson sent word to Graham by Daniels that he should do no such thing.[25] Instead, Wilson's message to Graham was that he should remain at the university and prepare men to serve their country. Graham complied and arranged for the formation of a voluntary training program in advance of the day when military instruction would be formally added to the curriculum. Plans were laid for a reserve officers program to be launched in the fall. In the meantime, when the first call came for participation in the hastily organized training program on campus, almost half of the student body turned out and they were organized into four companies.

By the time the United States formally entered the war on April 6, 1917, men were already reporting twice weekly for marching drills on an athletic field behind South Building that had been illuminated with electric lights. Julius Cone of Greensboro, whose nephew Ben was among the recruits, purchased 250 Civil War-era rifles for the men to use in the drills. The campus armory was later increased by fifty modern Springfield rifles that were secured for target practice. Some volunteers took up flag signal drills and "wireless telegraphy."[26] Officers of the National Guard back from the Mexican border duty served as drill instructors.

That April, a visiting war correspondent, Frederick Palmer, drew a crowd of about five hundred to Memorial Hall for his talks about life at the front in the Somme region of northern France, where the British army had suffered 57,470 casualties in one day. He illustrated his presentations with pictures and vivid descriptions of the new machines of war, including airplanes, machine guns, and tanks. He held his crowd for three hours.[27]

Two weeks after Congress declared war on Germany on April 6, about twelve hundred people packed into Memorial Hall to hear President Graham commit the university to the war effort. "The single thought of the University is to co-operate in every intelligent way with the government."

"Ours is a larger task than that of the French Revolution, the American Revolution or the American Union," Graham said. "It is the continuation of the supreme issue for which those great causes were fought—the structure of steps toward a permanent peace that all nations 'under God shall have a new birth of freedom,' and toward a world unity of the great common cause of living together for all mankind."[28]

Coates blended the same theme and historic references into his own text a week later in Greensboro, where he won the sixth annual Intercollegiate Peace Oratorical contest. His manuscript was submitted to the twenty-second annual Peace Conference at Lake Mohonk, New York, the sponsor of another oratorical contest. A few days before the conference was due to open, Mary Helen Seabury of New Bedford, Massachusetts, wrote to tell Coates, "The idea of a united world is indeed a grand idea and we wish it could be, to use one of Mr. Beals' original expressions, a 'pan-human kingdom.'"[29] The conference didn't convene that summer because of the onset of war, and Coates lost the opportunity to win a $100 prize for his work.

He had other honors aplenty. Before the 1917–1918 academic year ended in somewhat ragged fashion for those who were already in uniform, Coates completed his term as class president and was chosen for the Order of the Golden Fleece. He was also elected president of the Athletic Association, which ran the student publications as well as the campus athletic program. By the time the juniors met for their last event of the year, the class was down to only 80 of the 278 men who had arrived in 1914. Thirteen had been accepted into the army's new Reserve Officers Training Camp program at Fort Oglethorpe in northern Georgia, along with seventy-nine other

Carolina men, including graduate students, students in the professional schools, and alumni. Fort Oglethorpe, active in the Spanish-American war, had been recently reopened as a training camp. Those in the Class of 1917 who left the campus ahead of graduation for military service were given credit for the remainder of the term if they were accepted into officer training. Inductions were completed so hastily that men were asked to provide their own uniforms, if possible.

The commencement ceremonies in June became a full-blown patriotic rally. Graham urged alumni to return to campus to hear Navy Secretary Daniels and Secretary of War Newton D. Baker. Memorial Hall overflowed with visitors to the campus.

Coates did not return to Smithfield and the family farm at the close of the term as he had for the two previous summers. Instead, he remained in Chapel Hill, where he assisted President Graham in recruiting the freshman class due to arrive in September. One of the concerns of the president, and other academic leaders across the country, was that enrollment at colleges and universities would suffer from the patriotic enthusiasm of young men eager to get into the fight in Europe. Graham was also making preparations for a more structured assistance to the war effort, including military training that would be offered for course credit. Throughout the summer, Graham was often away as part of the education committee of the Council of National Defense.

When classes resumed in September 1917, the ranks of students and faculty had been thinned. Ten faculty members, including Coates's freshman advisor, Oliver Towles, had been given leave for military service. Frank Graham had enlisted as a private in the Marines. One hundred fifty former students were in training at Oglethorpe. Coates remained with his class and paid ten dollars for a uniform and cotton leggings and joined the ranks of the third platoon of Company A, one of four companies organized as part of the new military training program under the command of Captain J. Stuart Allen, a Canadian and twice-wounded veteran of the fighting in France. Coates and more than half of the student body participated in a far more rigorous program than the one that had been hastily organized in the spring. At the outset, most of the activity consisted of squad and platoon marching movements. Two-hour afternoon drills were held on Mondays, Wednesdays, and Fridays. At 8 a.m. on Tuesdays, Thursdays, and Saturdays the men gathered for another two-hour session. Lectures in military subjects were given three days a week. In October, the governor came to Chapel Hill for an official review.

The military exercises would expand throughout the year as men built trenches and barbed-wire emplacements and then performed simulated assaults such as those Allen had led in France. No one seemed to mind the effort, even when the school's fall intercollegiate football program was suspended for the duration. The students made do with inter-company rivalries. Fifty men turned out to continue practicing in anticipation of an eventual renewal of the hard-fought rivalry with the University of Virginia.

In his senior year, Coates lived in Battle Dormitory, one of the residential halls that had opened in 1912. He shared room 11 with C. G. Tennant of Asheville, the editor of the *Tar Heel*. Close by in other Battle rooms were his friends Albert Oettinger, Robert Madry, and an ambitious young member of the *Tar Heel* staff who would later succeed Tennant as editor, a sophomore named Thomas C. Wolfe of Asheville.

Coates was one of the leading men on campus and he seemed to be everywhere. As head of the Athletic Association, he participated in the decision to cancel the football season. Once again, he introduced freshmen to their duties as Carolina men and delivered a recruiting message for volunteers for the YMCA and its programs in rural Sunday schools, Negro night schools, Corn and Tomato Clubs, and a Boy Scout program.

He was president of the North Carolina Club and launched it into what would prove to be its most productive year. Sixty counties were represented at the organizational meeting that Coates called to order in late September 1917. His remarks were straight from the heart of one of President Graham's speeches and included the essence of what eventually would become Coates's own life's work. The club connected the university to the local community, he told the new men. "With the [club's] aid," Coates said, "the students may find the facts as to where their home county leads, where it lags, and the way out, and by conveying this knowledge to the people back home render a great service. In doing this work the students will also train themselves in details of citizenship."[30]

Over the coming months, Coates would bring to the campus a wide range of speakers for the club's monthly meetings. In October, a superior court judge talked about courthouse customs. The following month the group heard about local taxation. Before the end of the year, the subjects would include home demonstration programs that were improving the quality of rural life, public health, juvenile delinquency, the adequacy of the state's bridges, and problems in rural school districts.

It was a heady time for Coates. As Branson's chief assistant, he was charged with greeting each of the visiting speakers, showing them around the campus, and generally attending to their needs while they were in town. The added exposure to the guest lecturers further encouraged Coates to pursue his own curiosity about his native state. The research of the club members formed the basis for a 188-page report on the state's counties that would be published in October 1918.[31] Seven years later, E. C. Branson would resurrect the subject and make it part of a major reform of county government under Governor Angus McLean. It also would be reflected in Coates's own missionary work in aid of local government in the decade thereafter.

At the same time that Coates was driving the North Carolina Club forward, he was trying to reform the Phi. As its new president, he pushed through new rules for collecting fines from men who missed meetings as a way to erase a debt of $75. (The Di Society had a healthy bank account of $700.) The purpose of the society, Coates told the Phi's 120 members, is self-expression, something that he clearly enjoyed. "What the society needs today more than a purely selfish or mechanical interest in her work, more than a cold understanding of her methods, more than a desire for applause under her standard, is men to love her, and in this love to work."[32]

It was a busy year as Coates collected more honors, from the distinguished to the sublime. Just before the Thanksgiving holiday he received detailed instructions to be at an old schoolhouse at nine in the evening, wearing the oldest clothes in his wardrobe, for induction into Epsilon Phi Delta, a small but distinguished fraternity with a unique mission. After being approached by a "spirit" who draped him in a white robe, he was taken for initiation, where he was administered an oath: "That I shall strive to achieve the purpose for which the organization was founded: Namely, to promote understanding and friendship between Japan and the United States by a diligent study of and continuous interest in Japanese-American relations, and Japan." Coates also had to swear never to reveal the secret motto, grip, and password.[33]

Among Coates's mates in the Class of 1918 was Kameichi Kato from Hiroshima, Japan, who had been honored by his countrymen for organizing the fraternity during the course of his studies in America. Kato, the first

Asian student to earn a four-year degree from the university, also was one of a dozen or so men, including Coates, who were members of Amphoterothen, a club of juniors and seniors that had been organized by Joseph Gregoire DeRoulhac Hamilton, the university's distinguished history professor, to encourage extemporaneous debate.

Coates also was a member of Tau Kappa Alpha, composed of students who had participated in intercollegiate debate, and Sigma Upsilon, a writing club that later added Thomas Wolfe and Paul Green to its membership.

Four years earlier, Coates had embarked upon his studies at Chapel Hill with trepidation, not quite sure he could match what he saw as the best of the best students in North Carolina. Among his classmates were men with more formal academic training, more social skills and money, and more promising prospects than a boy from a farm in Johnston County who depended on loans and self-help jobs to remain in school. Certainly any insecurity was all behind him by the time his years as an undergraduate were drawing to a close.

He had done well in his studies, although he never reached the heights of his friend Albert Oettinger, who was elected president of Phi Beta Kappa in his junior year and had already begun his first year in the law school. (Law school entrance at the time didn't require a college degree.) He had thoroughly invested himself in university life and had left his mark on campus publications and organizations, and in the university's record books. Over the Christmas holidays, Coates was the toastmaster at the Johnston County gathering of university alumni at the Red Men's Hall. His final honor was selection as the winner of the Willie P. Mangum Medal for oratory. It was the university's oldest student award, and Coates's name was added to a list of his personal heroes, including Governor Charles Brantley Aycock and Edward Kidder Graham, the winner two decades earlier.

Coates had grown into a handsome young man of twenty-one. He had arrived as a gangling youth with his suits a bit tight and his pant cuffs riding high on his ankles. He now presented a striking image with a high forehead, deep-set soft eyes, and full lips. His face had filled out, adding a bit more proportion to ears that seemed more prominent four years earlier. The part that had been firmly planted in the middle of his black hair in his freshman photographs had migrated to the left side as he grew older, lending him a more mature appearance. In posing for his pictures in the *Yackety Yack*, he stood erect to his full five feet, eight inches with his head cocked slightly forward and a bit to the side, almost as though he were waiting to respond to an opponent on the debate platform.

Commencement week for the 123rd graduating class of the university opened on June 2, 1918, with a vespers service by the Reverend W. D. Moss under the Davie Poplar, the old tree where legend said William R. Davie had tied his horse as he looked for a spot on which to locate the nation's first state university. Coates's attention was focused on the program for Monday, which was Senior Class day in Gerrard Hall, when he was scheduled to deliver his oration in the competition for the Mangum Medal. There were banquets and reunions scheduled for the classes of "the eights," from 1858 on through 1908. Alumni from 1913 and 1917 were also expected to attend.

These were days of celebration and Chapel Hill was at its most delightful. A southeasterly breeze kept the temperatures comfortable and the skies were clear. The Class of 1918 pledged a gift to their alma mater of $2,500, with the class co-signing a note to return to the university $500 a year for the next five years. The seniors also arranged for the planting of a rooted shoot from the Davie Poplar, which had been struck by lightning, causing some to worry that its days were numbered. William Long of Chapel Hill had nurtured a grafted shoot from the old tree, and he gave it to the class to be planted following the chapel service. (Poplar Sr. and Poplar Jr. are still standing in the twenty-first century.)

But, beyond the peaceful glen, and the nostalgia of the Old Well, and the warmth of reunions, the world was a very troubled place. As the commencement program proceeded, the front pages of the *News & Observer* were filled with news of attacks and counterattacks that shifted the lines slowly to and fro in France. Secretary of the Navy Daniels ordered the port of New York closed on Monday, June 4, and sent warships on the hunt for German submarines off the American coast. Shells were falling at the rate of two a minute on the trenches as British and French soldiers fell back in the Soissons region. U.S. troops were now in the thick of the fighting. One account highlighted a charge led by a Lieutenant Watson of North Carolina, who stood atop a parapet encouraging his men and yelling, "Stick to it boys. Give'em hell. They can't drive you out. No boche ever lived who could lick an American."[34]

The appearance of men in uniform changed the atmosphere in Chapel Hill as the graduates prepared to receive their diplomas. Twelve members of the faculty were in military service. Of the 278 students who had begun the journey with Coates four years earlier, only 81 remained in the senior class and, of these, only 49 were on hand to receive their diplomas. Thirty-two were already in France, or in the training camps, having volunteered or answered the draft. Many more were due to leave soon. Coates read the class poem composed by his roommate, C. G. Tennant, who was already in service. The call for the allotment of men, white and Negro, by each county in North Carolina was published in the newspaper. The state's contingent was part of another nationwide mobilization, this time for two hundred thousand men.

Instead of the usual four contenders for the Mangum Medal, there were only two, Coates and W. H. Stephenson of Raleigh. Both talked about the world conflict. Coates chose as his title, "America's Message to the World." It was a stirring piece of oratory in praise of American ideals of freedom over the despotism of imperialism. He combined bits of history, current events, and even the story of the crucifixion of Jesus Christ. Ideals, Coates said, will prevail.

"It is the infinite yearning of the human spirit to realize in its own life the vision that has glimmered before it that America has expressed," he said. "What others have dared to dream of America dares to do. The men who scoff at and scorn her action as a foolish dream are the men who held the vinegar soaked sponge to a suffering Christ on Calvary."[35] The *News & Observer* carried Coates's full text in the Sunday paper following graduation.

President Graham announced Coates's selection for the Mangum Medal and also his selection for the William Jennings Bryan Prize in Political Science. The awards must have bound the two even closer together. No member of any class since Graham had taken office had so closely followed the president's own interests and accomplishments. The two had become close friends during the time together, and the president asked his protégé to serve as his secretary until mid-summer, when Coates was due to leave for Camp Gordon, Georgia, to begin his military training, first as a private and then in officer training school.

Coates appeared to have no plans beyond his military service. There was no indication of how much longer the horrible war in Europe would rage. He did not know if he would be shipped overseas, or if he would return. His friend, mentor and professor, Horace Williams, had planted the idea of continuing his studies at Harvard University, but Coates had no money for such a step. He still had debts remaining from his undergraduate years to consider, as well as his obligations to the state in exchange for his student loans. None of these concerns made a lot of difference in the summer of 1918, when the uncertainty of war lay ahead.

THREE

One of Dean Pound's Boys

1918–1923

OF ALL THE DEATHS SUFFERED by the university during World War I, none was more deeply felt in Chapel Hill and throughout the state than that of President Edward Kidder Graham, who became one of the thousands of victims of the Spanish flu pandemic that devastated homes and communities across the nation in 1918.

Graham died in the president's residence in Chapel Hill on Saturday, October 26, around eight in the evening. The previous Monday he had left the campus, where the number of flu cases was subsiding in the wake of a crisis that had confined up to three hundred students in makeshift infirmaries. He arrived in Raleigh, where flu deaths were still being recorded daily, and boarded a train for New York to attend to his duties as the academic director of the Student Army Training Corps (SATC). The SATC was in control of five hundred college and university campuses whose academic programs had been supplanted by military training that regulated everything from a student's free time to course offerings. By the time Graham returned to Chapel Hill at the end of the week, he was ill, and death followed shortly thereafter. This virulent strain of flu struck quickly and, unlike earlier outbreaks, it was especially deadly for men between twenty and forty years of age. The grim reality of Graham's death was well understood in households across the state. The day before he died, the *News & Observer* reported that health officials estimated a hundred thousand cases of influenza in North Carolina.[1] By the time the pandemic would run its course, it would claim fifteen thousand victims in the state, and touch Chapel Hill deeply yet again.

Graham's death was not officially included among the university's war casualties. Of the twenty-two hundred students, alumni, and faculty members who had answered the call to arms, forty-one had died while in uniform. Yet, Graham was as much one of these casualties as any soldier or sailor. His presidency had begun within weeks of the assassination of a European prince that provoked a conflict that would mire the world in the most costly slaughter ever seen. Over the next four years Graham transformed the university and prepared it in such a way for future demands that when America entered the war, students and faculty were ready to serve. He devoted his own tireless energy to the war effort only to die just two weeks before the armistice ended the fighting on the front on November 11, 1918.

Albert Coates learned of Graham's death while he was midway through his training to become a second lieutenant in the army. He was posted at Fort Gordon, Georgia, and scrambling through the piney woods and leaping from trenches topped with barbed wire. He later wrote that he received the news of Graham's passing while sitting in his rough wooden barracks on the post. "I knew and felt that there had passed away a glory from the earth," he later wrote.[2] It would be more than six weeks before he could return to Chapel Hill. While the official period of mourning was over by the time he arrived, the loss still hung heavy upon him and others who had placed so much hope in Graham's leadership.

Military service had shaped Coates into a handsome man of twenty-two. He had never been overweight, although he enjoyed all manner of food, especially ice cream, but the rigors of training had trimmed off any excess weight, leaving him lean and fit with his facial features more defined. He appeared stronger and more manly pictured in his uniform than he did in his college days. Coates concluded his training just as the war in Europe was coming to an end. His 17th Company was demobilized on November 30 before he was ever assigned to active duty with a line company.

Coates lost friends and classmates in the war. Four members of the Class of 1918 died in military service, three of them from disease. Another casualty was a companion from Smithfield. Ensign Edwin S. Pou was a hydroplane pilot and was killed during a landing near Brest, France. In March 1919, Coates delivered a memorial address on the grounds of Turlington Graded School, the former Turlington Institute, where both had attended classes. "We have seen boys who played about our streets show the stuff of manhood and the mystic fire of heroic souls," Coates said in the eulogy he delivered that day. "There is one among us, Edwin Pou, who rose with the crest to a height from which he would not descend, and there wreathed himself in the glory of a people's affection."[3]

By the time Coates was mustered out and reached Chapel Hill in mid-December, he found university leaders hastily preparing a return to normality under new leadership. The trustees had named Marvin H. Stacy, the dean of the college of liberal arts under Graham, as acting president. He was appointed chairman of the faculty and temporarily given all the powers of the presidency until a permanent replacement could be found. The university community enthusiastically received Stacy's appointment. He was an engineer, rather than a man of letters like Graham, but he embraced Graham's vision for the programs of outreach and university involvement in the state. Despite his technical training, he, too, was a decorated speaker and had won the Mangum medal as an undergraduate. Stacy and Coates had become good friends during their years together in Chapel Hill, and the two had often shared the dais in presentations about the traditions and responsibilities of students to themselves, to their university, and to their state.

Stacy and his colleagues faced immediate challenges. The campus military program was disbanded on December 9, the day after a memorial service was held for President Graham, with a formal lowering of the colors and the distribution of discharge papers. The faculty had until the middle of January and the start of the new term to arrange class schedules, reassign lecture halls, and revive organizations whose activities had been put on hold in favor of the war effort before students who had shed khaki for civilian garb returned to campus. In the midst of all this, discussions had begun about building a lasting memorial to Graham. A week after his memorial service in Gerrard Hall, a special committee of trustees and faculty members met to consider suggestions offered by Louis R. Wilson. One of the boldest of Wilson's ideas was the construction of a campus student activities building dedicated in Graham's name.

Wilson's idea caught fire immediately. Graham had talked for years about the need for such a center for student life and campus activities.

He considered the absence of a central meeting hall, a "living room" as it were, for students and their visitors, and for alumni, to be one of the major shortcomings of the Chapel Hill campus. Graham had called the spacious lounge he wanted for the building to be a place where a student might "loaf and invite his soul."[4] Graham also believed that since student government and student organizations played such an important role in the quality of campus life, as well as its governance, such a building ought to provide a home for these groups as well. A campus student center, similar to the Harvard Union, had long been an item in Graham's "want book," a compilation of projects for the university that he always kept handy on his desk.[5] This new building would replace the YMCA building, a combination of gothic and Tudor design that served as a catchall for all organizations. The Y included meeting rooms, a small auditorium, and even some sleeping rooms for students. The student bookstore was also in the Y. It was much too small to accommodate a growing student body.

Graham had seen money for replacement for the YMCA slip through his fingers five years earlier. During his first year as acting president, he had talked with the Rockefeller Foundation about a grant to build a student activities building. The foundation was agreeable to giving the university $50,000 if the state would match it. The proposal ran into opposition from Governor Locke Craig and other trustees who "took the position that the University should not accept 'tainted' money," according to Wilson.[6] The opponents agreed only to offer land for such a building and a modest $600 a year to go toward its maintenance. When John D. Rockefeller learned of the snub, he withdrew the offer.

Wilson would have been one of the first to see Coates when he arrived in Chapel Hill after his trip home from Georgia. And, as the two talked, Coates would have learned then of these early discussions about a memorial. For Wilson, Coates's appearance on campus must have seemed providential. He would need someone to devote his time to a fund-raising campaign to underwrite construction, and there was no better candidate than Albert Coates. He was confident he could not find any other person who was immediately available and who would invest his full energy and spirit to prosecute a persuasive and successful fund-raising campaign.

Coates brought other credentials to the task. His devotion to Graham was well known; the two had worked closely together in the months preceding the president's death. Moreover, he was a recognized leader among the students and alumni and was known as a booster of the university. He also brought a statewide perspective to the task, largely through his work the previous year with Branson and the North Carolina Club. While his own travels had been limited, Coates knew North Carolina and, through his association with the extension program, knew something about how to reach people well beyond the boundaries of his own hometown.

Most important, perhaps, Coates was available. His old mentor, Horace Williams, was encouraging him to consider further study, perhaps at the law school at Harvard University. If he were to follow Williams's advice—and his limited financial resources made that doubtful—then the young man's schedule would be open until the next opportunity for admission of first-year students in the fall of 1919. When Wilson presented the assignment to Coates, he accepted immediately, and a few weeks later the committee announced his appointment as executive secretary of the Graham Memorial Committee.

The official launch of the campaign was set for February 10 with a student rally on campus. The committee believed the effort should rise from the campus. It hoped that the solidarity of the student body would engage those most likely to lend support and engage their families at the same time. After spending the Christmas holidays with his family in Smithfield, Coates was back in Chapel Hill making preparations for the campaign at the same time that Dean Stacy was completing his plans for returning the university to civilian control. On January 14, Stacy was delivering his report to the trustees on the dismantling of the SATC program and his plans for the future when he fell ill and was forced to leave the meeting. A week later, on January 21, Stacy succumbed to pneumonia. Once again, the campus was in shock over the death of a young leader.[7]

Students, faculty, and friends gathered once again for a memorial service in Gerrard Hall. On March 2, Coates was one of three speakers chosen to remember Stacy. The others were former president Francis Venable and a childhood friend. Speaking for the students, Coates recalled Stacy as a fair and trusted advisor "who through these intimate personal relations gained and held the esteem of every man and the friendship of every group; a man against whom the charge of unfairness was never brought; a man who, rooting his life in such things as these, could but grow in stature and favor with us all."[8]

The loss of Stacy and Graham in so short a period was compounded two weeks later by the death of former president Kemp Plummer Battle. He had just celebrated his eighty-seventh birthday when he died peacefully at "Senlac," his home at the edge of the campus. It was almost too much to take. Within a brief period, the university had lost those who had seemed so well prepared to carry the institution boldly into a new century as well as the man who had resurrected the university itself and set it on its course following Reconstruction. Battle's death was the end of an era; his years at the university connected him with the institution's earliest days. He had not only done business as state treasurer with President Jefferson Davis and seen Robert E. Lee on the battle lines at Richmond, but, as a student, he had presided over a meeting of the Dialectic Society with one of the university's first students, alumnus James Mebane, on the platform beside him.[9]

In June, 1919, the trustees elected Harry Woodburn Chase as the university's new president. A native New Englander, Chase had blended well with his southern home. He joined the university's faculty in 1910, when he was twenty-seven, and taught in the department of education. He was one of four faculty members charged with developing the SATC and had succeeded to the chairmanship of the faculty upon Stacy's death. He was tall and slender, gracious, and, with his white hair, appeared older than his thirty-six years.[10]

Descriptions of the proposed student activities building were already common knowledge on the campus by the time the students gathered in Gerrard Hall on the night of February 10 to formally launch the campaign. The initial goal of $100,000 for the new building had been raised to $150,000, an amount believed necessary to build and to furnish the facility. Either figure was a formidable challenge, and full of political implications. Some trustees were concerned that a statewide campaign would irritate the leaders of the denominational schools who depended on public appeals to support their institutions. There was also concern that if a public campaign could raise that kind of money for the university then state legislators, who were just beginning their biennial session in Raleigh, might believe they could reduce state appropriations without any concern. Historian and faculty member R. D. W. Connor wrote Wilson to emphasize that the campaign was one that should involve all of North Carolina, not just those directly connected to the university. To do less would perpetuate the notion that the university was just for the sons of North Carolina's best families, not a university of the people as Graham had characterized it.[11]

Coates was mindful of these powerful political currents as the students and faculty gathered on the tenth. He opened the program with an inspiring appeal to students to continue to aspire to the greatness in themselves and the university that Graham had talked about. "Tonight we who saw him and we who heard him have the opportunity to express in terms that are definite and real whether or not we understood with our souls what our eyes saw and our ears heard [when Graham was here with us]. We have met in the interest of a movement which calls on us to say in the open and in language that all can understand what we thought and what we think of President Graham's meaning to us; of the cause to which he gave his life; and that cause: The cause of Carolina; the cause which is ours."

The building that would rise on the campus and carry Graham's name "would gather into it all the fine, free spirit of this campus through the men who make it what it is and the organizations and activities which they have built up; a building which would be a recognition and an approval of the student initiative and manliness and power which he did so much to encourage and promote; a Student Activities Building to be known as the Graham Memorial."[12]

Speakers who followed Coates to the platform reinforced the message that the new building was more than a monument to a fallen leader. Rather, they said, the building was one that was desperately needed to replace the YMCA building that had opened in 1906 when the student population was about a third of the current enrollment. Among the speakers that night were two who had followed Coates in the leadership of the campus debating circles—William H. Bobbitt, who would later become chief justice of the North Carolina Supreme Court, and Luther H. "Luke" Hodges, who would be elected governor at mid-century.

Coates closed out the evening with a stirring tribute that showed both the breadth of his devotion to Graham and the depth of his feelings of loss. It was a eulogy he had been preparing for weeks, probably from the moment when he learned of Graham's death down in Georgia. It was born of love and inspiration and sailed close to a comparison of Graham with Jesus Christ. Such were Coates's deep love and admiration for the man.

"To speak for the men of Carolina is to speak for men who shun affectations; who know not sham; who love naturalness; who seek the truth and when they find it follow it as their guiding star. To phrase the feeling of these men toward Edward Kidder Graham is to phrase the relationship of free men toward a life which lived with the freedom of the open air and the romance of the morning in a personality which breathed into their lives the inspiration to aspire. It is the revelation of leadership. It is the story of men who, free to choose, chose him as their leader.

"In resurrected strength his spirit touches ours as before, stirred us to depths before unsounded, revealed to us possibilities before unknown. And to-day on this campus, even as when he walked among us, he is still the living leader loved of men, inspiring them to that life which is the way the truth the light of the world. And he still glows with the glow of triumph, still grows in the affections of men."[13]

The evening was a resounding success. Coates's passionate and flowing rhetoric, and the more straightforward arguments put forth by Bobbitt and Hodges, encouraged the students to open their pocketbooks. By the time the meeting was concluded, student pledges and cash contributions amounted to $20,000. The members of the senior class averaged $70 per person.

Coates also enlisted the aid of the North Carolina Club in the campaign. With the start of the regular academic program in January, Coates had been assigned to work with E. C. Branson on a study of city government that was something of a companion to the earlier study of county government. At the Club's first meeting he encouraged members to make contacts with alumni and others in their home counties who were in a financial position to support the effort.

Working under Wilson's direction, Coates also traveled about the state on behalf of the memorial committee, paying personal calls on alumni and attending their meetings. Speaking to alumni in Goldsboro, the hometown of trustee Leslie Weil, Coates borrowed phrases from his opening night speech and recapped the progress of the campaign. The $20,000 pledged and given by students had been followed by larger gifts of $1,000 and $2,000 each from alumni around the state and as far away as New York. "It is the spirit of Edward K. Graham, the spirit of the University of North Carolina which calls to you and to me—not only now, but always," Coates said. "It is still the call to service wherever we are: for better roads, for better schools, for civic betterment in any form, for uplift everywhere. And as she calls she says to you: 'Even as ye have done it unto the least of these, ye have done it unto Me.'"[14]

He walked his listeners through the building with a detailed description of the recreation hall, barbershop, bowling alley, and cafeteria that would be located on a level below ground. The main floor was the one that Graham had envisioned as a social center for the campus, with comfortable chairs where students could greet visitors or alumni could congregate when they returned to the campus—a place for students to escape the Spartan confinement of their dormitory rooms, if only for an hour or two of relaxation. In addition, it would be large enough for speaking events, even dances. The building's second floor would have offices for student publications, organizations, and student government. The latter were especially important to Graham. This would be the busy working heart of the center and student life.

"We do not seek to raise $150,000 for this purpose in the spirit of a tax, or on the basis of assessment," Coates told the Goldsboro alumni, "for that is contrary to the spirit of the man whose memorial it will be. It must represent the loyalty and love as well as the money of men. It is in that spirit that the movement lives."[15]

By the time the deadline arrived on June 20, the campaign was well short of its goal. Only $70,000 in cash and pledges had been collected. It was a good start, but only enough to inspire the committee to press on. Faced with considerably more work ahead, Coates put aside his plans of entering law school in the fall of 1919 and agreed to work until the end of the year.

When the fall term of 1919 opened, Coates enrolled as a graduate student in English and was a teaching assistant under a new program of graduate fellowships. His service helped him fulfill his obligation for his student loans. Coates found it an absolutely fertile experience working under the direction of Dean Edwin A. Greenlaw. Among the men who roamed about the literary warrens of the campus were powerful writers-to-be, including Thomas Wolfe, Coates's friend from his senior year, and Paul Green, whose academic career had been interrupted by service in France. Like Coates, Green was devoted to Horace Williams and would return in 1923 to join him as the newest and youngest instructor in the philosophy department.

Coates found a room in the old University Inn, a tree-shaded wooden building on the edge of the campus described as "gray with age and neglect." There he lived with Dougald McMillan and Clement Eaton, who subsequently distinguished themselves as scholars. Wolfe had a room nearby on a porch that overlooked Alumni Hall. Coates was on the advisory board of *The Tar Baby*, a campus humor magazine that Wolfe contributed to with great regularity.

The fall's fund-raising activities were pegged to the popular football weekends when alumni filled the seats on Emerson Field. Coates also organized a special alumni gathering in October. By the end of the year, the committee's prospects were improved with pledges and cash of $120,000, but the campaign was short of the mark by $30,000. And that was the end of Coates's participation in the campaign.[16]

The campaign continued into 1920, but another man was hired to fill in for the rest of the academic year. Coates, meanwhile, continued to teach in the English department and made plans to enter Harvard Law School in the fall. In May he got a boost for his ambitions when he was awarded the James A. Rumrill Scholarship from the Harvard Law School. The $275-a-year scholarship was awarded annually to a graduate student from the Carolinas, Virginia, Florida, Georgia, Tennessee, or Kentucky.

The cash award was modest, but at least it would cover his tuition charges and leave him with $75 to apply to other expenses. Based on the estimates offered students entering law school in the fall of 1920, Coates would need a minimum of $350 more to make it through his first year. He returned to the bank in Smithfield, which had advanced him loans as an undergraduate, and got some support from James Abell, the bank's cashier, who offered him $100 a year. In mid-September he headed north on an adventure that would transform his life as much as his studies had at the University of North Carolina.

For Albert Coates, the Harvard Law School was the only place for him to train if he wished to become a truly great attorney. As the nation's oldest law school, it was the school whose professors wrote the books that were used by the law faculty throughout the rest of the land. During his first year alone, Coates would take a seat in the lecture halls of Samuel Williston, who was just publishing the first of his five volumes on contracts; Austin Scott, an equally venerated authority on civil procedure; and Joseph H. Beale, who was unsurpassed on principles of liability. Not only were these men *the* authority in their specialties, they were legendary in their teaching skill. Their use of dialectic swordplay tested the intellect, the reasoning, and the endurance of some of the finest college graduates in the country.

Not only had the faculty written the law—as it was taught—but the Harvard method of teaching, developed in the late nineteenth century by

Harvard's late Dean Christopher Columbus Langdell, was changing legal education. Langdell believed that the law is a science, in the way that chemistry or botany is a science. His specimens, and the building blocks of legal education, were the opinions of judges as they were found in the volumes of judicial reports from courts around the country. "The student of law, he thought, like the student of chemistry or biology, must learn the arts of close scrutiny and discriminating classification," Arthur Sutherland wrote in his history of Harvard Law School. "The student of the law, that is to say, must continually study, compare, and classify judicial opinions."[17]

The foundation of each course taught under the Langdell method was the casebook. Langdell knew he could not expect all students to be able to share the volumes of judicial reports found in the library. Instead, professors pulled together reprints of significant cases into one volume and that became the text for the course. One of Coates's classmates told him he was buying casebooks for every course he didn't take so he could carry the entire Harvard Law School home with him in his trunk.[18]

Professors like Williston and Beale were masters at using the Socratic method to dissect the cases under review in what Sutherland called "dialectical demonstration." Both demanded precision in the analysis of the chosen cases and they dealt quickly with those who missed the essential elements or wandered in their thinking. Beale "persuaded himself that some sort of necessity controlled law, that there was a cosmic logical sequence which could be perceived and stated if only one could think aright."[19]

Coates later recounted that on his first day in class his professor—he didn't say whether it was Williston or Beale or another known for sparing no pain—called upon him to state the first case. He gave his analysis, Coates later wrote, "with mounting blood pressure." When he was through, his professor asked, "'You don't mind if I criticize you right sharply?' 'No, sir,' I answered, in as big a lie as I could have told at that time and under those circumstances. He took me at my word, fried the fat off my statement of the case, found no lean meat or even gristle underneath, went on to burn up the grease, and left not even a crackling to recall my maiden effort in the Harvard Law School."[20]

As the professor moved from one man to the next, and with each one bumbling before the master, Coates realized he had to change his approach to reading the case law if he was to weather the sessions in his Harvard classrooms. Up to that point, he had used the written word to arouse his listeners. Most of his compositions had been designed to dazzle the listener with literary footwork and stir the passions. That strategy had been his stock-in-trade for debates, where the object was to capture the spirit and persuade to a point of view. He learned that the casebook was not the place to appreciate the literary flourish or oratorical phrasing. The premium now was upon the words that provoked the mind.

"I had underscored the fine phrases, the flowing sentences, the atmospheric paragraphs, and completely missed the point of the case." He later wrote that he could track his own evolution as a successful law student from the underscoring in his casebooks as he shifted from the purple passages to "the meanings obscured and all but lost in the interstices of procedure, stated always without flourish and sometimes without grammar. I had heard about reading between the lines, and now I was learning how to do it."[21]

The exchange underscored the warning Coates had heard on his first evening in Cambridge at a meeting with the other first-year men. Professor Edward H. Warren—he was known among students as "Bull"—had announced: "Young gentlemen, if your moral character has not been nourished by your parents, the kindergarten, public school, and college, there is little the Harvard Law School can do for it this late in the day. What this law school is concerned with is your mental character, training a mind that refuses to do a sloppy piece of work." Warren's description added a new dimension to Coates's definition of the word "character" and came as a pointed reminder of the lesson in discipline that had been pressed upon him as an undergraduate by Professor Patterson and President Graham.[22]

Clearly, this was going to be a most challenging year. Coates was up against the best men from the best universities in the nation who all were working twelve hours a day just to keep pace. This was no place for the faint of heart. The classrooms were crowded, and the faculty was interested in winnowing out those who could not hold their own. A man got his walking papers at the Harvard Law School upon the failure of one course. "I was finding that the tortoise will always beat the hare if the hare is accommodating enough to go to sleep in the middle of the race; but God pity the tortoise when he runs up against a hare that does not go to sleep," Coates later observed.[23] At the same time, he had been well prepared by Horace Williams, who had toughened Coates to meet the rigor of the Socratic style. Williams would "incite disagreement if for no other reason than to fire up the lethargic minds of his classroom."[24]

A week after he arrived in Cambridge for the start of classes on September 27, Coates accounted for his first twelve days in the North in a letter to Williams. He said he had enjoyed a leisurely five-day trip that had included a stopover in New York City, where he saw his first Broadway play, John Drinkwater's *Abraham Lincoln*, a performance that had been running for two years. He told Williams that after his experience in his first week of classes he must begin thinking about his academic career differently. When he was at Chapel Hill he had devoted twelve hours a day to being a student, but his attention had not always been on his studies. "One [professor] has said outright, and the others have implied it, that it is the fashion to work here; and he gave impressive figures from the mortality of last year's entering class to show that only those who remain wear this fashion. For me is the Law School, the Law Club, the Law Review. Other things may enter—but to amplify, not to interfere."[25]

The law club to which Coates referred was the Parsons Club. It was one of a number of student groups, each composed of eight first-year, eight second-year, and eight third-year men. Coates had received invitations to join two of the school's clubs and had chosen the one named in honor of Theophilus Parsons, a leading figure in the school in the first half of the nineteenth century. Over the course of the year, club members studied together, prepared briefs, and organized teams in preparation for moot court appearances in the Ames Competition, one of the most prized honors of the school.

Teeming with the sights, sounds, and smells of competing races, nationalities, and languages, Cambridge must have seemed strange to a young man from rural North Carolina, a state that took pride in its homogeneous population. But Coates was not alone; he discovered there were a dozen North Carolinians in the Law School. Of the first-year men like himself, two were from Trinity College in Durham and one was a Harvard graduate. Coates was well acquainted with two others, both fellow graduates from Chapel Hill. William T. Polk of Warrenton had edited the *Tar Heel* before graduating in 1917, and T. Skinner Kittrell of Henderson had finished in 1920 while Coates was teaching in the graduate school. Coates, Polk, and Kittrell all had rooms in a two-story frame house at 48 Buckingham Street that was being rented by Nathan W. Walker, who was on a year's leave from his faculty position in Chapel Hill. Another roomer at Buckingham Street was Thomas Wolfe of Asheville. He was an aspiring playwright and studying with George Pierce Baker at Harvard's 47 Workshop.[26]

Coates connected with another old friend from Chapel Hill. Sam J. Ervin Jr. of Morganton had graduated with Polk in 1917, having left early to report for military training at Fort Oglethorpe. Ervin had fought in the trenches in France and had been badly wounded at Soissons. On Armistice Day he was convalescing in a hospital in Brittany and did not return to the States until April 1919. In the fall of 1920, Ervin was beginning his second year at the law school as an "unclassified student" and was working toward a degree by a most unusual route—backwards. Before the war, Ervin had completed the equivalent of one year of law school at the University of North Carolina. In the summer of 1919, he had taken a refresher course and passed the North Carolina Bar on his first attempt. Ervin's sister was worried that he was not fully recovered from the trauma of combat and suggested he put off joining his father in his law practice and enroll at Harvard to "take some courses." Ervin completed the school's third-year courses, and then returned in the fall of 1920, as Coates was beginning his first year, to take the second-year courses. He would be back in 1921 to take the first-year courses and qualify for a degree, which he received in 1922.[27]

The experienced second- and third-year students provided the new men with a hand up where they could. Erwin had depended on his friend, Floyd Crouse of Sparta, North Carolina, for class notes as he made his way. Alfred Lindau of Greensboro, a 1917 University of North Carolina graduate, had recommended Coates for the Parsons Law Club. Such assistance was welcome in a world that was unlike anything these young men had ever seen. Gone was the easy nature and comfortable isolation of Chapel Hill and the somnolence of hometowns such as Henderson, Warrenton, and Smithfield. Of the four men living with the Walkers, only Wolfe had lived in a city with a population larger than the Harvard student body of six thousand. At the same time, even Wolfe was impressed with the size of it all. "There is no doubt of the greatness of Harvard. Her size is appalling but one can get here just what he wants under the biggest men in America," he wrote in a letter home.

Coates and his friends had entered a world where money, status, and class were far more evident than in Chapel Hill. Wolfe commented on men in "golf tweed and stockings" and students driving to class in a Packard or a Stutz. "It is a heterogeneous mass of humanity and if there is anywhere in America where you can get a national outlook it is here. Or, if you choose, you can become a first-class jack-ass in knee-breeches," Wolfe wrote to his mother. "The old democratic atmosphere of Chapel Hill is unknown here, not because these men are snobs, but because it is every man for himself and everyone 'tends strictly to his own affairs.'" Harvard, he said, "is for men who begin to 'find themselves,' who know what they want and are here to get it. If I had to start over again, it would be Chapel Hill first, Harvard later."[28]

In Coates's recollections of his three years in Cambridge, he left behind a few anecdotal snippets of his classroom experiences. There is no question it was a glorious time in his life and one that impressed him profoundly. He enjoyed the storied atmosphere of the Harvard campus, where he found history and tradition in virtually every building and at every turn. One of his favorite spots was the reading room in Austin Hall, one of the two law school buildings. It was only a short walk from his lodgings on Buckingham Street, and as pleasant a stroll under leafy maples as he would have known in Chapel Hill. At Austin Hall he could retreat from his roommates to a comfortable chair under high ceilings with images of wild boars and dragons carved in the beams and be but a few steps away from a library that contained all the reports from the American, English, and Irish courts. Nearby was Langdell Hall, with its larger library and special collections of legal treatises and decisions and volumes on the continental law of Europe. Austin Hall was older and well rubbed and it may have better suited Coates's romantic nature as he settled into a chair before a huge fireplace filled with massive logs and immersed himself in the tangle of legal issues that challenged his creative and nimble mind.

Hours upon hours of reading and researching cases suited Coates. While he had dashed from one student activity to another as an undergraduate, he had never given short shrift to his debate preparations. Once he recovered from the missteps of his early days in the law classroom, Coates pushed himself to devote the hours required to stay abreast of his assignments. He later said that armed with "main strength and awkwardness," he succeeded in developing that "mental character" that Bull Warren had talked about that first night.[29]

There was little time for anything other than study if he was to be ready for the verbal jousting and Socratic give and take of the lecture halls. His course work for the year included civil procedure at common law for two hours a week, contracts for three hours a week, property law for two hours a week, torts for two hours a week, principles of liability for three hours in the first half of the year, and criminal law for three hours in the second half. He took his meals at Memorial Hall, the main dining hall on the campus, where good food and plenty of it was available for $8 a week. And he made use of Hemenway gymnasium, where he kept a locker and got a free medical examination in the bargain. The school's Stillman Infirmary was available if he fell ill.

Despite the grind, it was an exhilarating time. Coates later compared Samuel Williston's "fine art of teaching" with poetry, art and music. "He taught easily, leaving me with the feeling not that culture could not afford to raise a sweat, but that with him it didn't have to." Joseph H. Beale's "mind played over everything it touched like a dancing ray of light that was up to no good. He out-Socratized Socrates in the Socratic method and attracted us like moths to the flame, and with similar results." Another of his favorites was Roscoe Pound, the dean of the law school. He didn't make it to Pound's classroom that first year, but Pound would take notice of this bright young man from the South. Coates certainly was impressed with the dean's work. "Trying to put Pound into the average student's head—I am referring to my own—was like trying to put an ocean into a quart pot."[30]

Pound was one of those rare men whose intellect spanned various disciplines, and he conquered them all. As a young man, he had wanted to be a botanist and was attracted to Harvard "as a botanical Mecca." He was nineteen when he arrived in Cambridge to study law and had already earned bachelor and master's degrees from the University of Nebraska. He was taken with the law, he said. "I belonged here." Over one Christmas holiday, rather than travel home to Nebraska, he stayed at Harvard and learned modern Roman law by reading Sohm's *Institutionen des Romischen Rechts* in the original German.[31]

Pound became dean at Harvard after serving in the same job at the law schools of Nebraska, Northwestern, and the University of Chicago. He professed to be able to fill in for any absent professor in any specialty, yet his students found him most approachable. He loved to sing, he occasionally bailed misbehaving students out of jail, and he ran an informal student loan fund, the latter being a service that would draw Coates to his chambers. Seated at his desk, he always wore a green eyeshade to protect his sensitive eyes as he pored over his work, but when a visitor knocked on his door, he was invited in and Pound was attentive. "He taught me the scarcity value of time," Coates wrote, "while at the same time he left me with the feeling that I could, and did, have all I wanted of his time, whenever I wanted it."[32]

Coates's first year ended in late June as Cambridge was growing warm under the summer sun. His dogged determination to succeed was rewarded with high marks. His average grade for the year was a 70, on a scale where 75 was perfection. Wolfe heard a report of Coates's grades from someone who was bragging about a mutual friend's success with a 64. He wrote to Coates, "Claude let one or two remarks drop which indicate that he doesn't think much of our Horatian method of generalizing but I believe it was your habit of thinking in this way combined with the steady and earnest digging you did this year that enabled you to make that splendid grade."

"I am bursting with pride for your splendid success," Wolfe continued. "If you are only half as proud of yourself as I am of you you'll have no buttons on your vest when this reaches you."[33] That summer the two met up with friends and spent a few days on a camping trip in the North Carolina mountains.

Coates had done well, to be sure, but his return to Cambridge in the fall was in doubt. He had his Rumrill scholarship money to cover tuition but his sponsor at the bank in Smithfield told him that he would not be able to support him to the extent he had the year before. North Carolina, and much of the country, was experiencing a serious recession. Johnston County farm prices were half what they had been a few years before, and banks in towns like Smithfield were feeling the pinch. Wolfe urged him to find a way to return. "Despite 'cotton tobacco or bankruptcy' you must come back here next year if you have to extract the money from a Smithfield bank at the point of a gun," he wrote in a summertime letter.[34]

Coates was at a loss about his future. Certainly, he could leave Harvard, take the North Carolina Bar examination and join a firm or open his own practice. The procedure for obtaining a law license was fairly simple. Candidates appeared in Raleigh on an appointed date in August or January and submitted to a written examination. If the North Carolina Supreme Court justices found them qualified, a law license was issued upon payment of $23.50. The nominal requirements called for candidates to have "read law" for two years, but having succeeded in distinguishing himself in the classrooms of the finest legal minds in the land, Coates could easily have answered the questions on the state examination and finessed that requirement.

There is no evidence that Coates ever considered changing course. A Harvard degree remained his goal and he surely talked about his situation with friends in Chapel Hill, including Horace Williams and Louis Wilson. He had been at home about a month when he got a telephone call from Leslie Weil of Goldsboro. Weil was a university trustee and had come to know Coates as a member of the Graham Memorial Committee (whose fund-raising goal was yet to be met). Weil said he was on his way from Goldsboro to Asheville, and he asked Coates to meet him in the office of a mutual friend in Smithfield. When Coates arrived, Weil told him he had heard from UNC President Harry W. Chase, who told him that he had been informed by Dean Pound that Coates would not be returning to Cambridge because he did not have the money. Weil asked Coates what he needed for a year's expenses and Coates gave him a figure. Weil immediately wrote him a check on a New York bank for half the proposed budget and told him to write to him when he needed more.[35]

Weil's generosity was Coates's bridge to the future. The loan not only guaranteed that he would finish his studies at Harvard, but, by extension, helped lay the foundation for his life's work. If Coates had not returned to Harvard, he probably would never have joined the faculty at the UNC law school and been able to use his law classroom as a launching pad for grand ambitions. With Weil's money in hand, Coates was back in Cambridge for the start of classes on September 25, 1921, and he took a room by himself at 1727 Cambridge Street on the northeastern edge of the main campus. (Neither Polk nor Kittrell was on the law school roster.) He was just minutes away from Harvard Square; the law school was two blocks from his door. A letter from President Chase reached him toward the end of the month and offered a ringing endorsement for the year. "We are all expecting such fine things of you that I certainly feel it would be not only a loss to you but to the state if you could not have continued this training."[36]

A short time later, Coates received a letter from one of his former graduate students, B. C. Brown, who also had studied at the feet of Horace Williams. He wrote Coates to ask about Harvard, where Williams was encouraging him to apply. In the letter, he passed on an appraisal of Coates from Williams, who told him, "Coates has as much ability as E. K. Graham."[37]

The range of the course work expanded in Coates's second year. He was in the lecture halls of Pound and Zechariah Chafee, one of the school's recently celebrated scholars. Coates credited Chaffee with showing him the merger of the liberal arts and the law. "I saw the 'inquiring mind' in his living presence before I saw it on the cover of his book," Coates later wrote, referring to Chaffee's book of that title.[38] Chaffee was returning to the classroom victorious after a year of examination and trial. In a *Harvard Law Review* article that he expanded and later published under the title *Freedom of Speech*, he had challenged a U.S. Supreme Court's decision upholding convictions in a sensational case brought under the 1917 Espionage Act. Chaffee challenged the court's decision just as the nation was reacting to the so-called "Red Scare" that produced police raids against suspected communists. Chaffee's study of the case, which questioned legal procedure as well as the constitutionality of the sedition laws used to condemn Jacob Abrams, provoked a university investigation and trial. He defended the rights of free speech, and in late May 1921 a committee acquitted Chaffee of charges that he had acted improperly. It was a decided victory for free speech.[39]

More thoroughly grounded than the year before, Coates found time to expand his social life. In October he joined the Southern Club of Boston, a social home away from home for men from the South. From November through April, the group held dances and programs monthly at the Copley Plaza Hotel in Boston. The mid-season program in January was a celebration of Robert E. Lee's birthday. In the fall Coates also turned out for a performance of Thomas Wolfe's *The Mountains*, the play Wolfe had been working on the previous year for the 47 Workshop.

Wolfe's Harvard experience was less rewarding than Albert's. He lived alone in a house on the north side of campus, several blocks away from Coates. The two saw one another from time to time, and may have slipped out on off-evenings for steaks and seafood at the Durgin-Park restaurant near Faneuil Hall or a sip of bootleg liquor at a speakeasy in the basement of the Palmer House, two haunts they had visited the year before with Polk and Kittrell. Their interests were diverging, however. Wolfe was becoming more and more disenchanted with his Harvard associates while Coates was building connections and relationships that he would call upon in the years ahead. Wolfe's critics found his plays long, tedious, and unbelievable. Coates had become one of Roscoe Pound's favorites.[40]

By spring Coates was beginning to think beyond the law school. Writing to Smithfield attorney H. B. Marrow, he spelled out some of his ideas about his duty to Graham and the vision of connecting the university more closely to the people of the state. Marrow wrote back to say that while his ambition was noble, Coates was not ready for such a challenge. He needed experience in the daily practice of law, and he hoped that Albert would come home to Smithfield and join his firm, or open a practice of his own, before embarking on his admirable mission. "Is this the work of a young man or an old man? If one is going to be enthusiastic in projecting the University law school upon the state, I mean the legal life of the state, must he not know of course first the law itself and second the law in the life of the state. As I see it, the job needs the zeal and enthusiasm of a young man and at the same time a man of experience who is already a part of the life of the state."[41]

Coates ended the year with another round of high grades; his average was a 66 out of 75 points. That summer he remained in Cambridge and worked in a Boston law firm. He was eager to finish his legal education when classes resumed in September. By the end of his time at Harvard, he had completed courses with all of the school's acclaimed faculty, including Felix Frankfurter, who would later be appointed to the U.S. Supreme Court by President Franklin Roosevelt. Frankfurter's course was advertised as the law of public utilities, but the subject matter ranged freely. Coates was not impressed with what Frankfurter called his "'method of approach', or a 'way of looking at things'. I was forever approaching and never getting there—whatever 'there' was. He gave few, if any, citations; had little patience with men who were 'always in earnest and always dull'; and was as likely to tell a student to read Trevelyan's *History of England* as a court decision, or to go out for a walk and look up at the sky, or read a novel, as to refer him to a statute."[42]

It wasn't until some years later that he found virtue in Frankfurter's approach, which sought to shake students free from the stiff regimen to which they had disciplined themselves for the sake of a Harvard degree. Indirectly, Frankfurter and Pound provided Coates with a vivid demonstration of how even the loftiest of academic institutions could connect with the community at large, an idea that was growing in his own mind.

Coates had been unable to take a course with Frankfurter in his second year because the professor and his colleague, Roscoe Pound, were away from Harvard at work on a landmark study of crime in Cleveland, Ohio. The study, the first of its kind, produced a mass of data about the law-enforcing process. It outlined the conflict of controlling crime while also controlling the over-reaching of law-enforcing agencies. There are no quick fixes to controlling crime, Frankfurter wrote in the preface to the 1922 report. In a line that would find its way into Coates's own arguments for improving law enforcement and all levels of local government, Frankfurter said, "the starting point of reform is the education of the public to the necessity of sustained interest." Rectifying the problems "will come if the community cares—or if only a small part of it cares enough."[43]

During his third year Coates was able to answer the call from his friends in Chapel Hill. During his absence, the university had succeeded in gaining unprecedented financial support from the state legislature. Enrollment was increasing and more new buildings were rising on the campus than ever before. The campaign for the Graham Memorial remained stalled, but new efforts were underway to reconnect alumni. One of the largest out-of-state alumni contingents was in New York City, and Coates was called on to make an appeal there for support.[44]

He made the stop in New York on his return from North Carolina, where he had traveled to apply for his law license. Before the end of 1922 he had secured the necessary personal recommendations and had even gotten some advice on the Bar examination from recent candidates who told him just to keep calm. The questions were no worse than any he had seen on a university test. Coates passed easily and he had his license to practice law before he got his degree from Harvard.[45]

Coates remained undecided on where he would settle once law school was behind him. He was ready to go back to North Carolina, he was sure of that. The three years in Cambridge had introduced him to a new world of big-city politics as well as the advantages of major cultural institutions such as the Boston Museum of Fine Arts and the Boston Symphony. All of this he had enjoyed. More important, however, the Harvard Law School "had given me a perspective on North Carolina and the South that I had not had before." Rather than being rocked, as Wolfe was, by those who characterized anyone from the South as slow, or impoverished, or both, Coates apparently rose above such snobbery and, possessed of his own deep self-confidence, never took offense. The years in the North had only strengthened his desire to take what he had learned and "go home and do more and better work because of habits formed and insights attained," he later wrote. "Somehow or other, the Harvard Law School had given me the feeling that I could get along without her. She had planted in me a power to go on my own, to work my way through a problem that came before me, within the limits of my abilities, no matter what the problem was. For three years, she had worked to make me independent of her, and not dependent on her, and in the process had drawn me closer to her."[46]

Coates faced difficult choices. Dean Pound asked him to remain in Cambridge, offering him a generous Langdell Fellowship that would cover all expenses and provide a stipend for a year of advanced study. Pound had told President Chase of his high opinion of Coates during a visit to the Chapel Hill campus in January 1923. Coates also had heard from Ed Abell, one of the leading members of the Johnston County Bar, who offered him a partnership. That held great appeal. Coates believed that after a decent interval as a practicing attorney, he might even parlay his standing in the community into a seat in the state legislature. His friend Sam Ervin had done just that. Albert had persuaded his brother, Kenneth, to enter the university at Chapel Hill with the notion that he also would become a lawyer and the two would one day work together.

And President Chase wanted Coates back in Chapel Hill to fill a vacancy in the faculty of the law school there. Chase was in need of a law teacher to fill in for Maurice Taylor Van Hecke, who was leaving Chapel Hill for a stint at the University of Kansas. In a story that Coates himself told repeatedly, and one that he finally put in writing in several of his books, he ran all the options for his future over and over in his mind. One lawyer, more or less, wouldn't make much difference, he mused as he walked along the banks of the Charles River in Cambridge. One more politician wasn't going to change the world, he told himself. "I had the feeling there was something I could do in Chapel Hill that I could not do in Smithfield, something I could do in a law school that I could not do in a law office, though I couldn't spell out the difference in words."[47]

FOUR

Home to Chapel Hill

1923–1926

"AND YOU, ALBERT, who carry so much back home with you, will be faithful to your best, I know," Thomas Wolfe wrote to his friend in September 1923. "You, and such as you—but there are none such—can save the state, if you be valiant. That you will discharge your professorship with tact and diplomacy, I have no doubt. But that you will never smile at the Philistine, that you will never truckle to materialism... of this I am as certain as I am of courage yet, and valiance in the hearts of primary people. And you are one of these."[1]

The University of North Carolina's newest and youngest assistant law professor left Wolfe behind in the North as he turned toward Chapel Hill with his friend's generous benediction. Old friends and admiring members of the faculty and university administration welcomed him there. Coates's brother, Kenneth, was beginning his junior year on the campus. Classmate Robert Madry was teaching journalism and running the university news service, while Paul Green was launching a teaching career in the philosophy department under their beloved mentor, Horace Williams. Faculty members E. C. Branson and Louis R. Wilson greeted Coates warmly, as did President Harry Chase, who was counting on Coates's leadership qualities to help press forward the improvements that he had in mind for the law school.

When Coates left for Harvard in 1920, Edward Kidder Graham's vision for the university was unrealized. Now, three years later, Chase was on his way to creating a modern university, using as his foundation the former president's ideas and an infusion of money from the state, the likes of which the university had never before enjoyed. This rebirth had begun in the early months of 1921 as Coates was falling into the demanding rhythms of Harvard Law School. Inspired by Wilson and led by Frank Graham, North Carolinians had rallied around a determined coalition of trustees, alumni, and campus leaders to create a groundswell of support for major capital improvements at all state institutions. By the time the 1921 General Assembly adjourned that spring, the university at Chapel Hill had $1.5 million for new buildings and a promise of more to come.

The money launched a building program that would expand the campus to meet growing needs and a student population that had more than doubled to 2,529 since Coates was a freshman. Workmen were erecting buildings for classrooms, dormitories, and faculty housing, and rehabilitating the campus's historic structures that were threatening to collapse. Included in the inventory was a new home for the law school. The sheer volume of building materials necessary to complete these projects was so great that the trustees paid for a temporary rail line to haul the bricks and steel from the railroad's end in Carrboro directly to the job site just below South Building.

The campus was expanding to the south, away from the historic grove with the Davie Poplar and the Old Well, into the old athletic fields where Coates and eager soldiers-to-be had drilled in mufti with their Civil-War era weapons in the fall of 1917. Three new buildings that went up simultaneously formed a quadrangle off what would become a grassy plaza crisscrossed with walkways and known as Polk Place. On the north and south sides of the new quad were Saunders and Murphey Halls with new space for the departments of history, economics, romance languages, and sociology. The eastern base was the law building, which would be dedicated in honor of a former dean, John Manning. Handsome it was, with a broad staircase, grand Ionic columns on the portico, and a cupola in the Colonial Revival style. The building was ready just in time for the start of classes in 1923 as Coates settled into his office and joined an expanded law faculty.

The north side of campus, between South Building and Franklin Street, maintained its quiet, park-like character. The solider atop the monument to the Confederacy still kept watch over Franklin Street, where Coates took a room at a boarding house at 411 E. Franklin. Even this pleasant setting would soon be disturbed. In the fall of 1923, the old University Inn would be demolished and a formal groundbreaking held for the new student center being built in its place in honor of E. K. Graham. The new hall was to be larger than originally proposed and the cost had swelled accordingly, to $400,000. Three years into the campaign for the Graham Memorial, the fund-raising goal had not been met, but the committee believed there were sufficient pledges and cash on hand to begin work on the first phase of the building.

Coates arrived in Chapel Hill at an exciting and transforming time, both for the village and for the university. One by one, sturdy brick buildings were replacing the small and dated wood-frame stores on Franklin Street. There was a new hard-surface road from the center of Chapel Hill to Durham, ten miles away. Franklin Street merchants had refused to underwrite the paving on either side of the eighteen-foot-wide concrete strip, so a muddy border remained alongside the new pavement. Louis Graves was just getting a weekly newspaper underway. It carried local items of interest and commentary.

At the university, President Chase had proved to be an inspired choice as Graham's successor. Though not a Tar Heel—he was a Yankee no less—Chase had the confidence and support of the faculty, trustees, and alumni as he pressed forward with Graham's ambitions, and his own, for the university. He was intent on finding the money and building the political support to enable the university to meet the demands of a student population growing rapidly as a result of the state's new emphasis on high school education. As Louis R. Wilson would later write, Chase was creating a modern university out of what had been essentially a good liberal arts college. Chase had become a fearless champion for this cause, and Coates would dedicate himself to it as well.[2]

Chase had made a compelling argument in 1921 when he and others demonstrated that while the Methodists and Presbyterians had invested $7 million in their colleges in recent years, the state had put less than a tenth of that amount into building up the Chapel Hill campus at a time when it was facing demands for admission from an expanding student-age population. As a result of the state's shortsighted budgeting over the years, some professors had to limit enrollment in their courses because there were not enough seats in their classrooms. There were only nineteen classrooms for general teaching on the entire campus. The aging Memorial Hall, grand in its Victorian Gothic design with towers and a soaring roofline, was without central heating and was usable only for daylight events in good weather. But, used it was because no other place on campus would accommodate the entire student body. Swain Hall was feeding 725 students a day though it was built to handle only 450. The walls of beloved landmarks such as South Building, Old East, and Old West were bulging, and immediate reconstruction was necessary if they were to be saved. Law school enrollment had doubled, yet classes and professors were functioning in severely cramped conditions in Smith Hall, a noble, ivy-covered building that had seen a variety of uses since it was built in 1851, including service as a ballroom and the university library.

The governor and the legislature had responded to the call from the Carolina crowd. The state's institutions of higher learning didn't get all they requested, but the new investment and indications of more to follow had produced a new spirit on the campus. Private investment was following the public money. Trustee John Sprunt Hill of Durham had begun construction of a new hotel at the campus's west entrance on Cameron Avenue. The Carolina Inn would rival any hotel in the state when it opened in 1924. Hill was one of Governor Cameron Morrison's new state highway commissioners, and it was he who had seen to it that Chapel Hill got its improved road, to Durham; a paved road to Raleigh was still some years away.

Chase wanted to build upon the best of the university—its dedicated faculty, its reputation for scholarship, and its alumni's love for what some considered heaven on earth—and bring Chapel Hill into the twentieth-century academic world. Among the improvements in the academic program was a new department of sociology led by Chase's former classmate from Clark University in Massachusetts, Howard W. Odum. A university press had been organized with Odum supplying manuscripts for the first releases.[3]

Also high on Chase's list was improving the law school. He had been a steadfast supporter of Dean Lucius Polk McGehee's steady efforts, which had begun under Graham, to raise the standard of legal education and secure accreditation for the law school by the American Bar Association (ABA), an honor that the law school at neighboring Trinity College (soon to be Duke University) had already achieved. The changes were not without controversy as McGehee and Chase challenged traditions that had governed qualifications for admission and faculty selection.

When McGehee assumed the deanship in 1910, admission was open to virtually any man of decent reputation who could read and write. Most students stayed only long enough to fulfill the North Carolina Bar requirements of two years of study and then headed off to take the bar examination administered by the state Supreme Court. Qualification was not difficult. Candidates all but memorized a rotating list of written questions that were readily available for review beforehand. In 1918, McGehee told the trustees, "We are too much inclined to regard the law course solely as a means of imparting enough knowledge to students to enable them to pass the bar examination of the state." At the time he was proposing that the university raise the qualification for admission to the law school to one year of college work while at the same time extending the course of study for a law degree to three years.[4]

Deans like McGehee knew their schools would be left behind if they did not conform to the new ABA standards. By the time Coates arrived in the fall of 1923, accreditation was available only for schools that required a minimum of two years of college work for admission and that conferred degrees after completion of a bona fide three-year course of instruction. Only thirty-nine law schools in the country met this standard. In the South that included schools at the Universities of Texas and Virginia, as well as at Emory, Washington and Lee, and Trinity.

McGehee designed a three-year program of instruction and received approval to increase the school's faculty from three to five, but the number of third-year men would remain small as long as the North Carolina standards for a law license required only two years of law study and passage of an examination. Among Coates's first-year students in the fall of 1923 were the last of those to be admitted who came with only a high school diploma and no college experience. At least one year of college would be required for admission in 1924, and McGehee had an understanding with the trustees that by 1925 no student would be accepted without at least two years of college.

Coates himself was an important part of the transition taking place in the law school. In hiring the twenty-seven-year-old Harvard law graduate, Chase was making a statement about the changes that he and McGehee had in mind, which included a faculty trained in the modern methods who were teachers, not retired practitioners. Coates was only the second faculty member who had been trained under the Langdell method developed at Harvard. More important, however, was the fact that Coates was joining the faculty with absolutely no practical legal experience. His only acquaintance with a client had come during the summer before the start of classes when a Smithfield attorney asked his help in settling an unpaid account for his client's meals at Swain Hall. That required no more than a bit of negotiation with Coates's old self-help boss, Charles T. Woollen, the university's business manager. Beyond that, Albert Coates had never set foot in a courtroom to represent a client.[5]

Coates's youth and lack of experience stood in stark contrast to those traditionally chosen as faculty members. McGehee was thirty years his senior and had practiced law in Raleigh and New York City before joining the faculty in 1904. Atwell Campbell McIntosh, older than McGehee, had several years of legal experience before his first law school appointment, while Patrick Henry Winston, nearly twenty years older than Coates, had been a member of the Asheville Bar and was definitely a product of another era. Winston didn't even have a formal law degree. He had attended the UNC law school for one year in 1905 and a summer program at the University of Michigan before taking his bar examination. More recent hires had spent most of their careers teaching law, rather than in private practice. Robert Hasley Wettach and Maurice T. Van Hecke had only limited practical experience when McGehee added them to the expanded faculty in 1921.

Chase's overhaul of the law school had proceeded with limited comment from the trustees until the fall of 1923, when McGehee died unexpectedly and the president set out to find a successor. By the time Chase reached the trustees with his recommendation in January 1924, there were already those who wanted to install a state supreme court justice or another candidate with years of legal experience in the job. Chase was unbowed. He boldly laid out his vision for the school to the trustees when they met in the governor's office. The changes in faculty, adoption of the Langdell method, and higher admission standards were part of a package, Chase argued. "The question at the root of the whole matter," he said, "is whether it is the function of the University Law School to prepare an inferior brand of lawyers for law as a trade, or whether it shall prepare men for practice and leadership in law as a profession.

"We must choose between a law school which is frankly a coaching school for bar examinations and a real professional law school in the modern sense. To choose the former course means to abandon all thought of leadership. A strong faculty can never be secured and kept in a law school under such conditions. Nor would the better type of students enter or remain."[6]

Governor Cameron Morrison was not impressed with Chase's plans and he recited the names of great lawyers who had never attended college. The discussion continued for some weeks as Chase responded to trustees and others who wrote to express their objections. Some discounted the case method of instruction that McGehee had supported. "I hope that the students are reading Blackstone whether it is taught or not, but a system of legal instruction which omits all instruction in one of the greatest legal classics of all time, because, forsooth, it is in the form of a textbook, is theory run to 'seed,'" one wrote. Nor did critics think much of Chase's plan to find a dean who was experienced in the teaching of law, rather than a man with practical or judicial experience. The character and standing of such a venerated attorney means more than academic standing, several argued. "I think you will agree with me that most men teach more by what they are than what they say, and the very presence of an able Judge at the head of a law school, a man who has been a vital factor in the life of the state, will mean more in the building up of the law school and in the life of the various students who will come in contact with such a character than any one subject, or any dozen subjects, that will be taught in the school."[7]

Alumni and influential members of the Bar rose to support Chase. "The University has been hidebound for 100 years by aristocratic and family and political ties," one wrote. "Because someone's grandfather has been Chief Justice, or a member of the Cabinet or a distinguished North Carolinian, such men have been put into positions where they taught well but where they missed the vision necessary in preparing their students for the different business eras in the growth of this country. We have graduated political lawyers."[8]

Chase prevailed against the opposition. In June 1924, as the trustees gathered for commencement and their annual meeting on the campus in Chapel Hill, they voted overwhelmingly for his candidate as McGehee's successor. He was Merton Leroy Ferson, the dean of the law school at George Washington University.

Commencement in 1924 was the first informal reunion of Coates's Class of 1918. Those who returned for the event found that Coates's enthusiasm for the university and the torch he carried for Graham's philosophy of extension and integrating the university into the life of the state had not dimmed in the intervening years. After just a year on campus, he had leaped from his lowly status as a junior faculty member into the thick of university affairs. Coates was once again on the platform on behalf of the wider university, pursuing his mission as vigorously as if Edward Kidder Graham himself had tapped him for a role in Chapel Hill's future.

The rapid growth of the student body and the expansion of the campus with new buildings had disturbed the cozy college atmosphere that had been one of the most charming characteristics of the Hill in the days before World War I. Students and faculty no longer needed to live within walking distance of the campus. Now, automobiles had opened new neighborhoods to development. The swelling population and the diverse new academic programs had further diffused student interests. The space set aside in New West and New East for the literary societies, once the most important and enduring threads in the university fabric, had been reduced as the demand for teaching space became paramount.

Chase was concerned about the changes wrought by a larger student body that no longer had the campus as its only focus. He hoped to recapture the spirit that had once been characteristic of the school. In the fall of 1923, he had challenged deans and department chairs to examine their course offerings, determine how they fit into the overall mission of the university, and then commit to using their classrooms to turn out citizen-leaders for the state. In February 1924, Coates had joined Chase and Student Body President Julian Allsbrook in a special chapel meeting in Memorial Hall to revive the flagging campaign to raise the necessary money to build Graham Memorial, which was presented as a new symbol of the university. The prospects for completion of the original design had been shelved and construction plans had been retailored for a smaller building. Work had begun on the exterior although there was no guarantee that money to complete even this reduced version could be raised.

The meeting was followed with a front-page article in the *Tar Heel* in late March in which Coates delivered a lengthy tribute to the university and the need to bring students together in the way that had prevailed before the war. The rallying point was a new "University Life Unification Plan," which showed all of campus and academic life radiating from Graham Memorial. The building was to be the hub for the campus by providing a home for campus publications, athletic programs, student government, and social life, as well as the point where the faculty members and the administration could connect with the student body outside of the classroom.[9]

The stilted language of judicial decisions and rigor of Harvard Law School had not diminished Coates's ability to create inspiring phrases and patriotic notes when he was writing for his platform appearances. His sentences in the *Tar Heel* ran on for dozens of words carrying his readers or listeners along with him. "With this purpose [of unification] and with these forces dedicated to it, is it too much to believe that we can build here in Chapel Hill a university that will see into and understand the heart of this new civilization, a university that will gather into herself and interpret in her teachings the tangled currents of thought and life which throughout the South today are uneasily struggling for expression and release, blend their varied notes into a prophetic chord in the lives of men who call this campus home, and send them away with minds keen enough to pierce through phrases to facts, powerful enough to cut through error to truth, and courageous enough to build on that bottom a South in the image and likeness they have developed here."[10]

Coates was a likely candidate for Chase to lean upon as he prosecuted his campaign. The young professor was not that far removed from his own student days and he had already demonstrated an ability to capture the spirit of Chase's efforts during his few short months on the law faculty. By the spring of 1924, Coates had revived the Law School Association and was using it to introduce the practical side of the legal profession to his students. His work dovetailed nicely with Chase's goals of the university serving the people.

The Law School Association had been organized in the 1919–1920 academic year by Oscar Ogburn Efird, who joined the faculty that year. He turned a loose system of moot courts into law clubs similar to those Coates had experienced at Harvard. These clubs organized in the form of appellate courts and took briefs and heard arguments of cases on appeal. Efird remained on the faculty for only one year, however, and after he left the vitality of the association had dissipated until Coates arrived in 1923.[11]

The association was organized to serve the students, but Coates found it of great aid to his own fledgling efforts as a teacher. While he approached his new job with excitement and enthusiasm, he also was burdened with self-doubt about his adequacy in the classroom. He enjoyed the platform provided him by his law classes, and walked his students through the cases with the same demanding questioning that he was subjected to at Harvard. At the same time, he was concerned that his lack of experience with real clients and real cases was a handicap. He believed he needed a way to introduce the insight of lawyers who had known the day-to-day challenges of the courtroom. He wanted to "bridge the gap"—a phrase that he would make almost synonymous with his own name—between the law as he found it in books and the law as it was practiced in cities and towns across the state."I could call on a student to state a case, ask him if he agreed with it, and then ask why he did or why he did not. I could then ask a second student if he agreed with the first one, and why or why not; and so on," Coates later explained. "But what then? I did not have much of anything to add by way of content or illumination. The shortcoming was not in my casebook, it was in myself. I was in trouble and I knew it."[12]

Coates felt himself in danger of proving Chase's critics right. In fact, the president himself had suggested to Coates that he could gain from practical experience in a law office and the courtroom, but he had hired him anyhow. The young law professor found a way around his difficulties, without raising any concern for Chase. He used the Law School Association as his calling card and appealed to the justices of the state supreme court for help. He told Chief Justice Walter Clark that he had no money to pay a speaker's fee, and certainly no funds to finance anyone's travel to Chapel Hill, but he wanted members of the court to come prepared to speak for an hour or more as if they were being compensated. The justices agreed to help and made their way to the law school to deliver one- or two-hour presentations that would eventually grow into two- or three-day sessions. The visits "helped me put meat on the bones I was feeding to my classes," Coates said. "They helped me to get the feel of the law, to catch and carry the tune, to weather the first big crisis of my teaching career."[13]

Over the next four years, Coates would develop the Law School Association into a vibrant student organization that would "bridge the gap" and serve as something of a prototype for his later efforts to connect his classroom with everyday needs of public officials around the state. He established the association's office in the basement of Manning Hall in space that the Carolina Playmakers were using for storage. After that proved to be too confining, he appropriated the unfinished attic of the building. The association's new stationery listed him as "Director" and, upon his invitation, attorneys and judges became regular guests of the law school, either making presentations to classes or speaking at special events. The lecture series raised the profile of the law school among lawyers and also unified students under a common banner. For the first time, law students from all three classes worked together on preparations of briefs, presentations for appeals, and arguments before a mock court chaired by state and federal judges. The annual Law School Association banquet attracted leading attorneys and others in the profession as guest speakers. In time, Coates would raise money to outfit a model law office—his laboratory, he called it—and stock it with the furnishings and paperwork (deeds, mortgages, surveys, criminal warrants, and such) that graduates would find when they arrived for their first day of work.[14]

Coates truly had found his home. After initial misgivings about his abilities in the classroom, he rebounded and expanded beyond the criminal law course that he was assigned to teach to establish courses in municipal law and legislation. The campus unification project that he had taken on for Chase also was making some progress. It had invigorated the student body and the effort to open the Graham Memorial building. Each morning, Coates walked past the site of the proposed building as he made his away from his room on Franklin Street along the edge of McCorkle Place to his office in Manning Hall.

"The campus today is rocking with an enthusiasm it has never known before," Coates wrote Gladys Jane Hall, a senior at Randolph-Macon Woman's College whom he had met a few months earlier. "And I feel glad: because it has all grown out of a lemon which was handed me some weeks ago, and I have turned it into an orange, and the folks who got rid of it with a wry face are claiming it again with a welcoming smile; because the boys who have nerve enough to join with me at the beginning are feeling to-day their faith was justified."[15]

Gladys Hall was becoming an important part of Coates's life. The two had met in Portsmouth in the summer of 1923 when Coates was visiting there with a mutual friend from Harvard. Gladys was impressed with the young law-professor-to-be; Albert was equally taken with the quiet studious woman who was a rising senior at Randolph-Macon, a prestigious women's college in Lynchburg, Virginia, with a reputation for academic rigor. Both enjoyed poetry, loved history, and, in time, would delight in each other's company. Albert initiated their exchange of letters late in 1923 when he wrote Gladys to recall their brief time together the previous summer. She was surprised, and pleased, that he had remembered her. Their relationship began to flourish in the spring of 1924 after Gladys took a teaching job in Kinston, North Carolina, a tobacco town much like Smithfield about eighty miles east of Chapel Hill. In the fall of that year, Gladys was Albert's guest in Chapel Hill, where she charmed his friends, especially the cantankerous Horace Williams, a childless widower who warmed to her as easily as he had to Albert.

Gladys had a full round face, a broad pleasing smile, and soft brown hair. She was a beautiful and talented young woman with a passion for books and the grace, refinement, and accent of Tidewater Virginia. She loved music and was an accomplished pianist. At the same time, she was athletic, enjoyed ocean swims, and took fencing at Randolph-Macon. Gladys had grown up in Portsmouth with a brother and sister. Her father was the son of a Quaker with family in Northampton County, North Carolina, and had been educated at a Friends school in the North. He was part owner of a company that manufactured tables and other furnishings. The family visited often in North Carolina, where her father's family had been early settlers.[16]

Gladys's friend in Portsmouth had described Albert as an accomplished orator, telling her, "Why he can turn a small town drinking fountain into the Lincoln Memorial." But while Coates was comfortable before a crowd of strangers—even when they numbered in the hundreds—he was anxious about his relationship with this intelligent, demure young woman who was all his equal when quoting Shakespeare, tracking the lineage of presidents, or recalling selected lines of the poets. Approaching thirty years of age, Coates was unprepared for a romantic relationship. He had never quite outgrown a youthful notion to "have a certain manly scorn for anything feminine" and to believe those who didn't "were unworthy of association with real men."[17] He had little to learn from at home. His mother was not at all demonstrative in her love for her husband or her sons. Once her boys were grown she never initiated physical contact. By the time Albert was in college, he had occasional flirtations, but none had ever developed into anything serious. He invested his energy in his campus affairs, and later in his teaching and the mission of the university. Gladys was the first person ever to distract him from his studies or his work.

She had a soft and quiet beauty that suited her gracious personality.

When she met Albert, she enjoyed socializing and, while reserved, was comfortable with people. She underlined a passage in *The Art of Attracting Men*, a booklet given her by a friend that read, "Use every method consistent with maidenly modesty to let men know that you are still alive, who you are, where you can be seen, and what you are worth."[18]

Early in 1924, Albert visited Gladys at Randolph-Macon, and she was in love with him before he left. He didn't write for a time, and she worried, but on Easter weekend she received a bouquet of flowers at her home in Portsmouth when she was home for a break. She was both pleased and surprised by his expression of affection. By the fall of 1924, Gladys was teaching history and romance languages in Kinston, and Albert was making regular trips by train to see her. She came to Chapel Hill for a football weekend that November and stayed at Mrs. Blanche Patterson's boarding house, where Albert took his meals with other bachelors and widowers who called themselves the "Old Soldiers' Club." That weekend in November culminated with a faculty dance after UNC's game against Virginia Military Institute.

"I told you, when I asked you to come to Chapel Hill, I wanted you to knock'em cold. You did," Albert wrote almost as soon as Gladys was on her way east. "Horace Williams frankly admits captivation. So do Mr. McKie and Dr. Moss. The rest of them admit it all the more plainly by trying to hide it. Add to that the further fact that two young ladies with whom Chapel Hill dames had predicted alignments, saw you with me at the VMI game, and immediately despaired."[19]

Gladys was equally taken with those she met. "I only wish I dared believe some of the lovely things you wrote about my visit to Chapel Hill. That weekend is certainly the most delightful I remember! I am frightened at the nonentity that I seem to have been here, before, and perhaps, still am! You remember you wrote of having buried me in a sea of music, flowers, and poetry and that you believe I've 'emerged.'"[20]

Chapel Hill in the fall and the crowd at Mrs. Patterson's were all Gladys needed to fall as deeply in love with the village as with her beau. She had been exposed to the heartbeat and history of the university during her stay. The men around Mrs. Patterson's table included Frank Graham and Horace Williams as well as Major William Cain, a venerated mathematician who at the age of fourteen was drilling raw Confederate troops; Vernon Howell, the dean of the school of pharmacy; and the Reverend W. D. Moss.

Mrs. Patterson presided with grace at the table and served as chaperone for the young couple.

The romance continued into the spring of 1925 when Albert finally declared his love as the two sat under an arbor near the house on Pollock Street in Kinston where Gladys had a room. The boundary that Albert had established between him and women was overcome, albeit slowly, by the patience and adoring persistence of Gladys. After more than a year of correspondence, Coates still signed his letters with his full name. It was only after he declared his love that he felt comfortable to close them with a simple "Albert." With what sounded like true relief, he called her sweetheart for the first time. "My dear, did you call me once," he wrote. "Then, let me call you sweetheart: I'm in love with you."[21]

Gladys was thrilled to find the man she called her "knight." "For me you are all people, all things, everything that is beautiful, noble or true." She closed her response with lines of poetry and the salutation, "I will follow your soul as it leads."[22]

She returned to her home in Portsmouth, a large frame house with a porch that wrapped around the front, for the summer of 1925. From her room on the second floor she could see a patch of water. Often, in the evenings, she walked along the edge of the Elizabeth River, whose waters lapped at the shoreline about a block away, and she gathered wildflowers for arrangements that she put in the home. In the evenings, she wrote Albert of her hopes and dreams in letters littered with quotations from her favorite poets. Albert would visit often, but their relationship endured for more than three years cultivated mainly by letters in which the two laid plans for a life together in Chapel Hill. Since he had taken his post at the law school, Albert had entertained invitations for jobs outside of the university, but he had turned down every one. He had no plans to leave. "Next to my own mother," he wrote Gladys, "my alma mater has meant the most to me."[23]

That same summer, while Gladys was in Portsmouth, Coates took a break from his work and planned to spend a few days on Ocracoke Island, at the outer reaches of the North Carolina Outer Banks. For the past two years, before his love affair with Gladys blossomed, his schedule had been full to overflowing. In the spring he had added more hours to his days as he shuttled to and from Kinston to see her. On weekends, he had often not returned until late Sunday evening and had spent that night preparing for his Monday morning class, arriving at Manning Hall just in time to open with his lecture after less than an hour or two of sleep. Exhausted from his schedule, he arrived on the isolated island for a few days. He soon extended his stay to three weeks.

It was the first time he had really escaped from his busy schedule to spend any time in reflection and self-examination. Now, everything seemed to be swirling about. Truths he had held firm up to that point were bending under the weight of his growing love for Gladys. His own determined sense of achievement, work above all else, was proving too much to bear. Over the past two years he had overcome the tribulations and uncertainty in the classroom, thrown himself into building up the Law School Association, responded to calls from Chase and Louis R. Wilson to push the Graham Memorial campaign, and even plunged into assignments at the Methodist church at the behest of Wilson, who was a loyal communicant. All the while, he had been counseling his brother, who had just graduated. Albert urged Kenneth to relax and enjoy life—never following his own advice.

Now there was a prospect of a future with Gladys. While the two were deeply in love and talked obliquely of marriage in their letters to each other, a wedding and making a life together in the near term seemed to be out of the question. Albert was deeply in debt. He owed small amounts to a loan fund at Harvard. The loans from the Smithfield bank that had paid for his undergraduate education were outstanding, and he owed larger amounts to Leslie Weil and other benefactors who had helped him complete his law school education. He also had borrowed against a piece of property he owned in Smithfield. The loans had gone unpaid, in part because he had helped pay college expenses for his brother and for a sister who was a student at Woman's College in Greensboro. His parents also needed occasional assistance. They had moved into Smithfield from the farm, and his mother was running a boardinghouse. "I fear life with me will be a stormy life, sweetheart," he wrote at one point. "Can we create a symphony out of its crashing discords?"[24]

The quiet and uncomplicated pace at Ocracoke suited him as he extended his visit once, and then again. He walked barefoot along the island's narrow sandy paths that were marked only by the footprints of the residents, a few geese, and ponies that didn't know they were wild. He fished with the locals, surprising his host one day when he dove unexpectedly off the side of the boat to retrieve a starfish from the bottom of the shallow sound.

He took a slow, but detailed, inventory of all that he found: a doctor who owned the pharmacy; a barber who could neither hear nor speak; seven cars—six Fords and a Dodge; and three or four soft drink stands. He wrote Gladys that at one of the stands no flag on the pole meant soft drinks only, but when the flag was up, milk shakes and ice cream were available. Life was lean and rugged on the islands and he seemed to thrive in the simplicity of it all. "Their life may be difficult, but it is no less life to them. There is no place here for reformers, and uplifters. These folks don't need to be 'prayed for.' I know most of them and like them."[25]

His time alone brought the realization that during his adult life he had never taken time to relax or have fun. In his usual style of one point flowing to another and on in a unified logical progression, as Horace Williams had taught him, he could construct a single paragraph that filled pages from margin to margin with his self-analysis.

He wrote Gladys: "And so I find out a new fact about myself: partly on account of heredity, partly on account of environment, partly on account of the nature of that part of us which is not to be ascribed either to heredity or environment and which we may call the original in us—the individual—the me or the you and the nobody else—I have for years generated a belief that work is the only part of life worthwhile; and in order to make that belief livable I have developed a philosophy that pleasure is to be found generally only in work. The result has been that I have played not for the love of play but for the love of work: and how on an evening off would more than make up for itself in terms of increased efficiency for work the next day. The result was: play was reduced from the level of pleasure to the level of exercise: exercise became a matter of duty rather than a matter of delight: duty, like obligation is to be entered into only as a matter of necessity: and so the story goes, so it went with me, tapering down to the point when I discharged my duty by calling my brother in once a week to lecture him on the value of getting out for recreation. The result of that was that I came near to running down because I wasn't running at all. And the result of that: instead of coming to Ocracoke for what is known as a 'hell of a good time' I came down here for what is known as 'rest' and relaxation."[26]

Coates finally pulled himself away from the pleasure he found on Ocracoke and returned to Chapel Hill to teach in the summer session of the law school. Yet, regardless of what he had written to Gladys, he found that he could not keep himself still. His Ocracoke epiphany faded before fall, when he returned to his busy life on campus, to the detriment of his health. By September, he was under a doctor's instructions to follow a more regular diet and a regimen that called for a light supper, warm milk before bedtime, and naps after his meals.

Coates seemed incapable of denying requests for public appearances. Regular calls for his oratory at convocations and graduations came from former classmates who were now school principals or otherwise involved with education. He was invited to special events in his hometown, where he spoke of the problems facing farmers' co-operatives and the needs of the university. He was in demand from alumni clubs around the state. Late in 1925, he made a special effort to speak before public groups when the university was under fire from conservative religious leaders who had failed in their efforts to outlaw the teaching of evolution in North Carolina schools and were taking out their disappointment in attacks on what they considered the deleterious effects of an education at Chapel Hill. (In 1925 the outcome in the legislature of the so-called Poole Bill prohibiting the teaching of evolution in public schools hung on one vote. Both President Chase and Wake Forest College President W. L. Poteat had opposed the measure as a restriction of free speech and academic liberties.)[27]

Coates's loyalty to the university and his kinship with Horace Williams would not allow him to sit silently on the sidelines in the face of controversy. The university and its faculty, especially Williams, had produced thinking men with a loyalty to the school who were deeply offended at the unreasonableness of the anti-evolutionists. Some of the harshest criticism had arisen in Charlotte and in Bible-belt cotton-mill towns such as Gastonia. Coates put off a post-Christmas visit with Gladys in Portsmouth to defend his alma mater at four alumni meetings held during that holiday season.

Critics claimed that the growth of the university had led to spiritual decline, outrageous student behavior, especially involving alcohol, and overall moral decay that threatened to undermine and destroy the religious faith of impressionable young men and women. Coates responded to each criticism, building his case on evidence that refuted each point. He took his applause in letters from some of the leading alumni in the state. Charlotte lawyer Charles Tillett Jr. wrote to Coates to say, "It is in all respects the best speech I have ever heard made to an alumni gathering by a professor from Chapel Hill." Later, in 1926, speaking at a convocation of the public schools in Wilson, Coates drew praise from an old friend. "The fundamentalists and liberals alike were loud in their praise of you."[28]

Albert was up for a fight to defend the university, but he particularly enjoyed the personal renewal he experienced at the public school events. He told Gladys: "There is a great deal of inspiration for me in the high school commencements—the look in the eyes of the boys and girls as they sit on the stage and as they get their diplomas. It isn't to be found anywhere else—it is only on a graduation evening. It is a peak—and they know it. And it is wonderful. It sort of gets hold of me."[29]

Despite advice from doctors, friends, and Mrs. Patterson to slow the pace of his life, Coates seemed to run at only one speed—wide open. He moderated his lifestyle on occasion, especially when he was thinking of Gladys. From time to time, he would wander off for a walk through the woods or into the fields at the edge of the campus—sometimes when he awoke in the middle of the night. One night he climbed the scaffolding of a building, perhaps the one at the unfinished Graham Memorial, and sat alone contemplating the evening sky, which he and Gladys often stared into as they sat quietly with one another. He wrote to Gladys that reading poetry eased the grinding wheels in his mind. Two favorites were Percy Bysshe Shelley's "Ode to the West Wind" and "The Skylark." As he wrote to Gladys, "The first somehow lends wings and a driving power to imagination; the second somehow gives a fine mist to thought. I reckon that's why I liked your idea of being 'sandaled with wind and with flame.'"[30]

In early June, Coates left Chapel Hill for a speaking engagement in Murphy, in the far western end of the state, even though a trip to Wilson the week before had left him sick and, once again, worn to exhaustion. His new aches and pains came in part from having had to change a flat tire in a drenching rainstorm on his return from Wilson. Albert had pushed on to meet his appointment in Murphy despite a severe head cold. He began to feel unwell as the trip began and when he reached Bryson City, west of Asheville, he got off the train and took a room for the night hoping to get some rest before continuing on his journey. The next day he arrived in Murphy but was still unsteady. That evening, he collapsed just as he was about to mount the stage to give a graduation speech. He ended up in a room at the Hotel Regal, under a doctor's care with a nurse at his side. For days, his fever hovered near 104 degrees and his head pounded with a headache. It was two weeks before he could hold down his first solid food, a boiled egg. Prior to that he had subsisted on glasses of buttermilk that he drank every few hours.

Coates spent nearly a month at the Hotel Regal before he regained enough strength for the return trip to Chapel Hill. When he arrived home, he was still weak. Doctors in Durham examined him thoroughly and concluded that he had worked himself into a state of complete exhaustion. "They only tell me what I have told you," he wrote to Gladys, who was beside herself with concern, "that I am tired—worn out—rundown—that I have for too many years been working too hard without taking care of my physical self—that I have all these years been drawing on my reserves until I have exhausted them—that I must build them up again—that I must rest."[31]

The experience shook Coates to his core. Never before had he been unable to meet challenges as they arose. He had had bouts with colds and other ailments—an injured foot had kept him on crutches the summer before—but he had always rebounded from sickness or injury. Now, he lay about all day on the sleeping porch at Mrs. Patterson's, almost too weak to do the modest exercises that his doctor recommended. He recalled earlier warnings from his landlady, who had told him he was headed for trouble, as a mutual friend reminded him in a letter. "Mrs. Pat tells me you do not like to be told your 'nerves' are involved. That's because so many folks' nerves and emotions are supposed to be exclusively feminine possessions. As a matter of fact, the basis of all health and happiness is the proper coordination of all the many organs of the body and that coordination is the function of the nerves and endocrine glands."[32]

Coates had planned to teach during the summer session, but in his weakened condition he had to cancel. In fact, he believed that he would not recover his health in time to prepare his classes for the fall. He told Gladys that he had sent a letter of resignation to Chase, but he asked the president to keep the matter private. "I shall be here for some weeks yet," he told Gladys, "and I do not want the sympathy of my associates—I do not need it."[33] He professed that all he needed was rest. His plans for the future remained uncertain.

He wrote to Gladys that he had offers from law firms in large cities but might open his own law practice in some small town. He warned that starting fresh he could not expect an income to equal his salary of $4,000 a year as a law professor; it would take time for him to regain what he was giving up in pay at the university. He was severely disappointed in himself. "The bitterness is intensified in the thought that my breakdown troubles you," he wrote. "Even if things had gone as they were going—as we had planned them, I could not have offered you the luxuries you are now enjoying—nor even the comforts. And now I have even less to offer."[34]

The recuperation at Mrs. Patterson's must have gone better than Coates expected. He got some encouragement from his friend Daniel Grant, who ran the alumni association. "You have the finest natural endowments of any young man I know but the finest have to be pampered a little, and greased and rested." And Chase was not going to be denied those talents. He arranged for a pay raise and tenured status as a professor of law. Coates was back in the classroom for the start of the fall term.

Coates, himself, was concerned enough about the episode to seek some answers. He asked a biologist friend to help him learn about how his body worked. He set about a course of reading that carried him into the fall. Later in the year he delayed his return to Chapel Hill after attending a meeting in Chicago of the Association of American Law Schools and traveled to Rochester, Minnesota, where, with the assistance of one of his former students, he scheduled a full physical examination at the Mayo Clinic. He spent several days there, and the results were no different from what he had learned at home. He had no illness or failure of critical organs. The experience of six months earlier was as simple as it had appeared. Coates had worked himself into exhaustion.

"They told me I was all right," Coates later wrote, "and, what is more, they proved it. More than that, Dr. [Charles] Mayo told me that I would stay all right, and that my body could stand up to the stress and strain of any amount of work, if I would accept and understand one thing: that I was a human being, with all the limitations of a human being, and that the only way a human being could transcend his limitations was to live within them. The process I had started as an intellectual enterprise turned into a spiritual experience."[35]

On his trip home, Coates weighed all he had heard from the Mayo doctors. Parsing his experience of the six days that he had been shuttled from one specialist to another, each with his own narrow field of interest, Coates marveled at the way Dr. Mayo had taken each of their reports and then organized their work to produce an analysis of the whole. Taken alone, the specialists' reports meant nothing. It was only when they were put together to produce a composite medical picture of Albert Coates that they proved worthwhile.

He was reminded of a similar demonstration just a few months back, when he had audited R. D. W. Connor's course on North Carolina history. It was a course that had not been available when Coates was an undergraduate, and in Connor's lectures he found a North Carolina that he had never really known. Born and bred in the eastern part of the state, Coates envisioned North Carolina not as a state, but as disparate parts, with mountainous regions as remote from the mainstream of the state as isolated islands such as Ocracoke. Connor brought the pieces together for him into a whole that he had never before seen.[36]

He began to see that there were linkages across the regions, and across academic disciplines, as there were within his own body, and that the whole needed consideration. It was not too far a leap from that kind of thinking to the challenges he had faced in his first law class and the progress he had made in bridging the gap between law student and law practitioner. He had his concept, or "begriff" as Horace Williams called it. Now he had to find a way to make it work.

The Coates family in Smithfield. Standing in the back row, left to right, are Albert's sisters Harriet, Bessie, and Dora. In the middle row, from left to right, are his sister Ethel, his parents, Daniel and Nancy, Albert, and his sister Eva. Albert's brother, Kenneth, is standing in the front with his sister Edna. Missing from the picture is his sister Elizabeth. (SHC)

Daniel Coates moved his family into this large plantation home with a storied past that stood on the outskirts of Smithfield. (SHC)

Franklin Street in Chapel Hill in 1914, the year Albert Coates arrived to begin his studies at the university. *W. Staley Wicker Photograph Album.* (NCC)

Aerial view of the University of North Carolina circa 1918–19. *Attributed to Belvin W. Maynard, "The Flying Parson."* (NCC)

University Day, University of North Carolina, October 12, 1917. In the front row are (left to right) University President Edward Kidder Graham, Governor Thomas Bickett, and Captain Stuart Allen. In the second row: Professor Walter Toy, Law School Dean Lucius McGehee, Graduate School Dean Charles L. Raper, former presidents Kemp Battle Jr. and Francis Venable, and Medical School Dean Isaac Manning. Professor E. C. Branson is in the back row in the upper right corner. (NCC)

Albert Coates on the far left at the head of a parade he marshaled on the campus in Chapel Hill, most likely during the July Fourth festivities in 1918. (SHC)

Edward Kidder Graham was president of the university for only four years before his untimely death in 1918, but his vision shaped the institution's future for the twentieth century. (NCC)

Albert Coates as an undergraduate at the University of North Carolina. (NCC)

Albert Coates was just finishing officer training in the army when World War I ended in November 1918. (SHC)

Members of the Order of the Golden Fleece at the University of North Carolina in 1920. In the front row, third and fifth from the left, are Albert Coates and Frank Graham. Thomas Wolfe, a friend of Coates at both Carolina and Harvard, is the tallest man in the back row. *Nat G. Gooding, photographer.* (NCC)

Horace Williams, pictured here in the late 1930s, was a beloved professor of philosophy whose teaching shaped the thinking of generations of students at the University of North Carolina. *Wootten-Moulton Studio, photographer.* (NCC)

In the summer of 1922, Albert and a group of friends, including writer Thomas Wolfe, spent several days tramping through the North Carolina mountains. Albert wore a tie. (SHC)

The Reverend W. D. Moss of Chapel Hill, the Presbyterian minister who was a favorite of students and who officiated at the wedding of Albert and Gladys Coates in June 1928. (NCC)

In the summer of 1927, before her marriage to Albert Coates, Gladys Hall took a tour of Europe. When she arrived at her hotels on the Continent, she was greeted by a bouquet of flowers ordered by Albert. (SHC)

During summer outings at the North Carolina coast, Albert Coates found rejuvenation from his exhausting schedule. This snapshot was taken at New River Inlet, Onslow County, in August 1921. (SHC)

During their first year of marriage in 1928, Albert and Gladys Coates rented the spacious home of a university colleague who was on leave. They would not enjoy such comfortable accommodations until they built their own house almost twenty-five years later. (SHC)

The Graham Memorial was originally designed to be three times as large as the building that was finally completed in 1931. (NCC)

The law school had just moved into its new home, Manning Hall, when Albert Coates joined the faculty in the fall of 1923. (NCC)

Albert Coates revived the Law School Association when he returned to teach at the university in 1923, arranging for donations from practicing attorneys to outfit a model courtroom and a model law office for law students. The courtroom was pictured in an article in the *Alumni Review* in 1928. (NCC)

As president of the University of North Carolina from 1930 to 1949, Frank Porter Graham, pictured here circa 1932, often intervened on behalf of Albert Coates and his Institute of Government. (NCC)

Albert Coates at his desk in his law school classroom. (SHC)

The law school faculty in 1933 included (front row, left to right) Albert Coates, Maurice T. Van Hecke, Atwell C. McIntosh, and Fred B. McCall and (back row, left to right) Robert H. Wettach, Millard S. Breckenridge, Frank W. Hanft, and James H. Chadbourn. (NCC)

Albert Coates, pictured here in February 1930, was then on leave from his teaching duties in Chapel Hill and was halfway through a year of graduate study at the Harvard University Law School. (SHC)

Sociologist Howard W. Odum, circa 1930. Though their shared interests were many, Odum and Coates differed too much in their approaches to local government—and were perhaps too similar in temperament and ego—for any real collaboration to be possible. *Underwood and Underwood, Washington, D.C., photographer.* (NCC)

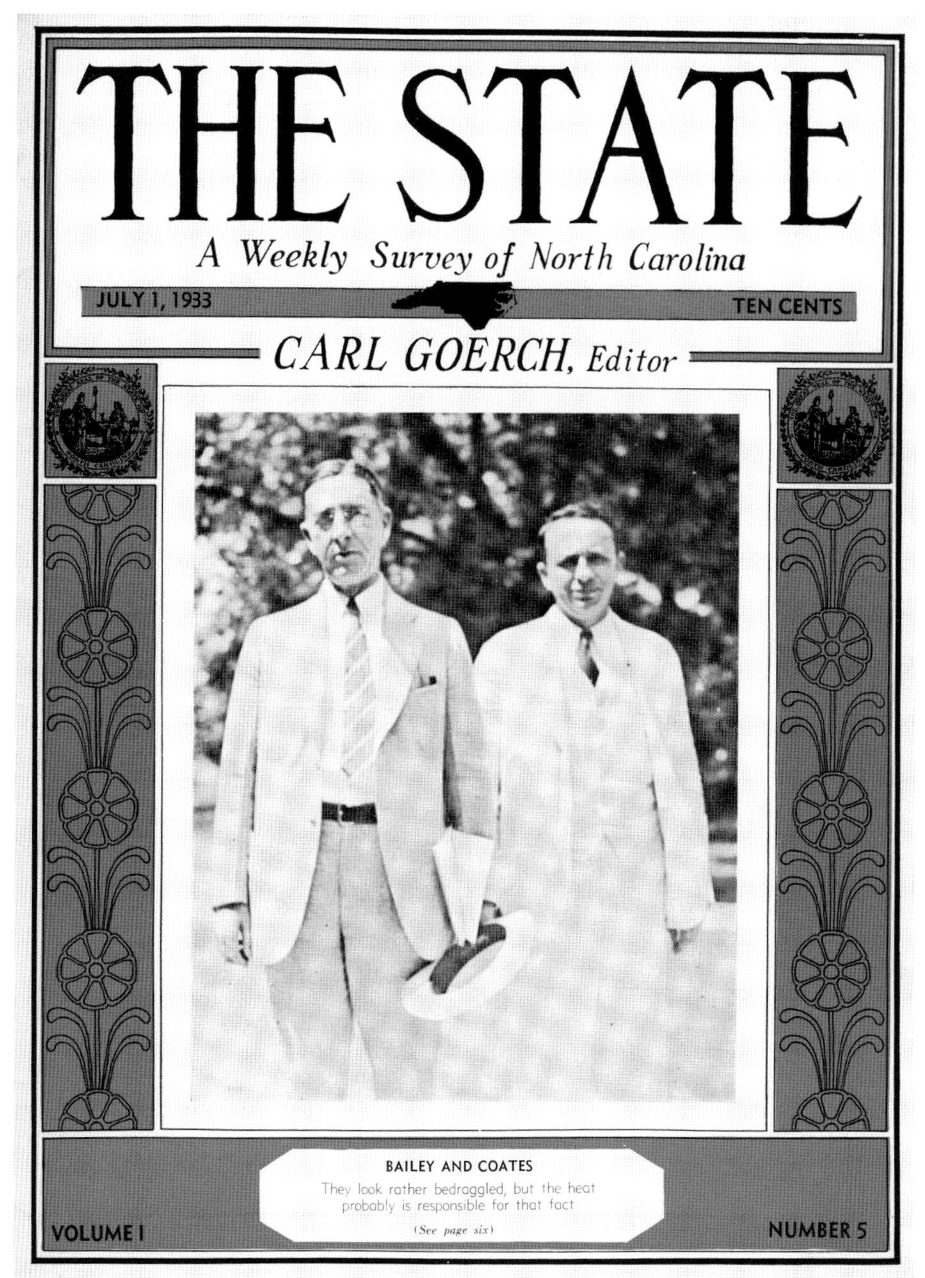

THE STATE

A Weekly Survey of North Carolina

JULY 1, 1933 — TEN CENTS

CARL GOERCH, Editor

BAILEY AND COATES

They look rather bedraggled, but the heat probably is responsible for that fact

(See page six)

VOLUME I — NUMBER 5

SUBSCRIPTION PRICE, $3.00 PER YEAR

Publisher Carl Goerch put his photograph of U.S. Senator Josiah Bailey and Albert Coates on the front cover of his new news magazine, *The State*, to mark a statewide meeting of the Institute of Government in July 1933 that drew hundreds of public officials to Chapel Hill. (NCC)

All meetings at the Institute of Government ended the same way—with a group photograph. This meeting on September 7, 1937, was with seventy-four state department and division heads and included Governor Clyde R. Hoey. Albert Coates chose an uncharacteristic spot in the shadows beneath the trees in the back right corner. (SHC)

The state's political leadership gathered for the dedication of the Institute's building on Franklin Street in 1939. Seated, left to right, are Governor Clyde Hoey, U.S. House Speaker William B. Bankhead of Alabama, and former governor O. Max Gardner. Standing, left to right, are UNC Chancellor Robert House, Coates, state Democratic Party Chairman Gregg Cherry, Congressmen Robert Doughton and Lindsey Warren, state Republican Party Chairman Jake Newell, and F. P. Coffey of the Federal Bureau of Investigation. (SHC)

The Institute of Government opened in 1939. The building stands across Franklin Street from Graham Memorial and was dedicated, years later, as the Albert and Gladys Coates Building. (NCC)

Visitors to the Institute of Government on Franklin Street found a welcoming lobby on the building's first floor, shown here circa 1940. (NCC)

Gladys and Albert Coates in front of the Institute of Government building on Franklin Street in 1944. (SHC)

Gladys Hall Coates was an accomplished scholar, musician, and writer who devoted herself to her husband's cause. (SHC)

Gladys Coates's favorite photographic portrait of her husband, Albert, was taken in 1940. *Fabian Bachrach, photographer.* (SHC)

One of the Institute of Government's earliest training programs was for members of the State Highway Patrol, who are pictured here in 1937. Without a building of his own, Coates used courtrooms around the state for his classrooms. (SHC)

Albert Coates, Governor Clyde R. Hoey, and Ed Scheidt of the Federal Bureau of Investigation, who was on leave to work with the Institute of Government (front row, left to right), with the North Carolina officers who completed the ten-day school for police instructors, January 14, 1937. (SOG)

Future governor Terry Sanford (front row, center) with Albert Coates (on his right) pose with the training staff of the expanded school for the State Highway Patrol that Sanford ran for the Institute of Government in 1946. *University of North Carolina Photographic Lab.* (NCC)

The Institute of Government revived the Boys State program after World War II. Included in this photograph of the Boys State staff are future UNC president William Friday, far left, and future governor Terry Sanford, who is standing to Friday's left and partially obscured. Sanford helped Coates manage the program in the summer of 1948, when Friday and the other staff members pictured here were law students or recent graduates who had not found jobs. *W. D. Patterson, photographer.* (SHC)

Robert Madry in early 1949. Madry was one of Albert Coates's mates in the Class of 1918. He ran the University News Bureau and served for nearly thirty years as Coates's unofficial and devoted publicist. (NCC)

Henry P. Brandis Jr. and Robert H. Wettach of the UNC law school faculty in 1949. (NCC)

In 1941 Albert Coates presented FBI director J. Edgar Hoover with a police training manual produced by the Institute of Government. (SHC)

The administrative careers of Robert B. House (left) as chancellor of the Chapel Hill campus and Frank Graham as president of the University of North Carolina—pictured here circa 1949—concurred with Albert Coates's tenure at the law school. Both men managed to contain as well as nurture Coates as he struggled through the creation of the Institute of Government. *William Stonestreet, photographer.* (NCC)

Thanks to a donation from the Joseph Palmer Knapp Foundation, the Institute of Government moved into new facilities on the University of North Carolina campus in the fall of 1956. (NCC)

The Institute of Government's new home, the Knapp-Sanders Building, as it looked from the air when it opened in 1956. *Monroe Campbell, University of North Carolina Photographic Lab.* (NCC)

UNC Chancellor William B. Aycock, U.S. Senator Sam Ervin Jr., Governor Luther H. Hodges, U.S. Senator B. Everett Jordan, and Albert Coates at the dedication of the Joseph Palmer Knapp Building, November 30, 1960. *Dave Windley, University of North Carolina Photographic Lab.* (NCC)

This photograph of Albert Coates with Chancellor William B. Aycock and John Sanders, Coates's successor as director of the Institute of Government, appeared on the cover of the September 1962 issue of *Popular Government* with the caption "End of an Era." (SHC)

One of the fourteen murals painted by Francis Kughler for the Institute of Government building was titled *Pageant of Dreamers*. Kughler depicted artists, writers, and other creative thinkers of the state, including Albert and Gladys Coates, whom he placed in the lower right corner. *Jim O'Neil, University of North Carolina Photographic Lab.* (NCC)

In 1975, the North Carolina League of Municipalities and the North Carolina Association of County Commissioners dedicated their joint offices in Raleigh as the Albert Coates Local Government Center. (SHC)

Albert Coates with Henry Lewis (left) and John Sanders (right), who succeeded him as directors of the Institute of Government. (SHC)

Albert Coates seated next to the bust created by William E. Hipp III on commission of the Dialectic and Philanthropic Societies in February 1976. *Howard Shepherd, University of North Carolina Photographic Lab.* (NCC)

FIVE

Out of the Classroom

1927–1930

IN THE FALL OF 1918, while Albert Coates was in the midst of his army training in Georgia, the university extension program published a comprehensive review of county government in North Carolina produced by E. C. Branson, Coates's friend, mentor, and former professor. Branson called county government the "least credible institution in America today" and backed up his claim with data collected by the men of the North Carolina Club who had worked under Coates during his senior year when he was leading the club through one of its most productive years.

Branson had long been interested in this political backwater. Until he came along, county government had escaped serious scrutiny, despite the taxing powers and potential for graft and mismanagement that existed for local officials who literally had control over one's life and property. Even if local officials were honest, and only incompetent, the casual or, as in some counties, the calculated mismanagement of property taxes showed how severely the public was being shortchanged in support for basic services such as schools, roads, and care of the elderly, poor, and infirm. The Great War, followed by an economic recession, and his travels abroad to study rural life in Europe, interrupted Branson's pursuit of this area of interest. He revived it in 1924 when the university's new Institute for

Research in Social Sciences took on county government as the focus of its first project and he was chosen to lead the research.

The Institute was the creation of Howard W. Odum, who had joined the university in 1920 in an arrangement largely engineered by Branson and blessed by President Harry Chase. Odum was asked to head the university's new school of public welfare, a name that had been agreed upon as less alarming than social science or sociology, which Branson himself admitted were fatally linked in the North Carolina mind with "socialism." (That association would soon fade and sociology would be accepted without controversy.) Odum, a Georgian, was teaching at Emory University in Atlanta when he was invited to come to Chapel Hill as one of the first Kenan professors, a position that included an extra stipend.

Odum proved to be one of the most productive members of the faculty. He worked on several books at a time, and the sound of his typewriter could be heard well into the night coming from his room in a farmhouse south of Chapel Hill. He liked living in the country, where he raised prize-winning Jersey cattle and was a bit of a social hermit. "He worked incessantly, as if every day was to be his last chance to get something done," Guy Johnson, one of his protégés later wrote. Odum had recruited Johnson to the UNC faculty and he and his wife, Guion, who taught journalism, lived on the Odum farm for a time when they first arrived. In the evenings, the three would talk about the future of the Institute. "We've all got to work hard," Odum told the Johnsons. "We've got to produce and publish, so that we can put this university and this Institute on the map. The university is behind us, and it is ready to go places. We have our chance, and if we don't make good, we will have nobody to blame but ourselves."[1]

By the time Coates returned to the campus from Harvard in 1923, Odum had launched *Social Forces*, a journal that reported on contemporary subjects. One of the early issues carried a scientific discussion of religion and provoked a stormy response from North Carolina churchmen, who demanded that he be fired. Simultaneously, he was organizing the Institute with an impressive grant from the Laura Spelman Rockefeller Memorial. In a short time, Odum had shown that he could recruit faculty, produce reams of copy for publication, and teach in the new discipline that everyone now called sociology, plus he was adept at raising money. The $32,500 from the foundation would fund the Institute's work for three years.

Branson and the Institute's researchers fanned out across North Carolina and made a detailed accounting of county government in forty-three of the state's one hundred counties. The study focused on the local power centers, the boards of county commissioners, and the results confirmed the range of behavior that Coates and his fellow students had reported on several years earlier. In a few instances, county government was run with modern efficiencies that were already in place as part of the reform movement of municipal governments. In other counties, decades of lax management had gone unchallenged. A researcher found one county where the commissioners held their regular meetings around a potbelly stove at a country store. Commissioners wandered in and out of the "meeting" to have private chats with onlookers. "Rarely were all three members at the table at once," Paul Wager reported in a published version of the study.[2] In another county, they found that the official minutes of the public's business consisted of notes that one board member scribbled on a scrap of paper that someone else later transcribed.

They found atrocious conditions in "county homes" maintained for poor and elderly men and women who had nowhere else to go. In some counties, the sheriff's treatment of prisoners on the county chain gangs was beyond the pale. Inmates were lodged in iron cages on wheels that were rolled from one road location to another. "Imagine eight or ten men with dirty, damp clothing sleeping in a poorly ventilated cage about 12 feet long, six feet wide and six feet high," Wager wrote. "There can be no toilet facilities except of an improvised sort. Some of the men are likely to be diseased. A man of any sensibilities would rather work a month at hard labor than spend one night in such an iniquitous trap."[3]

In 1925, Odum shared the findings of this research with a study commission that had been created by North Carolina's newly elected governor, Angus McLean. During his first year in office, the governor answered the call to make reform a priority. Government efficiency was just the topic for McLean, who put the brakes on the generous spending program that had been promoted by his predecessor, Cameron Morrison. In 1927, with the commission's recommendations in hand, McLean delivered a special address to the General Assembly and put forward a range of changes in state law to impose more fiscal discipline on county government. It was aimed at improving the financial strength of the counties, some of which were woefully in debt simply because the local officials had mishandled their taxing authority. In one county, the board of commissioners had taken out short-term bank loans rather than collect back taxes.

Branson's success in extending the resources of the university into the community, first with the North Carolina Club and later with Odum's Institute, was a perfect example of Edward Kidder Graham's vision for how the university—its faculty, students, and institutions—should serve the citizens of the state. Odum's Institute had merged academic research with reform to produce a higher standard of government in the state. The Institute's work came just as Albert Coates was trying to perfect his own vision of how he could use his classroom in the law school to serve the people of North Carolina.

The law school was growing in students and faculty and moving steadily along the path that Chase had prepared for it earlier in the decade. More students were staying for the third year, even though only two years of study were required to qualify for licensing. The quality of the faculty was improving with each new addition, and the summer school had been overhauled to include courses for credit, raising it from its previous service as a refresher program for candidates for the Bar examination. Among those invited to teach in the summer were professors of law from Yale and Columbia and the University of Pittsburgh. Coates and other regular faculty members taught courses, as did members of the state supreme court.

The standards of admission to the Bar, and the requirements for admission to law school, were still lively topics of debate among the trustees, alumni, and within the North Carolina Bar Association. In the fall of 1927, with enrollment at the law school up by 25 percent in just five years and the full-time faculty expanded to seven, Coates was completing an article on the bar standards for the *North Carolina Law Review*. In it he argued that a three-year course of study was necessary for licensing if a lawyer was going to be prepared for the complex new world of business and government in which lawyers would find themselves when they hung out their shingles.

Coates also believed he had struck a blow for boosting the stature of the profession when he created a major dustup among the first-year students. He would survive without major scars but at the same time the experience would leave him chastened. In February 1927, the students in Coates's personal property class were shaken and angry when they received their grades for the final examination. Out of a class of fifty-two, Coates had issued fifteen Fs and seven Es, thus flunking 40 percent of the class. Two of the failing grades went to men who had been tapped for Phi Beta Kappa. The class leaders confronted Coates with complaints that his grading had been too harsh, and they organized meetings to press their case. One of those speaking for the class was Dan K. Moore of Asheville, who was the second-semester president of the first-year class. (Forty years later, Moore would be governor of North Carolina and, subsequently, a justice of the state supreme court. Another member of the class was Susie M. Sharp, who would later be chief justice of the state supreme court.) The student committee argued that Coates should have used some sort of curve on which to measure the performance of his class. The young professor refused to budge, however, and took great umbrage at his students' challenge. He said he could not in good conscience give a higher grade than he thought was deserved.

The complaints spilled over into the campus at large. There was talk of boycotting his class and raising a petition for his dismissal. Some of the students took their concerns to other members of the faculty, where they found a bit of support. Coates was not roundly loved by his peers, and he was regarded as a challenge by his dean, A. C. McIntosh, who once said of him, "You can always tell a Harvard man, but you can't tell him much." Susie Sharp, the first woman to wear the robes of a superior court judge in North Carolina, said that the first time she ever heard that worn phrase was when McIntosh applied it to Coates.[4]

As Coates had gained confidence in the classroom, he had become known for his tough, even cynical, treatment of students. It was as if he were trying to outdo—or certainly equal—the probing questioning of Samuel Williston and Joseph Henry Beale at Harvard. Gladys Hall once sat in on a class and afterward expressed her concern about Albert's curt exchange with one student in particular. Yes, he told her, he is the best in the class.

Coates asked more questions than he answered in his verbal sparring with students. In his course in criminal law he liked to poke and prod students with questions that forced them to break down the basic elements of an offense. If a door was ajar and one entered, was he guilty of the offense of breaking and entering? There had been no "breaking"—or had there? Coates went relentlessly from one question to another, testing his students' ability to analyze the particulars of a case. One day, a frustrated student finally exploded at his professor. "You are undoubtedly the meanest son of a bitch I have ever sat in class with. I guess I can't be a lawyer." He was preparing to walk out of the class when Coates said, "Young man, wait a minute. Come back here and sit down. With that spirit you're bound to be a good lawyer. Sit down. Now, you're showing something."[5]

Susie Sharp was not the first woman to be admitted to the law school, but she was the only woman in the first-year class of sixty that began classes in September 1926. She suffered through harassment and insults in her early weeks and was thoroughly bewildered by Coates. In his course on personal property, the one in which he had delivered the disputed grades (Sharp got a D), Coates had used as an example a hunter who captures a wild animal. "The rule was clear," she said, "the hunter owned the animal when he reduced it to his possession—but when Oh! When was that accomplished? Mr. Coates paced the floor. Suppose the animal had walked into your trap a hundred yards away and you were hurrying toward it when another hunter took possession of it? Was it your mink? Mr. Coates didn't say—he just asked another question."[6]

Coates accented his lectures with generous doses of profanity, quotations from the Bible, Shakespeare, and Oliver Wendell Holmes, and even lines from *Alice in Wonderland*. His favorite question was, "Where do you draw the line?" Sharp wrote that for Coates success was not measured by the "right answer" to questions of law. "Your grade would depend on whether you could pierce through the phrases to the facts, isolate all the issues which lurked in his questions, and then draw the line *somewhere*."[7] Coates defended his style of teaching saying that he believed a question mark at the end of a sentence was more effective than a period. "One is a stopping point, the other is a starting point. One is the end of discussion, the other is the beginning. One is more likely to stuff the students, the other is likely to stir them. And teaching is more a matter of stirring than of stuffing."[8]

Coates's classroom performance looked like it had caught up with him by the time the *Tar Heel* reported on the uproar created by the students in his property law class. He met with the student committee and then called the entire class together for a meeting. He told them that the reason so many had done worse than expected was because they had failed to find the essence of the questions he had posed. They had responded from memory, rather than with answers supported by their own reasoning and creativity. With his mastery of a tightly wrapped argument that he cloaked in patriotism and appeals to the best of his alma mater, he succeeded in calming the waters. Coates said he had set high standards for his students because of his devotion to the university and to the law school. He refused to change their grades, but he did arrange for a new examination.

Some years later, however, Coates thought better of holding fast to his position. "I thought I was hitting a blow for higher standards in the law school," Coates wrote, "and then came the sober second thought: 'Old boy, those grades not only show how little the student learned but they also show how little you have taught.'"[9]

Coates had enjoyed considerable professional freedom since joining the faculty in the fall of 1923, largely thanks to requests from the president's office that he represent the university outside of the classroom. Chase called on him to fill speaking engagements, especially during the revival of the Graham Memorial campaign. Meanwhile, Coates ventured outside of his own discipline and audited courses in history and literature. At the same time, he expanded the list of his course offerings. He had begun with criminal law, corporations, trusts, taxation, and torts. Within two years he was teaching courses on equity, procedure, and property, and he had developed a new course on municipal corporations. Municipal law was one of his favorites, along with family law, and, later, legislation.

Despite the lowly reputation of criminal law within the legal community, it was the area that occupied most of Coates's time and attention. He later wrote that he had long heard that any self-respecting lawyer practiced criminal defense law only until he was able to make a living at something else. That attitude, he said, "explains the plight of criminal law enforcement now."[10] Yet, as much as he wanted to raise the level of appreciation for the subject, Coates felt limited by his own lack of knowledge and experience with the criminal justice system. He knew nothing of the challenges facing the policeman on the street and had never defended a client on trial. He had never seen the inside of a prison cell. Furthermore, he would explain later that for all the virtues of the case system he and his colleagues subscribed to, he was teaching criminal law based on too few examples and without any of the facts and experience that were part of the original criminal charge. If Coates needed more evidence of the short supply of valid cases to bring to his students, he discovered in one of Odum's studies that only four-tenths of one percent of the cases tried in the criminal courts of the state had even made it to the state supreme court. He was reminded of an article written by his law school dean, Roscoe Pound, titled, "Law in Books and Law in Action."[11]

Coates's interest in the challenges to the legal profession outside of the classroom was further sparked after a visit with James G. Hanes, the mayor of Winston-Salem. Hanes had come to the law school seeking help on how to raise the professionalism of law enforcement in his city. One summer afternoon, the two sat under a tree in Coates's front yard and talked for three hours about the problems of modern policing. The issue was more than cops and robbers and the difficulties facing the police officer on the beat. Hanes wondered how social conditions and the welfare of neighborhoods affected life on the streets.[12]

There were a number of city officials throughout America who were concerned that lawlessness was on the rise in the nation and that traditional policing was no longer adequate. Indeed, lurid newspaper headlines often told of crime in major cities such as Chicago, St. Louis, New York, and Cleveland, where organized crime organizations were robust and healthy. In the 1920s, some six hundred gunmen were killed in battles between competing mobs in Chicago, "but there appears to be a never failing source of recruits," a major crime study found. During that same time, not a single gang member was punished.[13]

The much-publicized crime study in Illinois, and others from Missouri and New York, not only examined the crime statistics, but looked beyond in an effort to determine if the criminal justice system was working. The findings were not encouraging. "The main feature of what is wrong may be put in one word—Inefficiency. No one part of the system of criminal justice works to maximum power, and most of them to less than moderate power—Inefficiency is everywhere," John H. Wigmore, the editor of the Illinois Crime Survey, wrote in his introduction.

North Carolina cities and towns weren't experiencing this level of violence, although there was no question that crime was a larger concern than it had been in the days before World War I. The state remained predominantly rural with a generous sprinkling of small towns. Urban areas were growing, however, especially around the textile mills that offered steady wages for men and women whose farms had gone bust, and crime was proliferating. Many lawmen in the state laid the blame on prohibition. North Carolina had been dry since 1909, but criminal activity increased after America outlawed booze in 1920 and legal out-of-state supplies were eliminated. The state's reputation for the production of illegal liquor in the backwoods was well deserved, as police raids and arrests of bootleggers became more commonplace in the 1920s.

The idea forming in Coates's mind—his "begriff," as Horace Williams would say—went beyond the notion of bringing lawyers and the legal profession into closer communion with his law students. Rather, Coates began thinking about how he could connect with public officials like Hanes who were responsible for the public safety in their communities and with the police officers who walked the beat. The growing urgency of his idea—Coates didn't want to be left behind by the work of Odum and his researchers—quickened his enthusiasm for the work of the Law School Association. That seemed to be the most promising vehicle immediately at hand for his aspirations. Coates shared his dreams and his frustrations with the confining nature of his classroom with Gladys Hall, who had become a steadfast and consistent confidant and cheerleader for his work, his ideas, and his ambitions. In the midst of the uproar over his grading practices, she had written him to say, "I know how you feel about the university and its law school. It is more to you than it is to anyone in that law faculty. And I do not think that I say that seeing it merely through your eyes, but I think I sense the spirit. The law school is sort of the heart of you—for you have injected in that school your thought and life freely and devotedly. I think you have triumphed—rightly and wonderfully—as you would!"[14]

Albert hopped the train for Portsmouth as often as his busy schedule would permit. Gladys came south when she could. In the fall of 1927, she spent a weekend in Chapel Hill when UNC hosted the game against the University of Virginia, a long-standing rivalry scheduled at Thanksgiving, in the new stadium built with a donation from William R. Kenan. It was one of their first weekends together since she had returned from a long trip abroad, an adventure she had planned for some time and paid for with savings from her teaching salary in the Portsmouth schools. (After one year in Kinston, she had returned home to Portsmouth and a teaching job there.) Albert had not been on hand when she sailed, but he had surprised her with bouquets of flowers that were delivered just as she arrived at hotels in London, Rome, and Paris. She had been overwhelmed and had written of conflicting emotions. She was thoroughly enjoying her trip, but she longed to see and hear from the man she loved.

The two had talked of marriage, but the matter never seemed to go further. He remained in debt and the trip to Europe had depleted Gladys's bank account. They must have talked about it again during that Thanksgiving weekend in 1927, because a few weeks later, just before Christmas, Gladys told her father of their desire to marry, with a wedding perhaps as early as the coming summer. Her only regret was that she had exhausted her savings on her trip to Europe months earlier, when it had looked like marriage was some time away. She wrote to Albert that if she had not spent so much on herself, her earnings would have gone into her life with him.

Gladys was so eager to marry that she told her father she planned to quit her teaching so she would have time to prepare. He advised her to keep her job, so each evening, after dinner, Gladys poured her every thought into the life she planned with Albert. She stitched *C*s onto her handkerchiefs and set about designing a home she wanted to build in Chapel Hill on one of the lots that Albert had purchased in Forest Hills, a residential development just south of Chapel Hill on the Pittsboro Road. She posted letters to Albert almost daily. He responded with one to her two, usually offering comment on her taste in furnishings and the various iterations of her design for their new home. At one point he encouraged her to go to an appliance store and take account of what they would need, "exclusive of music." She had planned a living room large enough to accommodate a piano. She also wanted a study with a fireplace, but she couldn't decide on whether the house should be one story or two. Then, as she was well into making her final choices, Albert brought it all to a halt.

Rather than build a house, he offered, why not rent a fine home that he knew would be available for the coming year. It was a large furnished residence on East Rosemary Street owned by Dr. James B. Bullitt. Building a house under their current financial situation was not practical, he said. They could postpone their wedding for a year and save toward a new house, or, he said, live in a rental and make their house plans from there. As eager as Gladys was to wed, it sounded from his letters that Albert knew she would choose to follow his lead.

Bullitt had joined the university's medical school in 1913. He was a member of a distinguished Kentucky family that produced a solicitor general under President William Howard Taft and would later produce an ambassador for President Franklin Roosevelt. He was one of those who had left campus while Coates was an undergraduate to begin his service with a medical corps that carried him to the front lines in France. He was a man of varied talents and interests. During faculty meetings he would quiet his nerves by whittling a hardwood rosette with his pocketknife. While in France, he had expanded his interest in history to include archeology and anthropology. His home reflected those interests as well as his passion for gardening.[15]

The Bullitts' home was everything that Gladys had dreamed of, from comfortable furnishings to an exquisitely tuned Steinway piano in a spacious living room. The house had bathrooms upstairs and down, two bedrooms opening onto a sleeping porch, an attic, and a basement. The rent of $100 a month caused her concern, but Albert said he had looked at small "cottages" that rented unfurnished for $85 a month. She finally relented despite the drain on their finances—$1,200 a year for rent out of his salary of $4,000—and put the plans for her home on hold. But she told him they would have to rent their extra space to students.

Albert did offer an additional option. He told Gladys he had received an offer to teach at the Tulane Law School in New Orleans. The job paid a thousand dollars a year more than he was currently making, and the school was offering to offset his moving expenses. Gladys was too much in love with Chapel Hill, she said. "I wouldn't have you leave North Carolina to go to Tulane for twice $5,000, my sweetest."[16]

The Bullitt house must have simply fallen into Albert's lap. He certainly had little time to look about Chapel Hill for rentals. His schedule was just as demanding in the spring of 1928 as it had been two years earlier when he had worked himself into exhaustion. When he wasn't organizing programs for the Law School Association, he was lining the halls of the law school with portraits of leading members of the North Carolina Bar and arranging short courses for students in office management and trial practice. Frank Graham had also recruited him to serve on a subcommittee on crime, correctional institutions, and law enforcement as part of a conference on social service that he was organizing.

Coates devoted not only his time to the Law School Association, but his own limited resources as well, as he reached into his pocket to pay some of its expenses. He was passionate about his efforts. Writing to a Greensboro attorney for a $120 contribution to continue outfitting the association's model law office, Coates said he had put $2,600 of his own money into the project over the past four years "because I believed in the ideas I was trying to work out and because I did not feel free to ask anyone to support them until they had proved their worth."[17]

Generally, his work met with the approval of the school's new dean, C. T. McCormick. Influential alumni such as Kemp D. Battle of Rocky Mount encouraged Coates to see that the work of the association attracted plenty of publicity for the law school. "As you know," Battle wrote Coates, "there is an influential group among the trustees who are very resentful of the fact that the law school is manned so largely by men of out-of-the-state affiliations, unacquainted and uninterested in the law of this particular jurisdiction. I do not adhere to their view, and I think their view should be combated at every turn."[18]

Coates was well supported in his efforts by Robert Madry, his former classmate, who ran the university news bureau and saw to it that the *Alumni Review* also included regular updates on the activities of the Law School Association. The June 1928 issue of the *Alumni Review* included photos of the new model law office and a model courtroom that had been created in Manning Hall and paid for by donations from lawyers around the state. "The two new acquisitions were hailed by university officials and leaders in the legal profession as a great forward step in legal education, enabling students to combine theory and practice in ideal proportions," Madry wrote in the accompanying article.[19]

Once Gladys and Albert had settled on where to live, they picked a date in late June for the wedding. The ceremony was to take place at her family's home church, Broad Street Methodist in Portsmouth, with the Reverend W. D. Moss of Chapel Hill officiating. "Parson" Moss had become as dear to Gladys as he was to Albert, and she insisted on his participation over the objections of her parents, who worried that their own minister might be offended by the choice. Albert presented Gladys with a ring in May and the wedding announcements went out in early June.

Albert completed his invitation list from a hospital bed in Durham. He had been on his way to Goldsboro, where he was to deliver a commencement address, when he suffered an attack of appendicitis. He didn't bother to notify his bride-to-be. Gladys learned he was ill when a telegram she sent him in Goldsboro was returned by the school principal with word that Albert was in Watts Hospital in Durham. After telephoning various places in Chapel Hill for word about Albert—the hospital was not forthcoming with information—she finally found a mutual friend who told her Albert's condition was not serious and surgery was unnecessary. (He would suffer another attack nine months later and that time surgery would be required.)

Albert casually brushed away her concern, as if his condition were a minor inconvenience. He said the episode had at least given him some quiet time to put the finishing touches to his invitation list. "The mild attack of appendicitis left without any adverse effects—there is no danger in postponing the operation until it gets worse. The chances are it may never hit me again, at any rate not soon. These are facts—not encouragements."[20]

As soon as he was on his feet, Albert bought an Essex roadster, gathered up his brother, Kenneth, and the two headed off to Portsmouth. Albert didn't know how to drive at all, and Kenneth was only slightly more experienced behind the wheel. Albert read the manual and "learned" to drive as they made their way through the countryside, although he turned the car over to Kenneth when they arrived at the towns along the way.[21]

Albert and Gladys were married on a warm, pleasant summer's evening on June 23, 1928, in the church that was just two blocks from the Hall home on Mt. Vernon Street. Gladys had planned every detail of the wedding, especially the music, which was a blend of familiar tunes, such as "Believe Me If All Those Endearing Young Charms" and "Annie Laurie," and the classical. She entered the church to the sound of the "Wedding March" from Wagner's *Lohengrin*. She had wanted calla lilies like those that Albert had had delivered to her in London, but they weren't available, so she chose the same flowers that Albert had surprised her with that Easter weekend three years before—roses, lilies of the valley, and orchids. Her sister, Marjorie, was her maid of honor. Kenneth was the best man.

Albert's proficiency with the automobile had improved by the time the couple arrived in the mountains of western North Carolina to spend their honeymoon in a cabin in the woods near the community of Tuxedo south of Hendersonville. It was a rustic outpost where they cooked their meals on a kerosene stove and bought provisions from a nearby country store. Albert's friend, Lassie Kelly, said a neighbor would be happy to dress a chicken or two for them. Albert had written to Gladys after an earlier trip to this part of the state telling her he wanted to build a mountain hideaway for them to use later in their years together.

Gladys felt immediately at home in Chapel Hill when they arrived in July to begin their lives together. She already knew all of her husband's friends, and the new couple became close with their next-door neighbors, the Lawrences, who lived in the rectory of the Chapel of the Cross, the Episcopal congregation whose church adjoined the campus a block away on Franklin Street. Mrs. Lawrence helped Gladys cook her first Thanksgiving dinner on a large wood-fired cook stove in the kitchen. It was the only time Gladys used it, she later recalled. She did not fancy herself a good cook and the couple usually made do on meals prepared on a small oil stove. She was pleased that the butler's pantry was equipped with a large electric refrigerator, an appliance that seemed to be a great luxury. Gladys served a lot of cold gelatin salads.

The Coateses' custom of long Sunday breakfasts began during their first week together on Rosemary Street. The newlyweds were set to enjoy one of the first of these occasions when they discovered that Chapel Hillians paid social calls on Sundays. Gladys had found an electric waffle iron in the pantry and planned to use it to prepare breakfast for the two of them. Before the first waffle was on the griddle, however, the parade of visitors began. Individuals, couples, and even groups of visitors followed one another throughout the day until it was nearly four in the afternoon. They had not yet eaten the first waffle.

The house became their home and they never resorted to renting rooms to students. Instead, Albert used the extra space to accommodate out-of-town speakers whom he invited to the law school. When Judge John J. Parker of the U.S. Court of Appeals came to the campus in the spring of 1929, Gladys prepared dinner for him and another honored guest, Horace Williams, who had taught both Albert and the judge. Williams had already entertained the Coateses at his home, his table elegantly set with fine china, silver and linen, and place cards. Gladys discovered that Williams could be unpredictable as well as gracious. Some time later, when she took her mother to his home for tea, the two arrived a few minutes late only to find that Williams had already had his tea and then gone about his business. "So we drank ours alone."[22]

Albert was absent from his classroom for much of the month of February 1929, recovering at home from an operation following another attack of appendicitis. As he convalesced, he waited for news that he believed would profoundly affect his future. He had finally produced a plan for a study of North Carolina's criminal justice system. His proposal came after conversations with Howard Odum and exploratory talks on law instruction in the fields of family and domestic relations and a wider use of sociology in the study of crime and penology. He had submitted his proposal to Dean Pound at Harvard in hopes of winning support for a year of graduate work at his law school. A few weeks before Christmas in 1928, Coates learned that with Pound's backing he was all but assured of a scholarship that amounted to at least half of his law school pay. In February, he received confirmation of the grant. President Chase also gave him his blessing and asked the trustees to grant him leave at half-pay so there would be no loss in income during his time away from campus.

Coates's area of study appealed to Pound, who had recently been appointed to the National Commission on Law Observance and Enforcement, later called the Wickersham Commission after its chairman, former Attorney General George W. Wickersham. By the spring of 1929, Coates also had a plan for teaching a course in what he called criminal law and administration. He got his first opportunity to test his efforts to connect the classroom with the judicial system during a visit by North Carolina Attorney General D. G. Brummitt. The attorney general talked with Coates and his students about the need for codifying the legal procedures for criminal trials in state courts. The American Law Institute had just issued a model code of procedure, and Coates decided it was time for North Carolina to compile its own procedures, which had evolved over a period of more than sixty years. New legislation was needed to organize them in one place in the statutes.

Coates immediately set to work. Once the spring semester was concluded he began organizing a Law School Association conference on criminal justice for lawyers, judges, law teachers, and others. There was nothing modest in Coates's plans for his meeting in Chapel Hill. Among those he wanted to speak at this event were none other than Pound and Newton D. Baker, Woodrow Wilson's secretary of war and a member of the Wickersham commission.

His ambitions outran his planning for the conference, however. It was a mistake that Coates would commit repeatedly in years to come. Invitations to Pound and Baker didn't get into the mail until a month before the event and even appeals from Governor O. Max Gardner and Judge John J. Parker could not convince Pound and Baker to reschedule and attend. Coates's boldness in proposing the two-day event drew a cautionary letter from President Chase, who advised Coates that he should be sure he had money to support such a conference and that he would do well to coordinate his efforts with Odum and the Institute for Research in Social Sciences, "which, as you know, has done a good deal in various directions with regards to the crime problems."[23]

Chase's advice came too late. Coates's first attempt at rallying the legal community was not rewarded with a large attendance. The meeting did attract a group of thirty practicing lawyers, judges, and state officials. Among those attending were Attorney General Brummitt and Supreme Court Justices George W. Connor and Willis J. Brogden, both of whom were teaching in the law school's summer program. There were one or two superior court judges, a handful of prosecutors, and an assortment of young lawyers, some of whom were just a year or two out of Coates's classroom. Out of this meeting came assignments for young lawyers to take sections of the model code and begin collecting information in preparation for a new code of criminal procedure for North Carolina. Albert then left the state for Harvard.[24]

Returning to Cambridge was bittersweet. Albert and Gladys found an apartment at 34 Chauncey Street on the north side of the Harvard campus, just a short walk from the law school's Langdell Hall. Albert was disappointed, however, that Pound, the man who had inspired his graduate work and helped make it possible, would not be on hand during the year. The dean would be absent because of his work on the Wickersham commission. Still, the year that Albert and Gladys would enjoy within reach of the cultural riches of Boston, with one of the world's great libraries at hand, was all but a second honeymoon for the two. The year would pass quickly and be marked with both success and sadness.

Albert found that Langdell Hall, with the hallway walls filled with portraits of English judges, was much changed since he was last at the law school. The building had been enlarged with the addition of lecture rooms and a courtroom for use for the Ames Competition, where his team had excelled. The new space was necessary to accommodate a law student population that now numbered 1,700. Even though Pound was not in his office peering from under his green eye shade and ever ready to talk with students, Coates found a renewed interest in criminal law among the Harvard faculty. Before he arrived in Cambridge, Coates received word that there was work underway to create an institute of criminal law that was to be led by another of his former professors, Paul L. Sayre.

Coates pursued his own independent studies and devoted himself to the perfection of a paper that he titled, "The Task of Legal Education in North Carolina." In it, he laid out his concern that the teaching of law had left the law student removed from the daily practice of law. Whereas at one time lawyers-to-be could see and absorb the daily activity of a law practice as they studied under a tutor, the modern law school classroom now separated students from the actual preparation of a case or management of a client's business, exposing students only to the law in the books and not the practice of law.

Coates wrote that it wasn't sufficient for the lawyer just to know the law. A legal education should be seasoned with the social sciences and the liberal arts. (A few months earlier, Coates had delivered a paper at the Association of American Law Schools on the integration of the study of criminology, a burgeoning science, into the study of criminal law.) "To bridge the gaps in legal education, to correlate these separated fields of knowledge and focus them upon the problems of the law and its administration, to bring out a cooperating relationship between the classroom and the courtroom—the law school and the law office, between the law teacher—the lawyer—the layman is the task of the modern law school. It is the problem of legal education in North Carolina."[25]

The paper covered a range of topics, not the least of which was Coates's own success with the Law School Association. Through the association's activities the "legal learning and the lawyer's techniques are brought closer together." He also reported on the work of the lawyers he had engaged for the study of criminal procedure and the improvements in the administration of justice that would rise from their research. Taking shape in his mind, however, was something grander. "The results of these studies, together with studies now being carried on by the Institute for Research in Social Science, the North Carolina Conference for Social Welfare, the state board of charities and public welfare, will from time to time be brought together in the Institute of Criminal Law which will provide a medium for the continuous study of our criminal law and procedure as it is and as it works." The "institute" that Coates referred to in his article was given no further reference or explanation.

Coates's commentary and his windy writing style drew a remark from his friend, W. Ney Evans, who would join the UNC law faculty for a time. Evans advised Coates to narrow his focus and figure out which audience he was trying to reach—the layman, the businessman, the lawyer, the law teacher. He also advised him to get to the point. "At the end," Evans told him, "you are writing for the oratory loving populace of North Carolina. I'd soft pedal that a bit."[26]

Early in 1930, Albert and Gladys used a portion of their university pay and Harvard stipend to have several hundred copies of Albert's paper printed as a booklet by Edwards & Broughton, a Raleigh printing firm. Albert then mailed copies to friends and associates in the profession and asked for comment. He got an encouraging reply from Superior Court Judge W. A. Devin, whom he had come to know through the Law School Association. "You have certainly apprehended what is, to my mind, the most serious problem of law schools. You are educating and training young men not only to go out into the world of affairs, and maintain high standards of learning and ethics, but also to equip them to make a living and put their knowledge into practice for the benefit of clients with advantage to themselves."[27]

Albert and Gladys returned to Chapel Hill before Christmas but were back in Cambridge for the holidays and hoped to see Thomas Wolfe while he was visiting relatives in Boston. Wolfe's first novel, *Look Homeward Angel*, was released in the fall of 1929 and it was received with grand reviews in New York. Some of those in the South who took personally his candid observations of Asheville, barely disguised as Altamont, were not so generous. Some regional editors regarded his work as nothing short of betrayal. Coates had written to Wolfe for a copy of his book and enclosed three dollars to cover the cost of the book and postage.

He got a prompt reply. "You certainly will not pay $3.00 for any book I write if I can be on hand to prevent it. By heaven, sir," Wolfe wrote his friend, "you must not, you shall not, you will not, etc. I am therefore *sending* your check back (please note that I do not say *giving*, for I shall expect you immediately to deposit these three dollars in a sound New England banking institution under the name of The Coates Fund for Hungry Novelists. I propose to visit the fair city of Boston, soon, and I expect you to be present with these three dollars and an invitation to the best $1.50 dinner in Boston.) Also, you should receive in a few days a copy of my book from Charles Scribner's Sons, handsomely inscribed with a touching sentiment (which I have not thought out yet)."

Wolfe asked for Coates's appraisal of his work. "The book has caused me a great deal of joy and pain—pain because some people in the South and in my home town have read it as an almanac of personal gossip, and have construed it as a cruel and merciless attack on actual persons, some now living.

"I know I can depend on your fairness and intelligence," he continued. "I have been much distressed by one or two Southern reviews which saw the book as an attack on North Carolina and the South. Of course, that is preposterous: the book is neither about North Carolina nor the South, nor any specific group of people North, South, East or West—it is about all the people I have ever known anywhere, and it simply says we are born alone, live alone, die alone, that we are strangers on the earth and never come to know one another. *You* will see that, and understand it at once."[28] Wolfe escaped from New York during the holidays and stayed with his family in Boston. He missed Albert and Gladys, however, and sent a note to say he hoped to see them soon in Chapel Hill.

In late March Gladys received word in Cambridge that her father was ill. He died before she could get to Portsmouth. While Gladys spent a couple of weeks in Portsmouth with her family, Albert went to Raleigh for his research on criminal procedure in his home state. Throughout his year at Harvard, he corresponded with the lawyers back in North Carolina who were gathering information for the new criminal code.

In preparation for his return to the UNC law school in the fall, Coates wrote to Dean McCormick with an update on his work at Harvard. In his letter, he expressed his desire to continue the survey of criminal procedure that he had started just before leaving for Cambridge. Coates remained intent on continuing his conferences and had promised those who had met with him in August that he would bring in Pound, Baker, and others as presenters for future meetings. McCormick was not enthusiastic about the diversions that Coates had planned. He feared Coates's extracurricular activities would take too much away from his law teaching.

In a letter to Coates in March 1930, McCormick noted that the law school was still competing for good students with the schools at Duke University and at Wake Forest College. He applauded Coates's success in the "promotional work" that he had earlier encouraged, but he told Coates that he feared it had taken too much away from his effectiveness as a teacher. The only way to maintain supremacy over their rivals and build a first-class law school was for the faculty to prove itself in the classroom.

"That requires great teachers," McCormick wrote. "That requires unremitting concentration on preparing for class. This is consistent with a substantial amount of writing on the same subject matter but not with a substantial amount of travel and organizing work. I am really anxious, then, not to see you placed in a position where you are going to be forced to allow class preparation to recede into second place. Consequently, I should like to see any work of organizing and holding institutes done in the summer at times when you have no classes."

McCormick also questioned the value of the survey work that Coates was then undertaking. "Frankly, I question whether unpaid, volunteer statistical work by officials will be of as great value or long continuance. You know from observation and experience the unreliability of that sort of assistance. Superficial results would not help us, but to the contrary.

"While good words from lawyers about the Law School are immensely helpful, in the long run we shall sink or swim according as the students say our courses are [more] substantial and worth while than those at Duke."[29]

Albert and Gladys returned to Chapel Hill in the summer of 1930 and found a rental house in the Westwood community south of Chapel Hill. When Albert resumed his teaching, he committed himself to the classroom, but he continued to work on the updating of the state's criminal code. He invited the young lawyers conducting the survey to a brunch at his home on a football weekend in the fall. That was enough for Robert Madry at the news service to get a lengthy story in the state's newspapers about the energetic young law professor who was mobilizing lawyers around the state to produce a new criminal code for North Carolina.[30]

The story must have suggested to McCormick that his advice to Coates had been in vain. The survey would prove just the start of Albert's troubles with his colleagues in the law school. All the while that Coates was coordinating his team of lawyers, he also was putting the finishing touches to the results of his work at Harvard—a seventy-page booklet that brought together under one title his earlier writing on legal education, his interest in criminology and penology, and a survey of the uneven distribution of justice in North Carolina courts. He titled the paper, "The Convict's Question." Albert and Gladys dug into their modest savings to pay the $1,500 cost of printing it themselves, publishing Albert's paper as Volume 1, Number 1, of a new publication that Coates called *Popular Government*.[31] Albert Coates, now a publisher in addition to his other activities, was not going to be confined to one classroom.

If Coates needed any more endorsement for his mission, as he saw it at the time, he got it from E. C. Branson, who wrote to him on his return to campus. "I have always felt sure that you would find yourself and your place in the scheme of things entire, and your place is that of trail-blazer and pace maker for bewildered humanity in its forward march. You begin where every effective genius begins, namely, with the folks and the big problem you best know. Such trails lead far afield and the big wide world at least claims such a man as its own. I am proud of you."[32]

SIX

Popular Government

1930–1932

IN THE LATE SPRING OF 1920, O. Max Gardner was in the closing weeks of his campaign for the Democratic Party's gubernatorial nomination when he visited Chapel Hill to make a campaign speech at Gerrard Hall and touch base with friends at the university. He was well known on campus, where he held the unique honor of having played football both for the university at Chapel Hill as a law school student, and earlier, as an undergraduate, for that other state institution in Raleigh. Gardner was in a tough race, and he was going to need every vote.

Gardner looked up Albert Coates, who was busy with the fund-raising campaign for the Graham Memorial, and he invited Coates to join him for a milk shake. When Coates said he didn't want one, Gardner loosed a hearty and robust laugh and said, "I know that, but I want you under obligation to me."[1] More than likely, Coates consented to the offer. He seldom turned down an opportunity for ice cream.

Coates was a good man for politicians like Gardner to know. His job on behalf of the university carried him out into the state, where he had contact with hundreds of alumni. A word here and there on Gardner's behalf was worth something in the days before political messages were carried far and wide in print and on the airwaves. In time, these early contacts paid off for Coates, who found that it was helpful for him to be on a first-name basis with men and women of influence and power in North Carolina. Throughout his career, he would cultivate such relationships, stockpiling them as he would money in the bank, and they would prove to be an essential underpinning for his vision of extending his law school classroom into the public life of North Carolina.

About nine years after Gardner visited Chapel Hill he finally made it to the governor's mansion. He lost the 1920 campaign, falling behind Cameron Morrison in a bitter second primary, but in 1928 he was the Democratic Party's undisputed choice. He won handily in the fall, even in the face of a serious party split over the candidacy of the party's presidential nominee, New Yorker Al Smith. Gardner took office in January 1929, just as Coates was making his plans to spend a year of graduate study at Harvard. Throughout Coates's absence from the state, one of his most important contacts was Tyre C. Taylor, who served as Gardner's private secretary. Taylor had been a campus leader during the year Coates was in graduate school and he later ran the alumni association. For Gardner's campaign Taylor created an army of foot soldiers who belonged to the Young Democratic Club. Another of Coates's chums, B. C. Brown, was on the staff of North Carolina's senior senator, Furnifold Simmons.

By all accounts, Coates was a Democrat, despite his grandfather's affiliation with Republicans. As an undergraduate, Albert freely used his middle initial, given to him in honor of William McKinley's nomination as the Republican presidential candidate in 1896. By the time he returned to the campus to teach in the law school, he had dropped the M from his signature. For the rest of his life, he would carefully navigate the waters of partisanship—both inter-party and intra-party—and maintain a judicious neutrality to avoid the shoals that could sink his ship.

When Albert and Gladys left Cambridge for Chapel Hill in the summer of 1930, Governor Gardner had his hands full. He had begun his four years in office pushing a progressive program and expended much of his political capital during the 1929 legislative session, during which he won passage of a worker's compensation law and the extension of the school year to eight months in every county. The governor also had continued the reforms of county government begun by his predecessor. The school bill, however, was not fully funded, and it would be the last major spending measure out of the state legislature until the end of World War II.

While much of the world marked the beginning of the Great Depression with the stock market crash in October 1929, North Carolinians were suffering hard times well before that. The state's textile mills were not running full time and tax collections were declining. A financial crisis for the state, as well as its cities and counties, was building and appeared unavoidable. State government had piled up a mountain of debt; obligations had risen from $13 million in 1920 to $178 million in 1929. Money had been spent with great exuberance for important capital improvements, including the new buildings at Chapel Hill and hundreds of miles of hard-surface roads. The road program begun in the 1920s and completed in Gardner's term would connect the county seats of North Carolina and, finally, make it possible to travel on a paved highway from Manns Harbor, at the edge of the Atlantic Ocean, to Murphy, deep in the Smoky Mountains near Tennessee, a distance of more than six hundred miles. It was a great achievement, but by the time the last mile was completed the average taxpayer was in trouble. Farmers and the mill hands who made up the state's working class were especially hard up.[2]

As classes at Chapel Hill were resuming in the fall of 1930, tobacco farmers in the east were organizing protest meetings and calling on the governor to do something to relieve their plight. Auction prices offered for North Carolina leaf that summer didn't even cover the cost of raising the crop. The Eastern Carolina Chamber of Commerce organized a Tobacco Relief Commission and called a public meeting at State College in Raleigh that September. Within a year, cotton farmers elsewhere in the South would be pushing for state laws to limit production in an effort to boost prices.

Hard times were leading to unrest in North Carolina towns and cities. They had swelled in population by the mid-1920s with the migration of former farm hands and sharecroppers, who had exchanged rural life for a regular paycheck at the textile mills and cigarette and furniture plants. Now, with short hours, there was wide discontent. Labor organizers were trying to make inroads and mill owners responded with quick and decisive action. In Greensboro, workers taking home less than $10 a week at Cone Mills plants found themselves without a job if they signed a union card. One supervisor fired his nephew after he learned he was a union member. A mother was threatened with eviction from her company-owned house if she continued to allow her son and grandson, both of them union members, to remain under the same roof.[3]

Violence had shattered some communities. The police chief was shot and killed in Gastonia in the summer of 1929, and the incident had received nationwide attention. Albert Coates's Harvard law professor, Felix Frankfurter, had called on Coates to offer some local assistance for the out-of-state legal counsel that had been engaged to defend the union organizers and workers charged in the police chief's death. Albert and Gladys were just leaving for Cambridge when the trial of those accused opened in Charlotte. Albert did not get involved.

Gardner's administration would be marked by both bold action and creative thinking to deal with these and other problems. His proposals alternated between the severe and the sublime. A year after taking office, Gardner issued his first round of budget cuts at the same time that he was attempting to inspire the home folks to do what they could to help themselves. Late in 1929 he launched his "Live-at-Home" campaign, calling on farmers to grow more food and feed and to reduce acreage for cotton and tobacco and make the state more self-sufficient. To promote his idea, he invited newspaper editors to Christmas dinner at the Executive Mansion. The menu included country ham from hogs raised on the state's Caledonia prison farm, oysters from the coast, Ashe County cheese, baked yams and crab apple jelly, turnip salad, corn pone, salted pecans and peanuts, and, for dessert, ice cream with a peach conserve from home demonstration clubs in the North Carolina sandhills.[4]

In January 1931, Gardner announced budget cuts in the face of declining tax collections. All state spending, including pay for employees—university professors included—would be cut by 10 percent beginning with the start of the fiscal year in July. The governor was also preparing a major reorganization of state government, and he delivered to the General Assembly a sweeping overhaul that rose out of a study of state agencies and departments by the Brookings Institution. It would become a model for other states whose leaders later called on Gardner to talk about the measures he had undertaken to maintain some degree of fiscal solvency.

Life in the state during much of Gardner's term would be tumultuous, disturbing, and dispiriting. Local institutions and leading community figures would be found to be lacking. Long-established banks managed by some of the state's leading businessmen failed. Scandal often ensued, as it did in Asheville when the mayor took his own life. City and county employees were indicted for embezzlement, and the state's crime rate easily kept pace with the rest of the nation, which also was in distress. County and municipal governments ran out of money and couldn't pay their debts. Asheville would not fully repay bonds sold in the 1920s until fifty years later. The hard times and alarming news made citizens all the more anxious as folks lost their jobs and their life savings.

Albert Coates could not have picked a less propitious time to attempt to expand his law school classroom into a teaching laboratory and resource for state and local government that he said would serve the most remote justice of the peace as well as legislators in Raleigh. In the months ahead he would present audacious plans and push his friends and colleagues, whom he badgered to join in his cause, to the point of frustration, all the while oblivious to threats to his career and financial security, not to mention the pressing needs and challenges facing the university, which was facing a budget cut of $200,000. It was not the time to be asking for money to establish a new institution or to underwrite a venture that by Coates's own reckoning would cost at least $50,000 a year just to get organized. At the same time, the urgency and difficulty of the times, especially the failure of local governments to live up to their obligations, underscored the necessity for what Coates proposed. There had never been a time when the state was in greater need of faith in public institutions or public officials who were better prepared to meet the challenges.

As Coates nursed his plans into shape, he had to be impressed with the success of Howard Odum's Institute for Research in Social Science, whose team of researchers was housed in Saunders Hall, just a few steps away from his own office in Manning Hall. Just as Coates was leaving for Harvard, Odum had secured a $240,000 grant from one of the Rockefeller foundations to pursue further studies of social and child welfare, studies of crime and justice, and a three-pronged study in the field of economics—taxation, industry, and cooperatives.[5] Odum's success included programs in the areas of public life that Coates was about to claim as his own domain.

There were other movements afoot that tracked what Coates had in mind and could drain away support. Maurice T. Van Hecke, who had succeeded C. T. McCormick as dean of the law school, wanted the faculty and students to serve as a legislative drafting service for the General Assembly. The new dean envisioned a joint effort with the state's other law schools to provide research as well as drafting services to help the state meet the demands of the modern era. North Carolina remained one of the most rural states in the South, but it was rapidly changing with the growth of an industrial base and advances in technology. Automobiles were cruising new highways and radio and telephones were connecting cities and towns, yet legislators were operating as though mud roads, kerosene lamps, and mule power were the order of the day.

After a year of unfettered study, research, and planning at Harvard, Coates returned to the classroom with his satchel full. That fall, he was scheduled to teach two of his favorites—municipal corporations and criminal law—but his mind was on what he considered far more important matters. While the rest of Chapel Hill settled into the Christmas holidays in 1930, Albert and Gladys were eagerly awaiting the delivery of the first issue of *Popular Government*, Albert's new journal. It arrived just before Christmas Day and before the end of the year, the two had packaged and addressed thousands of envelopes and delivered Volume 1, Number 1, to the post office in Chapel Hill.

The issue would not have gotten in the mail without a determined effort by Gladys. Albert finished writing the final draft of his manuscript while sick with a debilitating cold. She read and edited it, frying off the fat, as Albert would say, and then sat with him at a card table and together they addressed by hand two thousand envelopes for the lawyers, judges, and others on Coates's mailing list. She said later that exercise taught her the names of cities and towns across North Carolina. The Coateses paid for the postage and printing of *Popular Government* themselves, even though their own finances were barely sufficient to afford a small rental house as their home.[6]

There was nothing modest about *Popular Government*. Within its seventy pages was the sum of Coates's work on the criminal justice system of the previous six years, including his year of work at Harvard. But it was more than that. Never one to waste a phrase or flowing paragraph, Coates included sections from his earlier writings on the history of the law in North Carolina and the teaching of the law at the university. Portions also referred to the work of the Law School Association. But the underlying foundation was an argument in favor of overhauling the state's criminal justice system, from the cop on the beat to the judge on the bench.

Popular Government was a one-song hymnal in the Coates church of criminal law. He declared that the citizens of North Carolina were ill-served by a criminal justice system that suffered from the inefficiency of overlapping jurisdictions, the unfettered discretion of prosecutors and judges who dispensed unequal justice, and law enforcement officers who were not properly trained to do their jobs. The pamphlet was Coates's call for a detailed analysis of the entire justice apparatus. He argued for the application of scientific methods in the analysis of how police answered calls and handled arrests, the decisions of district attorneys in prosecuting crimes, the sentencing behavior of judges, as well as the fairness of the penal system. In later years he would say that his approach was no less exacting than the one the doctors at the Mayo Clinic had taken with him when he went there seeking a diagnosis of his medical problems. Just as the Mayo doctors had examined each part of his body in an effort to find what ailed him, Coates called for a thorough examination to determine the weak links in the criminal justice system, and then changes to produce a complete and finished whole.

The proposition Coates posed in *Popular Government* built like a tidal wave that then swept over the shores of all of local government. He began with a detailed analysis of the state's criminal justice system, reciting forms of punishment from the colonial era to the present in an effort to answer the problem of two prisoners who were sentenced for the same crime but drew unequal terms in prison. Tracing the "unsolved problem" of unequal justice, as he called it, Coates reached a conclusion that the state was in need of "a critical analysis of our governmental structure as a whole." This examination would result in greater efficiency in government, more enlightened and knowledgeable public officials, and homegrown solutions for governmental institutions caught in the grip of great social and economic change. What the criminal justice system, and by extension the rest of government, needed was the same rigorous discipline used by scientists.

Future governors should be relieved of the need to go out of state for help with reform, as Gardner had done in hiring the Brookings Institution. This work could and should be done at home with honest, earnest, and intelligent North Carolinians. It was not impossible, he argued, to resolve the overlapping jurisdictions of law enforcement to make it easier to catch a criminal driving a fast automobile rather than hobbling along on foot. What was needed, he said, was for public servants at various levels to come together with their peers, share concerns, and find solutions by meeting first in the local community and then with their neighbors in adjoining counties and finally in a grand statewide conference. In his journal, Coates announced what he called a statewide School of Criminal Law Administration that he said was already planned for Chapel Hill in the summer of 1931. He said he was working toward the program with the assistance of the university's new president, Frank Graham, who had recently succeeded Harry W. Chase. Graham, Coates said, had offered up the university campus classrooms and dormitory space to accommodate all who could attend.

In making his case, Coates was untroubled by such apparent limitations as manpower, money, or institutional support. The state's economy was a shambles, the university's budget had been reduced, and taxpayers were struggling to make ends meet. Other great movements, led by men of grand ideas, had faced obstacles, including empty pockets, Coates said in his conclusion, yet these men had not been deterred in pursuit of their noble cause. "And in them is revealed the spirit of a people which sees in disaster only a challenge the brighter to burn and which when darkness hedges it about builds in itself a dwelling place of light. We are the heirs of that tradition."[7]

Sprinkled throughout the work were references to eight studies of different aspects of the justice system that Coates said were underway. Judges, prosecuting attorneys, law enforcement agencies, and attorneys were already cooperating to gather information and prepare reports. Thirty lawyers were working on a codification of criminal procedures, he said. In an article about his plans that he wrote for the *Daily Tar Heel*, and which found its way into some state newspapers, Coates said the criminal code recodification would culminate with an Institute of Criminal Law in the late summer of 1931, with final work completed by the time the 1933 General Assembly convened.[8]

The criminal code revision that Coates had declared as his own area of work was no modest undertaking, but with the release of *Popular Government* some readers drew the conclusion that this task had all but been completed and Coates was moving on to even greater challenges. Coates made such a convincing case about the progress of the criminal code study that the dean of the University of Wisconsin Law School, Lloyd K. Garrison, was eager to receive details of the findings in order to establish a similar effort in his state.[9] Coates declared his goal was to use the same approach underway in the examination of the criminal justice system for all other government functions at all levels. In addition, he proposed extending the product of the studies that would flow from this government laboratory into a new program of civic education for the high schools of the state. "On this platform I plant myself, my courses and my classroom."[10]

Coates's stirring conclusion to *Popular Government* was replete with passionate and patriotic phrase making. He drew upon a favorite anecdote to inspire readers to take up his cause, recalling a "son of the university" who before his death on the field at Gettysburg lived long enough to write a message in his own blood: "Tell my father I died with my face to the foe."[11] "The center of gravity in American life—in our social fabric, our economic order, our governmental structure—is shifting today with a meaning no less significant and far more real than in 1776," Coates concluded. "Here is a cause to which ourselves now, no less than our fathers then, are called upon to pledge our lives, our fortunes and our sacred honor to the end that popular government shall not vanish before our eyes; to the end that through its chosen representatives—from the policeman in our smallest town to the chief executive of our state, grappling with the fears and forces which beset it now, it may rid itself of inefficiency and waste and once more victorious ride the storm."[12]

Within a few weeks of the mailing, responses began arriving at the Chapel Hill post office. Most writers were complimentary and, they freely admitted, they were overwhelmed with Coates's exhaustive treatment of the subject. Some called his work genius; others said he'd never get local officials to give up power in order to achieve the efficiencies that would come with change. Lawyers and judges unburdened themselves to Coates with their complaints about the criminal justice system and their belief that hard times were breeding crime and destroying the fabric of government.

Coates had built much of his case for an overhaul upon a letter from a convicted felon who complained to the governor that a cellmate had received a lesser sentence for the same crime. Such a condition argued for limiting the discretion of judges in passing sentence, Coates had said. In his eight-page reply, Superior Court Judge M. V. Barnhill of Rocky Mount complimented Coates on his work, but took exception to this example of unequal justice. Judicial penal policy does not neatly lend itself to scientific comparison, he said. One man caught stealing a ham might be a habitual criminal and using the rewards of his theft for further bad deeds, Barnhill argued, while another caught stealing a ham was a first offender who found himself down on his luck with a hungry family to feed. The fix for this problem, Barnhill wrote, was to "eliminate the judge or presiding officer who is not conscientiously and properly administering the law rather than by changing the system."[13]

Fayetteville attorney Charles G. Rose, a former president of the North Carolina Bar Association, wrote: "I am especially interested in the suggestions about consolidating the law enforcement officers of the cities and counties. I can not possibly see any advantage under the present system of automobiles and good roads of having two, and possibly three, sets of such officers."[14]

An Asheville attorney, Junius G. Adams, wrote: "You have set a standard for your first issue that is going to be hard, if not impossible to live up to, as your handling of the shortcomings and need of reform in our penal policy and criminal procedure is nothing short of masterful; and is entirely convincing."[15]

Coates was aided in the promotion of *Popular Government* by the University News Bureau, where Robert Madry was becoming nothing short of Coates's press agent. In January, Madry arranged for Coates to speak to the university's annual Press Institute before all the leading newspapermen in the state. Complimentary editorial comment on Coates's plans followed when the newspapermen returned home to their typewriters. The governor's office also took notice. During the 1931 session, the General Assembly created a commission for the improvement of laws in North Carolina. Appointed to the commission were members of the state supreme court, superior court judges, attorneys, and representatives from the state's law schools, including Albert Coates, who was named executive secretary of the commission. The commission was directed to make a report to the 1933 General Assembly.

For all the attention that the journal drew to the young professor, *Popular Government* was just Coates's first shot. By the end of the spring term in May, he had produced two more lengthy proposals, both of them grand in scope and imagination. The first was an elaborate plan that expanded on the idea that Coates had touched on near the conclusion of the treatise on the criminal justice system—that is, to organize a "school of governmental officers for the study of governmental institutions and processes in North Carolina." While his reading audience mulled over that proposition, he wrote and published a small pamphlet that he called "A Plan for County, District and Statewide Schools of Law Enforcing Officers."

With his "police school," as it would soon be called, Coates proposed that judges, prosecutors, and law enforcement officers begin regular meetings in their local communities to talk about common problems. They should then meet with their law officers in adjoining counties and finally convene for a statewide meeting. These sessions could improve the communication within the law enforcement community but, more importantly, raise the level of training for local police. Coates wrote: "Our law enforcing officers must know and understand the laws they are directed to enforce and the policies behind them; the limits within which the law allows the law enforcing officer to enforce the law; the methods of crime detection and of crime prevention; the relation of the agencies for the investigation of crime and the apprehension of criminals to the agencies for criminal trial, punishment, pardon and parole."

"We are foolish," he wrote, "when we expect the change from a suit of overalls to an official uniform in some mysterious fashion to invest the wearer with all the qualifications of a law enforcing officer."[16]

Throughout the spring of 1931, Coates slipped out of Chapel Hill for speaking engagements to civic clubs in nearby cities. The North Carolina Association of Chiefs of Police invited him to their meeting in Salisbury where the law officers immediately warmed to his ideas for police training. Some warned that police chiefs and sheriffs would never sit down together, however. Coates set out to prove them wrong. Instead of calling his proposed meeting of lawmen a "school," which he thought might scare some away, he called it a "convention," which suggested more conviviality. He talked to lawyers, prosecutors, and lawmen wherever he found them. Coates was in one county talking with the sheriff about the meeting and promoting interagency cooperation when he found a parking ticket on his windshield. The sheriff, who had walked Coates to his car, said, "Give it to me. You have been talking about cooperation. Here is the way police and sheriffs cooperate in this town." The sheriff tore up the ticket. Later, Coates wrote, "A state highway patrolman actually picked up a county sheriff and a city police chief in his territory, and all three rode to the meeting in the same car!"[17] His missionary work had paid off.

On September 8, 1931, Coates opened his first meeting of local officials, which despite his promotion was called a "police school" in the newspapers. It began on a Tuesday morning during that quiet lull between the closing of the university's summer session and the resumption of classes. About fifty police executives, prosecuting attorneys, clerks of court, sheriffs, and judges arrived at Manning Hall, home of the university's law school, to register for the three-day program. Madry announced in the news releases, which were printed verbatim in the state's major daily newspapers, that it was the first time that representatives of city, county, state, and federal agencies had ever met under one roof. Brimming with confidence, Albert Coates had produced what only a few months earlier had looked like little more than a hopeful vision—a statewide conference on law enforcement.

Coates assembled an impressive lineup of speakers for the program, which was sponsored by the Police Chief's association, which made Coates an honorary member on opening day. Attending would be the governor and lieutenant governor, along with the attorney general and members of the state supreme court. U. S. Senator Josiah Bailey was scheduled for an address, and J. C. B. Ehringhaus of Elizabeth City, a candidate for governor and one of the local prosecutors, was on the program. Other speakers included chiefs of police, clerks of court, and a juvenile court judge. It was all that Coates could have hoped for, and he had his mentor, Horace Williams, on hand to witness this realization of his "begriff." Williams opened the second day of the session and talked not of law enforcement but of the desperate condition of many Americans. "There is bound to be something wrong with a country that sent six million people to bed last night without supper." The country needed someone to "lead us out of the present dilemma."[18]

Winston-Salem's police chief, J. B. Wooten, who was a leader in the association, echoed Williams's concern. With winter coming and unemployment high, he said he expected a jump in crime, as people were desperate for food and shelter. "If the captains of industry could see the situation as we do I believe they would do something."[19]

The lawmen felt under siege. As the session opened, one of America's most notorious gangsters, Chicago's Al Capone, had escaped conviction in an Illinois courtroom. At home, death row at North Carolina's Central Prison was full, and the daily newspapers carried reports of public officials charged with embezzlement, theft, and other crimes. Most troubling of all was enforcement of liquor laws. One speaker, Salisbury attorney Neill Sowers, reported that in the course of his study of the criminal justice system, half of the cases in federal court in North Carolina were alcohol-related. When he took the podium, Senator Bailey noted that more than half of the state's criminal convictions in 1930 were for violations of liquor law or for larceny and receiving, the crimes that brought the greatest financial rewards to criminals. At the same time, he urged calm and advised police not to overreact. He said violators made up less than one-half percent of the state population and that ought to be some comfort to society.

The meeting tapped into the great frustration of lawmen. Some pointed their fingers at defense lawyers, whom they accused of using the system to find a friendly judge to handle their cases, and at prosecutors, who dismissed cases without good explanation. Fayetteville's police chief, Foss Jones, blamed current troubles on lawyers "who will take any sort of case and resort to all sorts of unethical practices in defense of criminals, as long as they are being paid for their services." Ehringhaus highlighted one of the issues raised by Coates in *Popular Government*. He said the diffusion of enforcement among various agencies with overlapping jurisdiction "has almost reached the point of confusion of enforcement." He called for greater cooperation among enforcement agencies.[20]

In his opening address, Coates said the need for training and more sessions like the one just beginning were evident to the public. "Accusations, investigations and disclosures of the inefficiency and corruption are pointing warning fingers at the festering spots of our machinery of criminal law administration. We cannot let these warnings go unheeded in reliance on law abiding Anglo-Saxon instincts. We cannot take law and order for granted when we see our neighbors losing it before our eyes.

"It is all too apparent that failure to catch the criminal may destroy the effect of the most effective criminal courts; that uncertainty of conviction and punishment in the criminal courts may paralyze the efforts of the best police departments; that the achievements of both may be neutralized by faulty policies of punishment, pardon and parole. That no law is stronger than the police desk, the jury box, the judge's bench, or the governor's chair; that it is literally true that the chain of our law enforcing machinery is no stronger than its weakest link; that all are in danger of hanging separately because they are not hanging together; that all of them together are powerless without the understanding cooperation of informed public opinion."[21]

Some at the gathering, which grew to between seventy-five and a hundred by the time the program concluded on Thursday, were looking for more direct solutions. A clerk of superior court declared that the public was getting too sentimental. He bemoaned the prohibition against public flogging and against lawmen shooting at fleeing automobiles. At the same time, a prosecuting attorney from Kinston roundly condemned forcing confessions out of the accused, which the Wickersham Commission, the national crime group co-chaired by Coates's mentor, Harvard Law School dean Roscoe Pound, had found to be prevalent in other states. (The commission reported there was little evidence of forced confessions in North Carolina.) In the training sessions, Coates and other speakers talked about the proper legal procedures for arrest, searches and seizures, self-incrimination, and ways for law enforcement agencies to work together.

In his remarks, Governor Gardner applauded the work of the chiefs of police and said his administration was "determined to lend the full force of its influence to assist in stamping out stealing and to turn the public thought from stealing to honest work." The governor also singled out Coates for his efforts. "It is my considered judgment that this movement here inaugurated today has in it more potentialities for the welfare of North Carolina, her government and her people, than any movement heretofore inaugurated in the history of this university. And when I say that I am not unmindful of its long historic past. I congratulate you, Professor Coates, on these results of years of hard and painstaking labor."[22] For Coates, the governor's generous endorsement was all the reward he needed to justify his sacrifice and hard work and encourage him to press on.

The meeting was just the start of what Coates had in mind for law enforcement. In his opening remarks, he outlined a plan for continuing the education of local lawmen in a series of schools that would be held periodically in cities around the state. He urged judges, prosecutors, and attorneys to meet once a month with local law officers to help them learn more about the required elements for an arrest and the proper gathering of evidence that would stand up in court. Less than a month later, the first of the local police schools opened in a Raleigh courtroom. Coates showed up with his law students in tow. Other sessions followed in the next few weeks in High Point, Greensboro, Wilmington, Asheville, and Winston-Salem.

While Coates was winning praise from the governor and editorial endorsements for his police schools, his ad hoc extension program was deeply troubling to Dean Van Hecke. Coates's flurry of activity during the first half of 1931 left Van Hecke wondering whether Coates had returned to Chapel Hill to teach or to use the law school, as he himself declared in *Popular Government*, as a platform for his own purposes. A quiet and serious scholar, Van Hecke was a first-rate teacher and was determined to continue the improvements at the law school begun by his predecessors. Van Hecke had worked alongside Coates before becoming dean and knew of his love of extra-curricular activities. When President Graham offered Van Hecke the deanship, Van Hecke had expressed his reservations about Coates's fitness in the classroom, questioning whether such energy and enthusiasm could be contained there. The dean feared the mission of the law school—to train men and women for the legal profession—would be jeopardized if he could not count on the full time, attention, and energy of the entire faculty.

Van Hecke and Coates had talked at the end of the 1931 spring term about Coates's absences for civic club speeches and the time he was devoting to his new program. The dean told Coates that the outside activities were interfering with his responsibilities to students and would have to be curtailed. In a memorandum to Graham, Van Hecke reported that Coates had pledged to mend his ways and devote his full energy to the law school and to meeting his classes when they resumed in the fall. Apparently Coates failed to tell the dean about his plans for the September conference and the subsequent establishment of local police schools around the state. Van Hecke later told Graham that he didn't learn about the gathering at Manning Hall until he read a notice about it in the morning newspaper.[23]

Van Hecke's counseling clearly did little to reform Coates. He proceeded on his own course throughout the fall of 1931 as if his mission to reform North Carolina's criminal justice system was of far greater importance than his duty to the law school. Coates believed that all his work up to that point—the years of study, preparation, and personal sacrifice—had been leading to this moment. He had gone to Harvard rather than take a teaching fellowship at Yale, where the compensation was greater, because Harvard had offered more support for his work. Moreover, he had turned down better-paying jobs at law schools in Louisiana and West Virginia to remain in North Carolina and pursue his goal of extending the service of the university throughout North Carolina.[24]

"I know I can work it out in this state better than any other," he told James G. Hanes, the mayor of Winston-Salem and one of those who warmed to his cause, "because all over this state are scattered my college-mates and students, whose confidence I think I have won no less than you have won the confidence of your associates, and they will work with me as they have been working with me and as they are working with me now."[25]

Coates believed his work would not only raise the standards of government in North Carolina and bring credit to the university, but serve an even broader purpose in uplifting the South and restoring honor, dignity, and tradition in a region of the country beaten down since the Civil War. "Out of our own sweat and toil," Coates wrote of his plans, "we can together build a unique and distinctive governmental movement—the gift of North Carolina, her governmental institutions and her people, to America and the world as the South, after seventy years of war, reconstruction and rebuilding swims back into the full tide of American life." Coates believed the movement he was undertaking transcended minor inconveniences, which apparently included his personal financial welfare and the disruption of Van Hecke's administration of the law school. What he was doing was vital to North Carolina, and, by extension, to the entire nation.

"This movement inaugurated here in North Carolina will gather up the intense and flowing interest of the people in the workings of governmental institutions, turn their scattered efforts into constructive channels and through them build here a governmental institution—the South's distinctive contribution to the solution of American governmental problems today."[26]

Armed with such urgency and purpose, Coates's work could not wait. "I had found the answer to the question I had faced in my senior year in Law School in the spring of 1923," Coates later wrote, "the question I had talked over with myself in the night-time walk up and down the Charles River in Cambridge, the question that had been answered in the feeling that there was something I could do in Chapel Hill that I could not do in Smithfield, something I could do in a law school that I could not do in a law office. I knew now what that something was."[27]

Despite Coates's assurances to the dean, he was absent from the classroom for most of October as he made his way around the state opening the local police schools. Neither his students nor the dean, nor even his supporters, knew where to find him. Many of his contacts outside Chapel Hill started writing him letters after repeated unsuccessful efforts to reach him by telephone. The law school office gave up on tracking him down. Van Hecke noted in a memorandum that he followed Coates's travels by way of newspaper accounts of his appearances around the state. When Coates was in Chapel Hill, the dean said, his attention was not fully on the law school. Van Hecke also was annoyed that when the American

Association of Universities met in Chapel Hill in November in conjunction with the formal inauguration of Frank Graham—with Harvard dean Roscoe Pound in attendance—Coates had escorted Pound around the campus without bringing him by the law school for introductions.[28]

Van Hecke's measured temperament disposed him against precipitate disciplinary action. He was clearly unhappy with his professor's behavior, but he did little more than lay his problem before President Graham, who sympathized—but did nothing. Graham's election as president was an event that rose to favor Coates. The two had known each other for nearly twenty years, since Coates's undergraduate days when he roomed in the YMCA and Graham was the leader of the YMCA program. The two were close friends; Graham had even cosigned one of Coates's bank loans. Most important, the two shared Edward Kidder Graham's vision for the university and had worked side by side in the 1920s to see that vision take hold and flourish as the university grew and increased in stature. Graham accepted Coates's penchant for overreaching and hyperbole in trade for his energy and passion for the mission of extension. In the years to come, Coates would have no greater champion, or savior, than Frank Graham.

As for Coates, he proceeded with an understanding that Graham had given his blessing to his work during a meeting of the two in the fall of 1931, during which Coates said he reviewed his plans in detail with the president. "I went out from your office to win for this program the support of public officials and private citizens of the state," Coates later noted in a letter to the president.[29] It is unlikely that Graham frustrated his friend by telling him to rein in his ambition, but rather gave him encouragement, as was his nature, especially on a mission so close to his own heart. So, while the president might have sympathized with the dean's scolding update on Coates's performance in November 1931, it is no surprise that only a few days later he obliged Coates by inviting Pound to be his house guest should he be able to attend another meeting that Coates was convening at the close of the year.

Coates asked Graham and others of influence and position—the governor, Chief Justice Walter Stacy, and Judge John J. Parker—to write to Pound and urge him to be in Chapel Hill at the end of December for what Coates called an "historic" gathering. In his own letter to Pound, Coates gave him the credit for inspiring his work. "In the meeting at the close of the year we expect to consolidate our gains [of the police school] and perfect plans for extending this work during the coming year throughout the one hundred counties of the state. In the same meeting we expect to lay foundations for the extension of the coordinating movement throughout the reaches of our state and local governmental units."[30]

The meeting was called to discuss the plan written by Coates, the title of which was as windy as Coates himself: "Tentative Plan for County, District and State-wide Schools of Governmental Officers, for Continuous Study of the Structure and the Workings of Governmental Institutions and Processes in the Cities, the Counties, and the State of North Carolina." One early reader of the work, Judge Parker, encouraged Coates to produce a shortened version of the plan to encourage readership.

Pound was unable to answer Coates's call, but forty-five judges, lawyers, and lawmen from around the state responded to invitations issued by Superior Court Judge W. A. Devin of Oxford. Devin, who was respected by members of the Bar and those interested in local affairs, was a former mayor and state legislator and had been on the bench for nearly twenty years. Chapel Hill was in his judicial district, and Coates had captured his interest with the first issue of *Popular Government.* Coates had earlier invited Devin to speak to the Law School Association, and more recently Governor Gardner had appointed both men to the state commission on laws.

The meeting at the Carolina Inn began on December 29, 1931, and continued into the morning of the 30th as Coates outlined his plans for an expansive and complex program of training and educating public officials. There was interest, as well as great anxiety. Two men had to leave early after receiving news their local banks had failed. Coates had scheduled the meeting for an awkward time, but he had done that out of necessity. Meeting during the holiday interregnum allowed Coates to pay some heed to Van Hecke's requirement that he work on his projects outside of the normal law school calendar. Despite the awkward date and the interruptions, Coates must have been pleased with the result.

Coates's proposition was simple: elected officials and public servants who could be trained and educated for their jobs and responsibilities would produce more efficient and less costly government. Too often, office holders were elected to positions of public trust despite a lack of qualifications or experience. In hotly contested elections, they could not even count on help in learning their jobs. Defeated incumbents were not inclined to stay behind and offer assistance in a transition. Or, as was sometimes the case, those elected to office simply were not aware of the responsibilities they had assumed. While the newly elected might be dedicated and hardworking, they could not do their best work for the taxpayers because they didn't know what was required of them.

Coates's solution was myriad working groups, which would require the mobilization of hundreds, if not thousands, of concerned citizens. Coates proposed the creation of the North Carolina Association of Governmental Officers, which would be an umbrella organization for separate associations representing elected officials and public employees from throughout local government. County coroners would have an association, as would the justices of the peace, auditors, prison officials, teachers of government, and citizens at large. Tax collectors and city engineers would gather with their kind and share ideas as would county commissioners, city council members, mayors, judges, prosecutors, sheriffs, and welfare and health officers. Later, school superintendents would be added. At the outset, Coates even included a department of student government leaders, from the college level to high school. All of these associations would meet separately in local communities, consider an agenda suited to their interests, and then gather annually for a statewide congress.

To support this mass movement of concerned citizens and public servants Coates proposed a professionally staffed organization that he would later call the Institute of Government. The staff would serve the needs of the constituent organizations and compile guidebooks and training materials for use in each area of public work. These support publications would be written by staff members who would become specialists in particular functions of government and share their knowledge through a host of publications prepared for each position. As his example, Coates said a staff member would focus on the clerks of court, and at the outset spend time as an apprentice in one county to learn how the clerk did his job. The man—Coates didn't suggest women would be a part of his staff—would then go to the next county and work with the clerk there before continuing on to a third county, and so on through a hundred counties. At each stop the Institute's man would pick up ideas that he would pass on at his next stop as the progression continued throughout the state. It was a Johnny Appleseed approach that would be supplemented by periodic schools for clerks, who would be served with printed materials on the responsibilities of the position and the laws pertaining to the functioning of the office. Records, forms, and the other paperwork related to each public office would be gathered together and held for review at a central "laboratory" building, presumably in Chapel Hill.

Coates wrote: "We will simply gather up the ragged ends of old traditions native to this soil and through studies, guidebooks, laboratories, journals and schools of public officers organize and focus our steadily accumulating governmental experience, making it conveniently available for the immediate use of officials now in office, transit it to successive generations of governmental officers thereby enabling them to start nearer the point where their predecessors left off than where they began, minimize the lost motion involved in short terms of office, rotation in offices and amateur officers, begin to develop a governmental tradition and morale compelling in its encouragement and inspiration to public officers to leave the public service better than they found it, and thus sweep popular government to higher levels of effectiveness."[31]

This idea captured the attention of those concerned about the growing financial crises in many communities around the state. Counties and municipalities were in dire straits; by the end of 1932, thirty-nine counties and seventy-eight cities and towns would be unable to pay their debts and be effectively bankrupt. Coates argued that local government suffered from management that was not so much corrupt as it was inexperienced, inefficient, and ignorant of cost-saving measures that another community just a few miles away might be taking. Ignorance was expensive.

The new program all but overshadowed all the talk about updating the criminal code. Coates had an answer for those who questioned his priorities. It was a reply that would later characterize the Institute itself. There was a lifetime of work to be done on criminal law, but that was only one area in need of attention. All four of his course areas—criminal law, legislation, municipal corporations, and domestic relations—required attention. "If I stayed with one I would not get to the others," he later wrote. Why not start with cities and move from there to counties and then to the state? There is no way to segregate the functions of government, Coates responded. The laws of arrest apply to deputy sheriffs as much as they do to city policemen. The criminal code revision would never be completed.[32]

The men meeting over the Christmas holidays told Coates to proceed with his plans. At what Coates later would call the first meeting of the Institute of Government, Judge Devin was asked to gather a group of twelve persons representing various public offices and plan an organizational meeting for some time in the spring. Nothing was done to finance the work, however, despite Coates's projections that as much as $50,000 a year would be needed. At the suggestion of Judge Parker, Coates soft-pedaled the expense and worked first to gain the interest of men who could carry the movement forward.[33]

Devin's endorsement of his idea was all the encouragement Coates needed, although Coates had developed such a head of steam that naysayers could not have slowed his momentum. Within a month, Coates had letters on the way to hundreds of people from all across the state inviting them to attend a meeting in Chapel Hill in early May to organize what he called the association of governmental officials. He wrote to mayors and city managers, city auditors and engineers, leaders of the county bar associations, and county officials from the sheriff on down. Some letters went out over Devin's name; others were signed by Coates. The response was immediate, and encouraging. Devin got two hundred replies. Coates received as many of his own.

Local officials were looking for lifelines in the face of citizen anger and resentment over the scandals in municipal affairs. The reply from Mayor J. W. Hollis of Laurinburg was typical. "I have for some time been trying to secure a pamphlet covering the laws governing municipalities, but have so far been unable to secure it. An organization such as you propose would probably, as the first step, have the laws printed in pamphlet form for distribution, and this within itself would be of great benefit to all interested."[34]

Attorney George Pennell of Asheville wrote to say: "I recall two instances while I was city attorney for Asheville. One, where a man worked in a cotton mill until noon, was sworn in as a police officer at three o'clock, given a billy, a pistol and other paraphernalia of an officer and sent out as a peace officer in a city the size of Asheville."[35]

Some wrote to cheer Coates on but begged off from attending the meeting because of conflicts and lack of time. A. Wayland Cooke, the new clerk of court in Guilford County said he was too busy making changes in the office. "It was like a 'busted bank' with all of its depositors down on you at once and knowing not which way to turn."[36] He said he had sought help from the clerk in a neighboring county, much as Coates was suggesting that those in like offices share their knowledge.

Mayors and leaders in the largest cities in the state responded to the call. So did men in state government. The chairman of the state highway commission agreed to come, as did the state superintendent of schools, the head of the state medical society and a variety of businessmen who answered letters from Junius G. Adams, an Asheville attorney whom Coates persuaded to chair the organizing committee for the new association of public officials.

Adams was predisposed to listen to Coates. Asheville had suffered a complete collapse of its municipal finances. The real estate boom of the 1920s, of which Adams had been a part, had ended in 1928, and within a year the city's leading bank had failed, taking with it the cash deposits of city government. Many in Asheville had been ruined. Adams was a prominent figure in the community, and his most important client was Edith Vanderbilt, the widow of the man who had built Biltmore, the lavish mansion on the outskirts of Asheville. After Mrs. Vanderbilt remarried and moved away from the state, Adams became the local manager of the vast family holdings. The local losses would touch him deeply. The bank of which he was president would fail, and he would eventually lose his home in Biltmore Forest and move into a house on the estate.[37]

He was known as "Judge Adams" due to a brief stint as a criminal court judge early in his legal career and was one of those who had received the first issue of *Popular Government* a year before. Adams wrote to Coates to congratulate him on his work and volunteered to help in his cause, but cautioned that he had his own problems at home. "I wish I could say, 'What is required of me?' and be governed by your answer, but fate, stupidity and corruption in public and semi-public affairs, have given some God-awful twists to this community, into the soil of which my roots have sunk very deep, and I feel that I am entering a long period of involuntary servitude, in behalf of its rehabilitation. In your program of reform for our criminal code, I urge that you return to mutilation as the punishment for stupidity in public officials, thus obliterating the tribe—the crooked ones we will always have with us, but we can understand them, as their activities have some sense to them, and we can, in a measure, protect ourselves against them—but the stupid ones, God help us, are so 'unexpected' in their oblique methods and devastating accomplishments, there is no way to dodge them."[38]

Adams did not make it to the December meeting, but Coates pressed him to agree to chair a board of trustees for the enterprise. Coates envisioned among its members the state's top elected officials, judicial officers, and the leaders of municipalities and counties from across the state. The committee wanted Adams, Coates said, because of his experience in the law and business and because of his familiarity with the problems facing Asheville. Pressed by Coates, Devin, and others, Adams finally agreed to serve.

On May 6, 1932, a Friday, the new Graham Memorial of the Chapel Hill campus began to fill with out-of-town visitors. The meeting to create the association that Coates had been organizing for the past six months was only hours away from becoming reality. Earlier in the day, Gladys Coates had stood outside of Graham Memorial and wondered if anyone was going to show up for the barbecue supper that Albert had arranged to be served on the lower level of the building. She paced nervously; her husband reassured her that everything was fine.[39]

The venue could not have been more fitting for the launching of Coates's new organization. Campus leaders had struggled for more than a decade to open the student center that was to commemorate Edward Kidder Graham, whose vision of university service to the state ran through and through Coates's ambitions. Construction had continued with various fits and starts, and the building was finally opened for use in the fall of 1931. It was one-third the size that had been proposed at the outset, in part because more than $130,000 of the pledges made in the repeated campaigns of the 1920s had gone unpaid. The smaller size was the best that could be arranged, even with a final generous gift of $80,000.

Gladys needn't have worried. About two hundred people answered the call to organize the Institute of Government, a name that was formally adopted at this meeting. The mayors of the state's major cities attended and so did members of the council of state, legislators, judges, and members of city councils and boards of county commissioners. After a supper that was served cafeteria style, the group settled into folding chairs arranged in the large student lounge on the main floor for the evening program.

Adams convened the session, but it was Coates's "platform," and for more than an hour and a half Coates laid out his plans for the association of governmental officials, which drew the immediate endorsement of those attending, including the president of the North Carolina Association of County Commissioners. In his enthusiasm for the program, George Stansbury, the president of the county commissioners association, referred to Coates as "governor," which made Albert and Gladys nervous and uncomfortable. Albert had heard rumors that this statewide association was not all it seemed, that it might be the foundation upon which an ambitious young man would build a campaign for elected office. R. Hunt Parker, an attorney from Roanoke Rapids and one of Coates's steadfast allies, allayed such talk when he rose to speak. The man who conceived the idea of an association of government officials might well be governor some day, Parker said, but the "movement" was of such value to North Carolina that it went beyond any personal political ambitions. "His speech somehow freed the thought from the mistaken notion of political purposes," Gladys later wrote.[40]

The meeting continued on Saturday morning, and it wasn't until then that people on campus began to take notice of the hubbub at Graham Memorial. Coates had made no local announcement of the meeting and most on campus were busy with such end-of-term rituals as final examinations and social events. Undoubtedly, Coates was trying to keep as low a profile as possible during the spring, considering his troubles with his dean. The *Daily Tar Heel* reported in its Sunday edition that the meeting had been something of a surprise and the talk of the campus the day before. Coates was quoted as saying he had notified only those who had been involved in the formative stages of the program.[41]

The meeting adjourned shortly after lunch on Saturday. That morning, representatives of the various groups of officials met to talk about a larger meeting tentatively set for September. Those attending elected Adams to chair the organizing committee for the September session. Chosen to work with Adams were Devin and A. A. F. Seawell, an assistant attorney general from Raleigh. Coates was named secretary.

As those attending the meeting packed and headed home, Albert Coates rejoiced in the acclaim of a nucleus of enthusiastic supporters, the challenge of an undeniable mandate for government reform, and, in the following days, editorial endorsement from a few newspapers in the state. He also had a name for his dream—the Institute of Government. The new enterprise had no money, he and Gladys were its only staff, and he had a statewide conference to organize during the summer months. But Albert was undaunted. A new era had begun; Coates was ready for the thousand or more people that he anticipated arriving in Chapel Hill for the Institute's inaugural event in September.

SEVEN

"*Every Paling in the Fence*"

1932–1934

ALBERT COATES could not have asked for anything more from the first statewide school of governmental officers that he convened on September 9, 1932, in Chapel Hill. It was attended by about six hundred public officials and interested citizens from nine out of ten of the state's one hundred counties. University President Frank Graham opened the Friday evening session in Gerrard Hall and Governor O. Max Gardner introduced Harvard Law School Dean Roscoe Pound—long sought after as a participant by his protégé—who delivered the closing address the following day.

Coates had worked throughout the summer to raise a crowd for this inaugural event. It had not been easy as he continued to finance his nascent organization with his own meager resources. The most pressing need was for publicity, and he persuaded the editors of the university *News Letter* to allow him to fill the two July issues with his plans for the September conference and the Institute of Government. The university was low on funds and could not afford the overtime pay required to produce the 75,000 copies that Coates requested, even at the low rates charged by the state to pay the inmates who ran the presses at Central Prison in Raleigh. So Coates paid for the paper for the extraordinary press run, and he persuaded the inmates to donate their time in aid of his cause.

"I went to the prisoners and told them what I was doing and why I was doing it; that I had already put all my money in it and that my pockets were empty; that if they would help me I would get a room in the prison and eat, sleep, and work with them until the job was done," Coates later wrote.[1] When he had the copies in hand, he prevailed on the State Highway Patrol, whose officers had attended his police schools during the preceding months, to deliver the *News Letter* to city halls, county courthouses, state government offices, and civic organizations around the state.

With the endorsement of Asheville attorney Junius G. Adams, Superior Court Judge W. A. Devin, and others committed to his cause, Coates was beginning to accumulate a following of prominent citizens willing to endorse his program. A month before the September meeting he held an organizational session in Chapel Hill. Those attending included friends from the judiciary and the Bar, as well as businessman James G. Hanes of Winston-Salem; textile men Luther Hodges of Leaksville and R. Grady Rankin of Gastonia; Capus Waynick, the editor of the *High Point Enterprise*; and Richard G. Stockton, an executive with Wachovia Bank & Trust Co. in Winston-Salem.

Those who attended the September meeting paid their own way; a bed in a dorm room cost a dollar and meals were fifty cents each. As before, Coates opened the event with a buffet supper. The crowd was such that this time the meal was served outdoors on McCorkle Place under the Davie Poplar. The evening session featured a short welcome by Graham, an introduction to the weekend's program from Adams, and a presentation by Coates, who outlined the plans for the Institute of Government.

Graham compared the Institute attendance to a "commonwealth come back to its university to give it courage at a time when democracy is under attack. You men can keep democracy free and undefiled by keeping better trained officials on the job rather than by cutting into the budgets of the people." He was seconded by Adams. "The underlying purpose of this institute is to restore to the people confidence in and respect for government," Adams said. "There is a growing distrust of men in public office."[2]

The remarks from both men captured the uncertainty and disquiet of the times. That very weekend, strikers were on the streets outside the Thomasville Chair Company plants in Thomasville, North Carolina, where lines of State Highway Patrolmen used tear gas to break up an angry crowd. Graham himself was under attack from those who claimed that the university was a hotbed of socialism and communism. The charges were such that former President Harry W. Chase felt called upon to come to Graham's defense. The national political campaigns were about to reach full throat. Before the weekend was over, several thousand people would gather in Goldsboro, about eighty miles east of Chapel Hill, for a "Hoover-cart rodeo." The array of contraptions—two-wheel carts mounted on automobile axles and tires pulled by mules and horses—would form a parade several blocks long. One was pulled by its owner, who carried a sign that read: "Hoover got my mule."[3]

Coates believed that restoring confidence in government was essential for recovery from the economic crisis. He told the gathering that the Institute was a movement in that direction as he summarized a plan boiled down to four primary components: training public officials to avoid lost motion and wasted efforts resulting from short terms and rotation in office; elimination of overlapping and duplication of effort; use of local talent to obviate the need to go out of state for help in developing reforms; and the creation of a program of government education for high schools, colleges, and the professional schools in the state. Before the evening concluded, he won endorsements from a number of those attending who volunteered to support his work.

On Saturday morning, groups of public officials, representing twenty categories, held organizational sessions for their associations, but there was barely time to cover the detailed agendas that Coates had prepared. The conference concluded with Pound's address, a luncheon, and the approval of the "organizing committee" to hire a director (Albert Coates) and employ a staff for the Institute. All in all, the meeting had not been so much a school as a pep rally for good government. Coates hoped it all would lead to more productive working sessions in the future.

Pound's appearance helped expand the crowd for the Saturday session. All the seats in Gerrard Hall were filled. Governor O. Max Gardner, whose family was in Washington, D.C., that day taking a tour of the White House, introduced the dean. Once again, Gardner applauded Coates's work. "I seriously doubt if there was ever inaugurated a movement of more far-reaching import to this state."[4]

Pound had been but one of the national political and governmental figures who had received invitations from Coates and the governor. Others on the list were U.S. Supreme Court justices Benjamin M. Cardozo and Owen

J. Roberts; former governor Frank O. Lowden of Illinois, a noted state government reformer; Owen D. Young of New York, the founder of the Radio Corporation of America and a trustee of the Rockefeller Foundation; as well as Newton D. Baker, the Cleveland lawyer and former cabinet officer for President Woodrow Wilson. Only Pound made the trip.

Pound could not have delivered any more affirming address as he issued a blanket endorsement of Coates's plans. The dean deplored overlapping and duplication in government and called for more cooperation among levels of government. "We don't want a regime of highly organized bureaucracy but unless our present administrative officers learn to cooperate we will be driven to centralization."[5] When Coates forwarded a $100 expense reimbursement check to Pound several months later, Pound thanked him, applauded his work, and said he would have come at his own expense.

A few days after the event, Coates received a reassuring letter of praise from President Graham. "All that you have worked for, sweated for, despaired of, prayed for, and dreamed of, was realized in this meeting of the Institute of Government.

"Your exposition that night was one of the clearest, cleanest pieces of thinking that I have ever heard from that platform," Graham wrote. "I haven't had anything recently so to lift me out of the depths as the gathering of these men, and the purpose that lay back of them and the spirit that moved in the midst of them."[6]

With his commission to proceed and the freedom to use his time as he wished—Dean Van Hecke had approved an unpaid leave of absence for the fall term of 1932—Coates forged ahead. Over the next three months Coates spoke to any group that extended an invitation. He visited Parent-Teacher Associations (whose state president had endorsed the Institute in September), civic clubs, the medical societies in a few counties, and larger regional groups such as a national conference of state legislators meeting in Asheville. The North Carolina Federation of Women's Clubs invited him to its meeting, and he appeared on two ten-minute programs promoting the virtues of North Carolina that were broadcast by WPTF, the Raleigh radio station whose powerful signal made it the broadcast voice of eastern North Carolina. "I talked ad infinitum to all, and ad nauseam to some," he later wrote. "I was once asked how small a gathering I was willing to talk to, and I paraphrased the scripture by saying that wherever two or three are gathered together in the name of the Institute of Government, there will I be also." Just before Coates spoke to a Winston-Salem group, Hanes was told, "Tell Albert not to try to put every paling in the fence." [7]

He was a persistent and determined salesman who could convince donors that it was in their best interest to contribute to his cause, if only to get him out of their hair and on his way. Some may have even come away with the notion that the Institute—or at least some dimension of Coates's plan—was their own idea.[8] Robert B. House said of his old friend: "Albert would ask you to listen for five minutes and he would talk for three hours, literally. There were times when you would feel that you must rise up and kill him in order to breathe."[9]

Coates later wrote that the words "cease and desist were anathema to me. I ceased to be an individual and became a character; and the character became an institution. People quit saying, 'here comes Albert Coates', and started saying, 'here comes the Institute of Government.' This label not only came with me, it ran ahead of me and headed me off from many a dinner party and social gathering which did not want to run into the Institute of Government at that particular time and place."[10]

Coates made the case for the Institute by declaring that 30 to 40 percent of the state's public officials took office knowing little about the positions they had been elected to fill. The claim was not unjustified; on-the-job training was part and parcel of a citizen-led government. This was particularly true in a rural state such as North Carolina where men shouldered the responsibilities of local government along with their regular work on the farm or in small businesses. Coates was not endorsing professionals for the job, but he argued in favor of doing a better job of preparing amateurs for their assignments. The Institute would make these transitions in public office work more efficiently, he said, and help the non-incumbents understand their duties and responsibilities with less lost motion and time. Coates also continued to drive home the need for change in the criminal justice system. At a meeting of public welfare officers in Gastonia, he said a scientific approach was necessary to track the work of judges and prosecutors. He said the discretionary powers allowed to sentencing judges were too broad and resulted in capital punishment being used in cases involving "poor white trash and Negroes."[11] The Institute's ongoing criminal justice study would help remedy abuses.

Coates came face to face with examples of such injustice during his break from the law school. As Governor Gardner neared the end of his term he had grown increasingly concerned about conditions in the state's prisons and reports of unequal sentencing, such as the case of two men who were charged with the same crime but received vastly different sentences that Coates himself had used in the initial issue of *Popular Government*. The governor asked Coates to be one of eight members of an ad hoc committee he assigned to look into claims for parole or clemency. Coates immersed himself in the committee's work and even spent a night in a cell at Central Prison. The conversations he had with prisoners added to his own appraisal of the inequities in the criminal justice system and confirmed his belief that it was not properly serving the citizens of the state. The committee forwarded its report to the governor in early December and he was prompted to go beyond the routine end-of-term paroles. He ordered all men out of "the hole," the cells used for solitary confinement, and he released a number of what he called "forgotten" men and others whose sentences were considered too severe.[12] Among those released were men convicted of manslaughter and murder, including one man who had been on death row. The governor also included one or two bankers who had gone to jail following the collapse of their institutions. Upward of a hundred grants of clemency were announced as Gardner's term came to a close in December 1932.[13]

Coates's speech-making drew public attention to the Institute, but nothing raised awareness more than an event he orchestrated for early December. Working with WPTF, Coates arranged for a statewide network of five radio stations to carry a swearing-in program that would reach virtually every courthouse in the state. The program was a bipartisan homage to local government, complete with an address by the newly elected governor, J. C. B. Ehringhaus, as well as remarks by Clifford Frazier, Ehringhaus's Republican opponent in the November elections. Both men heartily endorsed the Institute of Government, as did Chief Justice Walter Stacy of the state supreme court and Kemp D. Battle, the president of the North Carolina Bar Association.

The radio broadcast demonstrated Coates's promotional genius and his ability to capitalize on opportunities. The evening was to serve as a capstone to his organizing efforts throughout the fall to create county units of the Institute of Government. These local organizations brought out a number of interested citizens in some of the urban counties, such as Wake and New Hanover. Organizers at the county level were asked to contact every public official and ask them to be on hand at the courthouse for an organizational meeting that would be followed by the broadcast of the speeches and the swearing-in ceremony. This coordination of meetings was to constitute the "formal launching" of the Institute of Government.

On the evening of December 5, the designated date for sheriffs, coroners, county commissioners, and others entering county office to take their oaths, citizens gathered at courthouses from the coast to the mountains to witness the oath taking, and then listen to the broadcast from Raleigh, where most of the principals had gathered at the Wake County courthouse. (Ehringhaus spoke by way of a radio relay from Elizabeth City, his hometown.) "The formation of the Institute of Government is one of the most significant events in North Carolina in many years," the governor-elect said. "People are beginning to realize that good government is not inattainable. No man can take the oath of office tonight without an added feeling of responsibility. There is need that officers think of themselves as called to the office to which they are elected."[14]

All told, the *Alumni Review* later reported, 35,000 to 40,000 people gathered in large and small groups in county courthouses across the state to witness the swearing in of their local officers and to listen to the broadcast. In Rowan County, the *Salisbury Post* reported that the courthouse was crowded with office holders, farmers, truck drivers, salesmen, teachers, the sixth graders from the Spencer schools, and "young men who seemed to have leisure on their hands. All to witness an event . . . as being in conjunction with the Institute of Government, which is a training ground at Chapel Hill for officials."

The program may have raised the confidence of North Carolinians who were ending the year battered and shaken by continuing reports of local governments embarrassingly caught up in the failure of financial institutions. Banks were continuing to fail, although a third fewer had closed their doors in 1932 than in 1930, when eighty-one collapsed, often taking deposits from local government with them. Some of the state's proudest cities were in deep trouble. The boom times in the 1920s had left local taxpayers in Greensboro—the third largest city, with a population of 58,000—with a painful financial hangover. During the good years, the city council had expanded the corporate limits to include new residential developments, buoyed by the claim of boosters that the city would double in population by 1940. A municipal building had been built at a cost of

$1.6 million, and half of the city's nearly $16 million of debt had been spent on building and paving new streets. A third of that money went for the extension of water and sewer lines to proposed subdivisions. In 1931 these residential building lots were still empty; the developers were bankrupt. In the coming months, nearly 20 percent of the city's property owners would be found delinquent in their property tax payments. The city would eventually take over land in lieu of taxes, and large parcels would remain on the books until home building resumed after World War II.[15]

There was no question that Coates had succeeded in launching a program that captured the imagination of elected officials across the state. He had brought officeholders from all levels of government together and organized them in associations where they could share concerns and seek solutions. His speeches and radio broadcast had offered hope and promise of government reforms that might save taxpayers money and develop more responsible and informed elected officials. He had united Republicans and Democrats in a non-partisan good government movement. His work had drawn the praise of the state's top elected officials, principals in the nation's legal establishment, and business and civic leaders within the state.

Despite the broad acceptance from elected leaders across the state and the support that appeared to be growing among everyday people, Coates was in danger of becoming like the Wizard of Oz. After a year of intense effort, and more than three years after he had set out to update and improve the state's criminal code, he had nothing to show for his work beyond rhetoric and a demonstrated ability to rally people to a cause. He later admitted that he had started fires all about the state and hoped that they would keep going long enough for him to get back and provide more fuel. As he prepared to return to the classroom in the early months of 1933 with his leave of absence at an end, the Institute had no formal structure, such as a board of trustees, and no plan of governance. Moreover, Coates had no money to consolidate his gains or secure a future for the Institute. Despite all the trappings and organizations for public officials and civilian volunteers, the Institute was still being run out of Coates's hip pocket, with the director responsible only to himself and a loosely defined organizing committee.

Coates did have a plan for financing the Institute. At the outset, in the original proposal that he mailed to hundreds of people around the state, he had estimated that $50,000 a year would be needed. He had proposed that the Institute first rely on contributions from a small group of wealthy individuals and then make a transition to smaller contributions from a larger group of those who could afford to give. Finally, when the Institute was established, the annual budget would be supported by individual memberships of a dollar each sold to as many as 50,000 interested citizens who joined the local units. This would produce the money to pay the salaries and expenses of four or five staff members, cover the cost of publishing monthly issues of *Popular Government* as well as guidebooks for local officials, and eventually help raise a building to house the Institute offices and laboratory.

It was an ambitious plan, but it required a leap of faith for North Carolinians when a dollar could equal half a day's pay. Coates certainly was aware of the difficulties facing people as he continued to juggle a bundle of obligations. He had been living on borrowed money for nearly twenty years, and he continued to roll over his loans at the bank with the help of friends like Frank Graham. Albert and Gladys already had forsaken the rental house in Westwood for a single rented room with a shared bath.

Even in the face of the Depression, Coates had some reason to believe that his plan held merit. His organizing work in the fall of 1932 had produced a growing number of county organizations, and by the end of the year he had received a $1,500 contribution from his old friend, Ben Cone of Greensboro. It was an impressive sum and arrived just in time for Coates to pay the $325 due WPTF for expenses related to the radio broadcast. He used some of the balance to restore his bank account, which had been diminished by the cost of printing the *News Letter* and a second issue of *Popular Government*, which he had rushed into print after the May meeting with a detailed description of the Institute and the agenda for the September meeting.[16]

Cone and Coates had known each other as undergraduates, and later, when Coates was in graduate school, Cone had been elected senior class president. Cone came from one of the wealthiest families in the state. He was the second son of Ceasar Cone, who, with his brother Moses, had founded the Cone textile enterprises in Greensboro at the turn of the century. The business was on its way to becoming the world's largest producer of denim and one of the first textile operations to take raw cotton and manufacture yarn and produce finished cloth all under the same roof. In later years Coates would generously credit Ben Cone with inspiring his ideas about the Institute as a research center. He often repeated the story of his visit to the company's research department, where he saw technicians testing dyes and developing fabrics that resisted shrinkage. Cone explained the importance of developing new products and manufacturing methods in the face of changing consumer tastes and demands. Coates said it was during this visit that he began to consider how research could be applied to public affairs.

The Cones were known as progressive men. Since the very early days of the company's mill villages, they had provided workers with health care by company nurses. Their clinics had been the forerunner of the state's first county health department. Meat, produce, and dairy products from the Cone farms were made available at cost at company stores. The company paid to erect church buildings and supplemented the cost of operating local schools. Ben had a keen interest in public affairs and was active in the university's alumni affairs and the Democratic Party. As he listened to Coates's plans for the Institute he was preparing to run for a seat in the state legislature. He would later become mayor of Greensboro and a leader of the North Carolina League of Municipalities.

Ben Cone followed his initial gift with a pledge early in 1933 to support the Institute with grants of $5,000 a year for three years. That pledge, and the promise of an additional $5,000 from his brother Ceasar II, was extraordinary, especially in the face of the difficult financial conditions at the time. The nation's new president, Franklin D. Roosevelt, declared a bank holiday in March, and many banks in North Carolina failed to reopen, including one in Greensboro owned by the Cones. Coates solicited other potential donors with large bank accounts, but none responded as generously as the Cone brothers. In those early months, his only other contributor was George Watts Hill of Durham, who gave him $300.

It was a modest beginning, but the Cone pledges were large enough for Coates to hire Henry P. Brandis Jr., who came to work on April 10, 1933, as the first associate director of the Institute of Government. Brandis was a native of Salisbury and a graduate of the university at Chapel Hill. He had attended law school there before transferring to Columbia University, where he got his law degree in 1931. He had been working in a New York City law firm when Coates offered him a job at a salary of $50 a week. As soon as Brandis arrived in the state, Coates sent him to Raleigh, where the North Carolina General Assembly had been in session since January 4.

Coates had always put unreasonable demands on himself, and he did nothing less with Brandis. From a seat in the galleries of the house and senate, Brandis was expected to follow the debate in each chamber, retrieve a copy of every bill, prepare a summary, and then produce a comprehensive report, ready for publication, of the state's new laws as soon after adjournment as possible. When Brandis arrived in Raleigh, the session had been underway for three months, and he had no support other than what he could coax out of the chamber's clerks. He became buried in paperwork as he sorted through bills and their tortured track through the committees. As it happened, Brandis's baptism in legislative coverage came with one of the longest sessions on record. After convening in early January, the General Assembly did not adjourn until May 15, after 1,711 bills had been introduced.[17]

Meanwhile, Coates returned to the law school for the spring term with a full teaching load. He also had an abundance of Institute duties, including fundraising and preparations for the 1933 statewide meeting, which he wanted to hold the first weekend in June to coincide with the university's graduation ceremonies. He hoped to build on the strength of the year before with a program that would include the congressional delegation and the leaders of the General Assembly. The Roosevelt administration was producing new legislation aimed at economic recovery, and local officials, strapped for cash, would be eager to learn from their representatives in Washington how to capture some of the millions of dollars that had been earmarked for public works and economic relief. At a minimum, Coates wanted from Brandis an analysis of state tax legislation.

Brandis faced an impossible task in digesting all the new laws that brought major changes to North Carolina. The new governor had been forced to retreat in his opposition to a state sales tax, finally supporting a 3-percent levy that was necessary to balance the budget and fully fund the eight-month school term. Changes in other tax laws relieved local governments of some financial responsibilities but imposed restrictions on bonded indebtedness. Constitutional amendments were passed, subject to approval by voters in 1934; prohibition was repealed and beer sales approved; new banking laws were adopted; and the chickadee was first selected, and then rejected, as the official state bird. There would be a lot of questions for Brandis at the Institute's meeting.

Coates could not work out arrangements for early June, so he moved the program to June 23 and 24. Despite the last-minute scheduling, the Institute's second statewide conference drew more than a thousand participants to Chapel Hill. At Coates's behest, Governor Ehringhaus and Senator Josiah Bailey had asked President Roosevelt to make a special radio address to the group, but the president sent a letter of support instead. Roosevelt encouraged other states to take at look at North Carolina and replicate what had been started there.[18]

Attention from the White House created front-page news stories for the opening session on Friday night. Bailey and other members of the congressional delegation supplied even more copy for the daily newspapers on the following day when they went through the new laws aimed at rebuilding the nation's economy. Bailey was the featured speaker, and while he praised the president's prompt action to deal with the Depression, he sounded words of caution. He was a reluctant supporter of the president's program and would grow more uncomfortable with it in the years ahead. The national government's new role was changing the country, he warned. Never before had such power been vested in Washington. "We had placed our emphasis for 140 years on liberty," he said, "but for the last year or so we had realized that somehow or other liberty was not working. Are these emergency measures and this new philosophy temporary or are they fundamental changes in the world?"[19]

This Institute meeting was a groundbreaking event. Never before in North Carolina, and perhaps throughout the nation, had so many public officials from all levels of government gathered with private citizens to talk about their government and how they should deal with a modern era that begged for a greater degree of expertise in understanding fair taxation, managing the judicial system, policing the streets, and financing the ever-growing demands of citizens for paved roads and highways, public welfare programs, and services considered essential for growing cities and counties. Coates had been warned that the competing interests of the various governments would preclude any results from a joint meeting, but he had proved the naysayers wrong. Writing of the event some time later, Coates said he was told that if he could develop a working relationship across governments that he would accomplish something entirely new in the United States.[20]

The lineup of participants was impressive, as evidenced by the stack of photographs of association chairs that Coates supplied the daily newspapers in the days following the event. Among Coates's volunteer leaders were the presidents of associations for the state's bankers, attorneys, and the press, as well as the North Carolina Merchant's Association and the state medical society. The lieutenant governor and speaker of the house were on board as were the state Federation of Women's Clubs, the Association of University Women, the American Legion, Rotary and Kiwanis clubs, educators, prison officers, police chiefs, sheriffs, tax supervisors, and purchasing agents. Coates also enlisted participation from business leaders and the head of the state Federation of Labor.

As the meeting drew to a close on a very warm Saturday afternoon, the organizing committee instructed Coates to continue to build a staff and focus his attention in the coming months on a report on the proposed constitutional amendments as well as the creation of a guidebook for election officials. Also on the agenda was completion of the recodification of the state's criminal code, the project that Coates had used to rouse public response in his first issue of *Popular Government*. Beaming broadly in the warm glow of success, Coates stood with Senator Bailey for a photograph that appeared on the cover of *The State* magazine, a new publication from Carl Goerch that had a broad circulation.

Coates loved the camera. The photographs that he provided newspapers along with the written accounts of the meeting were just the first of an inventory of pictures that would grow over the years. Every group that met for a training session was photographed and a print sent to each participant. These often ended up hanging in the offices of county sheriffs and police departments around the state. A meeting or school was not concluded until the photographer had done his work. The pictures were a visual affirmation of the Institute's program and in later years would become part of elaborate displays of the Institute's history and record of service. Coates was often in the picture, easily recognizeable as the man in a three-piece business suit standing in the middle.

What should have been Coates's hour of greatest satisfaction and the high point of his professional life came in the midst of a professional crisis that shook him to the core and threatened to end his association with the law school. Coates had earned praise for his work from the president of the United States, two governors, and the president of the university. He had a working relationship with more judges, mayors, police chiefs, and men of substance in business and the law than any faculty member on campus. Yet, his dean and direct superior, Maurice T. Van Hecke, was not pleased with the way he was carrying out his responsibilities in the law school.

A month before the June meeting, just as the spring term was drawing to a close, Coates was called upon to defend his performance in the classroom. During the 1932 fall term, Van Hecke had reshuffled Coates's schedule to provide for a leave of absence on the condition that he return in the spring of 1933 and rededicate himself to law teaching. In the early weeks of the spring term Coates had done as he promised and delivered some of his best work. However, the commitment failed after a few weeks, Van Hecke wrote in a report to Graham. For most of the term Coates's performance was characterized by poor preparation, lack of organization, and inadequate attention to the affairs of the law school, especially as the preparations for the June conference grew more involved. Once again, the dean said, Coates was often absent from campus and failed to let the dean's office know where he could be found for the delivery of phone messages. His students liked him, Van Hecke said in late April, but he was not an effective teacher of the law. "They admire his mind and his enthusiasm but they regard him as misplaced vocationally. They think that he would be at his best as a promoter and as a speech maker. In addition, the dean said, Coates had failed to meet his obligations to prepare research for the constitutional commission that reported to the 1933 General Assembly—his work was due just a few weeks before the Institute's December broadcast—and his assignment had to be completed by the dean of the Duke Law School. In addition, Coates had not allowed Van Hecke or others in the law school access to the Law Improvement Commission, which had been created at the request of the law schools to aid the General Assembly in updating laws and which Coates served as the executive secretary. All in all, Van Hecke said, Coates was not only failing his duty to his students, but had damaged the reputation of the law school among its peers.

"I recommend that Professor Albert Coates cease teaching in the Law School after the close of the current semester, and that, should the University desire to sponsor the enterprise, his salary and his entire services be made available to the direction of the Institute of Government. No new member of the faculty would have to be added to take his place," Van Hecke wrote to Graham.[21]

Van Hecke's five-page report to the president was a stunning indictment. Coates learned of the dean's concern when a messenger interrupted his class and handed him a note from Robert B. House, the university's executive secretary, asking him to meet him at Kenan stadium, a location deserted during weekday hours. House, who on the university's other campuses at Raleigh and Greensboro would have held the title of chancellor, was a close friend of both Graham and Coates. The president often asked him to sort out difficult matters, and this one was fraught with all manner of complications. House told Coates of Van Hecke's report to Graham and that the president had directed Van Hecke to meet with Coates and discuss the matter with him before it was taken any further.

Van Hecke confronted Coates with his complaint and asked him to choose between the Institute of Government and the law school. He said he was convinced Coates could not do both. Before the two men met with the president, Van Hecke agreed to Coates's request that Graham be allowed to conduct his own investigation and talk to students to determine if Coates's classroom performance was as Van Hecke had described. It was near the end of term, and teaching evaluations were not uncommon, so such an inquiry would not raise suspicion. At Graham's request, Van Hecke provided a list of eighteen men for interviews. Meanwhile, with Graham's consent, the dean wrote to his predecessors who had worked with Coates and asked for their appraisal of his work. Van Hecke was as insistent upon action from the president as he could be without bringing formal charges against Coates. Had he taken that step, Coates, as a full professor, could have requested an academic trial, an exercise that would have been difficult for all involved. Such an affair would have been most embarrassing to the university in light of Graham's public applause of Coates's work and all the attention that the creation of the Institute had drawn to Chapel Hill.[22]

Graham proceeded quietly. The former deans were reluctant to join the fray, but M. L. Ferson, who had left Chapel Hill for the University of Cincinnati, and Leon Green, then at Northwestern University School of Law, responded with candor. Green compared Coates to a "young race horse with great possibilities for a fine record." He urged Van Hecke to get Coates's best friends "to give Albert a series of good talks for his own good."[23] Ferson said he liked Coates and during their two years of association "we never had a personal jar," but, he conceded, Coates did not patiently concentrate his industry. "Albert is inclined to be very enthusiastic about a given subject or a given movement. He burns up with it for a time. It may be a subject the mastery of which calls for years of study. But he loses interest without seeing it through and turns to something else. It seems to me that Albert would be better placed in some work where his personality and power of persuasion could be capitalized but where consistent, plodding scholarship is not essential. He has a fine sense of the dramatic. I know of few men who could equal him in reaching and stirring the general run of people."[24]

Despite Graham's efforts to keep the matter private, word of Coates's difficulties became known within the law school. A group of students circulated a petition on his behalf and sent it to the president's office in South Building over thirty-one signatures, including one from a future attorney general of North Carolina, Malcolm Seawell. The petition was not effusive in praise of Coates, but the men said, "the ability and professional efficiency of Professor Coates ought not to be questioned."[25]

During their private conversation at the stadium, House had advised Coates not to do anything hasty, reminding him that his tenured position was not to be discarded without long and deep consideration. In time, he might find another arrangement with the university, should the Institute succeed as he hoped, but for the time being his professorship would provide an income and he should protect it. Perhaps the most disturbing prospect for Coates was the loss of association with the law school. It was his identity within the university and the place where he had declared that he would take his stand in advancing the vision of Edward Kidder Graham. Nonetheless, about two weeks later, Coates dictated a letter of resignation and asked House to deliver it to the president. In a cover letter to Graham, House said Coates was "out of town on business" and he had been asked to write the following on the law professor's behalf:

"A question having arisen concerning my status in the University, I stated to you that my primary concern was not to preserve my professorship as such but to preserve my good name and the integrity of my work. I wanted it particularly demonstrated that I spoke the truth when I reported to you that I was doing better teaching in my established law course than I had ever done before and that I was laying the ground in my new courses for better work than I had ever done before.

"You have been my severest critic and I have absolute confidence in you as my fairest judge. I, therefore, hand you, herewith, my resignation, leaving my future absolutely in your hands."[26]

Meanwhile, Van Hecke's frustration over the entire affair was building, and he tendered his own resignation as dean. On June 6, Coates, Van Hecke, and another faculty member, Millard Breckenridge, met in Graham's office in South Building. By the time the meeting was over, both Coates and Van Hecke had withdrawn their resignations. Van Hecke agreed to another leave of absence for Coates for the fall term and that he was to be given another opportunity to prove his value to the law school. Coates also agreed to distance the Institute from the university and not use, advertise, or claim the law school or the university as a sponsor of his work.

Graham defused the crisis in the law school, but the settlement with Van Hecke did not entirely resolve the matter of what to do with Albert Coates and his institute. It was being run independently of the university, but it had become associated with the institution because of Coates's professional affiliation and the Institute's use of university facilities for its meetings. Coates's dream was to make the Institute a part of the law school and an extension of his classroom, much as the Law School Association had been. Van Hecke had made it clear he did not want it there.

A year earlier, in the fall of 1932, Graham had urged Coates to merge the Institute with the new School of Public Administration that was just getting underway after three years of discussion and planning, most of it by Howard Odum. It was a logical outgrowth of Odum's work at the Institute for Research in Social Science (IRSS) and followed the vision of E. C. Branson, Coates's mentor and Odum's colleague. Odum had convinced Governor Gardner of the school's value and had even secured a small state allocation that he hoped to match with a grant from the Rockefeller Foundation. The strength of Odum's connections with the foundation was demonstrated in May 1932, on the same day that Coates convened his first conference of public officials, when the foundation announced a grant of $30,000 a year to underwrite the IRSS work. Graham supported Odum's efforts and three weeks later the two announced that W. C. Jackson, the chair of the history department at the Woman's College in Greensboro, would become the school's new dean.[27]

Odum's school and Coates's institute were branches of the same tree. E. C. Branson had recruited Odum in 1920, and out of their collaboration had come the School of Public Welfare and IRSS, both of which were an extension of Branson's philosophy of the university in service to the community. For ten years, Odum and his researchers had undertaken studies on county government, local taxation, and the state's penal system. The latter included a damning report on county chain gangs. Since many of the topics that Coates had on his agenda dovetailed with the work of IRSS, it made sense to Graham and others that Coates should merge the Institute into an organization that had a record of work and demonstrated success in gaining foundation support.

A merger was not impossible, but highly improbable. Both Odum and Coates were men with towering egos. Neither man would have tolerated subordination to the other. Coates also disagreed with Odum's approach to local government. IRSS studied an area of government with or without cooperation from its subject and then produced a report that could be used to form government policy or legislation. Coates believed in a more cooperative approach, and he emphasized the Institute's training function and its potential as a service bureau for local officials. He believed the Institute of Government could help public officials achieve a higher level of performance by answering their questions about laws and regulations and helping them become better informed. Meanwhile, Odum's studies had alienated local officials whose shortcomings were held up for public criticism. Coates believed that working hand-in-hand with local officials created confidence and generated mutual problem solving. "Albert didn't go at it 'that there is something rotten in Denmark' and we are going to find out what it is all about," Gladys recalled some years later. "Albert was working with people in the field and finding out what their frustrations were."[28]

There was another overriding issue. For Coates, independence was paramount. He had created the Institute of Government as an extension of his classroom and thus it was an extension of himself. His vision and ambition were driving it forward and he was reluctant to put his creation under the control of others who did not share his philosophy of service or appreciate the value of using the resources of the law school to train non-students. There were those in the academic community, including Van Hecke, who considered the Institute's training component beneath the dignity of the law school. In a merger, the training component of the Institute's program would be in peril.

Van Hecke wasn't his only critic. Others on campus believed Coates had appropriated the name for his institute without regard to their work. Coates called it a "battle of academic imperialism." Did the Institute of Government poach on public administration or political science, he later asked? "I agreed with the objectors that any one of several departments might register a valid claim to the sort of work that I was doing under the label I had chosen, that all of them ought to have been doing it for a hundred years."

Coates held firm to his claim, however, arguing, "I ought to be accorded at least the dignity of 'squatter's rights' in territory I had already occupied."[29]

With hopes of Coates finding a higher level of comfort within the new School of Public Administration, Graham had arranged in the fall of 1932 for Coates to become a trustee of the new program. The trustee group included members of the campus establishment such as D. D. Carroll, the head of the School of Commerce; historian R. D. W. Connor; Graham; and Van Hecke. Familiarity did not move Coates. After nine months on the board, Jackson wrote to Graham to say it was clear Coates preferred to remain independent and he would like to proceed with plans for the School of Public Administration without regard to Coates and his institute.

Coates was at an important crossroads. He had put his appointment in the law school in jeopardy because of his preoccupation with the Institute. The settlement with Van Hecke essentially left him on probation. In the coming year, he would need to convince the dean that he could be a contributing and supportive member of the faculty. At the same time, the Institute was at an important stage of its development. He needed to push ahead and demonstrate that it could be more than promises and public meetings. The advisory committee had issued assignments and that work would require additional staff and time, something Coates had in short supply. Coates told Graham and Van Hecke that if he could have another leave of absence for the fall of 1933, he would have the Institute established and running on its own by the first of 1934. The claim was certainly ambitious, but his superiors agreed nonetheless.

Brandis was worn thin by the end of the summer of 1933. He had buried himself in the work of preparing the legislative summary and rose from the pile of papers and note cards he used to catalogue each bill long enough to present a report on laws affecting clerks of court at the June meeting of the Institute. He also prepared for that meeting a handout that indexed the new laws affecting sheriffs, registers of deeds, and tax supervisors. It was not what Coates had promised, but it was something tangible to present to local officials. Brandis remained in Raleigh and worked steadily through the early fall to complete a summary of local laws affecting each county and its cities and subdivisions. His report was sent to legislators for their review and comment. While he was awaiting replies, he started on a summary of statewide legislation, organizing it by category. This task would occupy him until the end of the year.[30]

Coates also had his hands full. He was eager to add to the Institute staff and make good on his promises. In the fall of 1933 he and Gladys moved to Greensboro, where they rented a room at 1030 W. Market Street in the home of Mrs. Katherine C. Gregory, a recently widowed schoolteacher whose daughter still lived with her at home. The large, two-story house, located on a rise two blocks west of the Greensboro College campus, became not only the Coates's residence but also the base of operations for the Institute for a number of months as Coates worked with officials in Greensboro and Guilford County to gain a better understanding of their work. He and Gladys were joined by Henry and Martha Brandis and, before the end of the year, Dillard Gardner, the second Institute man to be hired, and his wife, June. The Brandises and Gardners lived on the third floor of the rambling house, which remained quite cold in winter. Gardner called their rooms "Little America," after the Antarctic exploration base established by Admiral Richard Byrd in 1929.[31]

Guilford County was a good spot for Coates's apprenticeship in local government. Officials with the city of Greensboro and Guilford County were working through a tangle of problems, from delinquent payments on the city's bonds to property owners forsaking their property in payment for past due taxes. Coates had heard that the county had hired a new employee in the tax office to find unlisted property and that in one year he had identified millions of dollars' worth of property that formerly had not been accounted for. The posting to Greensboro also put Coates close to his principal benefactors, the Cone brothers, whose contributions accounted for more than three-quarters of all of the money deposited to the Institute's account at the Bank of Chapel Hill. Albert spent his days in the city and county tax offices; Gladys monitored sessions of the juvenile court.

In November, Coates broke from his work routine long enough to deliver an uplifting patriotic speech on the fifteenth anniversary of the end of the Great War. His speech was preceded by a parade of military units from Greensboro, Reidsville, and Leaksville that filled the city's main thoroughfare, Elm Street, on a delightful November morning. Veterans of several wars, including the Civil War, stood with their families and hundreds of others on the curb as the marching units and bands passed by. The Red Cross, the Guilford Peace League, and the Salvation Army marched in the parade as well. The anniversary fell on a Saturday, the busiest shopping day of the week, but merchants closed their stores from ten until noon in honor of the occasion.

At the Armistice Day ceremonies at the Carolina Theater later that day, Superior Court Judge Hoyle Sink introduced Coates as director of the Institute of Government at Chapel Hill. In his speech, which was reminiscent of the eulogy he had delivered fifteen years earlier at the post-war memorial service for his friend Ensign Edward Pou, Coates wove together phrases and thoughts that ran throughout the lengthy papers he had written in support of the Institute. Although he never specifically referred to the Institute of Government by name, he issued a subtle call to rally behind movements like his own. "Today in the hunger, thirst and tumult of communism sweeping through Russia, fascism sweeping through Italy, Nazism breaking out from German centers, socialism eating at the roots of English institutions, above the repercussions of these movements breaking on American shores and rumbling in the bread lines of the land, like a bell from distant hill tops we can hear our fallen comrades calling to us now, to re-examine the foundations and the superstructure of our own government institutions to look to the rock whence we are hewn and build upon it."[32]

Dillard Gardner began work about three weeks after the Armistice Day celebrations, leaving behind a law partnership in Lenoir, North Carolina. He had been one of the young lawyers whom Coates had recruited in 1930 to work as a volunteer on the revisions of the state's criminal code. Gardner was troubled that this project remained incomplete. In a letter to Coates a year earlier, he quoted a Chapel Hill professor who had told him that Coates needed to show results more than anything else. "Here is one such which is ready for, and should be easy of, achievement," Gardner wrote Coates.[33]

Coates assigned Gardner to the criminal code revisions and told him he wanted him to complete his work in time to prepare recommendations to the 1935 General Assembly. In the meantime, Coates had two other pressing items on his agenda. He had been working with faculty members at State College in Raleigh, where he hoped to produce a statewide school for police officers over the Thanksgiving weekend. At the last minute, the school was rescheduled for late in December so that the U.S. Department of Justice could make available a display of its crime detection exhibit. Coates hoped that the devices and techniques being developed by the Federal Bureau of Investigation would be a lure for lawmen to attend.

Coates's other urgent task was to build on the financial support that he had received from the Cones. Coates's appeal to wealthy contributors had produced disappointing results; even those most closely aligned with the

Institute had not opened their wallets. None of the members of his organizing committee had made contributions, nor had any of the chairs of the constituent groups whose names and pictures had appeared in the state's newspapers. James G. Hanes had done some work on Coates's behalf in Winston-Salem, but those who traveled in Hanes's circles were reluctant to make an investment until Coates could demonstrate that his program had statewide appeal.[34] As Coates neared the end of 1933, all of the Institute's money had come from just three men: Ben Cone, Watts Hill, and J. G. Millis, a High Point hosiery manufacturer, whose $1,000 arrived just ahead of Coates's Armistice Day speech.

In November, with help from Robert Madry, Coates arranged for a story to be fed to the state's leading newspapers that he hoped would produce a wave of contributions. Coates announced that he had pledges of $50,000 in support of the Institute of Government that would be available only if the Institute could raise a like amount from individual supporters.[35] This stretched the truth a bit, but Coates thought he could come close to that figure. The Cone brothers had pledged $15,000 each, Hanes had indicated he might be able to raise $10,000 out of Winston-Salem under the right circumstances, and assorted other pledges took Coates close to the $50,000 he announced. Emphasizing that this money would be available only if matched by citizens of the state, he called on the county units to meet on December 12 to collect a dollar each from members.

The *Charlotte Observer* report on the proposed mass meeting quoted an unnamed "representative of the public officers of North Carolina" whose syntax and rhetorical flourishes sounded a lot like Coates. "If the officers of North Carolina want to improve the workings of the government they administer, if the citizens of North Carolina want to acquaint themselves and keep themselves acquainted with the actual workings of their government from day to day, if the youth of North Carolina want to bring with them to the ballot box an adequate understanding of the government, whose destinies they must determine, here is the opportunity to do so through a program which has grown out of their own experiences, which has been studied and approved by over 2,000 people from every section of North Carolina, by governmental leaders and administrators in 44 states, and by the President of the United States, who has sent his congratulations to the people of North Carolina on the building of the Institute of Government and expressed the hope that every state in the union would follow North Carolina leadership in this work.

"This is a great co-operative program. It is as great as government of the people and no greater." The remarks of the "representative" quoted in the *Charlotte Observer* were printed verbatim in the (Raleigh) *News & Observer.*[36]

Calling meetings of county units had to be one of Coates's most ambitious gambits, but there was nothing else he could do. Unfortunately, the December date came and went without a single dollar being added to the bank account. This public appeal might have produced better results in good times, but Coates was trying to raise money from average citizens when one quarter of them were dependent on some form of government relief. While the number of families receiving government support had begun to decline by the fall of 1933, the bitter memory of handouts and empty cupboards remained vivid. People just didn't have money for civic causes. A schoolteacher—perhaps a prime candidate for Coates's enterprise—was paid only $12.50 a week. In the late summer, when a hurricane raked the coast, calls went out for aid for those who had lost their homes in the storm. These efforts went unanswered. Even local Community Chest campaigns were falling behind their budgets. Coates would repeat this appeal in the spring of 1934, but the Institute would collect only $136 in individual memberships over twelve months.[37]

Coates's plea for financial support came at a time when he was all but incapacitated by a severe case of the flu. He recovered sufficiently to be in Raleigh two days after Christmas for the opening of the three-day police school co-sponsored by the Institute and State College, where faculty members had begun to gather data on traffic fatalities and highway safety. The turnout at the sessions held on the campus was impressive. A total of 165 officers from 75 towns and 67 counties attended.

Dwight Brantley, a special agent of the U.S. Justice Department, was one of the featured speakers and a popular man at the program. Brantley was one of a new kind of federal agent, or "G-man," who made up the FBI, which was emerging as a model of modern policing. The agency would capture the public's imagination a few months later with the bloody showdown outside of a Chicago movie theater with bank robber and popular national felon John Dillinger. For the time being the public was still singing songs about Oklahoma bank robber Charles "Pretty Boy" Floyd, who continued to elude lawmen. At least six killings and more than a dozen bank robberies were credited to Floyd.

North Carolina had escaped the attention of the likes of Dillinger and Floyd and other notorious outlaws who seemed satisfied with robbing banks in the Midwest. But that didn't mean that gangsters weren't active locally, Brantley said. He reported that a recent $100,000 mail robbery in Charlotte was the work of a gang called the Chicago Touhys. Brantley gave a rundown of investigations on other highly publicized crimes, including the kidnapping of the infant son of Charles Lindbergh. He brought to Raleigh an array of police hardware, including fingerprinting kits, ultraviolet lamps for reading secret messages, police radios, teletypes, and an eavesdropping device called a "detectophone." The display also included photos showing applications of scientific devices used in criminal investigations, as well as exhibits from recent high-profile kidnappings.[38]

Coates, State Highway Patrol Captain Charles D. Farmer, and Harry Tucker from State College took the lawmen to school on more prosaic matters: traffic safety and highway law enforcement. According to Tucker, 15 percent of all traffic fatalities were due either to drunken drivers or drunken pedestrians. About a thousand people a year were dying in roadway accidents as drivers roamed the highways without legal restrictions on who could drive or what they could drive. An effort to require drivers to obtain a license had been defeated in the 1933 General Assembly. Officers learned about retrieving stolen automobiles from a representative of the National Association Theft Bureau, while District Solicitor J. Will Pless talked about the need for uniform law enforcement to earn the respect of citizens.[39]

Coates felt a connection with the police officers, their chiefs, and the sheriffs and deputies who turned out for this school. He enjoyed their candor, their stories, and their interest in learning better techniques. He believed that working with law enforcement was the most direct connection with his classroom, where criminal law remained the mainstay of his teaching portfolio. Over the years he would write fondly of winning the confidence of crusty sheriffs and suspicious uniformed officers, some of whom had taken their jobs with a minimum of education and were suspicious of "schools."[40]

Despite the shortfall in his fundraising, Coates had to feel optimistic at the beginning of 1934. The police school was followed by the publication of Brandis's summary of the new laws passed by the 1933 General Assembly. Soon after release of this report—published as an issue of *Popular Government*—came the publication of the Institute's first "guide book," which was written for clerks of court. Altogether, these publications were the Institute's first major substantive products that could actually serve officials on the local level. Brandis and Gardner also were summarizing rulings by the attorney general, the Local Government Commission, the Utilities Commission, and other state agencies. These were condensed and published in a biweekly bulletin sent to local government offices.

Coates's success may have given him more confidence in the classroom. Throughout the spring of 1934 he was more successful in juggling his law school duties with his work for the Institute. Chastened, perhaps, by the showdown with Van Hecke a year earlier, Coates performed at a level sufficient for Van Hecke to inform Graham that while he did not believe Coates had done as well as other faculty members, he had made improvement. He told Graham, in person and in writing, that in "the opinion of the faculty and myself, [Coates] should be restored to his former status as a regular member of the faculty."[41]

Coates seemed to be bound for controversy, nonetheless. The organizing committee had asked for a study of the proposed constitutional amendments that were scheduled to be on the ballot in November. Dillard Gardner completed that report, and it was published as an issue of *Popular Government*, which now called itself a quarterly journal. Gardner was assisted in the study by Brandis and a new member of the staff, T. N. Grice Jr. Grice had come on board shortly after the first of the year. His friends called him "Buck" and he was a native of Elizabeth City. He was a 1928 graduate of the university's School of Commerce, and after graduation had taught accounting for a year. For the previous five years he had been on the staff of the accounting firm Price, Waterhouse and Company.

Coates's problems arose after he refused to involve the Institute in a partisan debate over the proposed constitutional amendments. The Institute had friends on both sides of the issue. Chief Justice Walter P. Stacy had chaired the commission that proposed the amendments. One of the most ardent opponents was Attorney General Dennis G. Brummitt, a man who had taken a keen interest in the Institute and had given it and Coates generous public support at the outset. The proposed amendments shifted power between the executive and legislative branches. Among the proposals were provisions for a gubernatorial veto and gubernatorial appointment of the state board of education. Other changes would give the legislature greater authority over the offices of coroner, sheriff, and clerk of court. In the judiciary, the chief justice would be given authority to assign judges, a power then held by the governor.

The first to urge Coates to take a position on the amendments were members of Stacy's commission, who were surprised that Coates would not commit the Institute to support changes designed to "modernize" the constitution, written in 1868. Coates refused, saying that the Institute must remain neutral if it was to perform any important service to the state. "Because this sponsorship would destroy the very foundations of our existence," he later wrote, "the Institute of Government will never lobby for or against anything or anybody, in the legislature or out, no matter how good or how bad. That proposition and the integrity of our work are the only things we are willing to fight about. They mean more to government in North Carolina than the success or failure of any particular venture we study and report on."[42]

According to Coates, Brummitt pushed the issue even further. Coates had already experienced one run-in with Brummitt, who had wanted to use an endorsement from the Institute in his candidacy for reelection in 1932. Coates had refused, explaining the need for neutrality. When Brummitt mounted his opposition to the amendments, he advised Coates to cancel informational meetings that Coates had planned for various locations around the state. Brummitt told Coates the amendments were a partisan issue, and if the Institute was non-partisan then it should remain out of the debate.

Coates proceeded against Brummitt's wishes and in mid-April he moderated a debate in the state House chamber before an audience of about 125 city, county, and state officeholders who had responded to an invitation by the Institute. Speaking in favor of the changes were Stacy and state Commissioner of Revenue Allen J. Maxwell, who had sought the Democratic gubernatorial nomination, without success, in 1932. Stacy endorsed the changes, even though he said he had reservations about some of the provisions. "Taking it by and large, I think it's better than the old," he told the officials in the House chamber. He said the changes generally gave citizens "freer self-government through their representatives."[43]

Brummitt said he opposed the amendments in the belief that they moved power away from voters and into the hands of the governor and legislators. He offered numerous changes that he said should have been included in the amendments approved by the General Assembly a year earlier. By shifting authority over local offices to the General Assembly, the amendments would allow the governor to use his influence to determine who held office in each county.

The April session was the first of several events where Brummitt held forth. Word reached Coates that the attorney general was telling his audiences that the Institute had justified the amendments by claiming the 1868 Constitution was written by "carpetbaggers." Indeed, the Constitution had been written in the wake of the Civil War when the state was under the control of Union authorities. Coates later wrote that Brummitt said that even though it was written during difficult times, it was the "best constitution North Carolina ever had." In fact, said Coates, Brummitt was lifting the reference to carpetbaggers out of context. Gardner had written in his report that the 1868 constitution was the state's best, but those words appeared on a page following the one from which Brummitt quoted. To prevent further misunderstandings, Coates appeared at public events where Brummitt was to speak and was prepared to defend the Institute. "I followed him, sitting on the front row in open view," he wrote. "He knew I was there to point out this fact and demonstrate his duplicity."[44]

The debate over the amendments allowed Coates to establish the independence of the Institute of Government, although the issue at hand became moot in September. Perhaps sensing that the amendments would fail in the referendum scheduled for the fall, the governor asked the state supreme court for an advisory opinion on whether a legislative mix-up had compromised the date of the election. The governor asked the court to advise him whether the amendments should have been submitted to voters in the fall of 1933, when the question of repeal of the Eighteenth Amendment to the United States Constitution was on the ballot. The court, led by Stacy, ruled that the state amendments should have been submitted at that time, and the referendum was pulled from the ballot for the fall elections.

The controversy was not without some worrisome fallout. For the first time, Coates and the Institute were the subject of critical editorial comment, including in the newspapers in Winston-Salem, one of the few cities where he had found financial backers. A *Winston-Salem Sentinel* editorial claimed it found bias in the Institute's pamphlets on the amendments that "was not even adroitly concealed. It gave the people no adequate conception of what they were asked to vote for." The editorial warned that based on Coates's pledge to be on hand when the 1935 General Assembly convened to assist in drafting legislation, "it appears that this bureau, commission or organization is assuming to perform governmental functions and to take over governmental powers. The next step, no doubt, will be request for an appropriation from state funds as a subsidy or grants in aid of the enterprise."[45]

A few days later, the city's morning newspaper, the *Winston-Salem Journal*, questioned the validity of the Institute's recently released guidebook for election officials, a project that had the endorsement of Republicans and Democrats. "Who furnished the money for this printing and distribution?" the editorial asked. "We readily agree that election officials ought to have guidance in these important matters. It is equally apparent, however, that this aid and guidance should be supplied by the officials of the state of North Carolina, and not by a voluntary organization such as the Institute of Government."[46] The *Durham Herald* editorial page rose to the Institute's defense.[47]

The negative commentary could have created real trouble had it appeared a year earlier, but the Institute's program was gathering momentum and Coates was increasing its financial base. While the public had not responded to his appeal for subscriptions or memberships in 1934, James G. Hanes and his friends in Winston-Salem contributed $1,400 and Ceasar Cone sent a check for $5,000. Subscriptions by cities and towns to the biweekly bulletins were also beginning to produce a small amount of income. There was sufficient income for Coates to increase the frequency of *Popular Government* from quarterly to monthly publication, with part of the cost of publication underwritten by advertising. The first monthly issue appeared in November and included ads from Jefferson Standard Life Insurance Company, the S&W cafeteria chain, a group of hotels, and Charlotte bond broker R. S. Dickson, whose firm specialized in municipal and state bonds. The ads for the cafeteria and the hotels may have been in exchange for room and meal expenses incurred by Coates and the staff as they traveled about the state.

The Institute's 1934 annual meeting was to have been held in early September, but many communities in the state were upended by a general strike of the textile industry that closed mills and put lawmen on alert from Charlotte to Durham. Coates postponed the session until November 15 and 16 in Raleigh and announced that the nation's first female member of the federal appellate court would be the principal speaker. The change cost him a return visit by Dean Pound, who could not reschedule for the later date. Standing in for Pound was Assistant U.S. Attorney General William Stanley.

The meeting focused on two themes, law enforcement and election laws, both of which were high on the Institute's agenda. Democrats and Republicans were represented with L. P. McLendon, a Democrat and chair of the state board of elections, and William C. Meekins, the chair of the state Republican Party, both taking part. They called for an overhaul of laws regulating primary elections and tighter restrictions on the use of absentee ballots, which had been introduced in 1917 as a wartime measure to accommodate men in uniform. In some counties, McLendon declared, 10 to 15 percent of the votes cast in some precincts were by absentee ballot. Such conditions, especially in counties where voter registration rolls had not been cleared of deceased voters in thirty years, could lead to fraud and manipulation of the elections. Primary elections laws needed examination, he said, after it was found that more than 1,700 persons voted twice on primary election day, once for Democratic candidates and again for Republican candidates.[48]

Stanley and Hugh H. Clegg of the FBI urged cooperation of all levels of law enforcement to combat crime. Clegg, who would soon organize the National Police Academy, also brought along a display of firearms and other hardware from the department's inventory.

About eight hundred people attended the sessions, which were held at various venues in Raleigh. The police school was conducted one afternoon on the State College campus. The public addresses and group meetings were held at Memorial Auditorium. Governor J. C. B. Ehringhaus was again present to give the Institute his endorsement. With highway safety a rising concern—North Carolina had the highest number of deaths in the nation by miles driven—the governor called for the legislature to enact a law, when it convened in a few weeks, requiring all drivers to be licensed.

The meeting closed a most successful year. The Institute was beginning to take shape as Coates had outlined it more than three years earlier. Public officials were meeting together and sharing ideas. Training schools had been conducted to improve law enforcement, election management, and tax administration. The Institute's guidebooks were in the hands of those in charge of the public's business. While the treasury was modest, Coates had enlisted the support of a handful of municipalities and counties that were paying for Institute reports. Coates also had survived the first serious public criticism of his program, as well as a showdown with a top state official, without any noticeable ill effects.

Nonetheless, the Institute remained a loosely run operation whose base was wherever Coates happened to be. His office, his classroom, and the small rental house that he and Gladys had found on East Rosemary Street were cluttered with publications, organizational records, and piles of materials submitted by lawyers who had been working on the recodification of the criminal code. Coates had borrowed some space on campus, first in the basement of Peabody Hall and later in an abandoned house on the old fraternity row in the northwest corner of the campus. Neither was a fit home, of course, nor qualified as the "government laboratory" that he talked about with great enthusiasm. The Institute's three staff members carried their offices with them and worked from rooms in boarding houses and hotels. As Dillard Gardner pushed ahead to finish the criminal law study, he imposed on local lawyers friendly to the Institute who gave him access to work space as well as their law libraries.[49] Coates knew that the Institute of Government would remain little more than an illustrated concept unless and until he found it a home. That was his next challenge.

EIGHT

A Home on Franklin Street

1935–1939

CONSTRUCTION ON the University of North Carolina campus in Chapel Hill was at a standstill in the early months of 1935. The last new building to open after the expansive years of the 1920s was Memorial Hall, where guests at the 1931 dedication ceremonies had to make do with the battered benches brought from the old building because there was no money for new seating. Scaffolding around other campus buildings stood abandoned. The university's accounts were so short there was no money for proper maintenance. Nonetheless, Albert Coates believed he could do what the university and the state of North Carolina could not—erect a $100,000 building on the campus and make it the home of his Institute of Government. Even his old mentor Horace Williams was incredulous on learning of his protégé's latest plans. "Mr. Coates's idea of the Institute of Government is a great one, but now he wants a cathedral," Williams told Gladys Coates.[1]

Though there was little reason to believe he could succeed, Coates was undeterred. After all, his institute had surpassed the critics' expectations. While the nation was struggling to repair battered civic institutions, he had produced measured success and had won applause from a host of state political leaders. His dean, and many of his colleagues in the law school, had discounted his work and raised doubts about his fitness as a professor, but the numbers of public officials and private citizens attending Institute meetings had continued to grow. His financial resources were thin, but he pushed on. He could transpose a businessman's impatience with his long-winded application for support into yet another donation. For Coates, a simple nod of agreement meant he was only a signature away from a check that he could carry to the bank. So why not a building, and a large and handsome one to boot, that would serve the civic-minded, the Institute staff, undergraduates at Chapel Hill, as well as policemen, sheriffs, schoolteachers, and public officials from across the state?

Coates had been talking with President Frank Graham about his "governmental laboratory building," as he called it, for months before the two men met in a more focused session in the early spring of 1935. He would raise the money to pay for the building, Coates earlier had told Graham, but he would like a piece of land at the edge of the university's property on which to build it. (He had his eye on a spot on the campus's western boundary, along the road to Pittsboro south of the Carolina Inn.) Graham was amenable but advised Coates that while he certainly held out a hand of welcome, and applauded his success in pursuit of E. K. Graham's commission of university service to all citizens, he could not make such a gift or even the promise of one. The Institute's request would require the approval of the university's trustees.[2]

For Coates, the building would be more than a headquarters and working space for a staff that would increase to five associate directors by year's end. The building would give the Institute permanence and represent the success of a movement that had grown out of his law school classroom and now was accepted by those managing the affairs of government across the state. The Institute was making a difference in the lives of ordinary taxpayers, Coates declared. He said new methods of listing and collecting local property taxes that had been passed on to tax officials by the Institute had produced more in savings and generated more new revenue for local governments than his new building would cost. The guidebooks and publications coming out of the Institute might disappear upon a library shelf, but the bricks and mortar of the laboratory building would serve as demonstrable public evidence of the movement's value.

That spring, as Coates talked to Graham about his plans for a building, he was on another unpaid leave of absence from the law school, his relations with the dean having once again become strained. Released from teaching responsibilities, Coates filled his time with Institute affairs, especially with the expanded coverage of the 1935 General Assembly, which had convened in January. This time, Dillard Gardner and T. N. Grice would support Henry Brandis and clerical assistants, among them Albert's youngest sister, Elizabeth, who was a recent graduate of the university at Chapel Hill.

Coates rented office space in the Raleigh Building, an office building a block south of Capitol Square at the corner of Hargett and Fayetteville streets. Before the session began, Coates and his men had called on legislative leaders to gain approval for their work. The lieutenant governor and speaker of the house endorsed the Institute's plans but warned that their work might not be readily accepted by members wary of "airing their soiled linen" in public. "We decided to assume the risk," Grice later wrote in his Institute report on the session.

The presiding officers turned the particulars of accommodating the Institute's needs over to the clerks, who were less welcoming. They "regarded us with a suspicion equal to or greater than that of a Kentucky mountaineer of the solicitous attentions paid his daughter by the traveling lightning rod salesman," according to Grice. The legislative staff in each chamber set out to make the Institute's job as difficult as possible because, Grice later determined, some of them were earning money on the side keeping certain special interests informed about legislative action. "So you can understand their fine spirit of cooperation," Grice reported.

Brandis asked for a seat at the press table. No, he was told. Too crowded. How about a chair in the foyer behind the rostrum? No, only members were allowed on the floor. Could they have copies of the bills when they were introduced? Only if the members provided an extra copy. Could they inspect bills in the clerk's office after the session adjourned? Well, they were told, the office closed for an hour at the end of the day's session so clerks could update their records, and then the staff had to eat. When the office reopened, they would be permitted to review the filings.

"Finally," Grice said, the Institute staff asked if they could sit "in the gallery, observe, make notes and get whatever information remained in the office after the employees had been fed provided we did not interfere with the leisure of the overstuffed office?"

"O! Yes! We'll be glad for you to try that."

Others would have been discouraged by such subterfuge, but they had not counted on what Grice called Coates's "bulldog tenacity."

Grice described their work this way: "It was no easy task to sit on straight back wooden benches with your knee for a table and record the legislative record of every bill introduced, sent to committee, reported out of committee, passed or voted down. In short, it was necessary, amid the clamor of visiting school children and in spite of the kindly old lady who wants to know the name of the tall gentleman in the third row two seats off the aisle, to record the history of every bill put into the legislative hopper. The task is more difficult since due to some reason, unknown to man, legislative reading clerks and railroad station callers generally enunciate the first syllable of the first word and follow through with a conglomeration of sounds, both guttural and nasal, which defy human understanding."[3]

The men tracked each bill as it made its way through the process, and with the aid of their own clerical help produced a bulletin of legislative action that was on the desk of each member when the next daily session opened. An expanded edition that included advisories on committee reports and summaries of ratified bills was mailed daily to state department heads and others, including a small list of paying subscribers. On the weekend, Albert and Gladys joined the staff in Raleigh to write and publish a weekly bulletin of bills having statewide application. This mimeographed report went into the mail on Saturday and was received on Monday morning in the offices of every daily and weekly newspaper in the state. The reporting served the state's citizens by providing unprecedented transparency to the legislative process, but it left some legislators wary of the watchdogs in the gallery.

Grice recalled an early confrontation with a legislator he called the "Bladen bombshell." The man burst into the Institute office and demanded to know why they were reporting on his legislative activity to his political enemies back home. The staff explained that the gentleman from Bladen wasn't being singled out for special attention. The bulletins that alerted his opponents were simply part of the total coverage. In addition, they pointed out, the Institute offered aid to legislators in drafting bills, another service open to all. This seemed to calm the man, who then asked if the staff would prepare him a bill abolishing every county office held by his enemies. Yes, he was told, and the bill was delivered. Grice wrote that the man kept the bill in his pocket for the balance of the session and spoke well of the Institute thereafter.[4]

As the 1935 session proceeded, the growing confidence of the legislative clerks in the fairness of the Institute's coverage eased some of the strain on the overworked team. The men were granted better access to materials, and with the creation of a shorthand of symbols and abbreviations on legislative action, they went from working twenty hours a day to only eighteen, Grice later wrote. They all contended with the long hours and the frustrations of unexpected emergencies such as the night the belt on the mimeograph machine broke and Elizabeth Coates had to repair it with a hairpin. By the end of the session, the daily bulletins had become a familiar fixture on the legislators' worn mahogany desks.

The Institute's daily and weekly bulletins were a burst of sunshine on state affairs. North Carolina's legislature, uninhibited by a gubernatorial veto, long had operated with little oversight. A bill could become law virtually overnight with no public notice or outside review. Newspaper reporters covered the major action of the day, but the Institute's bulletins exposed the legislative intent of all bills for interested citizens, state officials, and editors at weekly newspapers. For the first time, those responsible for the running of cities, towns, and counties had a fair and unvarnished account of legislative action in their hands in time to digest and respond to a bill before it became law. The Institute's summaries went behind a bill's sometimes misleading and innocuous title to its essence, often to the embarrassment of individual members. Grice recalled one bill whose titled purpose was to "correct a typographical error" but actually raised the salary of the mayor of the legislator's hometown by 30 percent.

"I think it can be said unqualifiedly," Brandis later wrote, "that the [Institute's] records were superior to any other legislative records available in one office; and more and more as the session lengthened many people, including newspaper men and legislators themselves, came to rely on our office for all types of information with respect to legislation."[5]

"Was it worth it?" Grice wrote, "It has certainly provided a needed service to give the people of the state a fuller knowledge of what the legislative mill is grinding. It has just about eliminated undercover spite legislation and probably has improved the general standard of all legislation."[6]

Coates had a capable staff in Raleigh. Brandis's earlier experience was invaluable, and both Gardner and Grice, while unfamiliar with the legislative processes, were eager and relentless in establishing the integrity and veracity of the Institute. Coates himself was never far from the action. He hustled between Chapel Hill and Raleigh throughout the spring as he juggled other chores and filled every speaking engagement that came his way. In March and April alone, at the height of the legislative action, he made more than two dozen appearances at civic clubs around the state. Each engagement, whether it was at a Rotary Club or a high school commencement, was a welcome platform for him to use to promote the name and expand the reputation of the Institute.

Coates was focused on his mission to the point of distraction. One evening he arrived in advance of an engagement and discovered that the 120-mile drive from Chapel Hill had left him with a rumpled suit. His host sent his trousers out to be pressed while he and Coates, who was offered a dressing gown, fell into conversation to await their return. When his pants had not arrived within an hour before Coates was due to speak, the host frantically began a search. He discovered that the cleaning establishment was closed and the owner had left for a business meeting in another town. The seconds ticked off as they searched for a way for Coates to appear fully clothed. The dry cleaner's wife finally called to say that Coates's trousers had been delivered to the wrong rooming house. With only three minutes to spare, Coates arrived on stage to deliver his address.[7]

Coates's appearances around the state brought complimentary newspaper coverage of the Institute's work, and Robert Madry at the University News Service added to the publicity with occasional news releases about the innovative Chapel Hill law professor who was working on behalf of better government. Late in the spring, Madry released a story about Coates forsaking the classroom for the life of a police officer. He reported that Coates planned to walk with the cop on the beat, ride with deputy sheriffs, and chase criminals with federal agents. "After that he plans to devote some time to 'sitting in' with a prosecuting attorney, a judge and the pardon boards of county, state and federal governments."[8]

With so many other duties pressing hard for his time, it is not clear how long Coates actually spent in police service. He prevailed on his friend, Frank N. Littlejohn, the police chief in Charlotte, to allow him to spend a few weeks in his department. Coates stayed in the field long enough to accumulate an inventory of stories that would work their way into his writing and his law school lectures for years to come. "I rode in a light Ford car geared up to go, and going, ninety miles an hour in pursuit of a fleeing Buick loaded down with liquor," he wrote in his memoir about the Institute. "When I saw my host pull out a rifle, draw a bead, plug a tire, and bring the car with a screaming zig-zag to a halt, I cried out, 'Good God, man, haven't you read the case of *State* [*Houston*] *v. De Herrodora*', a Supreme Court decision recently handed down prohibiting this sort of conduct?"[9]

All the while, Coates was overseeing the production of *Popular Government*. In late 1934 it had begun appearing monthly, and each edition featured on the cover a photograph of a government building, usually a courthouse, with a brief account inside of the county's history and assets. Copies sold for ten cents. For a short time, each issue included personal features, such as an obituary of Coates's nemesis, Attorney General Dennis Brummitt, who died in January 1935 and was hailed as an "evangel of democracy," and a profile of "Uncle Dan" Terry, the man who had been tending to the Capitol building and grounds since Coates was an infant in Johnston County. Some of the articles were written by George Bradham, a newspaperman from New Bern whose ad sales produced more than $10,000 in income for the year, more than enough to pay for printing and postage.

Popular Government focused on issues of interest to the Institute's principal constituency—county commissioners, mayors, city council members, tax assessors and collectors, city traffic engineers, clerks of court, and others who kept the machinery of local government turning. During the legislative session, it included an update on the latest legislative action and a longer article on a pressing state issue. The January 1935 issue offered arguments for and against the new state sales tax. Willard L. Dowell, the executive secretary of the North Carolina Merchants Association, wrote to urge early repeal. G. P. Geoghegan from the Association of Real Estate Boards wrote in support of the tax, which gave some relief to property owners.

A standing feature in each issue was a column that carried capsule summaries of opinions from the attorney general's office and rulings by other state agencies. This was the kind of inside information that seldom if ever reached the newspapers. The staff also passed along practical tips and suggestions for city managers trying to stretch their budgets. One idea advanced by the Durham public works director called for cleaning old sewer lines with a drag built from old timbers and barbed wire instead of replacing pipes that could have years of remaining use.

Coates took special pride in the April 1935 issue. In it he launched a public campaign to raise money for the Institute's new home. A draftsman's illustration of the proposed "governmental laboratory building of the Institute of Government" spread across two pages at the center of the twenty-four-page issue. The drawing was the work of the university's architects, the Durham firm of Atwood and Weeks, whose fees Coates had somehow managed to have paid by the university.[10] His excitement over the new building was evident in an over-reaching letter he wrote to Dean Roscoe Pound. Coates told his mentor in late March that he had "practically completed plans for a governmental laboratory building as the headquarters of the Institute of Government. The building will be approximately 45 x 100 feet and three stories in height. The business men of North Carolina in the building supply business are contributing all the materials going into the building." In celebration of the event, he asked Pound for a fifteen-hundred-word article for the next issue of *Popular Government* and, apologizing for his boldness, gave the dean a week to produce it.

"We want to carry the picture of the building in the magazine of *Popular Government* now going to press because it is a symbol of our movement and the culmination of these last years of struggle to build the movement, and along with this picture of the building we want to carry your appraisal of the movement together with a picture of yourself, which we have already.

"In my mind and in the minds of the officers and citizens of this state you are inseparably connected with this movement. When it was only a dream with us you encouraged it by granting me a fellowship. When it was getting under way and a lot of folks were still skeptical you came all the way to North Carolina to throw your power behind it. Within the next year when the building is completed we shall want you to come here to dedicate it and in the meantime we hope you will understand why it is that we feel the announcement of the building as a milestone on our way will not be complete unless it carries this message of appraisal from you."[11]

Despite the lateness of the request, Pound submitted a five-page memorandum on the tradition of independence of investigative and police agencies, closing it with the passage that Coates wanted most: "Everyone interested in American government must rejoice that the North Carolina Institute of Government is about to be suitably housed and provided with a governmental laboratory from which we may be sure great results will flow."[12]

The construction of the building would be a major achievement, but it would not come by the route Coates described to Pound. It would take more than four years for Coates to realize his dream as he bounded from one funding proposition to another, rising in enthusiasm and then sinking into desperation at repeated setbacks, only to revive at the slightest hint of support and continue pushing toward his goal. In the spring of 1935 his plans hinged on success on several fronts. In time, each would slip away.

Just as the General Assembly was settling in to begin work in January 1935, Coates traveled to Richmond, Virginia, to meet with Leo M. Favrot, the noted sociologist and Louisiana educator who was the man in the South for the General Education Board, a philanthropic venture started by John D. Rockefeller. Howard Odum had successfully tapped into the millions Favrot helped funnel into education, health care, and practical farming projects in the South. Coates was armed with what he believed was a powerful argument for reform of local government, and as he set out for Richmond he believed he could be as successful as Odum.

Coates pinned his hopes on the foundation being willing to underwrite the Institute's work in North Carolina high schools to improve and enhance the teaching of civics and public affairs. Education of young people in government and public affairs had always been an important component of Coates's plans, although educating high school students had not aroused as much interest as the training schools and research assistance he proposed for local government officials. Coates pursued his interest, nonetheless, and was then chairing a subcommittee on the revision of the school curriculum for the office of the state superintendent of public instruction. After his meeting with Favrot, which apparently Coates found encouraging, Coates quickly prepared a proposal that he supplemented with endorsement letters from Graham and the university's graduate school dean, W. W. Pierson. But even as he was writing to Pound in March of his news and optimistic outlook, his prospects with the General Education Board had already begun to fade. Among other things, Coates's hastily prepared appeal, along with his hip-pocket method of managing the Institute, didn't fit the foundation's culture, whose deliberative processes could stall a request for months or even years before money was released. "I have conferred with some of my fellow officers about the matter," Favrot wrote Graham in March, "and we are by no means sure that it falls within the present program of the Board."[13] Coates got a similarly polite but firm refusal.

Coates pressed on. He announced in *Popular Government* yet another statewide membership drive, this time asking for one-dollar memberships from high school students and teachers, who he promised would receive fair value in Institute publications. To add excitement and urgency to the appeal, he announced that each participating school would receive a free subscription to *Popular Government* for its library and the school that raised the most money would receive a $1,000 prize. Once again, individual memberships failed to flood the Institute's post office box in Chapel Hill. Over the course of the year these small contributions would amount to only $1,600. This was not an inconsiderable sum, but it would not pay for a new building.

As the legislature ground on, another fundraising option appeared. Among the bills highlighted in the Institute's bulletins were proposals to allow local and state governments to participate in a new federal program that was designed to put people back to work and improve government facilities at the same time. A late spring issue of *Popular Government* described the process by which state institutions could apply for Public Works Administration (PWA) grants. During 1934, the PWA had pumped nearly $9 million into federal building projects in North Carolina, including the Blue Ridge Parkway, a scenic highway that ran the ridges and mountaintops of western North Carolina. Now, money would flow to state and local governments.[14]

North Carolina moved slowly to tap this source of funds, and it was not until the fall of 1935, after legal issues had been settled in the state supreme court, that the way was clear for the University of North Carolina and other state agencies to submit requests to the PWA. The money would prove a blessing for the University of North Carolina, where major building projects had been put on hold. Between 1935 and 1941, the university would add thirteen buildings, using nearly $3 million in federal aid. Among the new structures would be a swimming pool, dormitories for men and women, and a dining hall to replace the outdated and inadequate Swain Hall.[15]

Coates was determined to be included in the university's program. He was at a disadvantage, however. No matter how closely he aligned the Institute with the public service traditions and practices of the university, the organization remained a private venture. With all of the trappings of committees and elaborate representation of various levels of government, the Institute was not even incorporated and had no bylaws or board of trustees. More than three years after an organizing committee had been formed in May 1932, the Institute of Government was little more than a bank account and the energy and enthusiasm of Albert Coates.

This absence of corporate structure had been a problem for Coates in his application for the Rockefeller money. At one point in the spring, he had assured Favrot that he would take care of these legal niceties. Even though nothing had been done to change the Institute's status by the fall, Coates asked Frank Graham and the university trustees to join with the Institute in a bid for PWA money. Generous to a fault, Graham agreed, but his aggravation with his friend's slip-shod methods was growing. For its part, the university, through the trustees, agreed to give the Institute the piece of land that Coates wanted on the western edge of the campus south of the Carolina Inn. In exchange, the building to be erected there would become the property of the university should the Institute cease to exist. The land was valued at $15,000.[16]

The news release that Madry put out on the Institute's behalf in early October 1935 implied that the Institute would have their building in no time. The building was "virtually assured," Madry wrote. The PWA had approved a grant of $55,498 to cover the costs of labor. With the $15,000 in land from the university, plus free materials promised by building supply dealers in the state, and informal pledges from some wealthy supporters, Coates believed he had almost all of what he needed to begin construction on a building then estimated to cost $123,000. "Only one condition remains to be met, and that is for the public officials and civic leaders to show the same faith in the program of governmental study and improvement they have inaugurated through The Institute by joining in sufficient numbers to guarantee its continuation."[17]

The PWA grant energized Coates and certainly boosted his spirits after what had been a troubling summer during which his differences with Dean Van Hecke had again threatened his position at the law school. Van Hecke's report on Coates's performance to Graham in May 1935 was even more critical and damaging than his complaints two years earlier, which had resulted in Coates being placed on probation. The dean came just short of asking for formal proceedings to strip Coates of his professorship. "I am sorry to have to report that during the school year just ended," Van Hecke wrote, "Mr. Coates' work has again been a failure. He has returned to the attitudes and methods, which caused my recommendation in 1933 that he be dismissed. The situation during the fall was so bad and so destructive of law school morale that I encouraged him to take a leave of absence during the spring."

Coates was totally absorbed in the Institute, Van Hecke continued, and that left the law school at a disadvantage. "The Institute is rendering a service to the people of the state but it is unfair to make the Law School, the law faculty and the law students pay for that service in crippled teaching and law school work," he wrote. "The experience of the last seven years compels the view that Mr. Coates is not interested in law school work and that any further experimentation to see if he will not devote himself to that work instead of to outside interests is futile."[18]

Van Hecke told Graham that while some members of the eight-man faculty had argued two years ago that Coates should be given a second chance, this time all of Coates's peers believed that the current situation was untenable. The dean laid out specific instances of neglect and disruption of law school programs caused either by Coates's absence or his performance. He told Graham that rather than continue to deal with the man's behavior for another term he had urged Coates to take a leave in the spring of 1935.

For the law school to continue with Coates on the faculty, even with repeated leaves of absence, was too disruptive, Van Hecke believed. He told Graham in a second letter two months later that the law school was not one of the top five in the United States, as some claimed, and that it would take a decade or more of "constant, painstaking effort before this Law School can approach the standard of faculty and student work maintained" at state universities, not to mention Harvard, Columbia, or Yale. "The Law School ought not to be asked to permit one-eighth of its instructional staff to be repeatedly absent one semester of each year and neglectful of primary Law School duties the other semester while the School is attempting to cope with the problem of improving its work." Van Hecke argued that the university would not allow a student to remain who failed to show up for class and performed below par, and the same standard should apply to a member of the faculty.[19]

In short, Van Hecke was through with Coates, whose performance had caused him no small amount of personal embarrassment. His letter to Graham in late July in which he renewed his objections to Coates's presence at the law school followed the dean's meeting with one of the top elected officials in the state whose son had been dismissed because of poor grades. The man had tearfully begged Van Hecke to readmit his son, but Van Hecke had refused. On leaving the office, the man told Van Hecke that the thing that galled him most was that the professor who had given his son a failing grade had not even showed up for class.[20]

Coates was outraged by the charges in Van Hecke's May report, and by a stern request from Robert B. House that he account in detail for his classroom attendance and teaching schedule in the fall of 1934. He responded with a report refuting all of Van Hecke's charges. He had met his classes, he said, except when he was either ill or away for special occasions, all of which were known beforehand by the dean. He had done some of his best work, he said, and added value to the law school by incorporating the law school into the work of the Institute. "I undertook to weave together the law in books and the law in action in my classes." He said other members of the faculty had taken leave for temporary assignments in federal agencies, all the while receiving their law school pay, yet his leaves of absence had all been without compensation. He told House that if law school morale had been destroyed, as Van Hecke claimed, then the president should launch an investigation and he would abide by the results.[21]

Graham had his hands full in the summer of 1935 and could hardly have welcomed a crisis in the law school in the summer of 1935. The university's budget had suffered more deep cuts, causing him to cancel programs and make cutbacks in others. In addition, the consolidation of the university that had been approved under Governor O. Max Gardner was underway and the reassignment of programs among the university at Chapel Hill, State College in Raleigh, and Woman's College in Greensboro had begun. At the same time that the Coates matter arrived on his desk, Graham was fending off angry alumni and trustees who were not taking the shuffling of courses and departments without a final fight. One of the most powerful among this group was state Senator John Sprunt Hill of Durham, whose generosity and service to the Chapel Hill campus were unequaled. Hill was pressing for a reversal of the decision to move the engineering program from Chapel Hill to State College in Raleigh. Still, Graham could not ignore the question of what to do with Albert Coates, so he leaned heavily on House to solve the problem.

House shuttled between the contending parties. In an update he wrote for Graham in mid-summer, he all but threw up his hands at finding a reasonable solution within the existing structure of the university. Coates would be a problem if he remained in the law school, House wrote. "His values do not fit in to the conception of law teaching, which dominates, and is likely to keep dominating the Law School. Let those who differ from Albert be his immediate administrative superiors and inevitably he will always fail, according to their standards." His answer was to make Coates a free agent. He would retain his professorship, but he would be relieved of teaching or any connection with the law school. He would be left to work on the Institute and could offer courses that would be open to law students as well as others in the university.

"This is not as chaotic as it sounds," House wrote. "It is manifest that social sciences and public administration are not perfectly organized exclusive of Albert. I see no great harm in placing him as one more unit in a University hospitable to all phases of social study. Theoretic rigidity of organization at this point in our development may prove detrimental to the very life of our manifest social interest."[22]

House's frustration was evident. Graham had tried to assist his friend for more than five years and nothing he had tried had worked. After Coates was unsuccessful in having the law school adopt the Institute, Graham had urged Coates to merge his program with the School of Public Administration, but Coates would not have anything to do with it. Coates would later assert that the new school had designs on the funds he was raising and would strip his programs of their intent. In any event, such a merger was no longer an option. The school had not received the state funding that had been hoped for and W. C. Jackson had returned to Woman's College in Greensboro as chancellor. (The school would be dissolved within the year.) House told Graham that there may be some other departments on campus with interests similar to those of the Institute but that if Coates was assigned under any department, it would just create "a whole new series of problems centering around Albert."[23]

Van Hecke endorsed House's recommendation to move Coates out of the law school. He sent Graham a formal request to that effect and it was seconded by all of Coates's law school colleagues. Van Hecke said "in order to permit Professor Coates to give the Institute and its work the guidance which it deserves, he ought to be free from all routine duties here at the University."[24]

After considering his options, Coates declared he would have none of it. He wrote to House that when asked at a joint meeting if the reassignment was for Coates's failure in the law school or for the advancement of the Institute, Van Hecke had replied that it was for both. Coates added that the dean had said, "For the purpose of public announcement I recommend it on the latter ground only." Coates told House that if he took this offer, it "would be an underserved reflection on my personal and professional character." He would demand an academic trial, if necessary, to protect his reputation.[25]

No one wanted a trial, and Coates probably knew that Graham would not let things go that far. It would be very awkward for the university, even in a more settled time. Van Hecke would have an especially difficult task in proving his charges against Coates after Graham had allowed Coates to continue his work on behalf of the Institute and had even praised Coates's efforts on numerous occasions, despite his awareness of Van Hecke's concerns.

Once again, Graham stood by Coates and declined to transfer him out of the law school. Van Hecke asked the president to reconsider his decision. After Graham declined, Van Hecke dropped the matter altogether. Coates's standing within the school was never raised again. As he had two years earlier, Graham again refused to accept Van Hecke's offer to resign the deanship and return to teaching. The entire episode was a tribute to Graham's talent for resolving issues without driving either party away. Coates and Van Hecke would remain under the same tent—neither perhaps entirely happy, at least as long as Van Hecke was dean. Van Hecke gave up the direction of the law school in 1941 and returned to teaching, which he did until his death in 1963. Coates continued his leave of absence for the balance of the year and returned in February 1936 to be part of the law school faculty, without interruption, for thirty years.

The absence of a regular paycheck had cut deeply into Albert and Gladys's finances by 1936. Time after time, Albert had used their money to cover Institute expenses. Some of these advances had been repaid, but he and Gladys were always short of money and had all but given up hope of building a home of their own. They now lived in a cottage built as servants' quarters at the rear of the home of N. W. Walker at 517 E. Rosemary Street. Walker was the dean of the summer school and the school of education and had been Coates's landlord once before, during his first year at law school in Cambridge. Walker had retired from the university in the summer of 1934 with a heart ailment. He died in early 1936, and the house later was sold to Guy B. Phillips, a professor in the school of education. The Coateses stayed on as Phillips's tenant.

The house was small, with only a few rooms, but it was snug and cheap and just a short walk from the campus. Albert and Gladys had gone without many pleasures during their years together, but they also had acquired a few prized possessions, including a Steinway piano. It came from the lobby of a resort in Pinehurst that had failed in the early days of the Depression. Gladys later wrote, "We managed the affair by not buying a much-needed new car. Instead, we put a new motor in our old car, and reasoned ourselves into being able to afford the piano."[26] Hanging over their mantel was a Trumble portrait that Gladys was keeping for a neighbor. She made window coverings from inexpensive theater gauze, and her dressing table was a travel trunk covered in fabric.[27]

Gladys was as devoted to her husband as the day she fell in love with him. She assisted wherever she could and from time to time contributed to *Popular Government*. She researched the history of North Carolina counties and created a family tree of sorts that traced their creation. The schematic appeared in the October 1935 issue, but it was put together so hastily that she failed to receive credit for her work. She also had begun a study of student government at Chapel Hill and research on Person Hall, one of the oldest buildings on campus. When she wasn't with her husband, she could usually be found in Wilson library bent over archival material. Years later, Gladys said the research allowed her to forget the "trials and troubles we were undergoing by losing myself, or finding myself, in the records."[28] Gladys was more than an aide-de-camp to her husband, according to Albert. She was an invaluable resource who edited "everything I wrote," Albert later said, "cutting out purple passages, frying off fat, and adding insult to injury by improving the final product in ways which could not be denied."[29]

Despite their modest circumstances, their home was a welcoming place. Early in 1937, Thomas Wolfe found his way to the door of their cottage during a visit to Chapel Hill. It was his first trip south since he had become a world-famous writer. He stopped in for a Sunday morning visit, and Wolfe and other guests were still sitting at the breakfast table until well into the afternoon. Wolfe did not stay overnight, but he returned late one evening after visiting others in Chapel Hill and said he was thirsty for a drink of whiskey. Albert and Gladys kept a small supply on hand for occasions such as this. Wolfe was then on his way. He would die the following year.[30]

Albert had overcome a major hurdle with approval of the PWA grant for the Institute's building. There were three hundred applications from cities and towns around the state and Coates had captured one of only fifty-two grants awarded. Half of the amount allocated for the Institute building would be enough to build a new town hall in Chapel Hill or update a water and sewer system in Sanford. The PWA granted money to build bridges and pay for street improvements in Greensboro and add to state facilities in Raleigh. (One proposal approved, and later rescinded, would have replaced the rock walls on the Chapel Hill campus with handsome new concrete, but the town and campus rose in arms to oppose the destruction of Elisha Mitchell's handiwork.)[31]

Coates had taken no chances on the prospects of his application being accepted. Over the years, he had carefully cultivated the state's congressional delegation, and all had attended the Institute's statewide meeting in Chapel Hill the previous June when the PWA and other federal legislation had been at the top of the meeting's agenda. When the university submitted his project, Coates asked his friends in Washington to write letters of support to the PWA regional administrator, H. G. Baity, who was on leave from the university's school of engineering and whose offices were in Chapel Hill. He also called on them to lobby on his behalf in Washington.

With the donation of the university land, and PWA cash to pay for labor, Coates now needed to collect on the promise of building materials from building supply firms in the state. The chair of the Institute's building committee was O. P. Makepeace of Sanford, North Carolina, president of Sanford Sash and Blind Company and also president of the suppliers' trade organization. He was helping Coates to redeem those pledges in the fall of 1935, but his work was inhibited by delays in the preparation of a complete list of the materials that would be needed. As was his usual habit, Coates had worked out the plan to combine the PWA grant with donated materials on the fly and in haste, with a schedule that allowed for no time lost due to the requirements of others. He was under pressure; to qualify for the PWA money by December 15, he needed to have a construction contract ready to be signed. With no such document in sight as the date approached, he feared his grant would lapse and be postponed indefinitely, or at least until Congress authorized more money for the agency.

The PWA's Baity was under pressure to get the federal money moving into the state's economy. The purpose of the PWA was to put Americans back to work, as well as to provide aid to local and state governments, so there was no tolerance for construction projects that could not begin immediately. Baity was under orders to release the Institute's money to others when he got word from the White House that the state's senior senator, Josiah Bailey, had won a thirty-day extension for Coates from President Franklin Roosevelt.

The additional time, coming as it did over the Christmas holidays, passed quickly, and Coates still did not have his commitments by the first of the year. He asked Duke Power Company to donate the wiring and electrical needs for the building, but was refused help. The state's leading brick maker—the three-story building would need 400,000 bricks—was ready to ship its contribution, but the promises of other materials remained unfulfilled. Coates asked for another thirty days and was given until February 15, 1936, to be ready to sign a contract and begin work.

Coates still did not have the materials or the money to buy what was needed by February 15, but Baity allowed a contract to be awarded for construction on the condition that Coates certify to the agency that he had the money in hand to pay for the building. This extraordinary allowance skirted the agency's rules and left Baity fending off demands from others above him who wanted to know why work had not begun.

Coates was out on a limb. He knocked on every door he could find. He even returned to the Rockefeller Foundation in a frantic effort to pull together the money he needed. At one point, he believed that he had achieved the impossible, but the pledges of cash faded away after a gift of $30,000 he was expecting from a large estate became tied up in tax court. In a frantic effort to save the project he proposed a joint bid with the town of Chapel Hill, which was seeking money for a town hall. Coates proposed that the town manager and his staff occupy a portion of the Institute's building.[32]

Baity was holding off the bureaucrats in the summer of 1936 when, unable to stall any longer, he rescinded the grant and released the money for other projects. Even that didn't stop Coates. He went to President Roosevelt again, first with a letter from Baity, who asked for an exception for the Institute. At the same time, Coates tried through his congressional allies to arrange for a personal meeting with the president as he made a campaign swing through the state in late summer. That meeting didn't take place, but friends in Washington did get him an audience with Secretary of the Interior Harold Ickes, who revived the project briefly in 1937. Coates remained unable to meet the financial requirements, however, despite this final extension.

The loss of the PWA grant was a deep disappointment. Coates believed he had come so close he could almost see construction beginning. He had traveled all about North Carolina to plead his case. He also made trips to New York City to visit expatriates, but William D. Carmichael Jr., a friend on Wall Street, warned him not to expect much there. He secured pledges for 80 percent of the money he needed, but that money would be available only after he had secured the total funds needed, which he estimated to be about $100,000. That amount would pay the cost of materials and furnishings and, as a condition of the grantors, provide some financial security for three years of operation. The pledges that he cobbled together came from James G. Hanes and Gordon and Bowman Gray in Winston-Salem; J. B. Millis, the High Point textile manufacturer; Ashley Penn of Reidsville; and Smith Richardson of the Vicks VapoRub fortune.

The money chase had been exhausting, and nearly fatal. In late February 1935, when demands on his time were at a peak, Coates and one of his assistants, Harry McGalliard, were returning to Chapel Hill after a long day on the road. McGalliard, who later would become state assistant attorney general, was in his final year in the law school and had been working for the Institute as a "special assistant" since 1934. The two had been calling on prospective donors and also promoting the September 1935 issue of *Popular Government*, which was entirely devoted to highway safety and included material on traffic fatalities gathered by McGalliard. (North Carolina was the deadliest state by motorist miles driven.) With financial support from the Standard Oil Company, the Institute printed 250,000 copies of the issue as a four-by-six-inch, thirty-two-page pamphlet. They were being distributed to high schools, police departments, civic groups, and others.

Coates and McGalliard were approaching Chapel Hill from the south in Albert's car. It was late at night, and Coates fell asleep at the wheel. The car ran off the road, crashed down an embankment, and overturned. Both men were knocked unconscious. When they recovered, they made their way to the pavement, where they flagged down a passing motorist. Gladys was waiting at home for Albert, who was often overdue on his return trips, when she got a call from the university infirmary. Albert called to warn her about his bruises and cuts before she caught sight of him. Albert was "in a fog," she later wrote, and it took nearly two weeks for him to recover from a concussion. Even in his woozy state, however, he had the presence of mind to send his men out to the crash scene to recover the copies of *Popular Government* before a newspaper reporter stumbled across what might have made an embarrassing story about a promoter of highway safety.[33]

Gladys was determined to avoid such an accident in the future. From that time on, she traveled with Albert or made sure another passenger would share in the driving (McGalliard didn't have a driver's license). She would drive while her husband worked on his lectures or prepared for a meeting with a prospective donor. While he was in his meetings, which could run on for an hour or more, she waited in the car and read Shakespeare or the Bible. She later recalled that she acquired quite a collection of inexpensive hand fans that she bought at nearby five and ten stores when the weather was warm. Whenever Albert drove at night, she made sure he remained awake and alert. On one occasion she even started an argument with Albert just to keep him awake.[34]

"The subject was the blanking of the Rivera murals in Rockefeller Center," she later wrote. "I took the position that the Rockefellers should have been magnanimous enough not to have destroyed the work of a great artist. Albert took the side that they had a right to do what they wanted with their property—particularly in this case. And so we argued for the two-hour trip until we reached Chapel Hill. I thought I was particularly good in my arguments, contrasting the Rockefellers with the Medicis to the Rockefellers's disadvantage, and so it went. Albert was tired and finally impatient but we both managed to keep awake and so my purpose was served."[35]

The Institute's work in highway safety, scientific approaches to crime detection, and training police in the law of arrest and evidence procedures were all popular topics with Coates. It was a fertile field, due to the increasing demands on local police departments, some of which were now supported by radio communications and beginning to use other new technology. Coates left the research on fiscal affairs to Brandis and Grice. They conducted a regular schedule of district meetings and one-day training sessions, and paid special attention to tax assessors, tax collectors, purchasing agents, and others involved with municipal and county finance. Grice spent months working in six counties examining their accounting and finance procedures as well as those of the incorporated cities and towns within their borders. It was the perfection of the plan that Coates had outlined in the beginning by which a staff member would move from place to place leaving improved methods behind. Grice spent nearly two years in the field and in that time produced eighteen reports on government finance and helped city managers and mayors deal with property foreclosures and debt defaults, which were the most pressing problems facing cities and counties. (More than half of the state's cities defaulted on interest payments.) He became so proficient in the subject of municipal finance that in the spring of 1936 he taught a course in governmental accounting at the university.

Law enforcement was Coates's personal bailiwick. The first statewide meeting for law enforcement was followed with regional and district sessions. These continued for a time, but it wasn't until early 1936 that Coates took all he had learned and began working toward offering a ten-day school that became the foundation for future work with law enforcement. The school was built upon Coates's growing acceptance among lawmen, some of whom did not naturally warm to a law professor claiming he could help their men do their jobs. Coates loved to recall the morning he was standing outside a courthouse in the eastern part of the state as officers arrived for a one-day school. A middle-aged member of the group approached Coates and asked him, "What are your qualifications for police instructor, young feller?" Coates said he decided the best defense was offense and responded, "I don't have a pot belly or a flat foot, but give me time."

"He flashed back," Coates later wrote, "'I had rather be a wart on a [clearly unmentionable but no less clearly discernible part of a dog's anatomy] than to be a college professor talking about something he don't know nothing about.' The answer came to me out of the blue, I didn't have time to think it up: 'I can understand that,' I said, 'You are better fitted for that position.' There was an explosion of laughter, the officer walked off, and the crowd went into the school. I have often thought: Suppose heaven hadn't taken care of me in that retort and his ridicule had worked on me—would those officers have gone into that courthouse with me or straggled off with him."[36]

Coates designed his sessions to accommodate an audience far different from the one in his Chapel Hill classroom. No matter how accomplished he was as a speaker, he quickly learned his lectures "handing down" the law did not work with this crowd, some of whom were barely literate. At his first session, he realized he was losing his audience and he shifted gears to win it back by putting the law into a context they could understand. Breaking from his prepared notes, he asked if an officer could use his firearm to bring down a fleeing suspect. Questions like that got the attention of the men. "They were on their own ground and not mine," he wrote. "I had run into these questions in the library while they were running into them on the firing line." Coates invited more questions from his students and, soon, he wrote, "we were going to school to each other. I might know more about the law in books, but they knew more about the law in action. From then on I began swapping my research for their experience."[37]

Coates opened the first ten-day school in January 1937 with sixty-one lawmen on hand. About one fourth of them were chiefs of police. A special attraction for this session, and several one-day sessions held in the following weeks around the state, was a team of FBI agents and other instructors on loan from the FBI's new National Police Academy in Washington, D.C. During its first year of operation in 1935, Coates had lectured at the academy on the legal elements of search and seizure, returning for a session in 1936. The academy's Hugh H. Clegg, who had spoken at one of the early police schools sponsored by the Institute, arranged with FBI Director J. Edgar Hoover for the agency to help the Institute with its program. Among the agents assigned to Coates was Edward Scheidt. He was one of Coates's former law students and was stationed in Charlotte.

Hoover was so impressed with Coates and his work with lawmen that he gave Scheidt a year of paid leave to work with the Institute. They produced guidebooks for law-enforcing officers that covered scientific aids to crime detection and guides to the limits of search and seizure, the law of arrests, and the law of jurisdictions. Coates had hoped that he would have enough money to hire Scheidt away from the FBI, but he was unable to raise the money to support his existing staff as the Depression continued its grip on the country.[38]

The financial burden of keeping the Institute afloat remained as heavy as ever. Coates struggled to meet the payroll of staff members whose paychecks arrived late. "While I am not yet having to go to the Community Chest for meals, I am in need of some of those little green pieces of paper upon which is engraved 'In God We Trust,'" Grice wrote to Coates from Asheville. "That's just the way the merchants in Asheville feel, and all others (including nationally known and justly famous members of the Institute staff) pay cash."[39] Dillard Gardner once found himself stranded with no cash in remote Cherokee County, his paycheck two months overdue.

Coates cast about for help. In 1936 and 1937, after the unsuccessful appeals to individuals for memberships, he put Dillard Gardner on the road to sell memberships to county and municipal governments, and the new income provided a temporary boost for the bottom line. He got the idea from a city manager who wrote to Coates to ask about a blanket rate that could cover the cost of all the Institute's publications rather than a charge for each guidebook or report. The result was "unit memberships," which were based on the population of a municipality or county. For example, Charlotte, with a population of more than 80,000, was asked to pay an annual fee of $413. The town of Taylorsville, a community with fewer than a thousand residents, was asked to pay a minimum of $7.50 a year. As members, the municipalities received all the guidebooks, a subscription to *Popular Government*, the legislative bulletins, and access to the Institute staff, who were available to answer questions.[40]

Gardner set out from Chapel Hill in the winter of 1936 to make calls from one end of the state to the other. He would not leave a county until he had contacted every municipality as well as all available county officials. That usually meant tracking down mayors and county commissioners where they worked. He talked to the mayor of one town while the man was repairing a vehicle at his service station. He found the chairman of the Camden County board of commissioners deep in a swamp where he was cutting timber. Gardner discovered that some municipalities had simply died from inactivity. He learned that the town of Norman had not held a mayoral election in ten years. Many of these small communities, perhaps those that could use the Institute's services the most, just didn't have the money to spend. In the town of Crouse, the $7.50 minimum was nearly 10 percent of the total budget. Gardner suggested the mayor save money by buying a personal subscription to *Popular Government* for a dollar.

Gardner filed detailed reports on his progress. His travels took him close to the life of small-town North Carolina where economic conditions were still dire. "The boys are 'depression commissioners' and the county is still in the depression," he wrote from Lincoln County west of Charlotte. A day later he reported that "The rest of the state may be 'looking up' but these three [county commissioners] are certainly watching the dimes. When I finally have to say '$130.00' they practically have heart failure. It would be easier to sell ice cream cones at the Arctic Circle than the Institute in Cleveland."[41] Despite the challenges, Gardner enrolled more than a hundred cities, towns, and counties as dues-paying members. In 1937 the income from membership amounted to more than $10,000.

The new man at the recently reorganized North Carolina League of Municipalities did not take kindly to the Institute's solicitation of its membership. The League had replaced the North Carolina Municipal Association, which had been founded in 1909. In 1934 the League's officers hired an aggressive and determined executive secretary named Patrick Healy. He set out on a program of expansion and development and was offering League members many of the same services that Coates promised. Coates believed he had a just claim for the support of local government since he had started the Institute before the League became more than a lobbying arm for municipal government. Healy, on the other hand, believed his was the proper organization to serve cities and towns. He was also under orders to raise money to match a $9,000 grant that the League had received from the Laura Spellman Rockefeller Memorial Fund. The North Carolina League was one of four such organizations in the country to receive a grant from the Fund. The League's success in gaining Rockefeller support surely had to stick in Coates's craw.

Coates and Healy found themselves at a standoff and the issue came to a head in the late summer of 1936, first at the League's annual meeting in Wilmington and later before the organization's executive committee. Coates believed the League should limit its work to lobbying the legislature and leave research and training to the Institute. Healy knew that he could not sustain a viable organization with such a limited purpose, but in a meeting that consumed all of an afternoon, a truce was arranged. Healy was told to work out details to support the Institute's police school and leave research and studies to Coates and his men. The League would continue to be an information center for local government. When Charlotte Mayor Ben Douglas became president of the League in 1937, he pledged the full cooperation of the cities in the work of the Institute.[42]

The local government memberships did not enlarge the Institute's budget; they simply replaced one-time gifts by supporters. In the past, benefactors had come through at the right time to avert crisis. Back in December 1934, Coates had been behind on the payroll and stopped in Greensboro to see Ben Cone, whom he found in a café. Cone told Coates about the 2,500 hams the company had just made available for employees at Christmas. Sensing an opening, Coates asked Cone to pay his 1935 pledge in advance so he could fill a payroll and catch up on back salaries in time for the Christmas holidays.[43] By the end of 1937, however, the Cone money had been spent and there was none to replace it. Coates had put his last available dollar into the enterprise, and he had borrowed against his law school salary. At one point, after his men had gone for weeks without a regular paycheck, they pooled their savings and distributed the money to each other as was needed for living expenses. "Years later I found out by accident," Coates wrote. "Their action struck deeper into my being than ever plummet sounded."[44]

Coates was facing a collapse of everything he had worked toward for nearly ten years. He recalled the dustup in the law school when his students had challenged his grading system and the later realization that their protest over the final examination reflected not the deficiency of the test but his own failure to adequately prepare his students. He despaired that once again he had failed because of his own shortcomings. Coates recalled the words of Justice Oliver Wendell Holmes, who wrote, "The best test of truth is the power of the thought to get itself accepted in the competition of the market place." Coates later wrote, "I had not met the test. It was just that simple, and just that profound."[45]

With the money gone, and no prospects for sufficient funds to continue, Coates was facing failure for the first time. The most crushing thought was that he had not matched the trust and confidence that had been given him in such generous measure by the men on the staff. He and Gladys had no children of their own and these men—Coates openly called them "his boys"— and their wives and children had become an extended family. No matter how cramped the quarters in the cottage on Rosemary Street, there was always room for one more at a meal as well as at celebrations of holidays and late-night discussions. They had shared trials and struggles, late meetings in remote areas, and exhausting work together. They had enjoyed victory and success as the Institute's reputation had grown. "Without precedents to go by," Coates later wrote, "these men had blazed their own paths under mentally wracking, physically exhausting, and long continuing strains that no other group of staff members of the Institute of Government from that day to this has been called upon to face."[46]

His men felt the loss as well. Gardner later sent Coates a poignant essay about the "death of an idea" in which he recalled that in the depths of the Depression he had found men to share his dream. "On a bare subsistence and the enthusiasm and fire of religious zealots, able young men still capable of a vision, joined with him in bringing this dream to pass. Night and day, heedless of personal comfort and neglectful of individual relaxation, these young men toiled to realize what is perhaps the finest idealistic conception of the aim of practical politics which any man has yet conceived."[47] With the money dwindling down to nothing in 1938, Coates helped most of the staff find other jobs, and he turned the Institute's dire situation into something of a public relations event. Brandis became research director of the State Tax Commission and Gardner joined the staff of the state supreme court, where he later became marshal and librarian. Grice joined the state auditor's staff. In his correspondence to prospective donors, Coates put as high a shine as he could on this turn of events. In a 1938 letter to Gordon Gray in Winston-Salem, he spoke of their being "called into state service" based upon the ability and integrity they demonstrated in their work at the Institute.[48]

Coates had told himself, and any who asked, that those who had found positions with other state agencies would be gone for a limited time, but he held to that dream with only the faintest of hope that they would return. He wrestled with the stamp of failure that was being prepared for him and the Institute. He grieved over local officials who had taken a stand on his behalf and colleagues who had put their faith in him. He knew his teaching had suffered because he had not been fully engaged; he knew that the Institute had suffered because he could not give it full time. Pouring himself into both had nearly destroyed both. Moreover, he felt disconnected from any fellowship of friends. That was "well nigh non-existent."[49]

It was not that Coates was without allies as he struggled to root the Institute deep enough to withstand strong winds. President Graham, Chancellor House, and others supportive of his efforts, including Governor Clyde Hoey, had offered a lifeline in 1936. One of the proposals had been for the Institute to become a part of the university's Extension Division. Hoey had even been inclined to include state funds to match the money that was coming from memberships from municipalities and counties. Coates had prepared a budget and sent it on to the governor. The idea had died, however, for the same reasons that previous attempts to shelter the Institute within the university had failed. Coates refused to relinquish total control of the program or even properly incorporate the Institute so that it could be considered for university acceptance. That was a "minimum for cooperation," Graham told Coates in 1936. The lack of structure was "a persistent defect," he added.[50]

With no money for a professional staff, Coates made do with a small team of law students who worked for pennies an hour. Marion Alexander and Harry McGalliard, among the youngest on the original staff, stayed with him at reduced wages. They helped get the last regular monthly issue of *Popular Government* mailed in January 1938 and produced another in late spring in which Coates announced that soon construction would begin on the Institute's building. While there was no money to pay operating expenses, somehow he had managed to keep a spark of interest alive among a few wealthy businessmen in Winston-Salem and Greensboro.

The news on the building was premature, as usual, although Coates was completing arrangements to purchase land on the north side of Franklin Street across from the Graham Memorial Building. (The university land that Graham and the trustees had offered earlier was no longer available.) The property he wanted included two building lots, one of which was "the Ledbetter property." The university controlled it, while the adjacent land, the "old Pickard Hotel property," had a private owner. The cost of both lots came to $8,700. The building plans Coates shared with Charles T. Woollen, the university's controller, called for a smaller version of the building that had been proposed three years earlier. It remained three stories tall, but the office wings on either side were gone and, as a result, the building was about one-third the original size.

Coates borrowed money to pay the expenses of clearing the land in late September 1938. In a short time, the old buildings were gone and a large hole had been dug to accommodate the building's lower level. Then work came to a standstill. Months passed without any activity. Chapel Hill experienced a particularly wet winter and town officials informed Coates that the pond forming in his excavated site was a public nuisance and the hole must be drained. Coates contacted workmen to pump out the water, but he told them to work slowly while he gathered the money he needed to sign a contract for construction. "The digging started and seemed to satisfy the most cynical; for who could be fool enough to dig such a hole if he did not have the wherewithal to fill it up? I was, in fact, so big a fool that they could not conceive how big a fool I was," Coates later wrote.[51]

Coates scurried about looking for ways to get construction underway. The promises of cash always seemed to be just beyond his reach. At one point, in an effort to shore up his position, he appealed for help from the National Youth Administration, a federal program that paid the wages of unskilled workers who learned a trade on the job. He discovered that the NYA couldn't help because the agency was prohibited from supporting projects on private property. "Well, I'll be back and I'll keep bothering you," Coates told the NYA.[52]

Once again, Coates's eagerness had outrun his resources. There had been frantic efforts on his part to underpin a promise of support from Winston-Salem benefactors Robert Hanes and Richard G. Stockton. With their help he had secured a $10,000 gift from Will Reynolds, the brother of tobacco baron R. J. Reynolds, but only after Coates convinced his congressman, William Umstead, to secure an Internal Revenue Service ruling that the Institute was a charitable institution. Coates later said the description of the Institute that he wrote for Umstead "made the University of North Carolina look like a commercial enterprise" by comparison.[53]

Reynolds's money covered the cost of the land. Pledges from Gordon and Bowman Gray, supporters of the earlier proposed building, amounted to $26,155, but Coates needed another $25,000 before he could sign a contract. Finally, with Umstead's help, he won an audience with Julian Price of Jefferson Standard Life Insurance Company in Greensboro. Price heard him out and advanced the money as a loan on Coates's signature under terms that claimed more than half of his law school salary. When friends told him "this building is your monument," Coates replied, "It may turn out to be my tombstone."[54]

NINE

Holding Buckle and Tongue Together

1939–1944

GLADYS COATES was on Franklin Street not long before America entered World War II in December 1941 when she was stopped by a friend who said she had been trying to reach her by telephone only to learn that the Coateses' phone service had been disconnected. Indeed, Albert and Gladys were without a telephone, they were behind on their rent, their taxes were overdue, and they were spending the few dollars they had available on things they needed most. A telephone failed the test of necessity.

"Evidently she did not know the straits we were in," Gladys later recalled, "or I am sure she would never have told me this. With a completely straight face I told her we had to be out of town so continuously that we had had the phone disconnected. We had little or nothing to say to friends about the troubles we were experiencing. Certainly this is the way I was brought up."[1]

Money had been hard to come by for so long that empty pockets were commonplace for Albert and Gladys. She never complained as Albert poured whatever he had, including much of his teaching salary, into the work of the Institute. When contributions to the program lagged in the late 1930s, the situation in which Albert and Gladys found themselves was nothing short of desperate. They had drained every available bank account and drawn the cash out of a small life insurance policy that Gladys's father had purchased for her. Though they were months behind on their rent, they held on to their small cottage on East Rosemary Street, largely through the compassion of the lawyer handling the estate of their former landlord. Sometimes they had no electricity in the home because that bill was overdue as well.

They depended on the grace of Franklin Street businesses and the assistance of friends to keep things together. Bruce Strowd, who owned a garage in town, extended credit for gas, oil, and repairs on a battered car that somehow Coates kept on the road. Their meals at the Carolina Coffee Shop went onto a tab that at one point amounted to nearly a thousand dollars, and this at a time when a full meal could be had for a quarter or less. Restaurant owner George Livas even advanced Albert cash against personal checks he would leave behind as collateral. (Livas waited for Coates to tell him when there was money in the bank to cover them.) If Albert needed to make a long-distance telephone call—and he substituted phone calls for personal visits when he could—Burt Linker let him add the charge to his bill.[2] When Albert did travel, he sometimes prevailed on municipal officials for the use of a bunk in the local firehouse rather than incur room charges at a hotel.

Any hope of building a home on the property in the Westwood subdivision that Albert had purchased in the 1920s had evaporated. The various building lots that he owned outright, or as an investment with others, were sold in 1938, 1940, and 1941 until there was nothing left but property taxes due to the town of Chapel Hill. The lapse on his taxes was a private embarrassment for a man whose Institute was known around the state for helping local governments improve their rates of tax collection.

As Albert himself later put it, he and Gladys were just "holding buckle and tongue together" and the Institute was suffering from "malnutrition." "Some of my more observant critics even noticed signs of scurvy. I understood the Confederate soldier who said that he was eating green persimmons 'so as to draw up my stomach to fit my rations.' I had the taste of green persimmons in my mouth."[3]

There was even a lien on the Institute's new building, once it was finally built. One of Albert's overdue notes was for $3,000 he owed a college friend who had loaned him money a decade earlier as he was getting established in Chapel Hill. Ironically, a portion of this money had paid for the printing of Coates's first treatise on criminal law, which itself was a forerunner to the lengthier outline that became his plan for the Institute. In 1939, the friend took Albert to court in an effort to collect and won a judgment against him.[4]

Their reduced circumstances affected more than their comfort. Years later Gladys said she and Albert put off having children during the Depression. "I just couldn't think of bringing children here with nothing to support them on. If I had had tremendous passion, I would have, I guess." The Institute and the "boys" who followed Albert's dream became their family.[5] Albert appeared to have no regrets about the course he had set for himself, even when he heard from a classmate that the average income of some men who had been with him at Harvard was between $25,000 and $30,000 a year.[6] From time to time, Albert and Gladys took solace in a quote from Shakespeare: "All these woes will serve for sweet discourses in our time to come."

The wobbly finances of the Coateses and the shaky condition of the Institute—the two were virtually one and the same—were obscured by the public attention lavished on both at the dedication of the Institute's new building over the Thanksgiving holiday in 1939. The event attracted hundreds of local officials, state legislators, as well as Governor Clyde Hoey and members of the council of state from Raleigh. Former governor O. Max Gardner came from Washington, D.C., where he had settled into a successful and lucrative career as lobbyist and senior counselor to Franklin D. Roosevelt. Eight of the eleven members of the state's congressional delegation attended and they brought along William B. Bankhead, the speaker of the U. S. House of Representatives, to deliver the keynote address for the occasion. At the time Bankhead was considered a possible contender in the upcoming presidential campaign. He would die within the year, however, ending twenty-three years of service in the House. Even with all these political stars on hand, the entire affair was produced modestly and inexpensively. For a three-dollar registration fee, guests got a bed for the night, three meals, plus a ticket to the university's annual football game against the University of Virginia. Coates arranged for lodging by asking young men in the dormitories to give up their rooms to accommodate guests from their home counties.

The construction of the Institute building had progressed in fits and starts as Coates struggled to get his finances in order. He had half of the

$50,000 he needed in gifts from brothers Gordon and Bowman Gray of Winston-Salem. Their pledges had been made in 1936, when Coates was desperately trying to hold the PWA project together, but these two men stood behind their promise of support after that effort failed. With the loan from the Jefferson Standard Life Insurance Company, Coates was finally able to begin construction in the spring of 1939. He hoped the building would be ready by fall.

Coates had reduced the building in size to fit his new budget. It was still three levels over a basement that was half above ground, but its width was cut by two-thirds. The front doors opened to a hallway that was flanked by offices and led to a large reception room with a fireplace on the facing wall. This room was large enough for conference tables and comfortable chairs and was designed to accommodate a meeting of up to seventy-five or a hundred people. Built-in racks held newspapers and magazines that came in from across the state and the nation. On the second floor, above the reception room, was the library, along with more offices for the Institute staff. A few sleeping rooms were on the third floor. There was more dormitory space in the basement, as well as restrooms and work areas for preparing publications. It was a handsome building with its Federal period design and stately portico. All in all, the new building in the block across from Graham Memorial on the campus's north side added to the dignity of Franklin Street. It was part teaching facility, part fraternity house for public officials, part research facility, and all Albert Coates.

Gladys still had a broom in her hand on the afternoon of November 29, 1939, the day before Thanksgiving, when the first of those invited for the dedication began to arrive. She had handled the final details, checking behind painters as they completed each room. She shooed them out in time for the paint to dry and not end up on the clothing of her guests. She worked with student help—that's all the Institute could afford at the time—to remove piles of debris and watched over a night shift of bricklayers who completed the entrance walkway. In the final hours, she hastily arranged for the resizing of frames that did not fit the array of murals and photographs of North Carolina scenes that her husband had ordered to provide a patriotic touch to the building's interior.

Speaker Bankhead opened the occasion with his speech on Thanksgiving eve. North Carolina had chosen to observe Thanksgiving Day on November 30, rather than November 23, the date that President Roosevelt had chosen in an effort to jumpstart the Christmas holiday season by a week. (About half of the forty-eight states had followed the president's lead.) Bankhead was an Alabama native, the father of actress Tallulah Bankhead, and he and Mrs. Bankhead used the occasion to spend the holiday with Mrs. Bankhead's sister, Mrs. Taul White, who was a friend of the Coateses and a resident of Chapel Hill. The Institute proceedings were to continue on Thanksgiving morning and end in time for a traditional meal before all headed to Kenan Stadium for the football game.

There was standing room only in Hill Music Hall when the evening dedication ceremonies began at eight o'clock. Upon his arrival following a low-budget and unremarkable dinner for the honored guests, Coates was welcomed with sustained applause. University President Frank Graham, the governor, and other speakers, including Bankhead, heaped praise upon Coates and the Institute before the two hours of speeches ended and a reception opened in Graham Memorial. The Institute was an example for the rest of the nation, Bankhead said, and, if developed to its fullest, "a startling recompense will come to our people in economy and efficiency in every branch of your government and practically an awakening of the consciousness of the individual citizen of his responsibility to his community."[7] His speech also touched on the state the nation had been brought to by reforms—experimental, controversial, and "some universally approved"—that the Roosevelt administration had initiated to lift the country out of the Depression and included a call for America to remain free from the entanglements of war in Europe. Just the day before, the *News & Observer* had carried photographs of French airmen flying American-made Curtiss airplanes engaged in a dogfight with German Messerschmitts. At the same time, Finland was on the verge of mobilizing to meet a threat from Soviet Russia.

With her husband seated on stage with the dignitaries, Gladys took a place in the audience with the Speaker's wife and her sister. Mrs. White was clearly moved by the event, although Gladys later noted she herself sat there dry-eyed. "I am easily moved to tears," she wrote, "and this was one of the most moving occasions of my life. But it was as if I were outside of myself looking on the whole thing. I think I was never more aware of everything that happened than I was on that occasion, and to me it was one of the most perfect performances I have ever witnessed."[8] In fact, Gladys was exhausted from the hard work and long days of preparation. After the

Thursday events concluded, and everyone had left Chapel Hill, she took a mild sedative and slept throughout the weekend.

Albert was irrepressible, as might be expected on this special evening. It was one that he had been anticipating for a decade. The opening of the building was the culmination of work that had begun fifteen years earlier in his classroom, had then been expanded with the creation of the Law School Association, and finally had taken flight as the movement he called the Institute of Government. The Institute had carried him to virtually every courthouse and city hall of the state, where he had prevailed on the leading business and political figures to lend their support. Now, the Institute's offices were undeniable evidence that his vision had become reality, and the handsome structure was a vivid response to doubters and critics, many of them right there in the academic community. He had battled the bureaucracy of the university and the red tape of federal agencies, and the struggle to fulfill his dream had led Gladys and him to the brink of insolvency, but in the end he had succeeded. He had, finally, joyously opened the doors on Franklin Street. Now, as he basked in the applause and accolades, he proposed an even larger and grander program for the Institute. On the eve of the dedication ceremonies, even as creditors remained at his door and the new building sat empty save for a few rudimentary furnishings, Coates declared he was ready to expand the building to provide more space for staff and research and the development of a governmental laboratory to serve the people of North Carolina.

Sitting with Coates on the stage were Henry Brandis, Dillard Gardner, T. N. Grice, Marion Alexander, and Harry McGalliard, his team of associate directors. "No teacher ever had a finer group of students," Coates told the audience in a familiar gravelly voice that stirred emotions among those who knew what these men had sacrificed. "And no teacher ever paid his former students a more ungrudging tribute than I pay these men tonight."[9] Brandis, Gardner, and Grice had succeeded to better-paying and more secure jobs. Now, their names appeared on the letterhead of the Institute as "consultants." Their places had been taken by younger men, most of them students in the law school, who were working part-time for fifty dollars a month, the going rate for the campus self-help jobs. Alexander remained as business manager of *Popular Government*, and he wrote the news releases on the ceremonies that went out to the state's newspapers. The October 1939 issue of the magazine that Alexander had carried to the printer would be the last for nearly a year. Despite the best efforts of Coates and his colleagues, at least one issue would be prepared but never published because of lack of funds.[10]

Coates had refused to let the Institute's research and services to local government lapse even as money for salaries became scarce. After his first team had departed for jobs that paid a living wage, he had corralled William Mitchell, a third-year law student and editor of the *Law Review*, to work with him on two special studies related to taxation. Earlier in the year, he had fielded a team to provide day-by-day coverage of the 1939 General Assembly, although the experience that had distinguished the reporting in previous years was missing.

Young Elmer Oettinger, whose uncle Albert had been one of Coates's roommates when they were undergraduates, led the legislative coverage. (Following a brief career as a lawyer in private practice, Albert Oettinger died just about the time Coates returned to Chapel Hill to join the law faculty.) The Oettingers were department store merchants in Wilson, an eastern North Carolina tobacco town not far from Smithfield. Elmer had already met his uncle's friend when Coates came to Wilson in 1930 to deliver his high school commencement address. Elmer Oettinger favored a career in the theater and as an undergraduate studied drama, following in the footsteps of his uncle, who had been in the Playmakers with Thomas Wolfe. He went to New York for graduate school and was working on a play when he had to return home for health reasons. Lacking any other direction, he entered law school, where he found Coates waiting for him. Elmer was just finishing his first year of law school in 1937 when Coates hired him to write an Institute guidebook for notaries public.

Oettinger's legislative team included George Riddle, Newbern Piland, Tom Alderman, and Bill Parker. The schedule was just as demanding as in previous years. The Institute's distribution list had grown to 7,000 names and Oettinger was putting bulletins in the mail to most of these each day. Toward the end of the session, two more law students, Terry Sanford and William Cochrane, joined the team. Cochrane called Coates "Captain" instead of "Mr. Coates," which was the title that virtually everyone else used until Coates's death. Cochrane recruited Sanford, a first-year law student, by convincing him that he would find more interesting work with Coates than at his campus job, which paid the same. Coates was a tough taskmaster, but he regarded these young men as dearly as he did his professional staff. When Sanford found himself short of cash to buy a Golden Fleece pin to give to his sweetheart, Margaret Rose Knight, Coates loaned him the money to pay for it.

Coates generally left the legislative operation to Oettinger—he had his law classes to meet—but he regularly checked on his progress. On one visit early in the session, he called Oettinger out of the House chamber for a profane woodshed rebuke after he looked down onto the chamber from his own perch in the balcony and saw Oettinger sitting at the press table just in front of the speaker's chair.

"We ain't got no privileges on the floor," Coates angrily told Oettinger. When the startled young man was given a chance to speak, Oettinger explained that the newspaper reporters who drew regularly on the details collected by the Institute staff had asked him repeatedly to join them at their table. He had finally accepted their request because of the added convenience it afforded. "I don't care," Coates retorted, directing Oettinger to return to the bench in the balcony. Recalling the incident some years later, Oettinger said he believed Coates feared that legislators would get the wrong impression about the Institute's role and that his efforts to provide impartial and non-partisan coverage would be in jeopardy.[11]

The legislative coverage was the Institute's major and virtually only contribution to the improvement of government for the year. Coates arranged to keep law enforcement agencies interested in the Institute's sessions, but he finally gave up on bringing a coalition of civic clubs and educators into the Institute's program. The great groundswell of support from average citizens, which he envisioned arising through the Rotary Club, Kiwanis, and like organizations for men and women, would have to wait. Worn to a frazzle by nearly constant travel, he shuttered that part of his program entirely.

Coates did not altogether forsake civic education for high school students, however. He entered into an arrangement with the American Legion's North Carolina post, which wanted to replicate a program called Boys State that had begun in 1935 in Illinois. The Institute was a perfect fit. The first session was held in late August 1939, when 135 teenagers came to the campus for a week of athletics, recreation, and up to three hours a day in a classroom where they talked about government and civic responsibility. Coates enlivened the sessions with appearances by state officials, highway patrol officers, members of the Institute staff, and coaches and athletes from the university. The program dovetailed neatly with Coates's desire to bring government closer to young people.[12]

Boys State ran for a week and featured a range of activities designed to keep the young men interested. Among Coates's speakers were Governor Hoey and Secretary of State Thad Eure, along with FBI agents personally assigned to the program by the top G-Man of them all, FBI Director J. Edgar Hoover. (With the capture of notorious bank robbers and desperados in the Midwest, the FBI had become the most highly visible law enforcement agency in the land.) The university's athletic department, including the coaches of the varsity teams, worked with the boys, while members of the teams and coaching staff served as counselors in the dormitories where the boys were housed for the week.

Young men would never forget their experiences. Douglass Hunt, a rising high school senior, was elected governor of Boys State in that first session. Coates presided at every session and introduced every speaker. Standing before them, he would grasp his lapels and launch into a round of stories, rising on the balls of his feet for emphasis. He seemed to be in constant motion and always in conversation, even as he walked with others about the campus. Hunt said he would exchange words with a man on one side and continue a separate conversation with a companion on the other side. He "pushed us to learn all we could, and prodded us with his questions. On the last evening, at dinner in the Carolina Inn, he said a succinct grace I have never forgotten: 'Thank God for the food. Amen.'"[13]

Boys State added to the reputation of the Institute, but it did little for the bottom line. Virtually the entire registration fee of $15 went to cover room and board. Operations of the Institute remained hand-to-mouth. Coates had hoped that the 1939 General Assembly might provide some relief. Governor Hoey seemed agreeable to a two-year subsidy of $25,000—money Coates said matched the Institute's receipts for memberships from cities and counties—but there was no such appropriation in the budget when the legislature adjourned in May. Once again, the roadblock was putting public money into a private enterprise, no matter how noble or valuable its civic intentions and service to the state.

After losing the round in 1939, Coates reluctantly reopened conversations in 1940 with the university about merging the Institute with the Extension Division. It was a move he had resisted earlier, claiming that members of the extension board were "hostile" to the Institute's program.[14] And he remained wary of the changes that he feared would be imposed on the Institute's research and programming by academics who had a notion of service different from his own. Coates had nowhere else to go, however. The Institute's receipts were not keeping up with expenses, no matter how hard he tried. When the books were closed on 1939, there was only $90.15 left in the bank account.

Gladys had begun to despair and later wrote of her disappointment in, and even resentment toward, Frank Graham, whom she believed had failed her husband by not finding a refuge for the Institute within the university's broad array of undertakings. Her mood swings went from high to low. She swelled with optimism and hope for the future the day she saw workmen installing the brass letters forming the words "Institute of Government" in the protection of the frieze on the building's portico. As each letter was put in place, Gladys said she knew in her heart that they would never be removed. At the same time, she could not shake a recurring dream of a ship anchored in a harbor that was ready for departure but which never sailed.[15]

She failed to see that Graham and Robert B. House were two of her husband's most steadfast champions and ready defenders of the Institute. Yet, they were equally frustrated. Time and again, the two had urged Coates to get the Institute's affairs in order by formally organizing a board of directors or trustees, preparing written bylaws, and legally incorporating the Institute. Coates had made promises to do just that over the years, and at the 1939 dedication of the new building the Institute's advisory board, which was a reconstituted version of the organizing committee from years before, was reorganized to include members representing the cities, the counties, and the state. It looked like a board of directors, and Coates all but called it such, but in fact the Institute's legal status had not changed. When Graham sent L. B. Rogerson, the university's assistant controller, to examine the Institute's books, Rogerson reported that the Institute was no more than "an operational name for some of the transactions of Albert Coates."

Incorporation was just the beginning of the housekeeping matters that would have to be resolved before the Institute could become part of the university, Rogerson reported. It was not possible for him to complete an audit because the financial records were incomplete. The financial documents that Coates and Grice pulled together for him in June 1940 only "reflected the items which Mr. Coates personally allotted to that part of his transactions which he considered the Institute of Government."[16] The finances of Coates and the Institute were so co-mingled that he found it impossible to tell the two apart.

Albert Coates's debts and those of the Institute were equally indistinguishable, Rogerson wrote. Among the obligations were the balance due on the note to the Jefferson Standard Life Insurance Company, the lien on the building from the uncollected debt due Coates's college friend, and much more. Altogether, the debts of the Institute and Coates that the university would have to assume, if the Institute were absorbed into the system, came to $58,104.49, an amount that included a current operating deficit of nearly $5,000. That amount was going to increase in short order, Rogerson said. If the Institute didn't become part of the university, the county tax supervisor planned to list the new building as Coates's own property and begin levying taxes.

These issues did not seem to matter to Coates, who had stubbornly defended the Institute's independence over the years, even at considerable cost to himself and to the future of the Institute. With bankruptcy looming, Coates remained defiant in his demand for autonomy. In a memorandum he prepared during this round of discussions with the university, he said, "I do not want my classroom, or the Institute of Government which has grown out of it, to become the victim of these department broils and therefore insist that it operate as a separate unit of the Extension Division, co-operating with all and receiving the co-operation of all, and subservient to none."[17]

There were political considerations, too. The tug of war between Coates and the League of Municipalities was not entirely over. The League's Patrick Healy continued to object to the Institute soliciting his members by offering programs and services that Healy believed were being taken care of by the League. Further, Healy argued that the university should not put itself in the position of producing training sessions and other programming for which it charged a fee. Those services should be provided free of charge by a state university. Healy proposed a coalition of the League and the Institute, with the Institute in a service role to the League and its membership. Such a proposition drew Coates's full wrath in a memorandum he sent Graham

"To Patrick Healy who has done the Institute this high honor of making it stop its work for cities and towns and let him do it, who threatened us that with the help of certain affiliated organizations he would put us out of business if we didn't stop of our own free will, who has sought to duplicate and take over programs he did not originate and call them his own, who has denied that the Institute would co-operate with the League at the very time he was copying our legislative service and sending it out as his own and taking our research and parading it as his own—to him and his associates who have joined him in his campaign of slander and deception I commend the solemn thought that two thousand years of the living Christ have taught mankind not only that 'thou shalt not steal,' but also that 'thou shalt not bear false witness against thy neighbor.'"[18]

The conversations continued into the fall and on into the early part of 1941 without a satisfactory conclusion. With nowhere else to turn, Coates began knocking on doors in Raleigh, where the Institute had earned considerable political support. He may have been close to working out a plan for state support when he got a visit from William D. "Billy" Carmichael Jr., an old friend who had recently given up a career on Wall Street to become the university's chief financial officer.

Carmichael was a Durham native, the son of the city's school superintendent, and a 1922 graduate of the university. When he was at Chapel Hill he was captain of the basketball team, business manager of the *Tar Heel*, editor-in-chief of the *Tar Baby*, and a social leader on the campus. He earned a degree in commerce and headed to New York, where he translated his skill in the advertising business and as an investor into a seat on the New York Stock Exchange. He was a partner in the firm of Carmichael and Carson when Graham and House persuaded him to give it all up to serve his alma mater. Carmichael had never lost touch with Chapel Hill. During his years out of state, he had helped raise money among New York alumni, and he was one of those Coates had approached about finding donors there for the Institute of Government. After conversations that went on for months, Carmichael decided in June 1940 to become the comptroller of the university. He succeeded Charles T. Woollen, who had died about eighteen months earlier.

Carmichael was a pragmatist and had a deep and unfailing devotion to the university and to the Catholic faith. He was an intense worker with a keen sense of humor and a feel for politics and people. He once said his mission at the university was to "humanize the scientists and Simonize the humanists." He approached problems with an eye to solutions and had enough contacts among the corporate chieftains and politicians in the state to make things happen. He built a large home on the edge of the golf course at the eastern edge of the campus, where, in later years, he would entertain the governor and the state budget writers with fine food and refreshment as they reviewed the university's financial needs. One year this cozy reunion failed to produce the state appropriation that Carmichael felt the university deserved. He sent a note to a colleague that read: "We done likkered up the wrong crowd."[19]

Coates later wrote that his fateful meeting with Carmichael came one evening when Carmichael was walking at the edge of the campus on Franklin Street and saw a light on in the Institute of Government. It was late, and Carmichael was curious. Inside he discovered Coates at his desk. He told Coates he had been going through the university's budget and was surprised to learn that the Institute was not receiving a dollar of support from the university. And it was from this meeting, Coates said, that a plan arose to achieve the goal that had been eluding Coates for so long.

In fact, Carmichael's visit probably was neither as casual nor as benign as Coates suggested. By the time he talked with Carmichael, Coates believed his efforts to become part of the university were at an end. In 1941 he had renewed his pleadings for financial assistance from the legislature, an end run that surely would have been a headache for Carmichael, who was facing his first session with the General Assembly. Carmichael had a tough enough job securing the university's appropriation without competing with an organization right at his front door. The urgency of the university's situation was compounded by orders issued to him and other state budget officers when the 1941 General Assembly convened. Governor J. Melville Broughton made it clear he wanted the biennial session to conclude business as soon as possible, and he had a heavy agenda for consideration. In fact, the session proved to be the shortest in more than a decade, but it also was one of the most productive. In little more than sixty days, legislators produced a state budget with new revenue to replace the sales tax on food, gave the governor authority to make over major state agencies, added the twelfth grade to public schools, and, among other things, designated the dogwood as the state tree.

The conversation in Coates's office was one between friends, despite any difficulties that may have lingered from the competing efforts in Raleigh. The two spoke the same language. Notwithstanding Coates's faculty appointment, neither man had much to do with the professoriate. Moreover, their frame of reference was the entire state, not the confines of the Chapel Hill campus. Carmichael also believed the university was a fulcrum for improving the quality of life in North Carolina, and he believed the Institute was a valuable asset that ought to be preserved and encouraged. If the Institute were part of the university, the university's standing in Raleigh would be raised. With these shared interests, Carmichael apparently convinced Coates that working together they could achieve what they both desired—placing the Institute under the umbrella of the university, with a more unfettered relationship than Coates would find if he had to depend on the ebb and flow of political fortune that came with direct legislative appropriations.

On October 9, 1941, Carmichael forwarded to the governor a plan for the Institute to become a part of the university. "We are happy that you are as determined as all of us that the work of the Institute of Government shall not fail at a time when the need for it is greatest." Under Carmichael's plan, the Institute would become an agency of the state, similar to the Extension Division, with a separate budget under the university administration. To clear up the Institute's financial affairs, the university would pay Albert Coates $6,000 a year, which he would use to reduce the Institute's debt of $61,000. Once the building was free of debt, Coates would convey title to the university.[20]

Carmichael's plan offered Coates virtually everything that he had hoped for. The Institute would have the imprimatur of the university, and its financial future would be secure. More important, while the Institute would be subject to budget review by the university, Coates would operate independently of other departments and be free to pursue research and programs that the Institute deemed appropriate. All in all, Carmichael persuaded Coates that the arrangement was as close as he would probably come to what he had hoped for over the years.

Just before Thanksgiving Albert received word that the executive committee of the university's board of trustees had approved Carmichael's plan. When Albert got the news he went looking for Gladys, whom he found in the reading room of the North Carolina Collection. It was her favorite haunt. From time to time Albert would drop by for a visit while she worked on her research. Their meetings caught the eye of a librarian who did not know either well, and she suspected they were using the library as a rendezvous for an illicit affair.

"It was incredible to me," Gladys later wrote of hearing the news from her husband, "and I took it on faith [that the full board would approve the plan] and I went down to the Bull's Head Bookshop and bought an art book I had been looking at longingly as my first act after the news!"[21]

In fact, the deal was not guaranteed. Carmichael added the Institute to the university's budget, but it was going to be eighteen months before the legislature would meet again to appropriate money to cover the cost of its operations. The Institute could easily fall into bankruptcy before that time. Before the full board of trustees met in January 1942 to approve the merger, Carmichael put in a call to an old friend, J. Spencer Love, whose Burlington Mills Corporation was one of the fastest growing textile operations in the South. Love's family had historic ties to the university and at the request of Carmichael and Graham, Love responded with a gift of $15,000, which was enough money to carry the Institute through the interim.[22] On January 20, 1942, the trustees met in the state capitol and approved the action of the executive committee.

Coates announced the change in the February issue of *Popular Government*, which was issued only twice that year. Coates called the trustees' action a "milestone in the life of the Institute of Government." He said that as part of the university, the Institute "is already drawing strength and vigor from its new associations—associations which will gather the growing resource of classrooms, libraries, laboratories, teaching and research personnel of the Greater University, and bring them to the aid of officials in every city hall, county courthouse, state department and federal agency in North Carolina."[23]

It was a solid victory for Coates, and just in time. When the trustees took their vote, the nation was at war on two fronts, and Coates was left virtually alone at the Institute. Soon after the attack on Pearl Harbor, William Cochrane and Elmer Oettinger headed to the navy, Samray Smith would soon enlist in the marines, and Terry Sanford left in January for Washington, D.C., to begin training as an FBI agent. (He remained in the FBI until the fall of 1943, when he resigned to enlist in the army, where he volunteered to become a paratrooper.) "For a long time," Coates later wrote, "I had had a staff without a building. Now I had a building without a staff."[24]

Prior to the attack on Pearl Harbor on December 7, 1941, sentiment was divided in North Carolina over involvement in the war in Europe.

U.S. Senator Robert R. Reynolds of Asheville was one of the most outspoken isolationists in the country, and the state's senior senator, Josiah Bailey, was just as strong in his conviction that the United States should remain out of the war. Nonetheless, Chapel Hill became a center of support for the Allies. One of the most vigorous organizers on behalf of the effort was banker George Watts Hill of Durham, who had begun working on behalf of the Allies in 1939. One of his first projects, pursued along with W. T. Couch, the director of the University of North Carolina Press, was raising money in support of Finland, which was fighting Soviet aggression in 1939.[25]

Hill and Frank Graham were among the first North Carolinians to lend their names to the Committee to Defend America by Aiding the Allies, or CDAAA, a nationwide group organized in 1940 that included Harvard President James B. Conant, financier J. P. Morgan, publisher Barry Bingham, and other leaders among the eastern political, social, and economic elite. CDAAA chapters were organized in Chapel Hill and in Asheville, with the one in the western part of the state accumulating an impressive list of members. At the same time, other sympathetic efforts were underway. In April 1941, the Chapel Hill British war relief committee raised $1,160 to purchase a mobile tea kitchen and a large supply of food for Londoners under attack from German bombers.[26]

Shortly after the collapse of the British forces in France in May 1940, Graham had offered the university's resources to the War Department in its defense preparations. That fall, the University of North Carolina received a WPA grant to improve an airfield on university property just north of Chapel Hill. Horace Williams, who died that year, had donated a hundred acres to the school to expand the field and it was named in his memory. (A photograph of a light plane taking off from the airport appeared on the cover of the January 1942 issue of *Popular Government*.) Training for prospective pilots from the university and nearby Duke University began as soon as the field was operational. In February 1942 the navy selected the university as one of its pre-flight training schools, and by the summer of that year there were 1,875 cadets on campus. Over the course of the war, 18,700 young men trained at the Chapel Hill campus, which came to be known as the "Annapolis of the South."[27]

Albert Coates's military service in the first war had been honorable, but short-lived. Just as he had won his bars as a second lieutenant in the army, the war came to an end and he was released from active duty. His patriotic fervor in the days leading up to America's entry into World War II was just as high as it had been in 1917 and 1918 when he mounted the platform to talk of America's duty as a beacon of hope and liberty for the world. In the months preceding the attack on Pearl Harbor in December 1941, Institute staff members had helped local officials manage the administration of the nation's new draft laws as well as other legislative changes regarding the debts and obligations of men in uniform. Coates also had set up schools to train local law enforcement officers, who were being called upon more and more frequently to work with military police as military convoys began to fill North Carolina roadways, especially around Fort Bragg, a once-sleepy army post that would soon transform the neighboring city of Fayetteville.

Coates received his own call to duty for World War II in the summer of 1942, when he was tapped for a War Department school in Texas where he was trained to teach civil defense programs. That fall, after he returned, he produced the "Defense Issue" of *Popular Government*, which covered a range of subjects including espionage, protection of water systems, gas attacks, and air raid warnings. All these civilian preparations were heightened in North Carolina by the sight of merchant ships and other Allied vessels as they were attacked and sunk off the mid-Atlantic coast throughout 1942, when the coastal shipping lanes became a favorite haunt for German submarines.

The press of new work came at a time when Coates and the Institute were most vulnerable. He had to fulfill his regular duties as a law teacher and the Institute's staff had dwindled to one or two young law students. Clearly, Coates could not carry on with the Institute's most productive service—coverage of the biennial sessions of the General Assembly—unless he found help, but it was not until December, just a month before the 1943 legislature was to convene, that he persuaded Peyton Abbot to join the Institute. Abbott would become his closest associate and most dependable surrogate throughout the war years.

A husky fellow, with rolls of short-cropped curly hair, Abbott showed the same devotion to Coates and the Institute that Coates had enjoyed from Brandis, Grice, and Gardner. Abbott had a keen sense of humor that he somehow maintained even in the face of the demanding work schedule handed him by Coates. Abbott had seen the Institute come alive in the early days when he and others from Coates's classroom gathered at the Coates home in 1931 to listen to Albert talk about his dream. Abbott had graduated that year and joined a Winston-Salem law firm where he had become a partner by 1942. His law practice was struggling financially when Coates called with an offer of $3,000 a year. On December 1, Abbott left his family in Winston-Salem and moved into a room in the Institute building, which became his temporary quarters until he could find a rental house for his wife and son in Chapel Hill.

Abbott picked up where Oettinger had left off and overcame Coates's objections to the Institute taking a seat at the press table. He even persuaded the bill drafters to provide a separate copy just for Institute use. His records of legislative action were so complete that he often answered inquiries from the clerks when they lost track of some detail of legislative business. Before the session adjourned, the members passed a joint resolution commending the Institute for its service to the General Assembly.

The legislative service remained the most important product of the Institute, but after the session ended Abbott became Coates's man in the field, where he found that the Institute and its founder were also held in especially high regard. In a report to Coates on a series of training sessions for city and county attorneys and city and county tax assessors and collectors, he wrote:

"The Institute is receiving some high praise. In New Bern yesterday when I declared the meeting was formally closed, Judge Nunn got up and gratuitously made a little speech on the work of the Institute—how reliable and helpful it was—and declared that it deserved support. They praise the things we send out, and it appears that we have a large number of cover-to-cover readers of *Popular Government*. Quite a number have introduced themselves to me, called me by name [saying] 'I recognize you from your picture in *Popular Government*.' It is a little disconcerting to see the disappointment and hear the all too genuine expressions of regret when the people look at me and find that Mr. Coates will not be present.

"Every group of public officials in North Carolina is confident that it has a first lien on Albert Coates, and they list that as pretty close to their No. 1 asset. It even gets a little tiresome, but as the realization of the strength of the ideas of one man grows on me as I go from place to place, I get prouder and prouder of being entrusted by that man with what is after all a pretty delicate operation—with what could at best strengthen the Institute a little, and could at worst darn near kill it."[28]

Lawmen, city attorneys, tax collectors, county commissioners, mayors, legislators, state department heads, directors of sanitation and the departments responsible for supplying water and other services to local citizens all had a stake in the Institute of Government now. After years of hand-to-mouth existence, and through persistence and bull-headed determination and no small amount of political cajoling, Coates and the Institute had become a valuable adjunct to state and local governments. It had become *the* resource to employ when a man in the provinces had a question about the intricacies of state law or needed an explanation of a ruling from the state attorney general, the best forms to use in listing taxes, and even the proper measure of chlorine in the water supply. If Coates and his "boys" at the Institute didn't have the answers, they knew enough public servants around the state with the expertise and the willingness to share what they knew. In Chapel Hill, Albert Coates wore the cloak of academe as a professor of law, but beyond the boundaries of the village he was the champion of better government who had brought the Institute to the aid of local officials, most of whom had never set foot in a college classroom or even strolled across the lawn of McCorkle Place but valued their ties to Chapel Hill nonetheless.

Coates had never failed to seize an opportunity for self-promotion, for himself or the Institute, but in the fall of 1943 he found himself in a national spotlight that even he could not have imagined possible. *Reader's Digest*, a magazine with a nationwide readership numbering in the millions, carried a feature story on Coates and the Institute that was written by the magazine's roving editor, J. P. McEvoy, a clever wordsmith whose magazine work included the *Saturday Evening Post* and *Cosmopolitan*. He was perhaps best known as the creator of "Dixie Dugan," a popular comic strip published for more than thirty years.

McEvoy showed up in Chapel Hill in the summer of 1943 and knocked at Coates's door. He left with stacks of material, among them samples of the Institute's work, testimonials from public officials (including FBI Director J. Edgar Hoover), and Coates's own story of trial and sacrifice. McEvoy's article, titled "Don't Shoot Your Sheriff: Teach Him," appeared in the magazine's October issue and captured the attention of everyday readers and others, including DeWitt Wallace, who with his wife, Lila Bell, had founded *Reader's Digest* in 1922. Letters of interest poured in to Coates, to McEvoy, and to the magazine. On the strength of the story, a representative from the president of the University of Rochester made his way to

North Carolina for a firsthand look at the Institute wanting to know how such a program might be exported to his state.

In June 1944, Coates wrote to Wallace that "last fall a friend of mine met me on the street in Chapel Hill and said 'I see you have made the *Reader's Digest*.' I assure you there was more than a grain of truth in my reply—'You haven't got your facts straight. The *Reader's Digest* has made me.'"[29] In the weeks following publication of the article, Coates was invited to Florida and Illinois to speak to the state conventions of the Rotary Club, where his story of the Institute was well received. He also traveled to Michigan, New Hampshire, New Jersey, Pennsylvania, and Virginia. The invitations were inspired by Coates's declarations in the article that what he accomplished at the university was no more than what concerned and involved citizens could do in their own communities, or could be organized by larger institutions for service to a state. Wallace was taken with Coates's suggestion and invited him to his country estate in New York, where he gathered a group of citizens around to visit with Coates and talk over plans. Wallace also had greater ambitions for the loquacious law professor from North Carolina.

That fall, Wallace proposed that Coates secure a leave of absence from the university and use the coming year to travel the nation and talk about the Institute of Government. Wallace told Coates that the magazine would cover his expenses and replace his lost wages with a generous stipend. As exciting as the offer appeared—Coates would have been paid for doing little more than making speeches and talking to citizens groups—he passed on Wallace's offer. There is no evidence in Coates's correspondence that he considered the proposal for long. He realized that if he set off across the country, no matter how satisfying that might be, he would return home to an empty shell. The Institute of Government remained a one-man band and when Albert Coates stopped playing the music was over.

There also may have been some concern about stepping out beyond his beloved North Carolina, where he knew the state's history, had an affinity with its people, and, most important, had a relationship with its political establishment and traditions. Wallace's proposal was not the first to come his way—he had received a serious offer to create an institute at the West Virginia University in the mid-1930s—but he had turned them all down. He said he understood North Carolina's governmental structure and its political history and preferred to plow the fields he knew best. While the

Institute's structure might be exportable, Coates would have been exposed to unknown territory had he agreed to Wallace's offer. Coates had an alternative that better suited his own situation. He proposed that he write the story of the creation of the Institute of Government and that Wallace pay for the publication of 30,000 copies that would then be distributed nationwide. Wallace agreed, and Coates settled in to work on what would be the first, but not the last, history he would write of the Institute.

Over the next four months Coates set down in longhand a very personal account of his challenges and conquests. He liberally salted his work with colorful language and heaps of citations, such as long quotes from E. K. Graham, as well as references to North Carolina history. The account began with the questions he had raised about his own readiness to meet students in his classroom, moved out to the early meetings with law enforcement, and then homed in on his vision of a broad-based citizen movement for better government. Coates made it an epic adventure, casting himself as the hero and his detractors as the luckless villains who had attempted to stifle him and his work, only to be chagrined at his success. "One day," Coates wrote, "the dean of administration (Robert B. House) encouraged me with the comment: 'Everyone admits a baby has been born. Everyone is swearing it's a bastard. But everyone is secretly hoping its paternity will be ascribed to him.'" Coates recalled the impatience of the professoriate who had sniffed at his meetings of public servants when they came to Chapel Hill to learn how to do their jobs better, all in the name of university extension. He referred to the "lifted eyebrows, distended nostrils, pawing hoofs, and wild alarums, as I led into 'these classic shades, these noble oaks, this quiet spot', policemen, constables, sheriffs, and their fellow officers from the farthest creeks in the commonwealth."[30]

There was also self-deprecating humor. He said he was not a martyr, sacrificing everything for a cause, as some had claimed. "Today they nod their heads the other way as they say that after all the Constitution of the United States guarantees to every man the inalienable right to make a fool out of himself if he wants to; and a newsman brings down a storm of approval and applause from a gathering of officials with the observation that the Institute of Government is living proof of the fact that fifteen years ago, 'Albert Coates got hold of an idea and went crazy.'"[31]

"Bridging the gap" was the theme of the seventy-six-page pamphlet published under the title of *Popular Government* and distributed under the auspices of the National University Extension Association Studies in University Extension Education and paid for by DeWitt Wallace. Coates recounted his early efforts to build cooperation among law enforcement officers from overlapping jurisdictions and breaking through the suspicions of public officials whose trust he finally secured with an earnest pledge that he had come to their offices as an apprentice, and not as a scold. He wanted to learn from their experiences so lessons in one city hall could be shared with peers in another. He traced each graduating step, from lawmen, to tax officials, to legislators, student government, civic club leaders, and citizens at large who gave their dollars to help him realize his dream. The Institute had succeeded because people wanted it to grow and survive, and it would continue to expand its reach.

Coates painted a broader picture of service than he had actually achieved. He often blurred the lines between what had been accomplished and what he hoped to accomplish. For example, Coates reported that the Institute's next step would be archiving the actions of city councils and boards of county commissioners in much the same way that the Institute had served the legislature. Such an undertaking would have been outrageously complicated and expensive and never went beyond assorted tips and comments shared between governmental agencies in the pages of *Popular Government*.

Coates circulated galley proofs of his work among the extension association board members, who generally applauded his effort but asked that he tone down his language. Colleagues at Chapel Hill who were given copies also suggested that he moderate his presentation. "I doubt whether the jokes, the poetry, the by Gods and damns, and the obviously rough quotations add to the effectiveness of your description. In some instances they will detract more than they will add, particularly as they are read by strangers," Louis R. Wilson wrote to his long-time friend.[32]

W. T. Couch, the director of the University of North Carolina Press, delivered to Coates an editor's critique as well as a mea culpa, for himself and his colleagues on campus. As an editor, Couch counseled Coates to closely edit his writing and avoid repetition, advice that could apply to most everything Coates wrote. "The first task is to get rid of the hypnosis which usually seizes authors when they read their own writings. You know, of course, as well as I do, that everything you say isn't true merely because you say it." He told Coates to "make every sentence you write stand up and answer questions. If your sentences can't give a good, full account of themselves, then they deserve to be rubbed out as nonsense. I would say you haven't been as tough with your brain children as their health requires." Rather than heap abuse on his critics, Couch urged Coates to answer them. "You would not hurt your case—on the contrary, you would help it—by assuming that the opposition was not merely ignorant, stupid, and vicious." He should take up their arguments and respond, rather than leave a void. "In failing to do this, you leave yourself without a basis for self-criticism. This sort of failure is very dangerous."

Indeed, Couch had been one of his critics—he considered Coates's publishing operation a trespass on the Press's turf—and he admitted mistakes. "I am convinced what you are doing is of significance. I consider it most unfortunate that some of us chose to try to block you completely rather than push you into a position such that the state and the region could profit from your marvelous energy and enthusiasm. If any of us ever concerned ourselves seriously and at a level worthy of university people, if we ever used any intelligence either in opposing or supporting you, I have not heard of it. In my opinion, this is one of Chapel Hill's worst failures."[33]

Coates stripped the final draft of profanity, and he answered Couch's call to give his critics at least some sort of standing. "In all fairness," Coates wrote in the published version, "I must admit that I am impressed with the amount of solid proof they have at times brought forward in support of their contentions; and with proper deference to these proofs I no longer pose in garments of lily white, but only of battleship gray, on the darker side."[34]

The pamphlet remained a victory statement for Coates, and the Institute's reputation was enhanced as word was spread across the nation. As American troops pushed across Europe in the fall of 1944, Governor Broughton called on the Institute—still strapped for manpower—to take a hand in the planning for life in North Carolina towns and cities after the war. The end of the war with Germany was expected, and the Institute was about to enter a new era with its future more secure than ever before. Coates had done his duty to his country.

TEN

"The Ugly Duckling"

1945–1952

IN A LETTER WRITTEN after the fall of Germany in the spring of 1945, but before the war in the Pacific had come to an end, Col. William A. Pritchard of the Army Service Forces in Raleigh presented Coates with as generous an honor as any Coates might have earned on the battlefield in World War I.

"During the critical days of World War II," Pritchard said in his letter, "the Institute of Government rendered outstanding service in aid of the defense of the soil of North Carolina against enemy invasion. The concept of amalgamating all local, municipal, county, and state forces with the federal forces in defense of life and property of the citizens of your state was your idea and was matured and made effective by you in the Institute of Government of the University of North Carolina. The service rendered was of incalculable value."[1]

Coates certainly felt special pride in the reference to the defense of his native state. The patriotic fires that had been ignited when he was an undergraduate and that inspired his oratory "on the platform" were stoked by his devotion to North Carolina. Coates loved his country, to be sure, and his building of the Institute was inspired, in part, as a way to bring recognition to a new era in the South. But Coates owed his allegiance first to his state, and second to his alma mater.

Indeed, Coates had performed a valuable service. By turning the Institute's attention to the war effort, he had added to its stature and aligned himself with the broader wartime mission of the university as Frank Graham had articulated it before Pearl Harbor. In the Albert-centric view of the world, however, the war had also been an aggravating interruption to his work. He had spent a decade securing the Institute's place within the university, and then, when that glorious day finally arrived, he was forced to wait again for years before he could turn his talent, his energy, and his dedication toward finding the resources necessary to build upon that success. That left Coates all the more impatient in the summer of 1945 as World War II came to an end and the campus at Chapel Hill became crowded with returning veterans who were just as eager as he was to resume their lives and pursue delayed ambitions.

Coates was probably still in his office on the evening of August 14 when the news of the end of hostilities in Japan began spreading through Chapel Hill. As word penetrated every home, store, and classroom, Franklin Street filled with jubilant townspeople, students, and men in uniform from the pre-flight school on campus. There was no confetti, and no high-rise office buildings to throw it from, so some in the crowd gathered rolls of toilet paper and tossed them back and forth through the air. Soon the trees were draped in white streamers. The pealing of the campus bells and blasts from the town's fire siren all became part of the celebration. Someone lit a bonfire at the west end of the central block, and Louis Graves of the *Chapel Hill Weekly* reported that when a police officer attempted to extinguish it he was pushed aside. Graves added that such obstruction of a lawman was permitted under the circumstances.[2]

The war was over, and a new life was beginning. Despite the obvious sacrifices, the war years had actually brought some financial relief to Albert and Gladys. The Institute's merger into the university called for annual rental payments from the university for the building, and the couple used this money to reduce their heavy debts. With his duties as a director of civil defense training, Albert had been more privileged than most during the war. His assignment provided him and the Institute staff with ration cards for gasoline, oil, and tires. Yet, travel was curtailed and there had been no extravagance. Peyton Abbott wrote his boss a tongue-in-cheek report on hotel accommodations, arguing that upgrading from a $1.50-a-night room to a $3-a-night establishment would at least have allowed him to leave his hotel each morning with "head held high full of confidence and self-esteem, radiating a fact that you are a minister plenipotentiary of a sovereign authority."[3] Albert's annual income from the university averaged about $4,000 during the war years and in the summer of 1945 he got a raise in his faculty salary to $5,000 a year. Moreover, the legislature appropriated $44,000 to pay off the balance of the mortgage on the Institute building. On June 30, 1945, Coates transferred title to the Institute property to the University of North Carolina.[4] With the extra cash, the two could have made some improvements in their own circumstances, but they remained in the cottage on East Rosemary Street, paying forty-five dollars a month in rent. The house wasn't much, but they did have full rights to an abundant scuppernong grape vine that grew nearby.

Coates was enjoying another round of national attention. In February 1945 the *Saturday Evening Post* published an article as flattering to Coates and the Institute as the one in *Reader's Digest*. The magazine's Warner Olivier portrayed Coates as the odd man out at the law school who had overcome all manner of obstacles and objections to succeed in an exercise in good government that was admired around the nation. The headline read "The Ugly Duckling at Chapel Hill," and the profile of Coates was as nicely tailored as if he had written it himself. The opening page carried a photograph of Albert and Gladys standing in front of the Institute building. Olivier wrote that the presence of the Institute within the arms of the university in 1945 gave no hint "of the toil, the tall talk and the tears, the patched and mended dreams, the monkly devotion and sacrifice, the austere living, the poker-faced bluffing and the prodigal generosity which went into every brick and splinter of it."[5]

The war work had allowed Coates to stabilize the Institute's operating finances with regular government payments for the civil defense training sessions and postwar planning that had begun in 1944 under Governor J. Melville Broughton. There was money enough to supplement his law school pay—he took a one-fourth reduction to recompense for his Institute work—and to provide regular salaries for a staff that included Abbott, John Fries Blair, and Clifford Pace. He was starved for manpower many times, however, and also for fuel to heat the building. The upper floors remained unheated until an extra ration of oil came available after a Red Cross unit moved into the space.

Coates was thankful for gas rationing in at least one respect. "It kept officials from coming to Chapel Hill," Coates later wrote, "to find out how little we had to work with, and it gave a satisfying, if illusory, explanation of why we were not sending out men we did not have, to hold district schools to which officials could not go. It did not keep the men on the staff from working overtime to keep the clearinghouse of information going and using the mails and telephones for all that they were worth to us, and we to them."[6]

With the war over, Coates would need more clients and income-producing projects, at least until the legislature returned in eighteen months. In spite of the uncertain future and no guarantee of work to pay their salaries, he warmly welcomed back to the Institute those who had left him in 1942 to serve their country. Two of his most able men—William Cochrane and Terry Sanford—arrived within weeks of the end of the war in the Pacific. Sanford drove into Chapel Hill in mid-September just in time to enroll for his final year in law school. After he took care of matters with the dean, his next stop was the Institute of Government building. Riding with him that day was J. Dickson Phillips, who was another decorated veteran from Sanford's hometown of Laurinburg. While Phillips pondered whether to enter law school—his prewar plan had been to teach history—Sanford pulled down a couple of mattresses from the attic at the Institute building and the two bunked on the third floor for the night.[7] The next day, Phillips, a Davidson College graduate, decided to study law and the dean accepted his application on the spot.

Chapel Hill was awash with veterans. Like Sanford, some arrived on campus straight from their demobilization posts and attended their first few days of class in uniform. Finding living quarters was the first priority; fashion could wait. With forty-five students, the law school enrollment was nearly triple what it had been the year before. It would swell to 113 by the spring of 1946, climb to 149 for the summer session, and be at 221 by the fall of 1946,[8] when the total university enrollment at Chapel Hill would soar past the prewar levels of 4,000, to 6,600. A quarter of the students were paying for their education under the GI Bill. Married couples would have to make do in temporary quarters, including twenty-foot-long "house trailers" and military Quonset huts erected on the campus tennis courts, while some single men slept in bunks set up in the "Tin Can," the campus gymnasium. Tent communities sprang up on the edge of the campus. When Henry Lewis, a new man at the Institute, arrived in Chapel Hill in the spring of 1946, the Coateses squeezed him into their cottage until he could find rooms of his own.

Chapel Hill was no longer a village, Louis Graves reported. With more than 13,000 residents when school was in session, it deserved to be called at least a town. He wasn't ready to shed the quainter title, however. After all, he wrote in late 1945, with all the trees and ample yards and gardens, "[Chapel Hill] still has the appearance and atmosphere of a village."[9]

Cochrane took up the editing and management of *Popular Government*, which had published only one issue in 1945 after a three-year hiatus. Beginning in January 1946, Coates and Cochrane were turning out issues on a regular schedule of nine a year. Until Cochrane would leave in 1955 for a new assignment in Washington, D.C., on the staff of newly elected senator Kerr Scott, he would serve as Coates's administrative assistant without title. He would develop an expertise in health care, but he also managed the Institute's day-to-day operations. If the mimeograph machine needed paper, Cochrane put in an order. If a secretary was absent, he shifted the clerical workloads. When the chancellor needed budget information, Cochrane provided it. He was devoted to Coates and made sure the Institute ran as smoothly as possible. During Cochrane's years at the Institute, he was one of the few who regularly filed the weekly work reports that Coates routinely asked for and which were often delayed by the writers, and then piled up on Coates's desk, leaving staff members wondering if they ever got read.

Sanford's return could not have been more timely, or appropriate, as Coates eagerly began expanding the Institute's training programs for law enforcement. He needed help, and Sanford's duty as an FBI agent, albeit brief, was an added advantage. Coates and Ed Scheidt, the agent who worked closely with the Institute before the war, had recommended Sanford for FBI training early in 1942, and he had served as a field agent for a few months before resigning to enlist in the army, where he became a paratrooper. Sanford's service in the nation's most-admired law enforcement agency gave him and the Institute credentials that added to its stature with local lawmen.

Sanford also filled in elsewhere. After he finished his law courses in the summer of 1946, he organized the Boys State program when it resumed after the war. Many of his fellow law students served as counselors. Among his hires was William Friday, who would later become president of the consolidated university. His first paycheck from the university was as one of Sanford's counselors. William Aycock, a future chancellor of the university, was another counselor.[10]

Coates had laid the foundation of the Institute upon the criminal law and its administration. During the 1930s, he had expanded beyond law enforcement as opportunities arose to develop a broader clientele and generate financial support from counties and municipalities. Institute men had developed solid reputations as experts on taxation at a time when citizens were clamoring for tax relief and local officials were looking for help. Coates never failed to use the results of their work as justification for the Institute. He claimed the savings that flowed to local government from ideas and recommendations put forth by the Institute more than covered the modest dues paid by local governments. The world of law enforcement was his first love, and the Institute's training schedule always included twice as many schools for lawmen as it did for other areas of public service. Coates especially cherished his relationship with the FBI, and throughout the war he had continued to travel to Washington, D.C., at least twice a year to lecture on search and seizure at the National Police Academy. Large photographs of J. Edgar Hoover and Hugh H. Clegg, the director of the National Police Academy, were prominent in what Coates called the Institute's law enforcement room.

As Sanford finished his final year of law studies he began working with Coates to capitalize on an opportunity for the Institute that had presented itself in 1945. As part of the post-war transition, the General Assembly had provided Gregg Cherry, the state's new governor and someone Coates knew well, with money to return the State Highway Patrol to its pre-war complement of troopers. That meant the Patrol would need forty-four new officers immediately. The Institute had conducted a series of one-day training sessions for the Patrol during the 1930s, and Coates had run a ten-day school for law enforcement, but he had never attempted something this large. Nonetheless, he eagerly declared the Institute capable of producing highway-ready officers with an eight-week program of instruction that would require the housing and feeding of about a hundred men.

Coates would have been sorely disappointed if the Patrol had asked for help from any other source. Over the years, beginning with that first session sponsored by the chiefs of police in 1931, he had carefully cultivated his relationship with the Patrol commanders. Even before the Patrol School opened in the fall of 1946, Coates began building the Institute's reputation for expertise in highway law matters. One of his best writers, John Fries Blair—he would later run his own book publishing house—filled three issues of *Popular Government* with exhaustive articles on the history of North Carolina roads and the evolution of traffic laws and enforcement, providing the perfect prelude to the creation of the Patrol School. Perhaps not surprisingly, Coates included sessions on public speaking in the training plans, despite the objections of Patrol leaders. He argued that troopers needed this instruction to enhance the public's image of the organization. The school also included training in firearms, self-defense, and pursuit driving. Sanford and Clifford Pace pulled it all together under Coates's watchful eye.

The Patrol school had all of the features that Coates loved. It was a high-visibility program that directly responded to an urgent need of the state. Moreover, it allowed Coates to expand the Institute's physical presence in Chapel Hill. In the summer of 1946 Coates received approval to begin construction of the Patrol training camp on the eastern edge of the campus on the south side of Raleigh Road at Country Club Road. Coates arranged for housing for the trainees to come from Camp Mackall, an army post near Fort Bragg where Sanford had trained as a paratrooper. Seven wooden barracks built by the Civilian Conservation Corps nearly a decade earlier were lifted off their foundations in the Sandhills by crews from the State Highway Department and delivered to Chapel Hill, where they were arranged in a U around an assembly area and exercise yard. Workers began making the necessary electrical connections and extending water and sewer lines from the university gymnasium. As was often the case with Coates, whose schedules allowed no room for error, the school opened two weeks late because of delays in the installation of water and sewer lines to the barracks.[11]

On the evening of October 12, with patrol classes due to begin the next morning, Coates arrived at the opening dinner straight from an inspection of the Patrol school. In his welcome to the new men, Coates said that over the years he had been able to hear the finest orchestras in the land, conducted under the baton of the leading maestros, but "no one of these orchestras, nor all of them together, have ever made music as sweet as forty flushing commodes and the sound of running water made to me as I came by the barrack latrines on my way to this meeting."[12]

Coates drew upon all his contacts for instructors. He called upon the FBI for help in classes on crime detection and he received instructors from the State Bureau of Investigation. The Traffic Institute of Northwestern

University and the Center for Safety Education of New York University provided instructors to supplement the classroom training that Coates himself—he considered himself an expert on laws of arrest, search, and seizure—and his two assistant directors conducted. Of the hundred-odd candidates accepted for the school, who had been selected from thirteen hundred applications, fifty-three men graduated, and of these forty-four were sworn in as officers of the State Highway Patrol on December 7, 1946. Within the year, the nine who were not immediately offered jobs were taken into the patrol as vacancies occurred.[13] The following year, Sanford and Pace directed two more training sessions after the 1947 General Assembly appropriated money to double the Patrol's strength in an effort to stem the alarming increase in traffic fatalities due in part to speeding drivers freed from the war-time speed limit of 35 miles per hour. Thereafter, for nearly thirty years, the Patrol school was part of the Institute's portfolio of service to the state.

The development of the Patrol school affirmed what Coates had been preaching all along. There was no assignment or challenge that was too big for the Institute to handle. He had taken his experience with one-day training sessions for experienced troopers and expanded it into an eight-week program that admitted raw recruits and turned out men ready to take an oath and pin on a badge. This was more than mere classroom work. Troopers learned self-defense, perfected their marksmanship, and experienced the challenge of handling a speeding automobile in a high-speed chase. All in all, it was hardly the sort of thing found in the curriculum of a law school, but for Coates it was a logical extension of his classroom and suited the Institute's purpose as Coates had always envisioned it. He was eager to exploit other opportunities.

Coates was proud of the Institute's improvisational style. He would tell the young lawyers he recruited to the Institute staff that he was offering opportunities where a man would have the "freedom of a country lawyer with the backing of an institution."[14] Another favorite of his declarations was a belief in "individualism to the point of anarchy."[15] By that he meant that he, and each of the assistant directors at the Institute, should feel free to follow a line of study or inquiry into any field and cut across any governmental boundaries that might inhibit their reaching a logical conclusion. He once lambasted a staff member for failing to exercise such unbridled curiosity. When the man protested that he had done just as he was asked,

Coates told him, "if you haven't got any better sense than to do as I say, you haven't got enough sense to be on the Institute staff."[16]

This freewheeling expression of the Institute's mission aggravated his critics on campus. During the late 1930s, men from Frank Graham on down had tried to get Coates to define the Institute's plans for programs and its field of work. In response, Coates usually recounted the history of the evolution of the Institute as if describing these broad parameters was in itself a definition of the Institute's program. He was loathe to put any field of study out of reach, lest it inhibit his taking on a project that piqued his interest or limit his ability to gain financial support. He had refused to be corralled in the 1930s, and he was not about to allow it to happen a decade later as the Institute regained its footing and solidified its importance within the governmental community of the state.

As long as Coates believed he was in control, he cooperated with other university departments and volunteered men and material from the Institute for use within various academic disciplines. Institute men produced training sessions for supervisors of municipal water service in conjunction with the university's School of Public Health. Coates also had been involved in the creation of a department of city and regional planning—one of its sponsors was the Tennessee Valley Authority, whose chief executive was Coates's Harvard classmate, David Lilienthal—and William Cochrane had taught courses there in planning law. The Institute's volumes on taxation were used as texts in political science courses that Institute men taught during the war. Paul Wager, one of the department's leading faculty members, had even written a generous article about the Institute for the *National Municipal Review.* The piece gently chided Coates for not using the Institute as more of an agency for reform rather than a training ground for public servants,[17] an observation that demonstrated the difference between the approaches used by Odum, with whom Wager had worked earlier in his career, and Coates.

In 1945, Wager and the chair of the political science department, Charles B. Robson, renewed their interest in creating a graduate program in public administration. Their meetings with Coates never got very far, however. Coates never refused to help, which would have left him open to the charge of being an obstructionist. He never endorsed their plan either. "He wouldn't let them say a word," recalled Donald Hayman, who at the time was working toward his doctorate under Wager's supervision. "If they started talking he'd just keep talking and they politely would shut up. He didn't want to do what they wanted him to do."[18]

Robson and Wager did not give up. When they learned that Coates was interested in hiring a political scientist—a clear departure from his routine of hiring only lawyers—they encouraged Hayman to apply for the job. Hayman was a soft-spoken Kansan who had years of government experience, including extensive service handling personnel matters for the U.S. Labor Department. He had prepared a grant proposal to fund a survey of personnel administration in state, city, and county governments when the Institute opening came to his attention. "They encouraged me to infiltrate the Institute of Government and try to get the Institute to cooperate with them to start a masters of public administration program and to beef up the political science department," Hayman later recalled.[19]

Unanticipated circumstances had prompted Coates to look outside the legal profession for help. After running three sessions of the Patrol school, Coates and the Patrol's commanders were concerned about the high failure rate of recruits. It was expensive to train a trooper, and Coates believed that the testing and screening process was not adequately weeding out those least likely to succeed. Coates happened upon Robson on the street in Chapel Hill and asked if he had someone who might be able to help. Robson recommended that Coates call Hayman, who was close to finishing his doctorate.

Coates arranged for a 3 p.m. appointment with Hayman at his office. Hayman arrived on time, but it was more than two hours before Coates caught up with his own schedule and invited Hayman into his office for an interview. Hayman found an engaging and gregarious host who delivered up his history of the Institute with recruiting-office enthusiasm. He also found a man who was deeply interested in Hayman's research and his plans. He frequently interrupted Hayman as he described his grant proposal, saying, "'The Institute should be doing this.' Everything that I proposed, 'the Institute should be doing this.'"[20] Coates offered Hayman a job on the spot, and he joined the staff on April 1, 1948. He was the first nonlawyer to become an assistant director since T. N. Grice, an accountant, had been part of the original team a decade earlier.

Hayman replaced Terry Sanford on the staffing chart, but at two-thirds the salary that Coates was paying Sanford, who had departed for Fayetteville to open a law practice. Hayman discovered that work had piled up around the Institute. He said Sanford left behind an unfinished study on pensions and retirement for law enforcement officers. The pension report was long overdue so when Hayman finished Sanford's assignment and one other in short order, Coates found new confidence in his political scientist, and raised his pay. Coates was as surprised at Hayman's success as he had been by Grice's. "Both proved their abilities equal to any lawyers on the staff, [and] I was astounded as completely as my old teacher Horace Williams had been when he had gone to Harvard for graduate work in the 1880s and discovered for the first time that God was not a Methodist."[21]

Coates had gathered up other projects in recent months. The 1947 General Assembly had requested a study on the increase in local, private, and special legislation, and the larger question of home rule. Looming even larger on the Institute's agenda was a commitment to report on the potential for consolidation of city and county government functions in Charlotte and Mecklenburg County.

Consolidation of local government had been a lively topic in North Carolina for nearly twenty years. The city and county of Durham had investigated consolidation in the mid-1930s, and in 1936 members of the Duke University Law School faculty had produced a merger option for local governments. That report was received favorably by government reformers around the country, and in the intervening years had become a starting point for cities and counties considering merger. Durham voters were not inclined to agree to its value, however. By the end of the war, the only governmental units merged in Durham County were the city and county health departments. A Mecklenburg County legislator, Carrie McLean, had introduced bills in the mid-1920s that would have enabled consolidation, but none had been passed. The issue began to build public support again in 1946 after the *Charlotte News* produced a series of articles that were tilted heavily in favor of merging tax departments, zoning and planning departments, courts, law enforcement, schools, and even governance. Just days after the last of the articles appeared, Charlotte Mayor H. H. Baxter and S. Y. McAden, the chair of the county board of commissioners, pushed through requests by their respective governing boards to ask the Institute of Government to begin a consolidation study.[22]

Coates had courted the Charlotte decision makers for several years and had fed information to *Charlotte News* general manager J. E. Dowd, the man who hired writer Burke Davis to produce the newspaper series. He also had talked with R. W. Flack, an old friend from Durham who was city manger in Charlotte during the war. When the Charlotte political leaders asked Coates to produce a study on consolidation, the Institute's staff was so thin that there was no way Coates could produce it in time for immediate action. But Coates didn't tell the Charlotte officials that. He accepted the invitation and tended to it as best he could. From time to time, Coates dispatched men to begin work using the methods that he, Henry Brandis, and the early staff had perfected. As best they could, with other obligations piling up in Chapel Hill, Sanford, Cochrane, and Lewis began taking a complete inventory of each department's assets and responsibilities. By the early part of 1948, more than a year after the work began, Sanford had completed a study of the county and city police departments and Cochrane had prepared some reports on the health departments. At the current rate, however, these early reports would be out of date by the time the rest of the areas of interest were completed. Coates needed more help.

Coates could add to the Institute staff only when he had some prospect of paying the salaries of new employees. Hence, he shopped the law schools for new men but often didn't buy, unless he saw an opportunity he didn't want to see slip away or a need he could not ignore. Until Hayman joined the staff in April 1946, Coates had hired only Sanford, Cochrane, and Henry Lewis since the end of the war. Now, with more work than his staff could handle, Coates went looking for talent as good as he had in these three, especially Lewis, who was a 1940 graduate of the Harvard Law School.

Lewis and Coates had more in common than their shared experience at Harvard. Lewis, a 1937 graduate of the university, was a cousin of Coates's friends William Polk and Tempe Boyd, now Mrs. Arthur Dugan, with whom Albert and Gladys had enjoyed weekend visits in Warrenton, North Carolina, since the days of their courtship. Lewis grew up in Northampton County and as a youngster he had spent his summers in Warrenton, not far from his home. Lewis was at the Dugans' home in New Orleans in the early days of the war when Albert and Gladys stopped for an overnight visit on their way west and they were all introduced. Albert continued the relationship with Lewis, whom he saw off and on during the war, usually when he was in Washington, D.C., where Lewis was posted with the army. When the war came to an end, Coates offered Lewis a job.[23]

Coates looked for men—he had hired only one woman, who did not stay long—who were much like him. He was partial to natives of the state, but a man from another southern state was acceptable. He wanted men who could share his passion and his vision for the Institute and for improving the level of government services. That also meant they would be willing to work for less money and less job security than they might find at a successful law firm. He considered only candidates who had finished at the top of their class, unless, of course, they had graduated from Harvard. When he interviewed in Cambridge, he didn't bother reviewing a candidate's academic standing.

The three years Albert Coates spent at the Harvard Law School left a profound imprint on him. His time in the classroom there influenced his own teaching style, although he infused his Socratic exercises with more bombast, profanity, and down-home humor than "Bull" Warren and other storied Harvard professors ever did. Coates was convinced that a well-trained Harvard lawyer was a superb generalist who could take any issue, parse it, and always find a solution. But it was the sociological school of jurisprudence developed and promoted by his dean, Roscoe Pound, that truly shaped Coates's life and fueled his ambition to bring the law closer to those who were charged with its administration.

Pound instilled in Coates the importance of viewing the law within a broader social context. Pound's philosophy was as much a part of the foundation of the Institute of Government as the lessons Coates had learned at the feet of E. K. Graham and E. C. Branson. The familiar phrase "bridging the gap between the law in the books and the law in action" that Coates used so liberally in everything he wrote sprang from Pound's own writing following his experiences in Nebraska and Chicago before he got to Harvard, and it encapsulated the Harvard professor's mission. The dean even provided an institutional model of sorts for his student. As Coates was beginning to plan his Institute of Government, Pound was implementing a pilot program at Harvard in which he sought to "bridge the gap" with special courses designed for correctional administrators. Coates proved more successful than his mentor. Pound's experiment in bringing "civilians" into a program of training within Harvard ended after just two years.

Lewis had met each of Coates's criteria and he became one of his most faithful followers. Unlike new men who were assigned by Coates to a particular area of work, Lewis picked his own field. He told Coates at the outset that he had never really liked criminal law and his army service had convinced him he had no aptitude for personnel issues. As an alternative, he chose election laws, and after he arrived he began updating the guidebook for local election officials. When Peyton Abbott left the Institute at the end of the 1947 General Assembly to become an assistant attorney general, Lewis assumed Abbott's coverage of tax matters.[24]

Pressed for more men like Lewis, Coates made a recruiting trip in the spring of 1948 to Harvard, where several promising candidates responded to a posted notice on the law school bulletin board announcing that Albert Coates of the Institute of Government at the University of North Carolina was conducting interviews. J. Alexander McMahon, a Duke University graduate who had been raised in Pennsylvania, and George Esser, a Virginian and graduate of the Virginia Military Institute, were two men who "answered the siren call," as McMahon later put it. "The Institute sounded to me like an ideal opportunity to do some things that were useful, not torts and contracts, but other things putting my law degree to good use," McMahon said.[25]

Esser believed the Institute would be an opportunity to be a part of the changes he saw ahead for the South. His wartime experience and time at law school had opened new challenges for Esser. "I could see that race and poverty were going to be tough issues for my generation, and so I came back to the South with a desire to be involved in solving those problems," Esser said. The Institute was not involved with these particular social issues, which would later play a larger part in Esser's life, but "the Institute was interested in good government and in a way that I felt was both necessary and challenging." One of Esser's law professors knew Coates and a little bit about the Institute. He endorsed Esser's decision to come south, but he told him to stay only for a year or two and then open a law practice. Coates sealed the deal when Esser made a visit in springtime, one of the prettiest seasons on the campus in Chapel Hill, and the two chanced upon Frank Graham during a walk across the campus. "I was very impressed with the warmth of the response of those people. I mean Frank Graham was a man of national stature."[26]

McMahon and Esser began work on the same day, October 1, 1948. They joined two other new men, Donald McCoy and Dickson Phillips. Both of them were from Laurinburg and had recently finished law school at Carolina. A few months later, these four were joined by Philip Green, a North Carolina native and a graduate of Princeton University and the Harvard Law School. They moved into offices in the Institute building on

Franklin Street and became part of the largest complement of assistant directors Coates had ever employed. Coates's prophecy that the Institute would outgrow its new home was proving accurate. The dormitory space on the third floor and in the basement was now used for staff offices. The clerical help had taken over the one and only classroom, leaving Cochrane to borrow classrooms and lecture halls on campus for Institute meetings and training sessions. The Institute's library spilled over into hallways and onto the shelves in the offices of the assistant directors. The print shop and mail room were in the basement hallway.

Coates's estimate of Harvard men proved accurate as he threw his new and expanded staff into the consolidation study and the completion of the other unfinished projects that had accumulated. Esser tackled the history of Charlotte municipal government while McMahon went to work on city and county finance. Cochrane continued his work on health care and picked up the law enforcement training component of the Institute's program. Lewis focused his attention on the tax structure of the city and county and even waded into the difficult subject of consolidating school districts. Hayman examined the personnel and purchasing departments, while Green began preparing reports on fire protection, building regulations, and water and sewer departments.

All the while Coates was fending off calls from Charlotte for updates on his consolidation work. "We would like to have your recommendation as soon as possible," Mayor Baxter wrote to Coates in the spring of 1948, just as he was beginning to recruit for positions at the Institute. "How's that report on city-county consolidation coming along?" the *Charlotte News's* Dowd probed nine months later.[27] When backed into a corner, Coates would filibuster and talk his clients into submission. He visited Charlotte late in 1948 and delivered an interim report in private that apparently won him more time. At the same time, he also secured a contract from the city and county to contribute $10,000 each toward completion of the study.[28]

He needed the money to cover the cost of his new hires. Coates's approach to the financing of this project was symptomatic of the way he had handled the Institute's finances for nearly twenty years. He had never managed a budget before the Institute became part of the university and only paid lip service to one after 1942. Coates had raised money as he needed it before, and he continued to do the same as the Institute expanded. "When the Institute of Government came into the University in 1942," he would later write, "I looked on the money allotted to it in the budget as a floor and not a ceiling—a starting point and not a stopping point for raising money."[29] Somehow, he managed to keep the operations out of the red, but the haphazard, even hand-to-mouth, style was disconcerting to men whose job security was no greater than the boss's success in finding new income.

On the first of November 1949, almost three years after the *Charlotte News* had stirred the local governments into pursuing a study of consolidation, Albert Coates delivered the first public report. The event drew large headlines in the newspapers, along with photographs of Coates reading from a lengthy introduction that was, essentially, an exhaustive account of the history of both the city and county, noting the historical details of the growth and evolution of each governmental unit, beginning with the first settlers. Eight more such events were scheduled over the next four months as assistant directors delivered reports on each of their subject areas.

Nothing like the study had ever been produced in North Carolina. Each function of municipal and county government was described in detail, with commentary noting areas of overlap or duplication. Accompanying charts and tabulations itemized operating expenses. It had taken Coates and his men far longer than anticipated to get a report to Charlotte, but they made up for their tardiness in volume. Each of the nine reports came with a 10,000-word summary, which the city's newspapers carried verbatim.

Over the years, Coates had carefully cultivated the Institute's reputation as an independent agency whose only goal was to provide solid information that political leaders could use to make informed decisions. In the Charlotte study, the Institute did not present a case for or against consolidation, although some of the language in the reports certainly led the reader to see the benefits of eliminating duplicative efforts through the merger of departments. This neutral approach set the Institute above the fray, and out of the way of political consequences if things didn't work out. Apparently this approach did not disappoint. A *Charlotte News* editorial called the work "monumental" and said it would "be of keen interest not only to Mecklenburgers but to the other metropolitan counties in North Carolina and, indeed, the nation."[30]

The result was a testament to Coates's belief that he could take any good lawyer and produce solid work, even if the man doing the work was learning as he went along. Despite their boss's confidence in their abilities, this introduction to local government was a shock to some. Esser and McMahon were assigned to review a collection of consolidation studies from other states. Esser wrote to Coates that they were at a disadvantage. "In view of the fact that both of us lacked any background in the administration of local government and many of the legal problems of local government, we had difficulty in being constructively critical of these studies."[31]

Henry Lewis had no experience in school management and approached his assignment to study the city and county school districts with some fear and trepidation. He interviewed the leaders of the school systems and through their answers tried to understand the fears and concerns of those in charge. "I was overwhelmed with ignorance of the technicalities, and I was fearful that whatever I wrote could be decimated by both sets of school officials. In desperation, I decided to try to analyze the problems posed by the two school systems from the point of view of the private citizen."[32]

Some changes flowed from the study, but not immediately. The city and county schools were consolidated about a decade later. The work probably had a greater impact on the way the Institute of Government looked at local government from then on. At the outset of the Charlotte study, Coates had applied his template of studying government by function rather than by political organization. This proved insufficient when the questions involved policy issues and went beyond the rudiments of better bookkeeping, detecting crime, and tax listing. Going forward from the work in Charlotte, some of the staff began to develop specialty areas. Esser became the Institute's man for cities and urban affairs while Alex McMahon concentrated his efforts on special problems related to county government. This assignment also moved the Institute into new areas of government operations. Having started from scratch with the consolidation study, Philip Green was on his way to becoming a nationally known specialist in zoning and planning law. His 430-page guidebook, published by the Institute in 1952, was the first publication of its kind for local zoning and planning boards in the state.

The expansion of the staff, together with the promotion of professor of law Henry Brandis to dean of the law school in 1949, allowed Coates more freedom for the Institute. Coates had long and often used his staff to fill in for him when he was absent from his classroom, a practice that, under

Brandis, had the dean's approval. The Institute and the law school established a closer working relationship, which became more pronounced as men at the Institute established their credentials in municipal law, urban affairs, planning and zoning, domestic relations, and other areas. It was always clear, however, that the Institute staff members were in the law school classes as Coates's surrogates; they had no academic standing of their own.

The arrangement pleased Coates and saved Brandis from some administrative headaches. Brandis let Coates know his goodwill was not to be taken for granted. Before the start of the academic year, not long after he assumed the deanship, Brandis announced that the law school would hold Saturday classes. When he met with the students and faculty on Friday evening before the start of the fall quarter, he urged everyone to be on time. The next morning Brandis was informed that Coates's classroom was full of students but their professor was absent. The dean asked the students to remain in their seats and marched back to his office.

He knew right where to find Coates. Brandis "picked up the telephone and he called Coates at the Institute of Government building," recalled William Aycock, who had recently joined the faculty straight from his term as a student. When Coates answered, Brandis braced him with a question: "Can't you read? Classes start today. You're supposed to be here."[33] Coates flew across the four hundred yards or so between Franklin Street and Manning Hall rummaging through his mind for excuses and anecdotal material that might produce a lively response from his students.

If Coates owned a watch, it served more as an ornament than as a tool for meeting a schedule. He thought nothing of working well past suppertime during the week, and he and his men were usually at their desks on Saturdays and sometimes on Sunday. Coates made light of the way he extended himself, saying he was grateful that the government had mandated a forty-hour workweek, since it allowed him to hold down two jobs at the same time. He expected the same commitment from those who worked at the Institute and was quite blunt about a staff member's obligations. "I did not want men with conflicting loyalties," he later wrote. "I wanted men on the Institute staff who found their fulfillment of the creative efforts in the day's work undistracted by competing sideline activities."[34] Again, he wanted men as dedicated as he was, but to only one master—the Institute.

Such dedication brought rewards. On March 22, 1952, the university trustees presented Coates with the O. Max Gardner award, which had been created according to the will of the former governor, who had died in 1947, just as he was about to leave for London as ambassador to the Court of St. James. Gardner had been present at the birthing of the Institute in 1932. In a joint statement, Governor W. Kerr Scott and J. Spencer Love, speaking for the trustees, said "no greater joy could come to the donor of this award, himself a life-long public servant, than to see Albert Coates, servant of all public servants, adjudged by the unanimous vote of the Board of Trustees, to be 'that member of the faculty of the Consolidated University of North Carolina who in the current scholastic year has made the greatest contribution to the welfare of the human race.'"[35]

Coates said he accepted the award, not as an individual, but "as a symbol of the Institute of Government." The award was a generous recognition of achievement for Coates, someone who had created so many headaches for his friends Frank Graham and Robert B. House but who also had brought national attention and praise to a program many on the campus had believed would never survive the Depression.

The university produced a booklet of the remarks made by Coates and the presenters, and Coates mailed copies around the country to friends, colleagues, former staff members, and others. By return mail came a flood of congratulatory letters, including some from staff members who had been recalled to active duty during the Korean conflict. Among those who sent congratulations were the FBI's Hoover and Clegg.

Along with the plaque and public recognition came a cash award of $10,000, which arrived just as Albert and Gladys were moving into their new home. In 1949, the two had moved from the cottage on East Rosemary Street to a rental house on Boundary Street that was owned by the university and made available to faculty members.[36] The move was temporary, as the two had finally begun making plans for a home of their own. Two years earlier, they had bought a lot on Hooper Lane in what had once been the back garden of the home of Edward Kidder Graham. The former president's two-story frame house, with its Victorian lines and a broad porch across the front, stood on the corner facing the eastern edge of the campus.

Gladys had begun planning her own home during her engagement to Albert nearly twenty-five years earlier. All the dreams that she transformed into plans in the spring of 1928 were never realized, but she had kept hope alive even as they had shuttled from one rental to another, each one smaller than the last. Gladys had added to her home whatever touches of grace and elegance their circumstances would allow. All the time she had maintained a warm and comfortable retreat for Albert with little assistance from her mate. Albert usually deflected Gladys's calls to handle even minor household chores by saying, "Can't we do that tomorrow?" Her sister-in-law once remarked, "Albert Coates is a guest in his own home."[37]

That was not to say that Albert was without his own ideas as they began working with two architects, brothers Jim and John Webb. The Webbs were known for bringing contemporary design to their work and had introduced the Bay Area architecture of the West Coast to the sleepy haunts of the South. The Webbs designed houses from the inside out, a notion foreign to Albert, but he and Gladys went ahead and provided their ideas for the interior. The architects returned with a floor plan but no rendering of what the exterior would look like. "The exterior is the function of the interior," they told Albert. "Well," said Albert, "I've heard of predestination in religion, maybe it will work in architecture." They proceeded with the rest of their work, but the contemporary styling that they produced was too far off the mark for Albert.

"I won't live in it," he declared. "My father might have paid five hundred dollars for a tenant house in that general form, size, and dimension, but he wouldn't have put thousands of dollars in it, and I'm not going to."

The architects repeated their mantra: the exterior is the function of the interior.

Finally, as Gladys would later relate, Albert said, "I've heard that one time too many. There is not a word of truth in it. I can show you two girls with the same interior floor plan, functions, mechanisms, and objectives—one is pretty as she can be and the other is ugly as hell. Don't tell me the exterior is the function of the interior!"[38]

The result was not the contemporary styling of the West Coast but the steady beauty of the traditional Georgian. Gladys added a flower garden and other plantings that recalled her romance with the man to whom she had devoted her life. In one corner of the yard she planted a bay tree to remind her of the bay blossom she picked and pinned to her suit on her way to church the Sunday of the week of their engagement. Albert's favorite spot, especially in spring, was a screen porch on the side of the neat two-story home where he could settle into a comfortable chair with a notepad in his lap and write.[39]

ELEVEN

The University of Public Officials

1952–1956

SHORTLY AFTER Gladys and Albert Coates moved into their new home on Hooper Lane in September 1952, Albert invited J. Spencer Love, the nation's leading textile executive, to bring his wife and daughter to Chapel Hill for a celebratory Sunday morning breakfast. The date hinged on Love's busy schedule, as Love was the honored guest at this housewarming. When Love's acceptance arrived, invitations also went out to President Gordon Gray and his wife, William Carmichael and his wife, and Chancellor Robert B. House and his wife.

Ten years earlier, Love had saved the Institute with the $15,000 that he provided to pay expenses until the cost of operations could be included in the state budget. Albert reminded Love of this in his invitation, and he told him that by saving the Institute he had prevented "our own household economy from going out in the wash. I am quite sure that the house we invite you into could not have been built. So, in a very real sense, you have brought this invitation on yourself."[1] More recently, Love had sent Coates another $50,000, with instructions to use it at his discretion. This gift—impressive in size and generous in its application—only heightened Coates's feelings of gratitude.

Indeed, there was much to celebrate. Albert had more money at his disposal than ever before, he had the home that he and

Gladys had postponed for a quarter century, and he was still basking in the university's presentation of the O. Max Gardner Award, a long-awaited recognition of two decades of difficult and sometimes heartbreaking work. It was all worthy of a Sunday morning breakfast, the preferred time for entertaining in the Coates home ever since Gladys had cooked her first meal on the waffle iron in the Bullitt house years before. Over the years, these Sunday breakfasts had become treasured occasions as the house filled with the aroma of warm waffles and the pleasure of long, unhurried conversation.

The occasion was equally joyful for Gladys. Over the years, she had made do in the cramped quarters of the cottage on East Rosemary. Now, with a home of her own, these gatherings allowed her to present herself in singular fashion. Those who knew Albert had long been aware of the important role she had played in his life. She smoothed the rough edges from a man whose profanity often seemed to have no bounds, whose bold challenges could infuriate his peers, and whose peripatetic and untimely schedule could leave his colleagues bewildered and confused. Gladys had a selfless nature along with an inner calm and grace that set all in her presence at ease. She filled their home with art, music, and intelligent conversation. Gladys, Albert would say, was the one person with the ability to bring him up short.

The two were more than a union of "tidewater Virginia and branchwater North Carolina," as the story went. Certainly, she was refinement, manners, and a touch of class and soft beauty. Her husband, by contrast, could leave battered relationships and a boil of discomforting language in his wake. Gladys was a serious and appreciative student of the university whose scholarship had not ended with commencement at Randolph-Macon Woman's College. Over the years, she had made their home a safe refuge for her husband, pitched in unstintingly when needed at the Institute, and served as an unflinching editor of his prolific pen. In her own hours, she had undertaken exhaustive research on projects that drew her closer and closer to the campus, its people, and its history. She had come to love Chapel Hill as dearly as did her husband. She would become engaged by Albert's bursts of enthusiasm for a variety of subjects—with him anticipating a quick conclusion to the research—and then make them her own, devoting the time that was actually required for good work. The history of the law school published in 1947 bore Albert's byline, but it was Gladys's carefully annotated research drawn from records from the colonial era to the present that had given his work its depth. Likewise, when Albert had launched into a study of student government in the mid-1930s, the research had driven Gladys deep into the university archives. She spent five years thumbing though *Yackety Yacks*, *Hellenians*, the *Tar Heel*, faculty minutes, trustees' minutes, and the records of the student literary societies, as well as students' letters, diaries, and assorted papers collected in Wilson Library, to produce a worthy product that would later be published in both of their names.[2]

She loved poetry and lifted favorite passages from Shakespeare and other writers, placing her transcriptions in a spot where they could not be missed by her husband. He, in turn, gathered them up and fed them into his seemingly endless reservoir of quotations and snippets from the classics and scripture that he would later retrieve for just the right occasion. Gladys composed Christmas music and songs for her alma mater from the bench at her beloved piano. She also had an eye for the substance and subtlety of artists that was often lost on her mate. "She has lit the path we have traveled with music and art and heartening observation," Albert wrote of her contribution to his life. "Once when we were driving over a river the wind had stirred the water into ripples which caught and reflected the morning sun, she said: 'It looks like a place where bright angels' feet have trod.'"[3]

Yes, the housewarming at the Coates's two-story home on Hooper Lane, sitting as it did just a stone's throw from the edge of the campus and on land once owned by Edward Kidder Graham, had been a long time coming for Gladys. All the while, she had never complained about her dream deferred or the sometimes desperate conditions forced upon them by Albert's single-minded devotion to the Institute. Each of their various addresses along the way had been "home" as much as she could bring the definition to bear in the face of heavy debt with only nickels and dimes remaining in their bank account.

Left behind in the Depression, too, were any thoughts of raising children. Instead, she had adopted the "boys" of the Institute as her own, and even became godmother to some of their children. As the Institute's new men and their families arrived in Chapel Hill in the years after World War II they all received a warm welcome from Gladys. Her annual Christmas party around a punch bowl, with the house festooned in her own unique seasonal decorations, was an anticipated affair. She had devoted her life to the Institute and its people as much as she had to Albert. If Edward Kidder Graham was, for her husband, the greatest man who had ever lived, then Albert Coates was clearly no less for her.

By the 1950s, the age difference between Coates and his staff was greater than it had been at the outset, when less than a decade separated him from Brandis, Gardner, and Grice. Another generation had come aboard and these were men young enough to be Albert's sons. They came because of him and caught the dream and stood somewhat in awe. "It was respect, a little bit of fear and anxiety," recalled Robert Stipe, an assistant director in the 1950s. Men worked for the idea of the Institute of Government, not the paycheck, he said. "The vision was articulated very clearly, and you either felt it or you didn't. If you didn't, you didn't go there. Or if you didn't, you didn't stay there very long."[4] It was an opportunity to "combine the science of government with the art of government," recalled Clyde Ball, who joined the Institute in the 1950s.[5]

Those who took up Coates's invitation were expected to give the Institute their all. He would not tolerate a man working outside of the Institute, even though the time was his own. Whether he appreciated the irony of this—the Institute would have never survived if Albert Coates had not used time that belonged to the university to organize and proselytize in the 1930s—is not clear. Institute men were expected to work at least some time on Saturdays, and some returned on Sundays to stay abreast of their assignments. Coates even questioned George Esser about the hours he devoted to preparing for and teaching a Sunday school class at the Episcopal Church. Moonlighting for pay to supplement an Institute salary was beyond the pale. Paraphrasing the Bible, Coates told his disciples that he wanted them to "love the Institute of Government with all their heart, with all their mind, and with all their soul."[6]

Indeed, in a memorandum to his staff, he wrote, "That this was the first and only commandment—and perhaps the last, and that the only thing any colleague owed to me as symbol of the Institute of Government was the same thing he owed to the Lord God Almighty—to get out of himself everything that the Lord God Almighty had put in him and to get it out as fast as he could and a little faster."[7]

The challenges were great, but the staff grew and men eagerly accepted the jobs they were offered, even when they could find more promising opportunities elsewhere. They developed a fraternity of sorts, with shared interests and objectives, and gladly became members of an organization where Coates was at the top and all were equal below. They believed there were few things more important than the work of the Institute and they carried on in sickness and in health. When one of the assistant directors, Basil Sherrill, was confined to bed to recover from pneumonia, Coates came to his home to check on his condition. Coates wouldn't enter the room—perhaps mindful of his own debilitating bouts in the past—so he stood at the door to comfort and console. Before long, Coates began suggesting that as Sherrill lay in bed with nothing to do, perhaps he could think about this issue or consider that problem related to his work. Before Coates left the house, Sherrill later related, he had outlined a year's worth of work.[8]

Though the complexity of the assignments had increased, and the number of workers was four times what it had been in earlier years, Coates's management style remained the same as when he could haul the entire staff around in his battered automobile. Coates ran the place from his vest pocket. He depended on the assistant directors—the designation given all the professional staff—to maintain their equilibrium even when he might find himself off balance. From time to time, he would issue directives designed to keep him better informed, such as his request for memos in which the men reported on their activities and contacts. Some filed these reports regularly while others delivered something quarterly or even only once a year. Mostly, Coates kept in touch by calling men into his office, where more often than not his guest was expected to be a listening post, saying little, as Coates talked through whatever was on his mind that day. These sessions could last up to an hour or more.

Coates held these conferences daily when he was in Chapel Hill. If he didn't catch a man in the morning, he would ask him to stop by late in the day. On occasion the line at his door in the evening would grow long. Stipe once found himself waiting for his time in the office as the afternoon closed in on evening and his usual dinner hour. Coates, finally taking notice of those waiting, told Stipe to meet him the next morning at 6:30 at his home on Hooper Lane. It was summertime, and the windows were open in the Coates house as Stipe headed down the front walk at the appointed hour. When he got to the front door he could clearly hear the sound of his boss's snoring coming from an upstairs bedroom window. His knock at the door was answered by Gladys, who said Albert would be down presently.

Covering without shame for her husband, she said Albert had been up for some time and needed only a few minutes to finish shaving.[9]

Coates did what he could to inculcate his men with his personal virtues as well as his philosophy. Mindful of the suspicious and unlettered county officials he encountered in the 1930s, who braced themselves against the condescension of a "college professor" come to right some wrong, Coates insisted that guidebooks and other published materials be written so they could be understood by the garage mechanic, insurance agent, butcher, or barber who might be serving his first term on a city board or holding county office. All instruction and personal contact with those in the Institute's classrooms was to be conducted with honesty and without pretension, however wide the gap between the educations of the Harvard men and a clerk in a tax office. If a staff man didn't have an answer, Coates insisted he say so. Once Coates overheard a conversation between one of his assistant directors and a highway patrolman who was asking about a mountain featured in one of the large photographs that hung on the Institute's walls. The Institute man identified the peak as Mt. Pisgah, only to concur a few minutes later when another trooper asked if it was Mt. Mitchell. "[Coates] said don't try to ingratiate these people by pretending to be something you're not," recalled Ernest Machen, an assistant director. "We don't, any of us in the Institute building, know what that damned mountain is. He was trying to pretend he did and he wanted the man to feel flattered that he called it right. There's no point in that. He was a lot better off to say 'I'll tell you honestly, sir, I don't know what that mountain is.'"[10]

Coates wanted strong-minded men who could not only think for themselves but were willing to stand behind their convictions. As a law student, Jack Elam caught Coates's attention as just such a man. When Elam found he was arriving late at his next class because Coates's lectures usually ran long, he brought an alarm clock to class and set it to ring when the class was supposed to end. Coates continued to talk after it rang and when he was finished asked Elam to remain behind. Instead of dressing Elam down for insubordination, Coates asked him to work for the Institute. Elam reminded Coates that he wasn't in the top 10 percent of the class, the group from which Coates made his selections, and Coates told him, "I need bastards to build the Institute of Government and you're one of those bastards."[11] Elam later became the mayor of Greensboro and legal counsel to Cone Mills Corporation.

Coates even attempted to impose his distinctive writing style upon the initiates. His words on the page captured the forensic flourishes born of his oratorical experience, where incantatory phrasing and repetition were essential to imprint an idea upon an audience. Coates's lyrical prose produced lengthy sentences that were complicated in construction. It was a style that was hard for others to replicate if they did not share a similar background or love of the spoken word. During the preparation of the reports on the Charlotte-Mecklenburg consolidation study, Coates drove George Esser and Alex McMahon to distraction with his constant call for revisions in a document that ran to 100,000 words or more.[12]

Coates's men either bent to his will or devised ways to a keep his extraordinary demands at bay. One man told his secretary not to tell Coates that he had departed for vacation until three days after he was gone. Otherwise, the director would load him up with work to get every ounce of energy before he left to spend time with his family. Alex McMahon warned Bob Stipe that Coates would often grab whoever was handy when he needed transportation to Raleigh for a meeting or a lift to the airport. The only way to avoid a second request was to make sure the first trip was one he would never forget. Sure enough, Coates commandeered Stipe for chauffeur duty not long after he arrived and the two headed off in Stipe's Volkswagen two-door sedan. The car was one of the early models and tiny in comparison to the familiar American land yachts of the late 1950s. Stipe said later he was sure Coates had never ridden in one before the younger man pulled the car to the curb to pick him up.

"Well," Stipe later reported, "N.C. 54 was narrow, uncertain, twisty, congested and so on. I followed Alex's advice very strictly, managed to slip off the road once or twice, and by the time we got to the airport, Mr. Coates was singing out loud, 'Jesus Loves Me.' I think he was genuinely frightened."[13]

Traveling in an automobile to distant meetings with Coates was a mixed blessing. The driver often was stuck with the tab when Coates suggested, as he frequently did, that they stop for a milk shake from a favorite spot. He seemed to know where all the best milk shakes could be found, from one end of the state to the other. Coates also could ride in silence, and appear to be distracted as he mulled an issue or problem, only to break loose with an exclamation or aphorism such as, "Oh Lordy, it's a great life if you don't weaken, and not so bad if you do."[14]

Despite the eccentricities of a man who could drive his associates to hair-pulling frustration, the men of the Institute would sacrifice time with their families and postpone development of their own careers, interests, and pursuits on his behalf. "He was the most self-centered person I ever dealt with in that he saw the world in terms of its relationship to him," said John Sanders, who joined the Institute in 1956 when Coates was at the pinnacle of his career. "There was never any question that he lived in an Alberto-centric world, and everybody who dealt with him recognized that and accepted it. That was part of his personality." But Coates had such a persuasive sense of mission, Sanders said, that other people normally put off by such egotism would remain steadfast. "They realized that while they had to put up with a lot in order to deal with him, there was enough there that was worth putting up with."[15]

There was little that was more important to Coates than the Institute's reputation for impartiality and fairness. He had guarded against any taint or suspicion of bias or hint of self-serving motive since that first meeting in 1932 when some suggested that his organizing efforts were nothing more than the first step in building a political organization. Coates had stood down the state's attorney general in the 1930s when the Institute's study of proposed constitutional amendments was called into question. Over the years he had carefully cultivated the support and good will of both Democrats and Republicans. Even though there were few Republicans in Raleigh to offer aid and comfort, he needed them in provinces where Republicans might hold a majority on a board of county commissioners. Coates kept his political preferences to himself. He was probably a registered Democrat, but he remained silent during the political season. After the election, he was always fulsome in praise for those who had been elected to public office. The papers and files that he left behind include only one partisan speech. It is a defense of Frank Graham that Coates apparently wrote some time in 1950 during Graham's bitter primary contest for the United States senate.[16] It carries no notation as to whether Coates ever delivered the long and passionate address. (Henry Lewis also produced a study of the election returns in this race, but the study was never published.[17])

The Institute's reputation for unvarnished facts and balanced reporting served the organization well, especially in Raleigh, where Coates depended on legislators and partisan budget writers for continued financial support. To choose sides, or even create the impression of having a partisan point of view, could be fatal to the Institute's welfare. At the same time, the Institute's reputation for impartiality allowed public officials to safely sidetrack an issue that had not fully ripened. When political debate became too heated, or when competing sides could not find common ground, the Institute was called upon to examine the arguments and present the case. The Institute's analysis didn't necessarily settle the matter. Coates carefully avoided offering recommendations, even when his interests could be served. Nonetheless, the Institute reports could bolster a case on one side or the other. In the late 1940s, for example, municipalities were stretched to the limit to maintain city streets and made a bid for a larger share of the gas tax being collected by the state. The effort was resisted by legislators from rural counties as well as by Governor Kerr Scott. The Institute considered all sides of the debate and its report sharpened the focus of the issue, which was one close to Ben Cone, Coates's longtime friend, generous benefactor, and, at the time, Greensboro's mayor. The analysis was evenhanded, but the numbers made a convincing argument for the cities' case. That didn't prevent Governor Scott from using everything in his arsenal—including political intimidation of some Greensboro council members—in his opposition to a bill giving municipalities a share of the gas tax rather than a lump sum.[18]

In the late spring of 1954, there was no bigger challenge facing North Carolina, and the rest of the South, than the one that the United States Supreme Court addressed on May 17. On that day, Chief Justice Earl Warren read the Court's decision in the case of *Brown v. Board of Education* rejecting the segregated schooling of whites and blacks. The decision overshadowed everything on the front pages of the newspapers. North Carolina was in the midst of a spirited contest for the Democratic nomination for the United States Senate, and the state and the nation were reeling from the specter, raised by Senator Joseph McCarthy, of communists in the government. On top of it all, North Carolina was suffering from its most devastating drought in years. Nothing was more important, or more emotionally charged, than the Supreme Court's decision. Albert Coates was not going to be left out.

North Carolina's governor was William B. Umstead. Coates had known all the state's chief executives for the past thirty years, but none of them as well as he knew Umstead. His relationship with the governor dated to their days as Carolina undergraduates (Umstead, too, had won the Mangum Medal). Over the years, Umstead had repeatedly responded to Coates's calls. When Umstead was a prosecuting attorney, Coates asked him to speak to his Law School Association. Later, after Umstead was elected to Congress, Coates prevailed upon him to secure favors to aid the Institute. Now, as governor, Umstead was the one person Coates could use to put him on the "platform" regarding what he considered the most important legal decision of the century.

Umstead had not joined the chorus of condemnation that arose from the South almost within minutes of Warren's reading of the Court's decision. In fact, Umstead was caught completely off guard. An assistant had to retrieve the language of the decision from a wire service reporter. The governor's office issued a brief statement saying Umstead was "disappointed." Almost a month passed before Umstead delivered a more thoughtful response that he wrote by hand on a legal pad. This statement was measured and lengthy, replete with a history lesson that included references to the state's stormy days of Reconstruction. Finally, he concluded, "The Supreme Court of the United States has spoken. It reversed itself and has declared segregation in the public schools unconstitutional. In my opinion its previous decision on this question was correct. This reversal of its former decisions is in my judgment a clear and serious invasion of the rights of the sovereign states. Nevertheless, this is now the latest interpretation of the Fourteenth Amendment."[19]

Umstead, like all in the South, was uncertain about what lay ahead. The Court had spoken to the central issue and determined that separate was not equal in the cases that arose from four separate states, but it did not prescribe a remedy in its May 17 decision. Instead, the Court called on the parties directly involved, as well as any of the states affected, to participate in further hearings with amicus briefs from participants due in December. The governor was faced with multiple challenges: how to deal with orders to dismantle a dual school system and the more immediate question of whether North Carolina should participate in the second round of hearings that would determine implementation.

Coates wanted to be part of what he called "the most compelling question of this generation," and he believed that he had just the man on his staff who could bring the right experience and expertise to the task. James C. N. Paul had been an assistant director for about six months when the Supreme Court ruled in May. He had come to Chapel Hill from Washington, D.C., fresh from two years as a clerk at the Court for former Chief Justice Fred N. Vinson, who had died in September 1953. As soon as Coates was given an open spot on the governor's calendar, he and Paul headed to Raleigh.

Paul was more familiar with the case history than perhaps anyone else in North Carolina. Because of his service with Vinson, he knew the chief justice had wrestled for nearly two years over how the Court should handle what all knew would be a most difficult decision for the nation. Vinson, a Kentuckian, was ambivalent about how far the Court should go, but he also was worried that some on the court might even uphold segregation.[20] The case was pending an early rehearing on questions posed by Justice Felix Frankfurter when the chief justice died and Paul's service at the Supreme Court came to an end. He had offers from private law firms and some corporate opportunities to consider, but he succumbed to the arguments of Albert Coates in favor of the Institute and the beauty of Chapel Hill in the spring. In March, two months before the decision, he had written to the Supreme Court clerk to ask for a copy of the decision as soon as it was rendered. He had not quite settled into an area of work when Coates appeared at his office door and told him they had a meeting with the governor.

Umstead's silence masked his private anger. He was just as upset at the Court's intrusion on the Southern way of life as any of those loudly demanding defiance and urging North Carolina to join the "massive resistance" movement that was building elsewhere, including neighboring Virginia. Umstead believed that North Carolinians paid the taxes for their schools and the Court had no business telling them how to run them. His initial response, one that he expressed only privately, was to ignore the Court and let the justices enforce their ruling while the states proceeded as before, but he had too much respect for the rule of law to declare his feelings openly.[21]

At the same time, Umstead also was hearing a different point of view from within the state. Immediately after the Court's decision, the board for the Greensboro city schools adopted a resolution instructing Superintendent Ben Smith to study "ways and means of complying with the Court's decision." An influential voice of moderation and restraint was Winston-Salem attorney Irving Carlyle, one of the most highly regarded lawyers in the state. Three days after the Court's decision, Carlyle declared in a speech to the state Democratic Party convention that "the Supreme Court of the United States has spoken. As good citizens we have no other course except to obey the law as laid down by the Court. To do otherwise would cost us our respect for law and order, and if we lose that in these critical times, we will have lost that quality which is the source of our strength as a state and as a nation."[22]

Coates and Paul made an unlikely pair. Paul was a Yankee, at least by southern standards, educated at Princeton with a law degree from the University of Pennsylvania. He had grown up in Pennsylvania, but during his service at the Court he had been drawn to the eastern shore of Maryland, which he considered his home. He had never set foot in North Carolina. One of Coates's men, V. Lee Bounds, had told Coates about Paul after the two got to know each other while Bounds was working on a graduate degree in law at Penn.[23]

Coates, of course, was steeped in the traditions and habits of the South. He had been raised in an era of racial separation decreed by North Carolina law and generally unquestioned by whites like him. He never spoke out on his feelings about race to those with whom he worked any more than he declared his political preferences. Those who knew him described his opinions on race as reflecting an era where whites and blacks had little more than perfunctory social interaction. Anything beyond that was suspect. The university had upheld its segregationist traditions and in the 1940s didn't even allow dance bands that included white and black musicians to perform on campus.[24] As an undergraduate, Coates had written a passionate objection to an initiative to mandate segregated neighborhoods in rural communities. This initiative was led by Clarence Poe, publisher of the Progressive Farmer, and gained some traction in the years before World War I. Coates did not object on moral grounds but founded his opposition in a fear that segregated neighborhoods would lead to all-black areas that would require political representation. A Negro district would be corrupt and immoral and "a thorn in the sides of the adjoining white community," he wrote.[25] He was not forced to adjust to dealing with whites and blacks on an equal footing until the first African Americans were enrolled in the law school in the fall of 1951 and took their seats in his classroom.

Donald Hayman, who worked with Coates for fifteen years, said his boss was in favor of integration because he opposed discrimination and inequity under law. However, Coates accommodated segregationists whom he had to work with in the General Assembly; nothing was to get in the way of securing their support for the Institute. That accounted for his anxiety one week in the late 1950s when he learned that an African American city council member had been booked into a room in the Institute's building, at a time when public accommodations in the South were still segregated. The registration was complete by the time Coates learned that it had occurred, and he did not attempt to make any changes. "He swore under his breath, turned and looked out the window," George Esser said in recalling the incident. "He said, 'That's all you could do.'"[26]

As long as Coates was director, his associates were people like himself—white, Anglo-Saxon, and Protestant males, with one exception. That was Elmer Oettinger, a non-observant Jew, whom Coates hired twice. He offered little encouragement to the few women who served brief stints on the staff. Even those with law degrees didn't stay long.[27] African American lawyers were even harder to find than female lawyers, so there were few opportunities for Coates to hire a non-white assistant director had he been so inclined. All of the clerical staff were white, which was the case throughout the university. Blacks were relegated to menial jobs on the campus and that included Jack Atwater, the Institute's long-serving janitor and general factotum.

Umstead moved slowly in the weeks after the Court's decision and added nothing to his prepared statement. In early June, he met with other southern governors in Richmond, Virginia. Attorney General Harry McMullan also conferred with his peers. There was considerable sentiment in Raleigh, shared by Umstead and the attorney general, that North Carolina should not participate in the second round of hearings. McMullan argued that if the state remained silent the ruling would, somehow, fall less heavily upon North Carolina. When the governor met with Coates and Paul he asked them to study the ruling and report on "the proposals for preserving the substance of separate schools within the framework of this decision." Apparently, Umstead wasn't as interested in the point of view of Carlyle and the Greensboro school board as he was in hearing from those who believed there was a way "to beat the devil around the stump," as Coates often put it.[28]

Coates and Paul partitioned their research and worked steadily through June and July. Coates's contribution was a history lesson in the establishment and operation of public schools in North Carolina. As he did with any topic, he began at the beginning of applicable history, in this case with the arrival of Africans in the seventeenth century and the endorsement of the practice of slavery by the Lords Proprietors of the Province of North Carolina. He then traced the development of public schools, ending with a comparison of the state's expenditures on the segregated systems from the late nineteenth century to the present. Charts showing the distribution of the white and black population across the state, along with comparisons of expenditures for school buildings and teacher salaries over the years, accompanied his work. All in all, it was a narrative sympathetic to the state's support for a dual school system that showed—in raw figures at least—that the disparity in funding for the white and black systems had begun to close in recent years. His was not a scholarly presentation as much as it was a compilation of reference material. This kind of detail would later prove useful to illustrate the relative ease with which desegregation might be achieved in some mountain counties, where the black population was negligible, as well as the greater threat of white backlash in counties where the black population was nearly equal to or even greater than the white population.

While the Court's decision may have offended Coates, his displeasure did not show in his words. If he believed the Court was overstepping its bounds, he, like the governor, was too much a defender of the power of law to say so. He did remind the governor in his report that the decision should not have come as a surprise, especially in light of the Court's recent decisions that integrated his law school classes. "The spectre of a cloud the size of a man's hand in Justice [John Marshall] Harlan's dissent [in the *Plessy v. Ferguson* case upholding segregation] on the far off horizon of 1896 had been growing in the sky with court decisions handed down in quick succession since the Murray case of 1935. But all of these successive warnings in the swiftly cumulating cloud did not prepare the rank and file of people in North Carolina for the flash of lightning on the 17th of May. Many of us have been a little blinded by the light, and are groping for an answer to the question—Where do we go from here?"

He followed his own advice to his men and presented the range of reactions. Some see the Court's ruling as the destruction "of a social order handed down to them by their fathers," he wrote. "Others see it as a milestone in the struggle since slavery." Coates said the state would need to plot a middle course between what he called "extremists in the white and Negro races." To avoid a collision of these two forces, he expressed hope that the Court would allow time for implementation and take into account the differences among and within the states. As for North Carolina, the governor should look to the local schools boards that had been working with white and black educators and students. He called them "sources of light."

There were unmistakable Coatesian flourishes in the prose. "Abiding answers to the mysterious and tormenting questions, if found at all, will not be found in fighting phrases, or in stirring slogans, or defiant gestures. They will be found in the differing viewpoints and clashing opinions coming out of the mind and heart and conscience of our leaders and ourselves, colored with something of the gall and gorge of all of us, and tempered with the saving grace of charity that suffereth long and is kind."[29]

If the governor was looking for an easy path to maintain segregation without outright defiance of the Court, he didn't find it in Paul's analysis. Paul looked at the various options being discussed openly within the southern states to avoid integration and gave special attention to the notion growing in popularity in Virginia that the states abolish public schools in favor of a system of private schools funded with state vouchers. Paul carefully picked apart this strategy and others and concluded that the Court had clearly established that it would not tolerate any such subterfuge. Paul then turned to what North Carolina school boards could do to meet the Court's requirement.

It is impossible to read Paul's work without arriving at the conclusion that segregated schools were now a thing of the past, no matter what politicians from the courthouse to Congress might say or wish to do. The best that North Carolina, or any state for that matter, could hope for was that the Court would allow time to eliminate a dual school system. "It must be remembered," he wrote, "that it is the law of the *Brown* case that enforced segregation has been declared illegal." Anything that would follow in the way of pupil assignment plans, districting arrangements, or other locally applied measures, must advance that decision and be "a transitional means to meet this law, *not* as a method to preserve the status quo, permanently and totally."[30]

While he balanced his arguments in correct Institute fashion, there also is no mistaking Paul's conclusion that North Carolina should not shun the Court's request for further hearings, and would do so at its peril. None of the other states could present North Carolina's position as clearly or as well.

Simply avoiding the Court was not going to relieve the state of compliance any more than any other state. "The attorney general was a pretty smart guy," Paul said many years later, "but he came out with an astounding announcement that if the state filed amicus they could be made an immediate party. It was absolute nonsense. I wrote a paper refuting that although I didn't think it needed refuting."[31]

Coates respected the integrity of Paul's analysis. He did ask Henry Lewis to read behind him and suggest any edits necessary to sustain the Institute's reputation for neutrality. Anyone reading Paul closely and thoughtfully, however, could not escape the sum of his reasoning, or the sentiments of his boss. Coates wrote that the state "can take the course that the Supreme Court has made its decision—let it enforce it," a position that came close to the attitude of the governor and other hardliners. Or it could "swallow it without question, and proceed in the direction of mixed schools without delay and in unthinking acquiescence," which in many North Carolinians' minds was the position of the National Association for the Advancement of Colored People (NAACP), an organization that for some ranked right next to the Communist Party. The NAACP leadership was already circulating petitions calling on Umstead to integrate the schools immediately. Or—and this was Coates's obviously preferred option—the state could "take the course of playing for time in which to study plans of action making haste slowly enough to avoid the provocative litigation and strife which might be a consequence of defying the decision."[32]

On August 11 Governor Umstead took his first step to advance the state's position. He announced the creation of a special "advisory" committee to study the *Brown* decision and prepare recommendations for the 1955 General Assembly, which was due to convene in about six months. The nineteen men and women he chose for the task represented a broad cross-section of the state and included three black members. (They were the presidents of two state colleges and a home demonstration agent, all state employees.) The committee also included University President Gordon Gray, a local school board chairman, and three experienced and politically connected lawyers. The chairman was Thomas J. Pearsall of Rocky Mount, a former speaker of the state House. He was an attorney and an easterner whose vast family farming operation provided jobs and homes for hundreds of black workers and their families. The group met privately with the governor and Attorney General McMullan and took its commission to study the issue and find a solution to "preserve the state's public school system by having the support of the people." The first document they were handed in aid of their work was the report from the Institute of Government.[33]

After discharging his duty to the governor, Coates reprinted an abridged version of the report in the next available issue of *Popular Government.* Reading the copy along with the magazine's editor was Gladys Coates, who applied her own editorial touches. Her only substantive change was the choice of a cover picture for the issue. Paul wanted a photograph showing the words "Equal Justice Under Law" as they appear on the entablature over the entrance of the Supreme Court building in Washington. "I held out against it," Gladys later wrote. "It seemed silly and utterly foolish to me when feelings were running high and probably going even higher to go to this extreme. So we compromised on a distant view of the whole building on the front cover and a less obtrusive view of the entablature on the back."[34]

Coates made sure that the report received a wide circulation. Copies were mailed to the governors and attorneys general across the South with a request for reciprocation if any such work had been done in their states. (None had prepared anything like the Institute's report.) Newspaper editors on the Institute's mailing list received copies as did the Ford Foundation in New York, which was underwriting a news reporting service on school desegregation in the South. The report drew praise from southern moderates and compliments from the *New York Times,* which declared that "historically and statistically and for its educational value [it] is almost without parallel in this field of research."[35] Howard W. Odum, then in retirement from his years of scholarship on race and social issues, wrote to the governor to praise Coates. "I want to record how happy we are that Albert Coates and his Institute have done such a complete and satisfying job. It is not only the best thing that I have seen, but is better that I thought anyone could do."[36]

Paul returned to other assignments at the Institute, including an emphasis on press law. The response to *Brown* by the newspapers in the South had impressed on him the need to provide more assistance to reporters called on to write about such difficult issues. He continued to consult with Pearsall and also helped the attorney general's office prepare for the coming round of hearings once the decision was made to participate. Assistant Attorney General I. Beverly Lake thanked Paul for his contributions.

Three years earlier, as a law professor at Wake Forest College, Lake had vigorously defended the state's right to maintain an all-white law school, and he remained as steadfast as ever in his support of segregation and North Carolina's ability to withstand a legal challenge to its dual system. In November, just before the deadline for the filing of amicus briefs, Lake was completing the state's submission when he wrote to Paul to say that the report is "a very fine objective study. If the state elects to operate mixed schools I am sure that a great many valuable suggestions will be found in this report."[37]

Paul prevailed on his contacts at the Court to secure a ticket for a seat in the chambers in April 1955 when the justices heard the arguments for *Brown II*. Just days before, the North Carolina General Assembly had adopted a resolution arising from the advisory committee's work that said the integration of the schools would face such opposition from citizens that their operation would be impossible. Lake carried that theme forward and predicted the Court's decision would be the death knell for public schools in North Carolina. He used the responses to a questionnaire circulated to school superintendents and sheriffs as evidence of the violence, disruption, and trouble that were sure to come with integrated schools.

"I know that if a decree should be entered by this Court, or any other court, requiring the immediate intermixing of white and Negro children in the public schools of North Carolina, those schools will be in the gravest danger of abolition," Lake told the court. "And the friendliness and peace which now characterizes the relations of white and Negro North Carolinians would be supplanted by racial tensions and bitterness and antipathies unparalleled in our state since those terrible days which called forth the original Ku Klux Klan."[38]

Paul listened to Lake from his seat in the chambers and watched Justice Frankfurter unfold the maps that he and Coates had prepared for their report as Lake pleaded his case. From his perch on the bench, Frankfurter took notice of Paul and scribbled a note to him saying he hoped he would be arguing before the Court some day. Shortly thereafter a second note arrived from the justice observing Paul certainly could do a better job than Lake.[39]

Coates never visited the subject of school desegregation again after his work during the summer of 1954. Pearsall's committee was reconstituted in 1955—this time no black members were appointed—and Pearsall relied on lawyers on the committee and the attorney general's office for legal support. This group put forth a plan in 1956 that bore Pearsall's name in common usage and was adopted during a special legislative session that same year. The Pearsall Plan provided for the integration of schools, but with so-called "safety valves," leaving to local school boards the option to close schools. Public schools were not closed in North Carolina as they were in Virginia, but nothing more than token integration occurred for a decade, and only after suits were brought in federal courts to compel local school boards to respond to *Brown*.

Paul left the Institute in 1955 for a teaching job in Pennsylvania as Coates's attention was turning toward the construction of a new building for the Institute. It was a one-million-dollar structure that surpassed anything that even he had talked about when the possibility of a bigger and better headquarters for the Institute was advanced in the late 1940s. The person responsible for the new quarters, New York publishing executive Joseph Palmer Knapp, would never see the building that would bear his name when it opened in 1956. In fact, his ashes were buried in rural Currituck County even before the foundation that oversaw his fortune agreed to split the cost of the building with the state of North Carolina.

Knapp was born in 1864 and grew up amidst luxury and the music of the Methodist church. His mother, Fannie Palmer Knapp, was an organist and composer of hymns ("Blessed Assurance"); his father was a founder of Metropolitan Life Insurance Company. Knapp chose the publishing business and became a multi-millionaire. As a young man he developed multi-color presses and fast-drying ink, and later he created the Crowell Collier publishing empire, which at one time was one of the largest in the world. A devoted sportsman who loved hunting and fishing, he had a hand in the founding of Ducks Unlimited. Knapp first learned about the waters of Currituck Sound and the fine hunting along this north-south flyway in the early years of the century. He later bought 2,500 acres and a "lodge" built by North Carolina writer Thomas Dixon, who had made a fortune from the release of *Birth of A Nation*, the movie version of his book *The Clansman*. The house was on Mackey's Island, a peninsula dropping out of Virginia south of the border with North Carolina. It had thirty-seven rooms, resembled George Washington's Mount Vernon, and came with a swimming pool and nine-hole golf course. In time, Knapp kept his hunting retreat open year round and employed a staff of sixty. It was just one of three homes he maintained outside of New York City.

Beginning in the 1920s and on through nearly three decades, Knapp developed a keen interest in the welfare of the people who lived around and near his estate. The residents of the state's northeastern counties were generally poor and education was limited for children whose families eked out meager livings as farmers and watermen. This was a virtually forgotten area of the state isolated by geography and a lack of thoroughfares. Knapp devoted his time and a share of his fortune to improving the county's schools and helping the local public servants get the county's financial affairs on a solvent basis. At one time in the 1920s, he sent Currituck County a check for $15,000 so that the county commissioners could balance the books.[40]

Near the beginning of World War II, Knapp was in a duck blind with a young local man with whom he shared his concerns about the county. What could be done to improve the skill and competence of public officials responsible for the local welfare? he asked. His companion, Frank B. Aycock Jr., told him what he knew about something called the Institute of Government in Chapel Hill. Knapp inquired about the Institute of his friend state Senator Dudley Bagley, and in time Knapp wrote to Coates for information. Coates responded but then heard nothing more. Aycock left for military service, and it was five years before Coates once again heard from Knapp about his desire to see that society trained its public officials just as it trained its ministers, lawyers, doctors, nurses, and others charged with safeguarding the public. Why not those charged with the care of the body politic, Knapp had asked in his first inquiry.[41]

Knapp may have pursued his interest in the university, and the Institute, without Coates's knowledge. Late in his life, Coates wrote to Aycock that William Carmichael and Frank Graham had tried to interest Knapp in endowing some other university needs, such as a building to house a number of centers and institutes on the campus, before Knapp insisted that his donation focus on the Institute of Government.[42] In 1948, three years before Knapp's death, Coates gave Graham a proposal for a new building and was counting on Knapp for the money to make it possible, either through an endowment to support a building paid for by the state, or by a construction grant of $500,000, with the state putting up the balance with an appropriation in 1955.

The need was certainly great. The Institute's Franklin Street building was designed to house a staff of five, and the number of assistant directors was already double that and growing. The Institute had to "muscle in" on the campus for university facilities that were already overcrowded. Coates told Graham, "I believe that the gift of a building to wear his name would broaden his activities in improving governmental processes from the crossroads of the county of Currituck to the crossroads of the commonwealth of North Carolina in Chapel Hill."[43]

It was another three years before the proposal reached its final shape and gained university approval. By that time Knapp had died, but Graham, and then Gordon Gray, Graham's successor as president, carried on the sometimes delicate negotiations with Knapp's widow Margaret, her stepson, and the Knapp Foundation, which would be writing the check. Coates was hoping for $500,000 to use as an endowment to accompany a million-dollar building to be paid for by the state. The endowment would relieve the Institute of suffering from financial slights by the General Assembly, he told Gray. Apparently, that had been Joseph Knapp Jr.'s preference as well. Gray, however, preferred a plan that seemed to have the most favor with Mrs. Knapp—a $500,000 grant that would be matched by $500,000 from the state to pay for the building. In November 1952, Gray got a commitment from the foundation for a $500,000 matching grant.[44]

It was probably just as well that Graham and then Gray and Carmichael handled most of the conversations with the donors. Coates's concept of fund-raising was to present the entire program of the Institute and then find a donor that either he knew, or his friends knew, who would buy into his vision. That had worked in the early days when he was largely calling on those close at hand who knew him. Meanwhile, he failed miserably in impressing strangers. Coates never quite understood how to tailor his desires, or specific research projects, to the interests of prospective donors, as Howard Odum had done successfully in the early days of the Institute for Research in Social Science. The down side to Odum's approach was that it produced swings in funding when money designated for specific projects ran out. Coates wanted to avoid these fluctuations and presented his requests as all or nothing. His technique, as well as his own missionary zeal to pursue his plans to the exclusion of others in the university, did not sit well with the Rockefeller Foundation, where he struck out in repeated requests over a decade.

When Coates received word from President Gray confirming the foundation's decision, he borrowed the letter from the president's office and carried it home to show Gladys. "We have 'put on the garments of rejoicing,'" Coates wrote Gray a few days later, quoting scripture, "and find ourselves quite willing to believe there are moments in this life when there is as much truth as poetry in the prophet's description of times 'when the morning stars sang together and all the sons of God shouted for joy.'"[45] He compared the succession of emotions that broke over them as they recalled the years of struggle for the Institute to listening to the Boston Symphony Orchestra's performance of Maurice Ravel's "Bolero" many years earlier when they were living in Cambridge.

The building that the foundation approved would accommodate up to twenty assistant directors, along with their support staff, and would have classrooms and assembly rooms, as well as a dormitory capable of accommodating up to 140 guests. The residential space remained as critical as it had been twenty years earlier, as there still were only limited hotel accommodations available in Chapel Hill. An auditorium with seating for up to 350 was added as plans progressed. The design was the work of the university's preferred architect at the time, Watts Carr's firm in Durham. One of Carr's men rendered a contemporary look for the building, but the one adopted carried through the pseudo-Colonial character of the campus buildings erected since the 1920s. It was believed that as the Institute building would be the first to be seen by visitors arriving at the eastern gateway to the campus, it should not contrast so dramatically with existing structures.[46]

There was some discussion about the site. Carmichael had preferred a location closer to the center of the campus near the Woollen Gymnasium. Coates and others lobbied for the hilltop on Raleigh Road where the State Highway Patrol training camp was located. That spot was distant from other university buildings and considered "out in the country," a fact that bothered Coates not at all. He saw the new building as just one of several that would later be needed for Institute work and he wanted room to expand. "I believe the Institute of Government is just beginning to hit its stride," Coates wrote to President Gray, "that the building now proposed will be the center of a cluster of buildings in the years to come; that the present working staff is only the beginning of a greater working staff; and that like the poor, but not the poor in heart, we will be forever with you asking for more and better facilities for rooting the University of North Carolina in the soil of the cities, the counties and the state of North Carolina."[47]

Coates's ambitions knew no bounds. After more than a decade within the arms of the university, he now saw the Institute as more than a resource center for mayors seeking interpretation of a statute, a training school for police officers and sanitation directors, a clearinghouse for information, and an accurate record keeper and occasional research arm of the General Assembly. The Institute was becoming something much larger and reaching further into the body politic than even Coates could have imagined in the early days. His "men" were now known around the state and in Raleigh for their expertise, and some of those who had spent time at the Institute had moved on to positions of influence. Among them was former assistant director Paul Johnston, who was Governor Luther Hodges's chief administrative officer. Johnston had moved to Raleigh after Hodges was unexpectedly elevated to the governor's office on the death of William Umstead in November 1954. Shortly after taking his new oath, Hodges, a political novice before he was elected lieutenant governor, called Coates and asked him to send someone who could help him govern.

When the Institute had come into the university in 1942, Coates called it the "public service department" of the university. Now it was much more. The Institute was a university within the university. As William Aycock was about to succeed Robert B. House as chancellor in 1957, Coates told him, "I caught the vision of the Institute of Government growing into a new University of Public Officials in the framework of the old University of North Carolina."[48] The new building was just the first that would serve his grand vision.

The arrangement of the new building was shaped more by the men who were handling the daily assignments and work than by Coates, who, along with Gladys, had handled every detail of the Franklin Street offices. A committee composed of assistant directors worked with the architects to plot the location of the offices, the classrooms, and the space for the support staff. The result was a building with an auditorium connected by an intersecting section. The south wing of the main building housed the dormitory while the north wing included offices for the staff and library. The classrooms and more offices were in an east wing that connected the other two wings to an auditorium. Once the various functions of the building were satisfied, then the exterior design was conceived. It was the same process that Coates had objected to so strenuously when John Webb first sat down with him and Gladys to plan their house on Hooper Lane.

Coates was involved with the new quarters, of course, but during the period of construction he was more preoccupied with arrangements for a collection of murals that Margaret Knapp had determined should be part of the building even before the foundation board had given final approval for the grant. The artist for the project was Francis Vandeveer Kughler, a New Yorker whose work she favored. There were other conditions, too. She wanted the university to display antique furnishings, rugs, and even the wood paneling from the drawing room of the Knapp's New York River House apartment in the university's new Ackland Museum of Art. The Kughler murals, however, were the focus of her attention and that of others in Chapel Hill.

Kughler, who produced a number of paintings of Margaret Knapp and her family and friends, was known for his murals, cityscapes, landscapes, and nudes. The Institute project, estimated to cost $100,000, was an extraordinary commission for any artist. There would be fourteen murals in all. In the end, twelve of them were eleven feet by eight feet, one was eleven by seven feet, and the final panel was eight by eight feet. Kughler would spend nearly five years on the project, working in his New York studio; in Williamsburg, Virginia; in Person Hall on the Chapel Hill campus; in Manteo, North Carolina; and in England.[49]

Carmichael wanted the murals to focus on the evolution of government in North Carolina and to feature the broad reach of the various forms of governmental authorities or councils over the centuries. He suggested they begin with a council of Native American chiefs and include images from colonial rule under Governor Tryon, display the early capitols of North Carolina, and end with a panel showing the meeting of the General Assembly in 1955.[50] In the end a panel of thirty art aficionados, historians, and others, including Gladys and Albert Coates, agreed on the subject of each panel.

Just where to hang these panels was resolved only after Mrs. Knapp arranged for immediate construction of the building's auditorium, which had originally been scheduled for another phase of construction. Once the dimensions of the auditorium were determined, Kughler began to paint. The finished works deviated from Carmichael's vision in that they focused on actual and imagined occasions in the state's history. North Carolina's English heritage was represented with panels of Queen Elizabeth and Sir Walter Raleigh and another showing Charles II and the Lords Proprietors of the Colonial era. One panel depicted Lafayette being entertained in a quintessential antebellum plantation setting, while another illustrated the charge of Pickett's brigade at Gettysburg. Additional panels represented the founding of the university as well as, more generally, education, art, industry, and even the space age. By the time Kughler turned his attention to current events the nation's first team of astronauts was using the university's Morehead Planetarium for part of their training.

Kughler placed in many of the panels the portraits of noteworthy current North Carolinians and dressed them in period-appropriate attire. For example, Frank and Marian Graham are among those watching as the cornerstone is laid for Old East, the first campus building, in the late eighteenth century; Mr. and Mrs. Knapp are the host and hostess for Lafayette when he visited the state in 1825; Albert and Gladys are part of the *Pageant of Dreamers* mural, along with writers Thomas Wolfe and Paul Green. Benjamin Swalin, the long-time director of the North Carolina Symphony, was included in the same panel as Playmakers founder Fredrick Koch, who, with a fanciful array of figures from fable and history, is directing a motion picture being filmed by Cecil B. deMille. The Cone brothers, Ben and Ceasar, are included in a mural entitled *Industrial Awakening* along with other friends of the Institute, J. Spencer Love, James G. Hanes, and Julian Price.

Paul Green spent some time with Kughler in Manteo, where actors in costume from his outdoor drama *The Lost Colony* posed for the artist. Green was struck by the homogeneity of those portrayed as contributors to the state's life and culture. He pointed out to Kughler that all of the principals were white. The few African Americans that he included were shown serving drinks in the shade of the old oaks on the plantation or driving a carriage and holding a lantern in the panel illustrating the Halifax Resolves. He told Kughler that certainly leading black educators, or at least a black schoolchild, would be appropriate. When he returned for a later look, he discovered that Kughler had included Dr. James E. Shepard of Durham, the founder of North Carolina College for Negroes (later North Carolina Central University) in Durham, in a far corner of the *Crusade for Education* panel.[51]

The final panel had nothing to do with North Carolina. Kughler produced it on his own, and its subject matter became something of a problem for the Institute's management. He called it *Pleiades, Mystery of the Future*, and it featured seven identical images of women in diaphanous gowns floating among the constellations. The historical panels were arranged chronologically around the walls of the auditorium, but *Pleiades* was placed in a commanding position above the center of the stage. In time, the images of the alluring statuesque figures—who all closely resembled a woman Kughler was seeing while he worked on the Chapel Hill campus—became such a distraction for the audience that an oversized North Carolina flag was strategically hung so as to obscure "Seven-fold Sue," as this mural was known by insiders at the Institute.[52]

The design and then the preparations for relocating to the new building brought to the fore a number of long-standing and smoldering issues among the staff about the day-to-day management of the Institute. The work assignments of staff members, the interaction of assistant directors, Coates's unilateral acceptance of large and small projects from outside, plus the routine administration of the Institute, were all on the table as Coates began a series of weekly staff meetings early in 1956. (He called these meetings for Saturday mornings at nine, and some sessions extended into the afternoon.) The new building was not due to be occupied until some time in the late summer or early fall. Some things just could not wait, however, as the university's new president, William Friday, and his staff were due to move into the Institute's former building on Franklin Street.

Coates sat through sessions of scorching criticism of his unstructured, *ad hoc* style of management. The year before Coates had asked Donald Hayman, whose specialty was personnel management, to prepare a memorandum on the qualities of a good supervisor. It is not clear from the minutes whether Coates wanted Hayman's advice to use himself, or if he planned to use it in the hiring of a new man to replace William Cochrane, who had left in 1955 to join the staff of the state's newest United States senator, Kerr Scott.

These staff meetings were open-ended collegial affairs where the men freely spoke their minds. Some complained that Coates took projects without first determining if the Institute had either the manpower or the expertise to produce good work. Others worried that the staff was losing its sense of unity of purpose as it grew larger and the range of work expanded. Royal Shannonhouse, a young man Coates often dragooned into buying his breakfast for their meetings at the Carolina Inn, told the group in June that he understood the difficulties of working with Coates but had simply resigned himself to bending his own ways to suit his boss. He wasn't going to try to change the director. Henry Lewis, the most senior member of the group, replied that everyone had done that, but men had always maintained their sense of purpose and devotion to the Institute.[53]

Coates was frank with his men. Administration was something that had "been either non-existent, or a sideline activity after the day's work was over and the week's work was done, or a red-headed stepchild with all of the dislike, distaste and neglect that apparently inspired this proverb." Coates insisted that he had always put the Institute's mission first, buying books before he hired a librarian, financing before he had a budget, messing up the floors before hiring a janitor. "I have often said that the question is not whether I am a good administrator or bad administrator, but whether I am any administrator at all."[54] Coates promised to give attention to the concerns and acknowledged that his shortcomings became a greater issue with a staff of fifteen or more, larger budgets, and operations touching all levels of government.

As he would often do on these occasions, Coates launched into a retelling of the history of the Institute as if he could imprint upon each man his own story and thus ensure continued operation. Lately, he had begun observing that the modest program that had grown out of his law school classroom to produce the Institute of Government now had a professional staff that was considerably larger than the entire law school faculty. "We are pioneering in several areas," he said, and went on to recount his vision of "the University of Public Officials within the framework of the old university, courses in local government, and training of students for public service in state and local government." He said there were ongoing discussions with the political science department about a joint program for students seeking an advanced degree in public administration. Institute men were teaching academic courses in University schools and departments on public health, city planning, and a range of other subjects.

As the day of the exit from the building on Franklin Street approached, many of these issues remained open for discussion, but attention changed to the task of relocating from one building to another. Coates began thinking about a formal dedication for the Joseph Palmer Knapp Building, as it was to be called. He proposed that an informal opening be held on October 12, 1956, the anniversary of the laying of the cornerstone at Old East, to be followed by a continuing program of dedication for his new "University of Public Officials" with events that recognized important dates in the University of North Carolina history. The governor and the council of state should come for an inspection on January 15, 1957, the same date that in 1795 the governor and council of state inspected the facilities of the university. If Mrs. Knapp was available, he wanted to hold the formal dedication on February 12. That was the date the first student had arrived in Chapel Hill in 1795. When the building's ceremonial cornerstone was put in place, he wanted it filled with photographs of the entire staff, of significant donors, and of the seats of local government—courthouses and city halls—from around the state.

The actual relocation to the large, handsome new home for the Institute of Government came just about two months after Albert Coates celebrated his sixtieth birthday. And it took place without the months-long array of ceremonies. The program he outlined would wait until the completion of the murals. Coates knew he was short on time if he was to accomplish his ultimate goal of bringing the Institute into the law school. He hoped to teach for some time, at least another decade, but the state's and the university's rule for administrators was clear. They must relinquish their jobs at age sixty-five. That date would come all too soon for Albert Coates.

TWELVE

Getting Off The Train

1959–1962

WHEN ALBERT COATES stepped forward in the late spring of 1960 to accept an honorary doctor of laws degree from Wake Forest College in Winston-Salem, he was at the peak of his career and the reputation of the Institute's work had carried him to venues across the nation as public officials and those who worked with them wanted to hear what he had to say. A few years earlier, the state of Georgia had opened its own Institute of Law and Government after sending a team to North Carolina to see what Coates had wrought.

The Institute's building in Chapel Hill was becoming known as something other than "that new building down by Woollen Gym with all the cop cars around it."[1] Law enforcement training for the State Highway Patrol and Wildlife Resource officers continued to occupy much of the staff time, but there also were a host of civilians around. The staff was busy with private citizens and public officials who were counting on help to resolve difficult questions about reorganization of state government, changes to the constitution, a major overhaul of an antiquated court system, changes in the tax code, and finding ways for municipal leaders to handle the problems of growing and expanding cities. Albert Coates's "classroom" was full to overflowing.

With a professional staff of nearly twenty to take care of business, Coates had reverted to a travel schedule reminiscent of his early days in the law school, when he accepted speaking engagements at virtually any whistle stop accessible from Raleigh. Now, airplanes carried him from coast to coast. Within a few months he had spoken to the National Association of County Officials in Portland, Oregon, and the American Bar Association meeting in Los Angeles. On the way he stopped to consult with folks at the University of Colorado. He was on the dais at the League of Virginia Counties meeting in Roanoke and participated in the Washington, D.C., meeting of the President's Committee on Traffic Safety. Then there were plenty of invitations to speak within North Carolina. Public welfare officers heard him in Raleigh and he drove to Kings Mountain to give a presentation on traffic laws. On one occasion, he gathered up two carloads of men from the Institute to meet with city and county leaders in Wilmington to fulfill a long-standing, and much-delayed, promise to consult with local leaders about the consolidation of municipal and county governments.[2]

His role as roving ambassador was made possible through the patience and generosity of Henry Brandis Jr., his dean at the law school. The man who had once been his protégé, the first member of the Institute staff and one on whom Coates regularly heaped praise for his forbearance in those hard times, was now his boss. Brandis gave Coates leave with full pay to focus on the Institute's work and brought into the law school men from the Institute to teach criminal law, domestic relations law, legislation, and municipal corporations, the courses that remained Coates's stock in trade. Coates's surrogates had already been doing much of the work in the classroom for the director; Brandis just made it official. They still had no status of their own in the law school, however.

Brandis was just one of Coates's "boys" who were making names for themselves. As Coates was picking up his honorary degree, Terry Sanford was capturing the Democratic Party's nomination for governor. Malcolm Seawell, another man from the early days, was attorney general. He also had been a contender in the 1960 gubernatorial primary. Other alumni were working under Seawell in the attorney general's office, while Dillard Gardner was the marshal of the state supreme court. In addition to picking up Paul Johnston as his chief administrative officer, Governor Luther Hodges had hired Ed Scheidt as his motor vehicles commissioner when Scheidt retired from the FBI. The Institute also had former assistant directors working as city attorneys or city managers in communities around the state.

The dedication of the new building was long in coming. When the staff moved into the new quarters in October 1956, Coates was unable to fulfill the historic program he had first outlined. One reason for the delay was the difficulty in finding a date to accommodate Margaret Knapp, whose health was fragile. By the time the building opened, she was traveling with a private nurse. She died in 1958 but had lived to receive a grand tour of the building. On that occasion, Coates turned on every light, from the lower-level offices to the cupola atop the administration wing, and drove her around it in the twilight.

Francis Kughler did not begin his work until the early part of 1956. He was still working on sketches for the second of the twelve huge panels with life-size figures when the building was first occupied. By the fall of 1960, his work was complete and the murals were all hung in the Institute's auditorium, where they became the drawing card for the long-awaited dedication, during which guests would witness their unveiling.

The event took place in late November 1960 and was produced in classic Coatesian style. He organized the program along the lines of the mass meetings that he favored in the 1930s. It was a gathering of government leaders spread over four days, with attendees asked to be on hand when their congressional districts were featured. Coates sent invitations to public servants from throughout city and county governments, to state officials in Raleigh, to the congressional delegation, and to friends of the Institute that he had accumulated over more than thirty years of its service. The state's senior senator, Sam J. Ervin Jr., stayed for the entire affair and day after day sat through the same lengthy introductions made by his old college chum Albert. From time to time, he tugged at Coates's sleeve to remind him that he had missed an anecdote or joke that was part of his presentation. The mighty production concluded on Wednesday, November 30, with Governor Hodges accepting for the state the Institute's million-dollar headquarters. His appearance was made all the more special since he was about to be named Secretary of Commerce by President-elect John F. Kennedy. Just the day before, Governor-elect Sanford had met privately with Kennedy to press his case for Hodges's nomination.[3]

"Albert Coates caught hold of a vision more than thirty years ago," Hodges said, "and he has never let it go. He dreamed, and by his own unceasing backbreaking efforts, his dreams were formed into substance. They were given life. We see a part of the culminating substance of that dream here in this lovely and useful building. We can also see a realization of that dream in one hundred counties of this State, in every courthouse, in every city hall, in the General Assembly, in every state government office in Raleigh—in every place where there are public officials. All of these officials are better public officials because of the work and labors of the Institute of Government. Because of the Coates dream come true, the administration of public affairs in North Carolina—at all levels—has been lifted up to standards of excellence second to none in the nation."[4]

Coates had always reveled in such occasions that brought the state's leading political figures together, and this event was perhaps the most meaningful of them all. He knew that he would not have another opportunity to showcase himself and the Institute in such a way. His retirement day was drawing near. University administrators had to step down on July 1 following their sixty-fifth birthdays; Coates would turn sixty-five in August 1961. If there was any disappointment for Coates as he orchestrated the grand meeting, it was the absence of FBI Director J. Edgar Hoover. Coates treasured his nearly thirty years of association with the nation's leading lawman, and Hoover's presence would have been an acknowledgment of that union. It also would have helped Coates close a troubling misunderstanding with Hoover and his top aides. The disturbance in the relationship was largely a clash of egos, but Coates believed his integrity had been questioned and he could not let that go unchallenged.

On numerous occasions, in print and in public meetings, Coates had been generous in his credit to the FBI for its assistance to the Institute in the early days when the training of law officers was the Insititute's leading service to the state. During World War II, Coates had printed a striking patriotic graphic illustrating the FBI's role in the war effort and circulated it widely in North Carolina at a time when the agency was being criticized for taking men off the front lines for service at home. Over the years, the Institute had mounted elaborate displays of the work of the training schools that highlighted the contribution of FBI agents who had brought hands-on training in scientific methods of crime detection to county sheriffs and local police chiefs. Beginning in the mid-1930s and continuing until the early 1950s, the FBI had reciprocated and had invited Coates to lecture on the law of search and seizure at the National Police Academy. When Albert and Gladys were in Washington, they were treated royally by the agency, which put a car and driver at their disposal. One year, their driver was also the chauffeur for U.S. Supreme Court Justice Harlan Stone and he provided Gladys with an insider's view of the Court while he drove her to Annapolis for the day.

In March 1947, Coates had personally delivered a copy of the Institute's guidebooks for law enforcement to Hoover and to Hugh H. Clegg, Hoover's man at the academy. A picture of that presentation became one of Coates's prized possessions and was prominent in what Coates called the FBI Law Enforcement Room in the Franklin Street building. Later that summer, while Albert and Gladys were vacationing on the Outer Banks, which was their habit at that time of year, Albert got a call from Clegg, who demanded that he meet him immediately in Chapel Hill. Coates obliged only to suffer through one of the most harrowing days of his life.[5]

The Saturday meeting began at 10 a.m. and concluded at 6 p.m. without a break for lunch. Coates did much of the talking as he responded to Clegg, who had arrived with a list of grievances against Coates and the Institute. Generally, the complaints were founded in Clegg's belief that the Institute had not properly acknowledged the contribution of the FBI. Moreover, he said, Coates had slighted the FBI in the feature articles about the Institute that had appeared in national magazines and had generally proved to be an ingrate as the Institute had grown and developed a national reputation. None of the allegations involved the exposure of national secrets or complicated any delicate FBI criminal investigations. Nothing even sniffed of criminal wrongdoing. The complaints were about image and touched on whether Coates was in league with Northwestern University, which had developed a law-enforcement training program that was competing with the National Police Academy for attendance from local law enforcement agencies around the nation.[6]

Indeed, in 1946 and 1947, Coates had worked closely with the Academy's competitor. The Institute had called on Northwestern University, as well as the FBI, for help with the Patrol School, and Coates had a job offer out to one of Northwestern's faculty. All in all, the perceived slights and charges of infidelity to the FBI appeared to be nothing more than Hoover's attempt to discipline Coates and keep him solidly in the director's camp.

Hoover would not tolerate an infidelity and jealously guarded his connections with graduates of the FBI's academy. Through them, he developed an intelligence network that reached into every city and county and most state policing agencies. Moreover, he dominated the International

Association of Chiefs of Police, and his liaison with the association, Quinn Tamm, who worked behind the scenes for the election of association officers whose work pleased the director. Those who pleased him won his quiet support. Those who didn't, such as the chief of the Los Angeles Police Department, were blackballed.[7]

Coates, on the other hand, was equally proud of the Institute's role in raising the level of professionalism of law enforcement in North Carolina. He could easily have taken more credit for the Institute than it deserved when speaking to public groups, although he never seemed to miss an opportunity to tout the Institute's association with the FBI. Nonetheless, while Gladys could edit the written Albert, there was no one to correct the spoken Albert.

Regardless of whether the accusations were valid, the meeting was a crushing blow to Coates. Clegg did not appear to be as troubled about the affair as Coates was; a few days after the meeting, he asked Coates to write a letter on his behalf to his ailing mother. For Coates, however, the very thought that the FBI did not hold him in the same high regard as he did the director and his agency was more than he could abide. Clegg's complaints—Coates called them "mud-splashing charges"—questioned his integrity, his loyalty, his honor as a gentleman, and just about everything else that Coates held dear. He took extraordinary measures to rebut the allegations and prepared a fifty-page response. In it he wrote: "My flesh crawls at the thought that these slanderous charges are lying in a file in FBI Washington offices today—(the word 'lying' carries a double connotation here), a time bomb ready to explode in my face or in my back if my integrity should ever be questioned in a direct or collateral proceeding in the future."[8]

According to internal FBI memoranda, Clegg and others, including Hoover, closed their doors to Coates. Coates continued to lecture at the FBI Academy, but he no longer enjoyed the easy access he once had to the director's inner circle. In what may have been an effort to reaffirm his loyalty, Coates threw himself into a lawsuit to defend the town of Weldon, North Carolina, where the city council was sued by a private citizen who questioned the town's payment of expenses for its police chief to attend courses at the National Police Academy. Coates won the case before the North Carolina Supreme Court and immediately sent word of his success to Hoover and Clegg. He later forwarded to them a copy of a *North Carolina Law Review* article on the court's decision.[9] He received a polite reply from Hoover, but FBI records show that Hoover and Clegg carefully avoided seeing Coates when he was in town. Penciled at the bottom of one memorandum, in which the director is told that Coates wanted four hours of his time to talk about the meeting with Clegg, is a notation by Hoover that reads: "It proves wisdom of my decision not to see him. I certainly couldn't waste any such amount of time."[10]

Although deeply troubling for Coates personally, the estrangement from the FBI didn't spill over into the Institute's business. That was not the case with the public embarrassment that surrounded the release in February 1959 of a state auditor's report on the Institute's financial records. Institute men were wrapping up their week at the General Assembly in Raleigh when they learned that the auditor had found "irregularities" in the Institute's accounts. Assistant director Milton Health Jr. was on his way to lunch when he saw the headlines in the *Raleigh Times*, the city's afternoon newspaper. He lost his appetite for a meal, as did others on the staff who were stunned to read the news stories that challenged the Institute's spotless reputation. Only the arrival of the weekend recess of the legislature relieved the Raleigh men of immediate embarrassment and the difficult task of explaining how the agency that had taken it upon itself to teach local officials proper accounting methods had failed to learn its own lessons.

State auditor Henry Bridges was sympathetic to Coates's predicament and took assistant director Joe Hennessee into his office and "soothed him" when he showed up at the auditor's office to get a copy of the report.[11] Bridges assured Hennessee that no money was missing and the matter turned on the Institute's sloppy bookkeeping as well as a failure to promptly deposit money collected for room fees and book sales. There was no criminal liability involved, but because the files were such a mess the auditor had to report a discrepancy of $5,064.32. The amount was significant, but not alarming when compared to the Institute's overall budget of about $360,000. Yet, if these same discrepancies had been discovered in a city hall or courthouse elsewhere in the state, the future employment of the local finance officer would be in question.

The root of the problem was Coates's failure to improve administrative procedures, which had long been a weakness in the Institute's operations. Some of the undocumented expenses arose from the staff's rush to prepare an elaborate display for a visiting group of county officials from across the nation. Assistant directors and other employees had worked night and day to gather photographs and publications to build a visual account of the Institute's programs and services that Coates wanted to use to impress his visitors. Certain questionable expenses resulted from Coates's efforts to help an assistant whose child was ill and required attention while she worked at the Institute at night. Coates used Institute funds to pay for a baby sitter and rent a television so the woman could remain on duty at odd hours. Other undocumented items included Coates's travel expenses, the purchase of football tickets for Institute guests, and sundry items that looked dubious without the necessary receipts and justification.

When the auditor's report became public, Coates was literally speechless; he claimed he had laryngitis. In a statement that was released in his name, he took the responsibility for the errors and said he would personally cover the undocumented claims. William Carmichael, the university's chief financial officer, explained away as much of the embarrassment as he could and stressed that the university was a good steward of state funds. Meanwhile, Bridges demanded immediate payment of the amount in question, and Coates delivered a check for $5,100. Most of the money came from a friend in Smithfield who wired Coates that he could have as much as he needed.[12]

The newspaper headlines created alarm and problems for everyone. George Esser was conducting a training session for municipal finance officers when the story broke. He later wrote Coates to say that if the Institute had been using the very procedures he was teaching that day, the problem would never have occurred. "I have always felt that the Institute, like Caesar's wife, should be above suspicion, and that our internal methods of management were completely inconsistent with the methods which we taught governmental officials."[13] The men in Raleigh were especially troubled. "Sitting on the firing line in Raleigh was definitely a traumatic experience," Hennessee reported to Coates. He said he nervously awaited the moment when the report would be raised in floor debate. To his relief, it never was.

Coates took his medicine from editorial writers without comment. Most newspapermen were generally sympathetic and took into account Coates's reputation for eccentricities. His friends at the *Greensboro Daily News* said, "Albert Coates, like the rest of us, is utterly human and his Institute has suffered such growing pains as to warrant closer attention to practices and procedures of management at home as well as abroad in

North Carolina."[14] Coates eventually submitted documentation for all of the expenses, some of which should have been paid out of the Burlington Fund that had been set up to cover such contingencies. In the end, Coates received approval for the expenses along with a full refund of the money he paid plus $438.79.[15]

The public quickly forgot the incident, but not the staff. The auditor's report exacerbated the Institute's unresolved management problems. Staff members were not only angry that the Institute had been embarrassed publicly and unnecessarily, but that Coates had not taken them into his confidence and informed them about problems with the accounts. Coates and the university had been notified about a potentially damaging report two months before it became public. Coates did not share the concern with his people so they could prepare for the bad publicity that was sure to come. "We have been assured on numerous occasions by Mr. Coates that the Institute is a partnership operation," Clyde Ball reported in a memorandum to his boss, "but here is a matter of great importance to the Institute, and many of us have not only not been informed, it appears that careful steps have been taken to make certain that information did not leak through to us by rumor."[16]

The uproar over the auditor's report was further evidence that the Institute was outgrowing its founder. This was no longer an enterprise that could be run part-time with one man managing the budget, directing the staff, presenting a public face of the program, and all the while holding down responsibilities at the law school. The auditor's report exposed unresolved tensions that ran deep. The corps of men that Coates had recruited set high standards for themselves, and for the Institute. The lawyers among them, and that included nearly everyone, had put their careers at risk in joining the Institute. Their future was not guaranteed at the Institute. Picking up the practice of law after an absence of several years was not an easy matter.

Coates's hyperbole offended those who believed that the Institute's future was jeopardized when the staff was unable to deliver on the promises made by the director. While the Institute received a wide array of publications (magazines, newspapers, and books dealing with local government), it was not the clearinghouse for information that Coates advertised. Publications and training programs were promoted, but never printed or organized. Esser told Coates he was taken aback by the "skeptical attitude taken of the Institute by many of the local officials to whom I talked at the League [of Municipalities] meeting in Winston-Salem. They have come to think that we talk a lot and offer little."[17] Esser expressed the concerns of others that the Institute's mission needed greater definition and a comprehensive plan of work adopted by the staff.

Esser was echoing words spoken decades earlier by men like House and Graham and others who had tried to find the boundaries in Coates's vision for the Institute. They failed, and Esser would fail, too. There were no boundaries in Coates's mind. The Institute moved like a spreading flow of water, touching everything. His university of public officials welcomed all disciplines.

The program was changing, too, beyond what Coates had envisioned. The primary focus of providing basic research and meeting the training needs of government remained as strong as ever, but local officials increasingly wanted a broader kind of support than simple interpretation of the law. Men like Esser and Philip Green Jr. had been moving into areas of policy and management of public administration that took the Institute beyond the "trade school" style of instruction that worked for new police officers. Esser was developing an expertise in urban affairs. A ten-week program in municipal management, taught on a series of three-day weekends, that he launched in 1955 was considered a must for aspiring city administrators. Green's specialty was planning and zoning, and along with Esser and Jake Wicker, another assistant director, he had helped write a new North Carolina law to facilitate municipal annexation. The legislation, written at the Institute for a state study commission, became a model for other states and remained in place without change for more than forty years. As a result, North Carolina cities avoided the balkanization of metropolitan areas that occurred in other states where satellite towns had incorporated to avoid annexation and had limited their growth. V. Lee Bounds was another innovative staff member who was building what some considered an institute within the Institute as he expanded services dealing with probation and corrections.

Esser and J. Alex McMahon broke the old model of focusing efforts on functions of government, say tax collection, rather than forms of government. Esser and McMahon had developed specialties in city and county government, respectively. McMahon's work with the counties had led to a fractious break with Coates when the director began to limit the range of services that McMahon believed the counties deserved. McMahon finally left the Institute to become the director of the North Carolina Association of County Commissioners. He never spoke with Coates again.[18]

Esser's work on urban affairs extended into other university departments such as political science, sociology, and social work. These were informal arrangements, and Coates encouraged Esser's efforts, harboring a notion that some day the Institute might take over the political science department. Coates did object when Esser proposed that he become more formally aligned with the Institute for Research in Social Science (IRSS). "His dream was involvement by invitation with control given to the Institute," Esser said.[19]

By associating himself with these other departments and programs, Esser brought home to the Institute a $130,000 grant from the Ford Foundation. It was part of a larger grant to IRSS for its work on cities, with the Institute of Government serving as the distributor of the information that was collected. Coates was amazed that Esser had landed the grant, and bewildered at why his own efforts with major foundations had always come up short. "He never got anything from Ford or any of the other [large] foundations, and it damn near killed him that they couldn't see Israel. He used to say that people did or did not see Israel, and Israel was the Institute."[20]

These adventures into new territory and expanding programming only encouraged Coates's vision of building his university of public officials within the University of North Carolina. While the frame of reference was changing—the university was not the compact institution it had been twenty years earlier—Coates understood that growth, which the Knapp Building had accelerated. The number of people attending events and participating in instruction had grown tenfold since 1956. Sixteen thousand people stayed overnight in the Institute's dormitory during the 1959–1960 academic year. This growth seemed to have no end, and Coates was quick to preserve his options. When he spotted surveyors hammering stakes into the ground in a wooded area just a hundred yards from the Knapp Building, he asked what they were doing. Picking a site for new dormitories, came the reply. "This is my land," Coates answered, ignoring the workers' rejoinder that they thought the land belonged to the university. Coates appealed to the chancellor, William B. Aycock, who allowed Coates to present his case to the university's building and grounds committee, whose job it was to pick the sites for new campus buildings.

When Coates appeared before the committee, he outlined his vision for the future of the Institute. The Knapp building was the start, he said. More buildings would follow. Did he have the money for these buildings, he was asked? No, Coates replied, but the Institute was growing and had always needed more space. The committee told Coates they would take his report "under advisement," a reply that Coates recognized as a polite brush-off. He quickly asked for a few minutes more and related a story he had heard years ago during his visit to the home of President Abbott Lawrence Lowell of Harvard University. Coates said he heard Lowell describe an optimist as "one who sees a light that isn't there" and a pessimist as one "who blows out that light." Recalling the incident later, Coates said he told the committee that "on that land out there I see buildings that are not there, and I am asking this committee not to tear those buildings down. They didn't."[21]

Coates was a man with unfinished business and that made the approaching end to his time at the Institute of Government all the more distressing. During the Depression, he had dropped his ambition of developing a program of civic education for young people. Also left behind was his dream of creating a network of civic groups to engage them more fully in the process of government. At the top of his list, however, was the merger of the Institute of Government with the law school. Whenever he told the story of the Institute he related how it had grown out of his law school classroom and had found its footing in the Law School Association. What he had never been able to do was to convince others of his vision of the law school and the Institute as one seamless element in the university's fabric of extension. He often said that if he had had his way there never would have been an Institute of Government but there would have been the most unusual law school in the nation.

Merger was always on his mind. During the early stages of planning for the Knapp Building he had proposed locating it behind Manning Hall and connecting it to the law school and the political science department with tunnels and walkways and a common library to create a center for law and government. In Coates's mind, the law school and the Institute were one and should "fuse into a single growing tree with the sap rising through it from the tap root to the top of the farthest leaf on the limb with the farthest reach," as he described it to Brandis in the early part of 1962. He even allowed as how he would forsake the Institute's name and even some members of the staff, as long as the work of the Institute was allowed to continue in the law school.[22]

With Brandis as dean, Coates believed he had his best chance of reaching the goal that had eluded him since the early 1930s. Certainly he felt closer to Brandis than any of his predecessors. The two men had worked alongside one another when Brandis shared Coates's vision for the Institute and had supplied Coates with one of his favorite quotes: "The difficulty of the Institute," Brandis said, "is there are no paths; the beauty of it is there are no fences." After Brandis was promoted to dean in 1949, he had asked William Aycock, then a member of the law faculty, to work with Coates to forge a closer relationship between the Institute and the law school. Out of that had come recognition in the university catalog of cooperative arrangements between the two and "research professor"—a status short of authentic professorship—as designations for Institute professional staff members. When Aycock later became chancellor, he obtained trustee approval in 1957 for the Institute's professional staff to become professors of public law and government, an important distinction that enhanced the Institute's standing within the university and aided in recruitment of staff members, since it conferred on faculty members the security of academic tenure.

In Coates's mind, and apparently only in his mind, each advance had strengthened his call for merger. In 1959, the possibility of merger provoked debate within both the faculty of the law school and within the staff of the Institute. When the votes were counted, neither the law school faculty nor the Institute staff looked favorably upon the possibility. The issue remained the differences between the role and function of a law school and those of a service and research institution. Asked anew were questions about whether an organization designed to teach the law to full-time students could maintain its national academic standing and coexist with an organization devoted principally to an off-campus constituency interested in training and applied research. More importantly for assistant director John Sanders was whether the Institute would survive to pursue the work for which it was intended if a merger took place. Inevitably, Sanders told Coates, the Institute would be subordinated to the needs and requirements of a law school and, in time, lose its unique identity and its purpose. Merger, he said, "would be for us to take the short road to oblivion."[23]

That seemed to be the end of the discussion for everyone except Coates, who persisted in his arguments to Brandis, even to the point of damaging their friendship. Coates's final appeal came in March 1962 in a pleading three-page letter accompanied by thirty-nine pages of enclosures. Even with the weight of his words, Coates could not persuade Brandis to consider the matter further. Brandis's patience was at an end. He said he had tried to accommodate the Institute within the law school, but when Coates returned to full-time teaching after his retirement as director, the law school would no longer allow Institute men to teach his courses. In a line that surely cut Coates to the quick, Brandis said that despite his hopes to the contrary, "the Institute's participation weakened rather than strengthened the School's instructional program."[24]

Coates's appeal to Brandis ran from the practical to the fanciful. The law school would gain from the Institute's connections in the General Assembly and a $3 million grant that Coates believed would soon be on the way from the Ford Foundation. It was a last desperate effort from a man who was fighting to continue his professional life as he had known it and doing everything possible to retain that which had sustained him through the most difficult of days and raised him to glorious acclaim. In the spring of 1962, Coates was anxiously confronting the end of his relationship with a child that he had raised from birth. For thirty years, the Institute had been the first thing on his mind in the morning and in his last fleeting thoughts at night. There was more. The university would allow him to continue to teach law until he reached the age of seventy, but his law classes would no longer be bolstered by their connection to city halls, police departments, county courthouses, and judicial venues via the Institute of Government. For the first time since the fall of 1923, when he had met his first class with no practical experience, he would once again stand alone before his students without a supporting cast. He would have only his course notes and a repertoire of stories with which to educate, illustrate, and entertain.

The war of words with Brandis was only one dimension of negotiations that were almost Shakespearean in their intrigue, nuance, and missed messages. The chancellor was charged with picking a replacement for Coates, and William Aycock was having no better luck than Brandis in bringing Coates's tenure at the Institute to a satisfactory conclusion. Aycock would later say that selecting Coates's successor was one of the most difficult, and time-consuming, challenges of his years as chancellor.

Like Brandis, Coates and Aycock had a long history together, as well as some shared heritage. Both were products of Johnston County, although a generation apart. Aycock had been raised in Selma and later moved to Smithfield, where his father, a lawyer, served as a county judge. Aycock entered State College (later North Carolina State University) in 1932 and after graduation began work on a master's degree in history at Chapel Hill. From time to time, as Aycock worked on his thesis in the law school library, he would catch sight of Coates, whom he recognized as the publisher of *Popular Government*, a magazine he often found on his father's desk. Aycock got his history degree and went on to teach high school in Greensboro before taking a job as the state head of the National Youth Administration (NYA), a New Deal program designed to hire and train young workers. The NYA paid the cost of labor for apprentice carpenters, plumbers, and electricians who worked under the eye of experienced laborers to erect small public buildings such as rural schools and community buildings.

In those desperate days during the Depression, Coates was grasping for a lifeline as he and his first Institute building were sinking in a sea of debt. "He came to Raleigh to see us," Aycock later recalled, "and I was already aware that he could talk for two or three hours without stopping about the Institute of Government. We couldn't stop him long enough to tell him that we couldn't build his building on private land." When Coates eventually finished his presentation, Aycock delivered the same verdict that he had warned Coates of before he began pressing his case. Coates was not put off. "Well, I'll be back and I'll keep bothering you."[25]

Aycock later found that Coates had not lost his ability to tie up an audience for hours on end, especially if it was an audience of one. After distinguishing himself as a battalion commander in World War II, Aycock returned to attend law school in Chapel Hill. Dean Robert H. Wettach was so impressed with his record that he offered him a teaching job even before he had finished his third year. He was away from the university in 1957, on a teaching fellowship at the University of Virginia, when William Friday, the university's new president, asked him to return to Chapel Hill as chancellor to succeed retiring Robert B. House. One of the first to contact him was Albert Coates, who attended a hometown celebration organized in Aycock's honor. When Coates noticed that Aycock's ten-year-old daughter was absent due to a bout with the mumps, he sent her a fulsome letter describing the proceedings. It was a nice touch, guaranteed to tug at the heartstrings of a parent. After Coates discovered that Aycock liked to begin his days early, usually by 6:30 or 7 a.m., he would be waiting outside the chancellor's door when he arrived, ready to talk about whatever item Coates had high on his wish list. "He was inexhaustible," Aycock said.[26]

Aycock and Coates began talking about a successor well in advance of July 1, 1962, the date when his service would come to an end. Time after time, Aycock pressed Coates for a recommendation, but he would never give a definitive reply. Coates, a disciple of Horace Williams, the master of equivocation, was still at the top of his form. Coates begged for more time, arguing that he had foundation grant applications and other internal issues that needed to be resolved before he could leave. In February 1962, Coates sent Aycock a lengthy letter—it was the same thirty-nine pages he later forwarded to Brandis—and laid out his case for selecting a man who would accomplish a merger of the Institute and the law school.

In his letter, Coates did offer some nominations. Paul Johnston had "the kind of mind" that was needed to run the Institute under the umbrella of the law school. So did Henry Brandis. He also said that John Sanders had "that kind of mind in the making." They were all choices without a choice. Johnston was not a viable candidate. After leaving the governor's office, he had launched into a business career. Likewise, Brandis was not likely to leave the law school deanship. As Coates himself suggested, Sanders had potential, but he was not quite ready. Coates was no more conclusive in his recommendations for a successor than an Institute of Government report ever was on an issue that his staff had been asked to study. He presented Aycock with all the measures to use in selecting a successor—seniority, ability, tenure—but never told Aycock which was the most important, leaving the chancellor with no guidance.

Aycock was working with James Godfrey, the dean of faculty and chief academic officer, to find the right person. They wanted someone from the staff because the Institute was unique and would require a person familiar with its mission. At the same time, Aycock wanted a director to bring order to the internal operations. They interviewed the entire staff individually and asked each person for his recommendation. Some returned for further conversations. As they narrowed their focus, they talked again with Coates, who would offer discouraging comments about this man or that man, but never deliver a clear endorsement of any of the names they put forward. Aycock believed that Coates was hoping that at the last minute the university would excuse him from the retirement rules and allow him to remain. He could not imagine the Institute continuing without him.[27]

Aycock had announced that a successor would be named by mid-May. That date came and went without any news from his office. When the academic year concluded and the campus emptied for the summer, Aycock was out of time. He told Coates that he would make a choice by the end of June, with or without his recommendation. He heard nothing more from Coates. Finally, Aycock told Coates he would be in his office at seven in the morning on Saturday, June 30, and that would be the outgoing director's last chance to weigh in. Coates presented himself at Aycock's office and the two talked until nearly one in the afternoon, again without a conclusion. Aycock finally said, "All right. We'll walk out to the car. When I get in that car, it's all over. I'm going to make a decision." Aycock drove away, and Coates still had not given him a name.

Aycock's choice was John Sanders. Sanders met with Aycock and Godfrey in the chancellor's office on Sunday and after five minutes of discussion accepted the job. On Monday, Godfrey called Coates to give him the news. Coates dropped the telephone, Godfrey later told Aycock, but retrieved it quickly and with Godfrey waiting for a reply, issued his judgment: "A magnificent risk."[28]

Sanders's appointment surprised others. Henry Lewis, the staff member with the most seniority, was seen as a likely successor. Philip Green Jr., also a senior member of the staff, was highly regarded and had served for a time as Coates's administrative aide. Meanwhile, Sanders had just turned thirty-five and had been at the Institute for five years. One of those five years had been spent on a special assignment for Governor Terry Sanford, who had drafted him to serve as executive secretary of a commission studying education beyond high school. His Institute work was impressive and had been concentrated largely in state government matters, including the legislative coverage, state government reorganization, and constitutional changes. His credentials were impeccable. He was a graduate of the university and had spent a year as a graduate student studying history before entering law school in 1951. He took high honors as a law student and, after graduation, had clerked for a year for Chief Judge John J. Parker of the Fourth Circuit of the U.S. Court of Appeals. He spent one year in private practice before joining the Institute in October 1956. Like Coates and Aycock, he, too, was a native of Johnston County. If Coates had any misgivings about the chancellor's decision, they never went beyond conversation with Gladys. He congratulated Sanders on the appointment and gave him his blessing.

Three days before Coates closed his years as director, the Institute staff honored Albert and Gladys. The event had originally been planned for

May, and was to have been the first celebration for Coates, but it had to be postponed when the naming of his successor was delayed. In the meantime, the State Highway Patrol had already expressed its appreciation to Coates. At the Institute that evening in August, Donald Hayman made the presentation from the staff of a silver tray and goblets. "Tonight, when the concept of a university of public officials is acclaimed throughout our nation and around the world, it is easy to honor you," Hayman said. "We believe that history will honor you as we honor you—for your creativity in adapting an idea, for daring to dream, and for your selfless devotion to that dream."

With Gladys beside him, Coates professed, "I am a moonlight, magnolia, and mint julep man. I love every one of these things for itself alone. Put them all together—in these silver julep cups, on this silver tray, in this golden company—and there is a mixture richer than the sum of all its parts." He went on to tell of a conversation about retirement that he had with Robert House, who had compared his leaving the university to trips home on the train when he was an undergraduate. House said along the way he would engage a stranger in conversation, but once the conductor announced his stop at Thelma, he would get up in mid-sentence and be off.

"And that is the way I find it now," Coates said. "I am getting off the train at Thelma, with my desk full of loose ends and unfinished business which will be picked up, carried on, added to and subtracted from by my successors who will go along in their own way as I have gone along in mine."[29] Three days later, on August 31, Coates unscrewed his nameplate from his office door, replaced it with one for Sanders, and carried the keys to the building to his successor's home.

THIRTEEN

The Truly Great

1962–1989

IN THE MONTHS PRIOR to Albert Coates's departure as director of the Institute of Government his staff compiled the Institute's record of work for a period of thirty years, from that first meeting in May 1932 when several hundred people gathered in Chapel Hill to learn of a law professor's ideas about improving local government to the day Coates left the Institute's million-dollar building and said goodbye to his staff. It was an impressive body of public work.

Assistant director Jake Wicker delivered more than two dozen reports to his boss. They detailed the content of training materials published in guidebooks for police officers, court clerks, tax collectors, and others in public service; the hundreds of articles ranging from a history of motor vehicle laws to studies in water treatment that had appeared in *Popular Government*; and the thousands of hours of training and special sessions that had been conducted in the name of preparing public officials to perform their duties more effectively and responsibly. In addition, Coates had on hand, probably for the first time, an accounting of the Institute's expenses and revenue from the early days of one- and two-dollar contributions from friends to the larger sums that flowed through the university to the Institute as it became a dedicated component of the university's budget. There was even a head count from the years of housing public officials and lawmen who traveled to the Institute for their meetings.

Much of the information found its way into a report that Coates delivered to Chancellor William Aycock in the spring of 1962 that he titled, "Report on the Beginning, Growth, Present Status and Future Needs of the Institute of Government." In this hefty document, which ran to 158 pages, Coates once again recounted the Institute's story and its development.[1] This edition—it would be updated and revised in succeeding years—was both a history and Coates's argument to Aycock that only he could carry the Institute forward and that the retirement rules should be waived on his behalf. When that effort failed, and retirement became a certainty, the report became the foundation for writing the next chapter in his life. He assured all who asked that he was soldiering on. Retirement, he said, was simply the name given the legal requirement that he leave his job as an administrator. He told the university's public relations office he had refused to join those who met monthly to study the aging process as they approached the age of sixty-five. "They call it 'geriatrics' or something like that. That's a disease I haven't got, don't want and don't expect to get."[2]

Coates was looking forward to many more active years. He told Aycock that his father had lived until well past eighty before his death in 1940. His mother also had enjoyed a long life. Accordingly, Albert believed he had at least another quarter century or more left to him. He would teach in the law school as long as university rules allowed him to—full-time until age seventy, and then half-time for two additional years. His black hair was now silver and his face bore the lines of his years. The slight paunch that he had carried for years was a bit more pronounced. But he was strong and vigorous. He compared his post-retirement ambitions to the steam engine that drove his father's cotton gin back down on the farm. When the day's work was over, the remaining fire continued to heat the boiler and a safety valve opened periodically to release the unspent pressure until the fire died and the boiler cooled. "In thirty years of working with officials on the job," he wrote, "I had built up a head of steam I did not want to see die down, evaporate, and go to waste for lack of use. I wanted to use it until the fire burned out and the steam went down to the point that it would not pull an engine or turn a wheel."[3]

As Coates prepared to leave the Institute, the chancellor offered him a six-month paid leave of absence, but Coates asked permission to avail himself of that at a later time. Leaving the Institute was difficult enough and he was not ready to remove himself entirely from the university, even for such a plum. He may have worried that simultaneously uprooting himself from both the Institute and the law school would be too much of a shock for a system that had been fed by the demands and the urgencies of an active schedule for forty years. Instead, he moved out of the Institute and took an office in Manning Hall, where he had begun his career as a law professor in 1923.

It was a difficult transition for a man whose "platform" had been removed without his consent. Coates could no longer snag available staff members for impromptu sessions that could run for an hour or more as he thought aloud about his dreams and ambitions for the Institute. Parked away in the law school, he found himself in a relative eddy of public life. When the General Assembly met in the spring of 1963, it was the first time in nearly three decades that Coates was not in the midst of the talk about laws that shaped North Carolina. The judges, prosecutors, and law enforcement officials who had flocked each year to Chapel Hill for their sessions now were a quarter mile away at the Institute while he labored in relative obscurity in Manning Hall.

The Institute building that he had built, and in which the men he had brought to his cause continued to work in dedication to his dream, was virtually off-limits. Coates had shown over and over through the years that he did not give up a bone easily, and there was a concern that he would figure out a way to reinstall himself there even after he left his office. He didn't darken the door now. Whenever his successor, John Sanders, needed information, he arranged to meet Coates outside of the building. Albert and Gladys even discontinued their annual Christmas party. Instead, they spent the holidays that first year on an extended visit to Historic Williamsburg in Virginia. The two didn't return to the Knapp Building for more than ten years until Benjamin Swalin arranged for a chamber music concert to be performed in their honor by musicians of the North Carolina Symphony.[4]

Coates was now just one member of the professoriate, a class in which he had never considered himself to be a fully participating member. Over the years he had declared his love of the law school and acknowledged that his life's work had been incubated in his classroom. What he left unsaid was that it was the work outside of the classroom, in the state at large, that had brought him the greatest satisfaction, enjoyment, and public attention. His classroom had been most important as the launching pad for his extracurricular activities. He cherished the law school for the job security that it afforded, but over the years he was usually delinquent in performing his duties to his students and to his colleagues on the faculty. It must have seemed confining in the fall of 1962 when he met his students and once again prodded and poked the neophytes with his insistent question, "Where do you draw the line?" Stories about Albert Coates would continue to abound in the 1960s as they did in the 1920s. He was now teaching the sons of those who had been there before.

Coates confessed that he was not fully prepared for his academic chores. He had not taught a class without the support of his Institute associates for more than a decade. In the two years before his retirement as director he had not met a single class at the law school. Dean Henry Brandis Jr. had approved arrangements for substitutes from the Institute to teach his classes in criminal law, municipal corporations, and family law. That exchange ended when Coates left the Institute. It also was not a particularly warm homecoming. In recent months, he had irritated some of his law school peers through his insistent lobbying for a merger of the law school and the Institute. Even his old friend Brandis was edgy.

Exiled from the Institute and uncomfortable with his circumstances elsewhere, it is no wonder that Coates became restless and started his search for a way to release his pent-up energies. He had said when he left the Institute that he planned to resume work on those portions of the Institute plan that he had been required to put aside during the desperate years of the Depression. That plan, hatched in 1932, had called for an association of high school teachers responsible for the teaching of civics and government as well as another association for those civic organizations that he saw as the heart and vitality of the volunteer life of local communities. He called these clubs and organizations the "flying buttresses" of local government. Associations for both civics teachers and civic clubs had been formed in the early days, but Coates had been unable to bring their leaders into participation in the Institute's program as full partners. Coates also told Brandis that he wanted to take what he had learned from bringing his classroom into the life of law enforcement and municipalities and prepare notes from his lectures that could be published and made available to those outside of the law school. Coates added another project, something he called "preservice" training of law students for participation in public life.

Coates had an agenda that was just as audacious as what he attempted in the 1930s. Back then, Coates had no money and had other limits to his resources, but at least he had the good offices of Frank Graham and Robert B. House to smooth over the difficulties he created with his colleagues and help him nurture his Institute. Now, he had no money and was limited in the time he could devote to building a new program. He also was facing administrators who had learned from experience about the problems that might arise if Coates was given his head to run.

Coates went looking for a home for his program. Neither the Institute of Government nor the law school proffered an invitation, but he did find a welcome from the university's Extension Division, whose director, Charles Milner, invited Coates to become part of the division's adult education efforts and base his new program, to be called the Institute of Civic Education, there. He would have to find the operating money on his own, however. After spending month after month knocking on doors, Coates finally found some support from the Richardson Foundation, which was being brought to life by his old friend Capus Waynick. Coates also camped out in the governor's office until Terry Sanford, then in his last year in office, approved a continuing appropriation for the Institute of Civic Education in the generous amount of $50,000 a year.[5]

By the summer of 1965 Albert Coates was back in business. It did not take long after the money started coming in for his notions of "pre-service training" of law students for public service to turn into a full-fledged proposal for a staff of four or five law school graduates and a program that was reminiscent of the early days of the Institute. In addition to the work with high school teachers and civic club leaders, Coates began making plans for his staff to extend the teaching and experience of his classroom into the academic program of the entire university. Coates proposed that his men would first work with him, spending a year assisting him, one man in each of his courses. The new men would then take what they had learned and be available to teach that course while Coates worked out new courses. In time, as his assistants became more experienced, they would reach out to other departments of the university and pollinate various disciplines with their law teaching. For example, the specialist in criminal law could teach in sociology, and the specialist in municipal corporations would be available to teach in the political science department. It was all very similar to what the Institute had done, and was continuing to do, in various disciplines.

The program Coates envisioned fit neatly within his view of his responsibility to the university. His classroom, and the law school, had long been a launching pad for those interested in public affairs. Over the years he had seen many students go out from the law school to hold major state offices and serve their communities. Terry Sanford had been elected governor in 1960. Dan Moore (one of those whom he flunked in his property course in 1927) had followed Sanford into office in 1965. Susie Sharp, the first woman to sit in his law classes, had become a superior court judge under Governor Kerr Scott, and a decade later Governor Sanford named her to the state supreme court. Countless other students had returned to their hometowns, where they were city and county attorneys, had been elected to the legislature, or had accepted calls to service on local boards and commissions. With the help of his new staff, he could extend his mission of preparing the state's new leaders by participating with other departments within the university. It was, Coates argued, the foundation for a master's program in public service.

His plans for his new staff died aborning. He did not get the approval he sought from the law school to supplement his course work with substitutes. His ambitions also ran afoul of ongoing discussions between the Institute and the department of political science over the development of a master's program in public administration. Coates was stung that his program was stopped short, but he proceeded with his efforts on the other fronts. In the summer of 1965 he conducted courses for high school teachers of civics and government, who came to Chapel Hill for his classes. The short courses delivered a heavy dose of North Carolina history combined with the particulars of local and state government, and examined the interlocking relationships between the two. The effort was designed to help teachers make city hall or the county courthouse, as well as the government in Raleigh, more familiar to young people who were approaching the age when they would be eligible to vote. To supplement his own extensive knowledge of state history, Coates hired history majors and law students looking for summer work to gather information on particular areas of law and history. Their reports went into his ever-growing files.

The fire remained hot under Coates's boiler, but in the fall of 1965, he finally took the leave of absence that had been offered earlier. Rather than bury himself in work, he turned his attention to Gladys and a travel adventure that was for her a dream come true. Despite their reduced circumstances over the years the two had enjoyed some special trips, usually related to Albert's evangelism for the Institute or to Bar association meetings where he was a featured speaker. During the 1930s, the professional excursions had included some summer cruises, both on the West Coast and in the Maritimes. The trip the two began in September 1965 was a special gift for Gladys as they headed to Europe and the cities that had captured her heart when she had traveled there with friends the summer before her marriage, with Albert's bouquets of flowers following her from hotel to hotel.

Their itinerary included England, France, and Italy and the museums that contained the artwork and sculptures that Gladys had admired in the many art books she had accumulated over the years. It was a leisurely trip that lasted through the fall. Once Albert put his work behind him, Gladys said, he became a great traveler. He was captivated by the masterpieces of art and sculpture and responded to them in his own unique way. In Florence he stared up at the brooding face of Michelango's *David* and told Gladys, "That man could handle my law suit." At another museum, Gladys later recounted, her husband was intent on a nativity scene. "He called to me and said he had never seen a stable that looked like the one in the picture. 'Why there are tapestries on the walls that are worthy of a palace,' he said. 'Mary is not sitting on a milking stool; she's sitting on a throne. And she's not dressed in calico, gingham, or percale; she's wearing velvet. There's an advanced contingent of United Nations from the East, and Mary and little Jesus are receiving them with all the aplomb of diplomats. The room is filled with gold and frankincense and myrrh, and Mary and Joseph and little Jesus couldn't qualify for federal aid under Lyndon Johnson's poverty program.' Needless to say, I did not try to shed any further light on the scene. It was far more enjoyable to listen to his interpretation."[6]

Their hotel in Paris was near the Louvre, and the two made frequent visits during the three weeks they were there. As a young man, Albert had seen a plaster cast of *Winged Victory of Samothrace,* an early marble sculpture of the Greek goddess Nike, during a visit to the Metropolitan Museum in New York. When he saw the original, Gladys said, it had for him "the very turn and twist of triumph." The Rodin Museum brought him face to face with other pieces seen only in books. The two were so enthralled with the work of French Impressionists in the Jeu de Paume Museum that when Albert returned home he enrolled in several classes in art to better acquaint himself with their work.[7] In Seville, the two found seats on the foot of the steps inside the Cathedral of Seville to see the choirboys dance before the high altar, a singular religious event.

The lease on his law school office was nearing an end in January 1968. He had given up full-time teaching the year before. In recognition, the school had dedicated the November 1967 issue of the *North Carolina Law Review* in his name. In addition, the North Carolina Bar Association had recognized him with the John J. Parker award, given in recognition of his "conspicuous service to jurisprudence." That same year, Governor Dan K. Moore had presented him with the North Carolina Award for service to the state. Coates continued to teach on a reduced schedule and was updating his history of the law school, as well as meeting a class on criminal law. In late January, he had finished his breakfast and had sat down to read the newspaper when he discovered that he could not move his right arm or leg. His speech was slurred when he called to Gladys for help. He had suffered a stroke that had come on him without pain. He was taken immediately to Memorial Hospital in Chapel Hill. His condition was listed as serious, and he remained in intensive care for a week or more, but gradually he began to improve. In addition to his stroke, there were other complications involving his heart. It was a month before Albert was able to return to his home on Hooper Lane.[8]

Albert's illness at age seventy-one arrived without warning. He had pushed himself to exhaustion as a young man, and he had suffered through bouts of pneumonia and appendicitis, but he had remained healthy through middle age and later. Throughout his life, he developed no troublesome habits. He hadn't used tobacco since he experimented with a bite of a plug as a youngster. He and Gladys imbibed only rarely. He was a voracious eater, however, and fed his roaring metabolism with such artery-clogging fare as ice cream and fried foods. His doctors put him on a strict diet and a regimen of physical therapy. His strength returned slowly and, in time, he began to regain use of his right arm and leg. On June 3, 1968, he was strong enough to accept an invitation to speak at the graduation ceremonies for the law school. His doctor had told him he should not plan on returning to the classroom, so Coates told the students that their invitation was well timed. "For I have taught my last class in the University Law School, you have attended yours, and we are going out together. I could not ask for better company."[9]

As was his habit with any life-changing experience, Coates prepared an account of his illness, his days of silent contemplation of his future years, and his subsequent recovery. He distributed it to his friends and the members of his criminal law class who had lost their professor before the end of the term. The University News Service received so many inquiries about his health that Coates's letter was reproduced as a ten-page news release and sent to newspapers around the state. Rising clearly from the pages is the image of an indomitable spirit in the face of debilitating adversity; Coates was no sooner going to be defeated by his illness than he had been at any other time in his life when he fought against long odds. He had been set back, to be sure, but he sized up his choices for the future: strain to do more than was physically possible and suffer a recurrence or "drop all ventures and all thought of them, and protect and prolong my life for preservation's sake." He said he could also strike for a middle ground. He said he planned to "work without worry, go through controversy without stress and strain," and his problem would be solved. "I have never done it in seventy-one years of life, but I am going to try it now. It involves a game and a gamble, with high stakes—for me."[10]

In the years that followed, Coates became a popular speaker for stroke recovery groups. He did not return to the law school classroom, but that didn't keep him away from students. In 1971, he began a six-week classroom session at Needham Broughton High School in Raleigh, where he produced a pilot program for teachers of state and local government. It was a continuation of the work that he had begun in the mid-1960s. The Z. Smith Reynolds Foundation of Winston-Salem underwrote his work and the publication of a series of books that were made available to teachers and students across the state.

The publications and classroom programs completed one of the assignments that he had proposed in the 1930s. As he returned to an active life, he also wrote a series of articles for newspapers that recounted the struggle for voting rights of women, poor whites, and African Americans. In 1975, he published *By Her Own Bootstraps: A Saga of Women in North Carolina*. This book was an extension of his study and teaching of family law and described the evolution of laws related to the political rights and domestic freedoms of women. A goodly portion of the book was devoted to the political debate over the Equal Rights Amendment, which Coates believed was just and long overdue. He also fulfilled his obligation to the civic clubs with the publication of *Citizens in Action: Women's Clubs, Civic Clubs, Community Chests*, which put into print information he had collected a decade earlier about the record and history of civic organizations in North Carolina.

In the years ahead he would complete yet another bit of unfinished business with the publication in 1985 of *The Story of Student Government in the University of North Carolina at Chapel Hill*, which he co-authored with Gladys. This was the culmination of the research Gladys had begun in the 1930s that had taken her deep into the university's archives and the records of the literary societies as well as into student publications. Her work, with chapters written by Albert, told the story of student government in the nineteenth and early twentieth century. Their work was supplemented with chapters written by student leaders and others whom they commissioned for more current campus activities.

All of these publications had a different tone from his memoirs, biographies, and accounts of the university that would make up much of his generous contribution to the bookshelf. In 1969, just as he was regaining his footing following his illness, he published a collection of autobiographical pieces that he titled *What the University of North Carolina Meant to Me*. The book began as a work faithful to the title but in true Coatesian fashion it grew to span far more than his relationship with the university. His chapters carried the reader through his childhood in Smithfield, his experiences as an undergraduate, his years at Harvard Law School and as a law professor in Chapel Hill, and the building of the Institute. Coates also added a lengthy tribute to his work with the FBI and to the period he was associated with the university extension division, two organizations with which he had had some differences over the years. (Coates sent a copy of his book to FBI Director J. Edgar Hoover. He received a polite reply signed by the director's secretary.)

Another deeply personal work was *My Brother, Kenneth*, a book that Coates published shortly after his brother's death in 1974. The collection of stories, letters, and reminiscences was an admiring portrayal of Kenneth's life. Kenneth, who had spent his career as a professor of English at Wofford College in Spartanburg, South Carolina, was eight years Albert's junior. Albert had planned for Kenneth to follow in his footsteps, enter the law, and become his law partner. Kenneth chose another path, entering a profession that was probably better suited to his more temperate personality and allowed him to flourish as a teacher outside of his brother's shadow. The two saw each other mostly at family gatherings where they would often compete in their verbal sparring. The book is largely a compilation of recollections about Kenneth that Albert gathered from his brother's friends, colleagues, and students. In his introduction, Albert confessed their words introduced him to a brother that he never knew.

Albert Coates's *finis coronat opus*, the book that had been his companion for half a century, was *The Story of the Institute of Government*. It had first taken shape in the letters he had written to potential contributors in the 1930s as he described his dreams for the Institute. It had been expanded and enlarged when published by the Institute for the National Extension Division in the 1940s, and then revised again in the report that he prepared for Chancellor William Aycock in the 1950s. The account of the Institute's early days is a tribute to the men who gave him five and six years of their lives during the depths of the Depression, and to Coates's determination to push on against the odds. The Institute's story in the postwar years is told in more programmatic fashion and serves as a founder's accounting of what he had wrought. He dedicated the book to those who had labored on the Institute's behalf over the years and to the University of North Carolina, which, he said, "gave me a classroom and a teaching job—the only job I have ever held and the only one I have needed in order to do what I wanted to do."[11]

Prior to publishing the Institute history, Coates circulated the manuscript to some of those who had accompanied him on the journey. In the late 1970s, Henry Lewis, who had succeeded John Sanders as director of the Institute of Government in 1973, read behind his former boss, made notes in the margins, and offered his comments. The revisions that Lewis gave to Coates went on for page after page. Coates had never let the accuracy of his reporting get in the way of telling a good story, and by the time he was in his eightieth year his recollection of some of the particulars was flawed. While he could portray with some accuracy the gist of events, his stories often veered off to enhancements that may or may not have been true. Once Gladys had brought home to him a quote that she lifted from Macaulay's essay on Samuel Johnson. The editor of Macaulay's essay could as easily have been talking about Coates when he added a note to the essay stating that it had been retained "... with a few trifling modifications in those places in which his invincible love of the picturesque has drawn him demonstrably aside from the dull line of veracity."[12] Many of Lewis's comments and suggested corrections were provoked by Albert's failing memory and his love of storytelling.

Coates produced a detailed response for Lewis and made some adjustments to his manuscript. Some of their differences fell into the category of misunderstood expectations. Coates, for example, lauded his associates for their work in his classroom; Lewis countered that when Coates hired men he did not make it clear to them that they were to be his surrogates. In his reply, Coates defended his interpretation of events saying that "there are things about the Institute which I have put into my story of the Institute known to me only—things which one who has not lived through them could not draw from found documents, and, without which, the story would have less life, less color, less passion, less truth, and less human interest."[13] Coates's history was published in 1981, fifty years after that first meeting that created the Institute.

Throughout his years of writing and publishing, Coates remained a visible and familiar figure in Chapel Hill. Albert and Gladys made a habit of attending open meetings of the University of North Carolina Board of Governors and board of trustees for the Chapel Hill campus. He was the only guest at either meeting who had known every president and chancellor of the Chapel Hill campus from the nineteenth-century's Kemp Plummer Battle on. His former law student, William Friday, who had become president of the University of North Carolina in 1956, asked Coates repeatedly to join him on his television show to talk about his life. Coates simply froze when the red light on the television camera came on. The man who could captivate hundreds with his speaking voice was unable to talk without a physical audience.[14]

Coates remained a popular luncheon speaker and enjoyed returning to a platform whenever the occasion presented itself. Usually, his talks were about the life of the university, which along with Gladys and the Institute was one of his three great loves. (His last book, published in 1988, was a loving tribute to Edward Kidder Graham, Harry Chase, and Frank Graham, three men who helped shape his life.) In his later years, Coates especially enjoyed his association with the Chapel Hill Rotary Club, whose meetings he first attended as an honorary member. After a few meetings, Coates told Donald Hayman, a club member, "This is such a God damn good organization that I want to be a dues-paying member." Hayman was one of the few men from the Institute whom Coates saw with any regularity. He would walk to the weekly club meetings at the Carolina Inn, where he would sit with Hayman, who would drive him home afterwards. The two would sit and talk for an hour or more, but never about the Institute. "He was moving on," Hayman said.[15]

Year after year, awards and honors came to Coates. In 1974, the University of North Carolina conferred upon him an honorary LL.D degree. Duke University had recognized him in the same way three years earlier. The 1975 General Assembly passed a joint resolution to recognize his contribution to state government. That same year, the North Carolina League of Municipalities and the North Carolina Association of County Commissioners announced that a new building in Raleigh that would serve both organizations would be called the Albert Coates Local Government Center. The North Carolina Citizens Association awarded him a citation for distinguished public service in 1978, and Albert received the North Caroliniana Society Award in 1979. Paul Johnston, his good friend and former colleague who had amassed a fortune as a businessman after leaving his service for former governor Luther Hodges, endowed a professorship at the Institute in Coates's name in 1979. A professorship honoring Gladys was created three years later. Johnston also commissioned a double portrait of Albert and Gladys. A bronze bust of Albert by sculptor William Hipp was dedicated in July 1977. In 1984, Coates received the William R. Davie Award from the trustees of the University of North Carolina at Chapel Hill.

Over the years Albert and Gladys continued to travel. Their destinations abroad included Greece, Turkey, Russia, and Ireland. One year they spent their Christmas holiday in Mexico. They also roamed about the United States. Gladys kept friends abreast of the events in their lives through Christmas letters that always included a remembrance from their childhoods or an update on their latest adventures. Her note to friends in 1987 recounted an earlier holiday season where their home on Hooper Lane was included in the Chapel Hill candlelight tour. A thousand visitors were treated to Gladys's display of Madonnas and Christmas cards that she had collected over the years. She also reported that in March 1987, at age ninety-one, Albert suffered another stroke. Though the attack was considered minor, Albert was hospitalized for six weeks, during which time he had a heart attack. By Christmas he was back home but, this time, the fire had cooled, the steam was gone. Just a little more than a year later, on January 28, 1989, Albert Coates died at home. He was ninety-two and he had made good on his prediction that he would live for another quarter century beyond "retirement."

Albert Coates's life spanned a remarkable period of transition for North Carolina, and for the university. He carried the vision of Edward Kidder Graham from the chapel talks of the years preceding World War I into the heart of the twentieth century. Throughout his life, Graham's addresses remained as fresh and inspiring to Coates as when he first heard him speak as an undergraduate sitting in Gerrard Hall. Those words took root in a young man who could have become one of the best trial lawyers in the land or one of the finest political orators of his day. Instead, he became a teacher, and his classroom became his platform for pursuing a dream that continues to serve virtually every citizen of the state in large ways and small.

He took the lessons he learned from creative and inspiring teachers and shaped and instructed the state during an astonishing period of growth. During his years, North Carolina moved from mud roads and horses and buggies to superhighways, suburbs, and industrial life. E. C. Branson presented the canvas when he introduced Coates to the state at large and offered up a palate of service by the university to the people who built and shaped local communities. Horace Williams trained him how to think and to find his "begriff" and then serve it as he would any master.

He remained true to his state, never straying, despite the lure of jobs paying more and with more prestigious institutions. His single-minded development of the Institute of Government brought to North Carolina a unique answer to the growing demands on government, especially at the local level. He helped turn citizen outrage over incompetence and inadequacies, if not outright corruption, into a learning process for both the electorate and the elected. He brought a new level of professionalism to local and state government that other states learned to appreciate only many years later. He pushed his ambitions forward during the early days, propping them up with the force of his promises of the days ahead by promoting his strengths and glossing over his weaknesses. His colleagues at the university and a constituency in the city halls and courthouses around the state did not fully realize for years what he had wrought, but the reputation of Albert Coates and the Institute grew steadily after his retirement.

He left casualties in his wake, including friendships and associations that he would bend to the point of breaking if it meant his Institute moved that much further along in its mission. Even those who worked with him for years addressed him as "Mr. Coates." He was "Albert" to Gladys and very few others. Always surrounded by people, Coates did not realize how isolated he had become until his colleagues were no longer there sitting at his desk late in the afternoon or early in the morning, listening to his plans. Leaving that behind in 1962 was far more traumatic than he let on to those who knew him. The degree of alienation he felt after he retired from the Institute did not become evident until twenty years later when Coates wrote what he called "The Great Reversal." He believed the Institute had traveled in the wrong direction under his successors and had failed to grow and expand. He enumerated areas of opportunity that he believed had been passed by, especially in the field of law enforcement. This diversion from the course he had set cut to the core and was as near a disappointment as his inability to convince his law school colleagues that the Institute belonged within its academic boundaries. Coates circulated "The Great Reversal" among a few men whom he considered faithful disciples, but not to his successor, John Sanders, who only learned of it twenty-seven years later. Finished in 1982, it was a great yawp that showed there was sufficient steam in the boiler for one last lesson from Albert Coates.

As usual he had the last word, even on his departure from this world. About a year before he died, Coates wrote to a nephew, the Reverend Phillip Washburn, who was a Congregational minister then serving a church in New York. Coates had been impressed with Washburn's rich baritone voice, which he had heard when the two had stood together to sing hymns at a relative's funeral. "I had nothing to say about how I came into this world, but I am going to have plenty to say about how I go out," he wrote. He asked Washburn to sing at his memorial service, without congregational participation, seven of Coates's favorite hymns. Just to make sure he had not chosen incorrectly, he asked Washburn to record all his selections and send the recordings for his approval.[16]

He and Gladys then met with Douglass Hunt to plan the rest. They had known Hunt since 1939, when he was just a teenager and elected to be the first governor at North Carolina Boys State. Hunt later enrolled at the university and became a student leader before leaving for law school at Yale. Hunt returned to Chapel Hill to a university post in the early 1970s and to a fast friendship with Albert and Gladys that flourished in their later years. Together, they fashioned a service that expressed Albert's devotion to the university, to Gladys, and to their accomplishments together. Hunt's task was not easy, he said. "If the idea of thinking emcompassingly of the long life, the torrential energy, the driving will, the upwelling humor, the channeled intelligence of this man is mind-boggling, the task of fitting him neatly into suitable words is staggering."[17] With Gladys, they remembered the words of Frank Graham, who said of Albert, "his loyalty and devotion have become as much a part of the traditions of the University as the ivy on the Old East Building, the shade of the Davie Poplar, and the moss on the rock walls of Chapel Hill. His perennial spirit is a resource of the aspiration of youth who keep this University as ever fair and as ever young as the newest freshman who comes to join the great pilgrimage of the sons and daughters of Carolina."[18]

Two months later, another memorial celebration for Coates was held by the university's student government. It was a tribute to a man who had been a lifelong champion of student governance, from his days as an undergraduate serving his class to the tribute that he and Gladys wrote together. This memorial service drew on the university at large, as students asked for remembrances from those who had known Coates in the classroom, in the Institute, and throughout the university. There were tributes and some laughs. Chancellor Paul Hardin said he had met with Albert and Gladys for two hours shortly after he took office. "Treat my university well," Coates told the new man. Hardin told those who had gathered, "He plainly doubted that I could do it, but equally plainly he was on my side."[19]

Historian H. G. Jones spent many hours with Coates in his later years. The two shared a love of North Carolina history and a lament that it was not as prominent in the minds of the professoriate as it had once been. Jones was retired as curator of the North Carolina Collection, a favorite haunt of both Albert and Gladys. "You are doing a powerful work," Coates would tell him when he came to visit Jones at the Collection. Jones gave a moving tribute to Coates and said in closing, "Albert Coates, North Carolinian—and every additional word is redundant."[20]

Throughout his life, Coates was a powerful presence whose appeal for loyalty to the state and to the university could not be denied. Over and over, beginning in the depths of the Depression and continuing even after he was gone, he inspired men and women to forsake their own plans, put their law practice careers aside, and take up his cause and make it their own. Twenty years, almost to the month, after Coates's death, Michael R. Smith sat in a conference room just down the hall from the office that Coates had once occupied at the Institute. Smith was only the third person after Coates to direct the Institute, following the administrations of John Sanders and Henry Lewis. The title now was not director, but dean, and the Institute of Government was the University of North Carolina

School of Government. Unlike Sanders and Lewis, Smith never met Albert Coates. In 1978 he had discovered the Institute of Government quite by accident while he was a student in the law school, which by then had relocated to a new home on a site just south of the Institute. Coates never achieved merger, but he lived to see the schools in close proximity.

When Smith talked about the School of Government of the twenty-first century, Coates had been gone from the campus for two decades, he had been away from his office for twice that time, and nearly all of the men that he hired had retired, some of them to "slipper'd ease," as the founder liked to say. Smith said the spirit of the founder remained alive and strong within the organization he now served. Coates would be cranky about some changes; the staff doesn't work weekends or come in on Sundays to catch up. Nonetheless, the men and women who carried on his tradition of service to local and state government were as dedicated as any who had come before and were worthy of the tradition of Henry Brandis in the 1930s, of Peyton Abbot in the 1940s, and of any one the assistant directors in the 1950s. Coates would also admire, probably as his own creation, the $24-million expansion that doubled the size of the Knapp Building as he had known it to accommodate a staff that had grown to nearly fifty professionals. (It was renamed the Knapp-Sanders Building when work was completed.) Build, grow, expand. That was Coates's measure of success. Most of those occupying offices were lawyers, just as in his day. (Smith, a lawyer, said such institutional bias drew a comment from a psychologist on the staff who preferred some other designation than non-lawyer. If she was going to be a non-something, she said she'd prefer to be a non-astronaut.) The Kughler murals, at least some of them, still hung in the common areas. "Seven-Fold Sue" was not among them, but the panel that included Albert and Gladys, the *Pageant of Dreamers*, was on public display. Smith said local officials and others continued to approach him with their Albert Coates stories much as earlier, in the 1940s, when Albert Coates was the very embodiment of good government, officials approached Peyton Abbott with their stories when he was filling in for his boss.

The School of Government remained focused on the mission that Coates had outlined three-quarters of a century earlier, and it ebbed and flowed with the needs of its constituency, the people of North Carolina and the public officials who serve them. From time to time, Smith said, he had reminded his colleagues that Coates set no boundaries for the Institute and often did not follow convention. Over the years staff members who did not know Coates have questioned him about the dignity of the Institute's fundraising or programs that did not hew closely to the service of public officials. Smith said he reminded them that the Institute would never have survived without Coates's own tin-cup efforts, and that a program in civic education was part of Coates's charter of service to high school teachers and their students. "I talk about Albert and Gladys and our history," Smith said. "He is very much alive here." From time to time, he even calls the place the "university of public officials," a line straight out of Albert's own book.[21]

Smith had been in the job only a short time—he was named director in 1992—when he received a call from Gladys Coates, who asked for an appointment. She came to offer a greeting to the new man who now was custodian of her husband's legacy. They had a pleasant visit and as she rose to leave, Smith asked if he could drive her home. Heavens, no, replied Gladys, who had recently turned ninety. She had driven herself to the office and she could certainly drive herself home.

For much of the coming decade, Gladys kept the flame alive. She was often asked to speak on various aspects of the university's history, including the early story of Person Hall, one of the oldest landmarks on the campus. She talked about her introduction to the university as a professor's young bride, and she served as a link to an era when Chapel Hill was a village, and a quaint one at that with its idiosyncratic mixtures of habits and personalities. One summer, the law clerks at the Institute invited her in to talk about the Institute's early days. She brought forth her research into campus life with a talk on women in the university, a subject she had studied since her early ventures into the North Carolina Collection.

In November 1977 the former Institute building on Franklin Street that Gladys and Albert had sacrificed their time and treasure to build was dedicated in their name. During his lifetime, the School of Social Work had offered to put his name on one of its new buildings, but Albert had asked not to be remembered there. The Franklin Street building had served as the headquarters for the consolidated university and then was used for other purposes over the years after the General Administration moved, in the early 1970s, into a larger building just east of the Institute on Raleigh Road.

In 2001, the university awarded Gladys, then ninety-nine, an honorary doctor of laws degree. Her other honors included the William Richardson

Davie Award, the Cornelia Phillips Spencer Bell Award, and the Distinguished Service Medal from the University of North Carolina at Chapel Hill General Alumni Association. She died on September 25, 2002, at the age of a hundred.

Over the years, she and Albert had attended either the Methodist church (his) or the Episcopal church (hers). She chose a simple service at the Chapel of the Cross and she was buried beside Albert in the Old Chapel Hill Cemetery on South Road. The burial grounds are just across from the School of Government and the stones carry the names of those whom Albert and Gladys held most dear—E. K. and Frank Graham, Odum, Branson, Koch, Paul and Margaret Johnston, and House, among others. Their stone stands near a path and carries the inscription, "Married June 23, 1928, and lived happily ever after."

She had taken part in the memorial service for her husband that the student government sponsored in 1989. She had been asked to speak, but demurred, and then changed her mind because of the deep respect and devotion that Albert had for this form of government, usually overlooked in the range of public affairs. She had read Frank Graham's tribute to Albert and recalled Thomas Wolfe's commission to him as he headed to Chapel Hill to begin his career as a law teacher. She recited words from Oliver Wendell Holmes, one of Albert's favorite jurists, and, finally, a poem by Stephen Spender called "The Truly Great."

> I think continually of those who were truly great.
> Whose lovely ambition was that their lips, still touched with fire,
>   Should tell of the Spirit, clothed from head to foot in song.
> The names of those who in their lives fought for life,
>   Who wore at their hearts the fire's centre.
>   Born of the sun, they traveled a short while toward the sun
>   And left the vivid air signed with their honor.

Notes

Chapter One

1. One of Coates's longtime associates, Elmer Oettinger, attempted to secretly record one of Coates's presentations and hid a microphone in a nearby potted plant. Coates discovered the microphone and told Oettinger to remove it. Elmer Oettinger, interview with Molly Matlock Parson, March 19, 2004, Southern Oral History Program, in the Southern Historical Collection Manuscripts Department, Wilson Library, The University of North Carolina at Chapel Hill (hereafter cited as Southern Oral History Program).

2. The Coates name enjoyed two spellings for no apparent reason. One had an *e* and the other did not. For example, the town of Coats in neighboring Harnett County was founded by Tom Coats in 1907.

3. Undated notes on John Rufus Coates, Albert Coates Papers, Southern Historical Collection, Manuscripts Department, Wilson Library, University of North Carolina at Chapel Hill (hereafter cited as Albert Coates Papers).

4. Bessie Coates Memoirs, Albert Coates Papers.

5. Ibid.

6. Albert Coates, "What Smithfield and Johnston County Meant to Me," *Smithfield Herald*, Harvest Edition, August 1969.

7. Albert Coates to Mrs. George T. Whitley, February 14, 1972, Albert Coates Papers.

8. Bessie Coates memoirs.

9. Albert Coates, *What the University of North Carolina Meant to Me: A Report to the Chancellors and Presidents and to the People With Whom I Have Lived and Worked From 1914 to 1969* (Richmond: William Byrd Press, 1969), p. 16.

10. Coates, "What Smithfield and Johnston County Meant to Me."

11. Ibid.

12. Ibid.

13. Coates, *What the University of North Carolina Meant To Me: A Report*, p. 14.

Chapter Two

1. Albert Coates, *What the University of North Carolina Meant to Me: A Report*, p. 25.

2. L. R. Wilson, *The University of North Carolina, 1900–1930: The Making of a Modern University* (Chapel Hill: University of North Carolina Press, 1957), p. 127.

3. Coates, *What the University of North Carolina Meant to Me: A Report*, p. 24.

4. Ibid., p. 26.

5. Ibid., p. 25.

6. Ibid., p. 50.

7. Albert Coates, *The University of North Carolina at Chapel Hill: A Magic Gulf Stream in the Life of North Carolina* (privately published, 1978), p. 22.

8. "Y.M.C.A. Offers Schedule Especially for New Men," *Tar Heel*, September 23, 1916, 3.

9. Wilson, *The University of North Carolina, 1900–1930*, p. 180.

10. *Yackety Yack*, 1914, University of North Carolina, p. 27.

11. Wilson, *The University of North Carolina, 1900–1930*, p. 183.

12. Ibid., pp. 184 and 185.

13. The exchange between Senators Robert Y. Hayne of South Carolina and Daniel Webster of Massachusetts in January 1830 arose over the question of western expansion of the nation and tariffs. Webster's response to Hayne's notion that states could act in their own best interests, regardless of the union, is considered one of the most eloquent defenses of the elements of a federal government.

14. Coates, *The University of North Carolina at Chapel Hill*, p. 27.

15. Albert Coates, *What the University Meant to Me From 1914 to 1918* (privately published, 1968), p. 5.

16. Ibid., p. 5.

17. Albert Coates, *Edward Kidder Graham, Harry Woodburn Chase, Frank Porter Graham: Three Men in the Transition of the University of North Carolina at Chapel Hill From a Small College to a Great University* (privately published, 1988), pp. 4–5.

18. Coates, *The University of North Carolina at Chapel Hill*, p. 8.

19. Ibid., p. 11.

20. Coates, *What the University of North Carolina Meant to Me: A Report*, p. 29.

21. Elmer Oettinger, interview with Molly Matlock Parsons, March 19, 2004, Southern Oral History Program.

22. Albert Coates, "The Phi Beta Kappa Society in the University of North Carolina at Chapel Hill," December 6, 1979, privately printed pamphlet.

23. "Albert Coates Discusses College Citizenship," *Tar Heel*, April 21, 1917.

24. Albert Coates, "America's Contribution to Peace," *University of North Carolina Magazine* 34 (May 1917), 300.

25. Wilson, *The University of North Carolina, 1900–1930*, p. 278.

26. "Companies Show Marked Improvement in Drilling," *Tar Heel*, April 6, 1917.

27. "Life in the Trenches Vividly Presented," *Tar Heel*, April 6, 1917.

28. "Over A Thousand Hear Dr. E. K. Graham Speak," *Tar Heel*, April 21, 1917. More information on the wartime preparations and training on the University of North Carolina campus can be found in the *Tar Heel*, *Yackety Yack*, and the *Alumni Review*.

29. Mary Helen Seabury to Albert Coates, May 2, 1917, Albert Coates Papers.

30. "County Clubs Hold a Miniature Convention," *Tar Heel*, September 28, 1917.

31. "County Government and County Affairs in North Carolina," *The University of North Carolina Record*, Extension Series No. 30, Number 159, University of North Carolina, October 1918.

32. Speech to Phi Society, Albert Coates Papers.

33. Note to A. M. Coates, Albert Coates Papers.

34. "Tar Heel Valor on the War Front," *News & Observer*, June 3, 1918.

35. "America's Message to the World," *News & Observer*, June 9, 1918.

Chapter Three

1. "Estimate 100,000 Cases Over State," *News & Observer*, October 26, 1918.

2. Coates, *What the University of North Carolina Meant to Me*, p. 50.

3. Albert Coates, eulogy delivered at Pou memorial, Albert Coates Papers.

4. Archibald Henderson, *The Campus of the First State University* (Chapel Hill: University of North Carolina Press, 1949), p. 216.

5. Wilson, *The University of North Carolina, 1900–1930*, p. 309.

6. Ibid., p. 249.

7. Ibid., p. 296.

8. Albert Coates, remarks prepared for the memorial service of Marvin H. Stacy, Albert Coates Papers.

9. Kemp Plummer Battle, *Memories of an Old-Time Tar Heel* (Chapel Hill: University of North Carolina Press, 1945), p. 186.

10. Wilson, *The University of North Carolina, 1900–1930*, pp. 306–309.

11. Minutes, Graham Memorial Committee, Louis Round Wilson Papers, Southern Historical Collection, Manuscripts Department, Wilson Library, University of North Carolina at Chapel Hill.

12. Albert Coates, typed remarks, Albert Coates Papers.

13. Ibid.

14. Albert Coates, remarks prepared for delivery to the University Alumni in Goldsboro in the interest of the Graham Memorial, Albert Coates Papers.

15. Ibid.

16. Minutes, Graham Memorial Committee.

17. Arthur E. Sutherland, *The Law at Harvard: A History of Ideas and Men, 1817–1967* (Cambridge, MA: The Belknap Press of Harvard University Press, 1967), p. 176

18. Coates, *What the University of North Carolina Meant to Me*, p. 123.

19. Sutherland, *The Law at Harvard*, p. 216.

20. Coates, *What the University of North Carolina Meant to Me*, p. 120.

21. Ibid., p. 121.

22. Ibid., p. 119.

23. Ibid., p. 122.

24. Richard Walser, *Thomas Wolfe, Undergraduate* (Durham, NC: Duke University Press, 1977), p. 124.

25. Albert Coates to Horace Williams, October 2, 1920, Horace Williams Papers, Southern Historical Collection, Manuscripts Department, Wilson Library, University of North Carolina at Chapel Hill.

26. C. Hugh Holman and Sue Fields Ross, *The Letters of Thomas Wolfe to his Mother* (Chapel Hill: University of North Carolina Press, 1968), p. 10.

27. Karl E. Campbell, *Senator Sam Ervin: Last of the Founding Fathers* (Chapel Hill: University of North Carolina Press, 2007), p. 46.

28. Holman, *The Letters of Thomas Wolfe to his Mother*, pp. 11–12.

29. Coates, *What the University of North Carolina Meant to Me*, p. 119.

30. Ibid., pp. 124–25.

31. Sutherland, *The Law at Harvard*, p. 237.

32. Coates, *What the University of North Carolina Meant to Me*, p. 125.

33. Thomas Wolfe to Albert Coates, Summer 1920, Thomas Wolfe Letters, North Carolina Collection, Wilson Library, University of North Carolina at Chapel Hill (hereafter cited as Thomas Wolfe Letters).

34. Ibid.

35. Coates, *What the University of North Carolina Meant to Me*, p. 57.

36. Harry W. Chase to Albert Coates, September 30, 1921, Albert Coates Papers.

37. B. C. Brown to Albert Coates, March 19, 1922, Albert Coates Papers.

38. Coates, *What the University of North Carolina Meant to Me*, p. 124.

39. Sutherland, *The Law at Harvard*, pp. 251–53

40. David Herbert Donald, *Look Homeward: A Life of Thomas Wolfe* (New York: Ballantine Books, 1987), p. 84.

41. H. B. Marrow to Albert Coates, April 29, 1922, Albert Coates Papers.

42. Coates, *What the University of North Carolina Meant to Me*, p. 123.

43. *Criminal Justice in Cleveland: Reports of the Cleveland Foundation Survey of the Administration of Criminal Justice in Cleveland, Ohio*, The Cleveland Foundation, Cleveland, Ohio, 1922.

44. Daniel Grant to Albert Coates, February 6, 1923, Albert Coates Papers.

45. Louis R. Wilson to Albert Coates, February 20, 1923, Albert Coates Papers.

46. Coates, *What the University of North Carolina Meant to Me*, p. 123.

47. Coates, *What the University of North Carolina Meant to Me*, p. 58.

Chapter Four

1. Quoted in Gladys Hall Coates, "Talk at the Memorial Celebration on the Life and Work of Albert Coates," March 29, 1989, private collection.

2. Louis R. Wilson, *The University of North Carolina, 1900–1930*, pp. 379–85.

3. Ibid., pp. 467–68.

4. Albert Coates, "A Century of Legal Education," in *A Century of Legal Education*, ed. Robert H. Wettach (Chapel Hill: University of North Carolina Press, 1947), p. 56.

5. Frank O. Ray to Albert Coates, July 7, 1923, Albert Coates Papers.

6. Wilson, *The University of North Carolina, 1900–1930*, p. 555.

7. Coates, "A Century of Legal Education," p. 59.

8. Ibid., p. 62.

9. "Graham Memorial Campaign Will Be Officially Opened at Chapel Period Monday," *Tar Heel*, February 22, 1924.

10. "History of the Unification Movement Given By Coates," *Tar Heel*, March 28, 1924.

11. Coates, "A Century of Legal Education," pp. 75–78.

12. Coates, *What the University of North Carolina Meant to Me*, p. 59.

13. Ibid., p. 60.

14. R. W. Madry, "Practice and Theory Join Hands in Law School," *Alumni Review*, June 1928.

15. Albert Coates to Gladys Hall, March 30, 1924, private collection.

16. Gladys Coates, interview with Sarah Wilkerson-Freeman, February 19, 1986, Southern Oral History Program.

17. Albert Coates to Gladys Hall, correspondence, May 6, 1925, private collection.

18. *The Art of Attracting Men* (St. Louis: The Psychology Press, 1922).

19. Albert Coates to Gladys Hall, November 24, 1924, private collection.

20. Gladys Hall to Albert Coates, December 6, 1924, private collection.

21. Albert Coates to Gladys Hall, May 4, 1925, private collection.

22. Gladys Hall to Albert Coates, May 26, 1925, private collection.

23. Albert Coates to Gladys Hall, December 1925, private collection.

24. Albert Coates to Gladys Hall, July 9, 1925, private collection.

25. Albert Coates to Gladys Hall, June 24, 1925, private collection.

26. Ibid.

27. Wilson, *The University of North Carolina, 1900–1930*, pp. 511–13.

28. Shepard Bryan to Albert Coates, June 11, 1926, Albert Coates Papers.

29. Albert Coates to Gladys Hall, May 22, 1926, private collection.

30. Albert Coates to Gladys Hall, April 13, 1925, private collection.

31. Albert Coates to Gladys Hall, June 1926, private collection.

32. Francis to Albert Coates, August 25, 1926, Albert Coates Papers.

33. Albert Coates to Gladys Hall, July 15, 1925, private collection.

34. Ibid.

35. Coates, *What the University of North Carolina Meant to Me*, p. 63.

36. Albert Coates, *The Story of the Institute of Government* (privately published, 1981), p. 2.

Chapter Five

1. Guy Benton Johnson and Guion Griffis Johnson, *Research in Service to Society: The First Fifty Years of the Institute for Research in Social Science at the University of North Carolina* (Chapel Hill: University of North Carolina Press, 1980), pp. 6 and 27.

2. Paul Wager, *County Government in North Carolina* (Chapel Hill: University of North Carolina Press, 1928), p. 89.

3. Ibid., p. 364.

4. Gladys Hall Coates, *The Albert Coates I Know* (Chapel Hill: North Caroliniana Society Imprints, no. 3, 1979), p. iv.

5. Ernest Machen Jr., interview with Montgomery Wolf, May 27, 2004, Albert Coates Project, Southern Oral History Program.

6. Gladys Hall Coates, *The Albert Coates I Know*, p. iii.

7. Ibid., p. iv.

8. Albert Coates, address to the Phi Beta Kappa Society of the University of North Carolina at Chapel Hill, December 9, 1979, Albert Coates Papers.

9. Albert Coates, "The Great Reversal," William McWhorter Cochrane Papers, Southern Historical Collection, Manuscripts Department, Wilson Library, University of North Carolina at Chapel Hill (hereafter cited as William McWhorter Cochrane Papers).

10. Albert Coates, ed., *Popular Government*, vol. 1, no.1 (January 1931).

11. Coates, *The Story of the Institute of Government*, p. 6.

12. Coates, *What the University of North Carolina Meant to Me*, p. 73.

13. John H. Wigmore, ed., *The Illinois Crime Survey*, Illinois Association for Criminal Justice, 1929.

14. Gladys Hall to Albert Coates, March 2, 1927, private collection.

15. Robert B. House, *The Light That Shines* (Chapel Hill: University of North Carolina Press, 1964), p. 98.

16. Gladys Hall to Albert Coates, April 18, 1928, private collection.

17. Albert Coates to E. D. Broadhurst, August 6, 1929, Albert Coates Papers.

18. Kemp D. Battle to Albert Coates, November 16, 1927, Albert Coates Papers.

19. Robert Madry, "Practice and Theory Join Hands in Law School," *Alumni Review*, University of North Carolina, June 1928.

20. Albert Coates to Gladys Hall, June 6, 1928, private collection.

21. Jack Aulis, "Albert Coates' Basic Rule of the Road," *News & Observer*, February 11, 1989.

22. Gladys Hall Coates, "Some Recollections of Early Days in Chapel Hill and the University," address to the Senior Citizens of St. Thomas More Catholic Church, September 17, 1992, private collection.

23. Harry W. Chase to Albert Coates, August 26, 1929, Albert Coates Papers.

24. Letters of invitation and Chase's notes to Coates, July and August 1929, Albert Coates Papers; "Confer on Criminal Law," *Daily Tar Heel*, August 30, 1929.

25. Albert Coates, "The Task of Legal Education in North Carolina," Albert Coates Papers.

26. W. Ney Evans to Albert Coates, June 25, 1929, Albert Coates Papers.

27. W. A. Devin to Albert Coates, March 26, 1930, Albert Coates Papers.

28. Thomas Wolfe to Albert Coates, November 29, 1929, Thomas Wolfe Letters.

29. C. T. McCormick to Albert Coates, March 6, 1930, Albert Coates Papers.

30. "Plans Announced for Revised Criminal Practice," *News & Observer*, December 16, 1930.

31. Gladys Coates, notes on the history of the Institute of Government, private collection.

32. E. C. Branson to Albert Coates, September 8, 1929, E. C. Branson Papers, Southern Historical Collection, Manuscripts Department, Wilson Library, University of North Carolina at Chapel Hill.

Chapter Six

1. Joseph L. Morrison, *Governor O. Max Gardner: A Power In North Carolina and New Deal Washington* (Chapel Hill: University of North Carolina Press, 1971), p. 31.

2. For an overview of the Depression in North Carolina, read John L. Bell Jr., *Hard Times: Beginnings of the Great Depression in North Carolina, 1929–1933* (Raleigh, NC: N.C. Division of Archives and History), 1982.

3. "Mill Operatives Get Out Of Union," *News & Observer*, August 28, 1930.

4. David Leroy Corbitt, ed., *Public Papers and Letters of Governor O. Max Gardner*, Council of State, Raleigh, NC, 1937.

5. Johnson and Johnson, *Research in Service to Society*, p. 65.

6. Gladys Hall Coates, notes prepared for a history of the Institute of Government, private collection.

7. Albert Coates, ed., *Popular Government*, vol. 1, no. 1 (January 1931).

8. "Plans Are Announced for Revised Criminal Practice," *News & Observer*, December 6, 1930.

9. Lloyd K. Garrison to Albert Coates, Albert Coates Papers.

10. Coates, *Popular Government*, vol. 1, no. 1 (January 1931): 66.

11. Ibid., 69. Coates used the anecdote regularly to underscore what he called the nobility and honor of the men of his native state. In this instance, he ended with the word "foe," but the closing word scribbled in an almost illegible hand by the soldier is believed to be "enemy."

12. Coates, *Popular Government*, vol. 1, no. 1 (January 1931): 70.

13. M. V. Barnhill to Albert Coates, January 30, 1931, Albert Coates Papers.

14. Charles G. Rose to Albert Coates, January 22, 1931.

15. Junius G. Adams to Albert Coates, February 7, 1931.

16. Albert Coates, "Preliminary Draft of a Plan for County, District and Statewide Schools of Law Enforcing Officers," Albert Coates Papers.

17. Albert Coates, *The Story of the Institute of Government* (privately published, 1981), p. 10.

18. "Law Enforcement Officers Hear Addresses At Meeting," *Greensboro Daily News*, September 10, 1931.

19. "Officers Score Third Degree," *News & Observer*, September 10, 1931.

20. Ibid.

21. "Law Enforcement Schools In Every District Planned," *Raleigh Times*, September 9, 1931.

22. "Governor Urges Rededication To Common Honesty," *News & Observer*, September 11, 1931.

23. M. T. Van Hecke to Frank Graham, November 30, 1931, Personnel Files, University Archives, Manuscripts Department, Wilson Library, University of North Carolina at Chapel Hill.

24. Albert Coates to James G. Hanes, October 5, 1931, Albert Coates Papers.

25. Ibid.

26. Albert Coates to Junius G. Adams, March 31, 1932, Albert Coates Papers.

27. Coates, *The Story of the Institute of Government*, p. 1.

28. Van Hecke to Graham, November 30, 1931.

29. Albert Coates to Frank Graham, April 26, 1937, Albert Coates Papers.

30. Albert Coates to Roscoe Pound, December 2, 1931, Albert Coates Papers.

31. Albert Coates, ed., *Popular Government*, vol. 1, no. 2 (June 1932): 17.

32. Ibid., 22–23.

33. John J. Parker to Albert Coates, November 30, 1931, Records of the Institute of Government, University Archives, Manuscripts Department, Wilson Library, University of North Carolina at Chapel Hill (hereafter cited as Records of the Institute of Government).

34. J. W. Hollis to Albert Coates, March 21, 1932, Albert Coates Papers.

35. George Pennell to Albert Coates, March 29, 1932, Albert Coates Papers.

36. A. Wayland Cooke to Albert Coates, April 17, 1932, Albert Coates Papers.

37. Howard E. Covington Jr., *Lady on the Hill: How Biltmore Estate Became an American Icon* (New York: John F. Wiley & Sons, 2004), p. 79.

38. Junius G. Adams to Albert Coates, February 7, 1931, Albert Coates Papers.

39. Gladys Hall Coates, notes prepared for a history of the Institute of Government, private collection.

40. Gladys Hall Coates, "Talk to Summer Law Clerks on Early Days and Events of the Institute of Government," July 19, 1993, private collection.

41. *Daily Tar Heel*, May 8, 1932.

Chapter Seven

1. Albert Coates, *The Story of the Institute of Government*, 1981, p. 28.

2. "Institute Begun by Government Group," *Greensboro Daily News*, September 10, 1932.

3. "'Hoover-Cart Rodeo' Is a Great Success," *Greensboro Daily News*, September 11, 1932.

4. "Pound and Gardner Heard at Institute," *Greensboro Daily News*, September 11, 1932.

5. Ibid.

6. Frank Graham to Albert Coates, September 15, 1932, Albert Coates Papers.

7. Coates, *The Story of the Institute of Government*, p. 30.

8. John Scarlett, interview with Molly Matlock Parsons, July 8, 2004, Southern Oral History Program.

9. Warner Olivier, "The Ugly Duckling at Chapel Hill," *Saturday Evening Post*, February 24, 1945.

10. Albert Coates to William B. Aycock, "Report To the Chancellor," 1961, Records of the Institute of Government.

11. "Dr. Coates Pleads For a Scientific Attitude in Study of State Criminal Code," *Gastonia Gazette*, October 23, 1932.

12. Morrison, *Governor O. Max Gardner*, p. 126.

13. "Gardner Frees Another Banker," *News & Observer*, December 29, 1932.

14. "Institute of Government Has Statewide Launching," *News & Observer*, December 6, 1932.

15. Howard E. Covington Jr., *Once Upon A City: Greensboro North Carolina's Second Century* (Greensboro, NC: Greensboro Historical Museum, 2008), p. 21.

16. Gladys Hall Coates, notes prepared for a history of the Institute of Government, private collection.

17. Henry Brandis Jr., "Report to the Director of the Institute of Government, Covering period from April 10, 1933, to June 1, 1936," Records of the Institute of Government.

18. Franklin D. Roosevelt to J. C. B. Ehringhaus, May 29, 1933, Records of the Institute of Government.

19. "Bailey is Speaker at Officials' Meet," *Greensboro Daily News*, June 25, 1933.

20. Albert Coates, "Report to the Chancellor," undated, Records of the Institute of Government.

21. M. T. Van Hecke, "A Recommendation to the President," undated, Albert Coates Personnel File, University Archives, Manuscripts Department, Wilson Library, University of North Carolina at Chapel Hill (hereafter cited as Albert Coates Personnel File).

22. Coates, *The Story of the Institute of Government*, p. 33.

23. Leon Green to Frank Graham, May 6, 1933, Albert Coates Personnel File.

24. M. L. Ferson to Frank Graham, May 10, 1933, Albert Coates Personnel File.

25. Petition to Frank Graham, undated, Albert Coates Papers.

26. R. B. House to Frank Graham, May 23, 1933, Albert Coates Papers.

27. Johnson and Johnson, *Research in Service to Society*, pp. 291–92.

28. Gladys Coates, notes prepared for a history of the Institute of Government, private collection.

29. Coates, *The Story of the Institute of Government*, p. 44.

30. Henry Brandis to Albert Coates, undated memorandum, Records of the Institute of Government.

31. Gladys Coates, notes prepared for a history of the Institute of Government.

32. "Parade and Service March Observance of Armistice Day Here," *Greensboro Daily News*, November 12, 1933.

33. Dillard Gardner to Albert Coates, November 16, 1932, Records of the Institute of Government.

34. James G. Hanes to Albert Coates, March 3, 1933, Albert Coates Papers.

35. "To Reveal Institute of Government Plan," *Charlotte Observer*, November 26, 1933.

36. Ibid.

37. Edward E. Hollowell, "The Four Eras in the Financial History of the Institute of Government," Records of the Institute of Government.

38. "Equipment Is Efficient," *Popular Government*, vol. 2, no. 2 (December 1934).

39. "Drivers' License For State Urged," *News & Observer*, December 30, 1933.

40. Coates, *The Story of the Institute of Government*, pp. 12–13.

41. M. T. Van Hecke to Frank Graham, May 23, 1934, University Archives, Manuscripts Department, Wilson Library, University of North Carolina at Chapel Hill.

42. Coates, *The Story of the Institute of Government*, p. 62.

43. "Proposed Basic Law Is Debated," *News & Observer*, April 14, 1934.

44. Coates, *The Story of the Institute of Government*, p. 41.

45. "Will Bear Watching," *Winston-Salem Sentinel*, October 24, 1934.

46. "Usurping a Governmental Function," *Winston-Salem Journal*, October 30, 1934.

47. "Anyway One is Needed," *Durham Herald*, November 1, 1934.

48. "The 1934 Institute Sessions at Raleigh, November 15 and 16," *Popular Government*, vol. 2, no. 2 (December 1934).

49. Dillard Gardner to Albert Coates, undated memorandum, Records of the Institute of Government.

Chapter Eight

1. Gladys Hall Coates, *Fifty Years with Albert Coates*, 1979, housed at the North Carolina Collection, Wilson Library, University of North Carolina at Chapel Hill.

2. Robert B. House to President Frank P. Graham, January 6, 1936, Records of the Institute of Government.

3. T. N. Grice to Albert Coates, "Report to the Director," undated, Records of the Institute of Government.

4. Ibid.

5. Henry Brandis Jr., "Report to the Director of the Institute of Government," undated, Records of the Institute of Government.

6. Grice, "Report to the Director."

7. "What? Coates Without Pants, Vest or Coat!" undated newspaper clipping, Albert Coates Papers.

8. Associated Press, April 16, 1935, Albert Coates Papers.

9. Albert Coates, *The Story of the Institute of Government*, p. 7.

10. Albert Coates to R. W. Gantt, December 27, 1935, Records of the Institute of Government.

11. Albert Coates to Roscoe Pound, March 26, 1935, Records of the Institute of Government.

12. Roscoe Pound to Albert Coates, undated, Records of the Institute of Government. See also *Popular Government*, vol. 2, no. 4 (April 1935).

13. Leo M. Favrot to Frank Graham, March 25, 1935, Records of the Institute of Government.

14. "PWA Projects in the State," *Popular Government*, vol. 2, no. 4 (April 1935).

15. Archibald Henderson, *The Campus of the First State University* (Chapel Hill: University of North Carolina Press, 1949).

16. R. W. Madry, "Building to House Government Institute Now Seems Assured," Records of the Institute of Government.

17. Ibid.

18. M. T. Van Hecke to Frank Graham, May 9, 1935, Records of the Institute of Government.
19. M. T. Van Hecke to Frank Graham, July 26, 1935, Records of the Institute of Government.
20. M. S. Van Hecke, son of M. T. Van Hecke, interview with author, October 15, 2008.
21. Albert Coates to R. B. House, July 9, 1935, Records of the Institute of Government.
22. R. B. House to Frank Graham, July 10, 1935, Records of the Institute of Government.
23. Ibid.
24. M. T. Van Hecke to Frank Graham, July 11, 1935, Records of the Institute of Government.
25. Albert Coates to Robert B. House, July 17, 1935, Records of the Institute of Government.
26. Gladys Coates, *Fifty Years with Albert Coates.*
27. Gladys Hall Coates, interview with Sarah Wilkerson-Freeman, February 19, 1986, Southern Oral History Program.
28. Ibid.
29. Albert Coates, "A Forty-One Year Record," private collection.
30. Gladys Hall Coates, interview with Sarah Wilkerson-Freeman, February 19, 1986, Southern Oral History Program.
31. "WPA in Full Swing," *Popular Government*, vol. 3, no. 3 (December 1935).
32. J. L. Caldwell to H. G. Baity, July 21, 1936, Records of the Institute of Government.
33. Gladys Coates, notes for a memoir, private collection.
34. Ibid.
35. Ibid.
36. Albert Coates, *The Story of the Institute of Government*, p. 41.
37. Albert Coates, *The Beginning of Schools for Law Enforcing Officers in North Carolina* (privately published, 1983), p. 6.
38. Coates, *The Story of the Institute of Government*, p. 50.
39. T. N. Grice Jr. to Albert Coates, October 24, 1934, Records of the Institute of Government.
40. Gladys Coates, notes for a memoir, private collection.
41. Dillard Gardner to Albert Coates, undated, Records of the Institute of Government.
42. Jack Aulis, *75 Years of Service: A History of the North Carolina League of Municipalities* (Raleigh, NC: North Carolina League of Municipalities, 1983), p. 61.
43. Albert Coates, *What the University of North Carolina Meant to Me.*
44. Coates, *The Story of the Institute of Government*, p. 74
45. Coates, *The Story of the Institute of Government*, p. 75.
46. Coates, *What the University of North Carolina Meant to Me*, p. 82.
47. Dillard Gardner to Albert Coates, attachment to letter, September 14, 1961, Records of the Institute of Government.
48. Albert Coates to Gordon Gray, September 23, 1938, Albert Coates Papers.
49. Albert Coates, "Report to the Chancellor," c. 1962, Records of the Institute of Government, p. 79.
50. Frank Graham to Albert Coates, October 17, 1936, Records of the Institute of Government.
51. Albert Coates, "The Great Reversal," Records of the Institute of Government.
52. William B. Aycock, interview with Molly Matlock Parsons, August 31, 2004, Albert Coates Project, Southern Oral History Program.
53. Albert Coates, "Report to the Chancellor," Records of the Institute of Government, p. 87.
54. Coates, *The Story of the Institute of Government*, p. 107.

Chapter Nine

1. Gladys Coates, notes on a history of the Institute of Government, private collection.
2. Albert Coates, "The Story of the Institute of Government, the University of North Carolina, Chapel Hill," *Popular Government*, National University Extension Association Studies in University Extension Education, no. 2 (July 1, 1944). Coates prepared various accounts of the Institute's history. This was the first extensive telling of the Institute story.

3. Albert Coates, *What the University of North Carolina Meant to Me*, p. 79.

4. L. B. Rogerson to President Graham, June 2, 1940, Records of the Institute of Government.

5. Gladys Coates, interview with John Ehle, November 13, 1990, North Carolina Collection, Wilson Library, University of North Carolina at Chapel Hill.

6. Nochem S. Winnet to Albert Coates, September 9, 1938, Albert Coates Papers.

7. Robert E. Williams, "Bankhead Lauds Institute Work," November 30, 1939, *News & Observer.*

8. Gladys Coates, notes prepared for a history of the Institute of Government.

9. Coates, *What the University of North Carolina Meant to Me*, p. 87.

10. Gladys Coates, notes prepared for a history of the Institute of Government.

11. Elmer Oettinger, interview with Molly Matlock Parsons, March 19, 2004, Southern Oral History.

12. Albert Coates to Ray C. Galloway, December 4, 1937, Records of the Institute of Government.

13. Douglass Hunt,"In Memoriam," private collection.

14. Albert Coates, undated memorandum, Records of the Institute of Government.

15. Gladys Coates, notes prepared for a history of the Institute of Government.

16. L. B. Rogerson to Frank Porter Graham, June 2, 1940, Records of the Institute of Government.

17. Albert Coates, undated memorandum, Records of the Institute of Government.

18. Albert Coates, "Memorandum on Exchange of Communications between Fesler–Healy–President Graham," October 3, 1940, Records of the Institute of Government.

19. William Friday, interview with author, December 19, 2008.

20. William Carmichael to Governor Melville Broughton, October 9, 1941, Records of the Institute of Government.

21. Gladys Coates, notes prepared for a history of the Institute of Government.

22. J. Spencer Love to Albert Coates, December 19, 1941, Records of the Institute of Government.

23. Albert Coates, "Institute of Government Joins Forces with UNC," *Popular Government* (February 1942).

24. Albert Coates, *The Story of the Institute of Government*, p. 112.

25. Howard E. Covington Jr., *Favored By Fortune: George W. Watts and the Hills of Durham* (Chapel Hill: University of North Carolina Library, 2004), pp. 209–210.

26. Thomas Vickers, Thomas Scism, and Dixon Qualls, *Chapel Hill: An Illustrated History* (Chapel Hill, NC: Barclay Publishers, 1985).

27. Ibid.

28. Peyton Abbott to Albert Coates, undated, Albert Coates Papers.

29. Albert Coates to DeWitt Wallace, June 12, 1944, Albert Coates Papers.

30. Albert Coates, "The Story of the Institute of Government."

31. Ibid.

32. Louis R. Wilson to Albert Coates, April 19, 1944, Records of the Institute of Government.

33. W. T. Couch to Albert Coates, July 7, 1944, Records of the Institute of Government.

34. Coates, "The Story of the Institute of Government."

Chapter Ten

1. William S. Pritchard to Albert Coates, May 24, 1945, Records of the Institute of Government.

2. Louis Graves, "Jubilation on the Village Street," *Chapel Hill Weekly*, August 17, 1945.

3. Peyton Abbott, memorandum to Albert Coates, undated, Records of the Institute of Government.

4. N.C. Session Laws 1941, ch. 279, s. 21.

5. Warner Olivier, "The Ugly Duckling at Chapel Hill," *Saturday Evening Post*, February 24, 1945.

6. Albert Coates, "Report to the Chancellor," Records of the Institute of Government, p. 85.

7. Howard E. Covington Jr. and Marion A. Ellis, *Terry Sanford: Politics, Progress and Outrageous Ambition* (Durham, NC: Duke University Press, 1999), p. 84.

8. Wettach, ed., *A Century of Legal Education.*

9. Louis Graves, "The Population of Chapel Hill," *Chapel Hill Weekly*, November 23, 1945.

10. Covington and Ellis, *Terry Sanford*, p. 91.

11. "State Patrolmen to Attend Safety Training School Here," *The Daily Tar Heel*, September 24, 1946.

12. Albert Coates, *The Beginning of Schools for Law Enforcing Officers in North Carolina* (Chapel Hill: University of North Carolina Professor Emeritus Fund, 1983), p. 48.

13. *Popular Government* (November 1946). The failure rate was something that was to concern Coates as time went on.

14. Roddey M. Ligon Jr., interview with Molly Matlock Parsons, May 27, 2004, Southern Oral History Program.

15. Coates, *The Story of the Institute of Government*, p. 152.

16. Ibid.

17. Paul W. Wager, "A North Carolina Experiment," *National Municipal Review*, vol. XXXIII, no. 2 (February 1944).

18. Donald Hayman, interview with Montgomery Wolf, March 3, 2004, Southern Oral History Program.

19. Ibid.

20. Ibid.

21. Albert Coates, "Report to the Chancellor," Records of the Institute of Government.

22. H. H. Baxter and Sid McAden to Albert Coates, December 12, 1946, Records of the Institute of Government.

23. Henry Lewis, interview with Molly Parsons, January 19, 2004, Southern Oral History Program.

24. Coates, *The Story of the Institute of Government*, p. 198.

25. J. Alexander McMahon, interview with Montgomery Wolf, March 17, 2004, Southern Historical Program.

26. George Esser, interview with Montgomery Wolf, April 2, 2004, Southern Historical Program.

27. H. H. Baxter to Albert Coates, February 24, 1948, and J. E. Dowd to Albert Coates, November 27, 1948, Records of the Institute of Government.

28. Joint Resolution, City of Charlotte and Mecklenburg County, March 16, 1949, Records of the Institute of Government.

29. Albert Coates, "The Great Reversal," William McWhorter Cochrane Papers.

30. "City-County Consolidation," *Charlotte News*, November 3, 1949.

31. George Esser to Albert Coates, 1948, Records of the Institute of Government.

32. Coates, *The Story of the Institute of Government*, p. 200.

33. William Aycock, interview with Molly Matlock Parsons, August 31, 2004, Southern Oral History Program.

34. Coates, *The Story of the Institute of Government*, p. 153.

35. J. Spencer Love, Governor W. Kerr Scott, joint statement, the Oliver Max Gardner Award presentation, March 22, 1952, Albert Coates Papers.

36. Albert Coates Personnel File.

37. Gladys Hall Coates, *The Albert Coates I Know*, North Caroliniana Society Imprints, no. 3 (1979).

38. Ibid.

39. Gladys Coates, notes for a memoir, private collection.

Chapter Eleven

1. Albert Coates to J. Spencer Love, October 18, 1952, Records of the Institute of Government.

2. Albert Coates and Gladys Hall Coates, *The Story of Student Government in the University of North Carolina at Chapel Hill*, privately published, 1985.

3. Albert Coates, *What the University of North Carolina Meant to Me*, p. 197.

4. Robert Stipe, interview with Molly Parsons, March 12, 2004, Southern Oral History Program.

5. Clyde Ball, memorandum to Albert Coates, February 19, 1962, Records of the Institute of Government.

6. Ernest Machen, interview with Montgomery Wolf, May 27, 2004, Southern Oral History Program.

7. Albert Coates to Staff Members, April 28, 1956, Records of the Institute of Government.

8. Basil Sherrill, interview with Montgomery Wolf, April 24, 2005, Southern Oral History Program.

9. Robert Stipe interview.

10. Ernest Machen interview.

11. Nancy Wykle, "Memorial celebration honors Albert Coates," *Daily Tar Heel*, March 30, 1989.

12. George Esser to Albert Coates, Special Studies Memorandum, 1948, Records of the Institute of Government.

13. Robert Stipe interview.

14. Roddey M. Ligon Jr., interview with Molly Matlock-Parsons, September 21, 2004, Southern Oral History Program.

15. John Sanders, interview with Montgomery Wolf, January 19, 2004, Southern Oral History Program.

16. Speech prepared for Frank Graham, Albert Coates Papers.

17. Henry Lewis to Albert Coates, October 22, 1954, Records of the Institute of Government.

18. Howard E. Covington Jr., *Once Upon A City*, p. 69.

19. Reed Surratt, *The Ordeal of Desegregation* (New York: Harper & Row, 1966), p. 4.

20. James C. N. Paul, interview with author, May 12, 2008.

21. Covington and Ellis, *Terry Sanford*, p. 136.

22. "Irving Carlyle's Leadership," *Greensboro Daily News*, May 22, 1954.

23. James C. N. Paul, interview with author, March 6, 2009.

24. William D. Carmichael to L. B. Rogerson, September 19, 1941, UNC Finance Office, University Archives, Manuscripts Department, University of North Carolina at Chapel Hill.

25. Albert Coates, debate booklet, Albert Coates Papers.

26. George Esser, interview with Montgomery Wolf, April 2, 2004, Southern Oral History Program.

27. Fannie Memory Mitchell, interview with Montgomery Wolf, June 23, 2005, Southern Oral History Program.

28. Albert Coates and James C. N. Paul, "A Report to the Governor of North Carolina on the Decision of the Supreme Court of the United States on the 17th of May, 1954," Records of the Institute of Government, p. i.

29. Coates and Paul, "A Report to the Governor of North Carolina," p. 43.

30. Coates and Paul, "A Report to the Governor of North Carolina," p. 168.

31. James C. N. Paul, interview with author, May 12, 2008.

32. Coates and Paul, "A Report to the Governor of North Carolina," p. iii.

33. James C. N. Paul, interview with author, March 6, 2009.

34. Gladys Coates, notes prepared for a history of the Institute of Government, Albert Coates Papers.

35. "A Southern Reconnaissance," *New York Times*, October 31, 1954.

36. Howard W. Odum to Governor William B. Umstead, August 30, 1954, Albert Coates Papers.

37. I. Beverly Lake to James C. N. Paul, November 1, 1954, Records of the Institute of Government.

38. *Brown v. Board of Education* (1954), transcript of oral arguments, U. S. Supreme Court Library, Washington, DC.

39. James C. N. Paul, interview with author, March 6, 2009.

40. Albert Coates, "Joseph Palmer Knapp in North Carolina," in "Dedication of the Joseph Palmer Knapp Building," Institute of Government, November 30, 1960, Records of the Institute of Government.

41. Albert Coates to Frank Graham, December 15, 1948, Records of the Institute of Government.

42. Albert Coates to Frank B. Aycock Jr., August 4, 1980, Albert Coates Papers.

43. Ibid.

44. W. Daniel to Gordon Gray, December 9, 1952, Vice President for Finance of the University of North Carolina, University Archives, Manuscripts Department, Wilson Library, University of North Carolina at Chapel Hill.

45. Albert Coates to Gordon Gray, December 13, 1952, President Gordon Gray Records, University Archives, Manuscripts Department, Wilson Library, University of North Carolina at Chapel Hill (hereafter cited as Gordon Gray Records).

46. John Sanders, interview with author, February 23, 2009.

47. Albert Coates to Gordon Gray, November 20, 1952, Gordon Gray Records.

48. Albert Coates, "Report to the Chancellor," Albert Coates Papers.

49. University of North Carolina School of Government, *Historical Murals*, http://www.sog.unc.edu/75/murals.htm (November 13, 2009).

50. William Carmichael to R. B. House, July 27, 1953, Vice President for Finance of the University of North Carolina System, University Archives, Manuscripts Department, Wilson Library, University of North Carolina at Chapel Hill.

51. Laurence G. Avery, ed., *A Southern Life: Letters of Paul Green 1916-1981* (Chapel Hill: University of North Carolina Press, 1994), p. 609.

52. Sanders interview with author, February 23, 2009.

53. Staff meeting minutes, Albert Coates Papers.

54. Albert Coates, memorandum to staff members, April 28, 1956, Records of the Institute of Government.

Chapter Twelve

1. "Informal Opening of Institute of Government," *Daily Tar Heel*, October 12, 1956.

2. Milton Heath Jr., interview with author, April 30, 2008.

3. Milton Health Jr. interview; "Dedication of the Joseph Palmer Knapp Building," Institute of Government, November 30, 1960, Records of the Institute of Government.

4. Remarks by Governor Luther H. Hodges, "Dedication of the Joseph Palmer Knapp Building".

5. Albert Coates to J. Edgar Hoover, September 4, 1947, William McWhorter Cochrane Papers.

6. Ibid.

7. Curt Gentry, *J. Edgar Hoover: The Man and the Secret* (New York: Plume Publishing, 1992), pp. 414–16.

8. Albert Coates, draft memorandum to J. Edgar Hoover, undated, Albert Coates Papers.

9. *Green v. Kitchin*, 229 N.C. 450, 50 S.E. (2d) 545.

10. H. H. Clegg to Mr. [Clyde] Tolson, March 31, 1952, Office Memorandum: United States Government, William McWhorter Cochrane Papers.

11. Joe Hennessee to Albert Coates, November 3, 1959, Albert Coates Papers.

12. Albert Coates, undated memorandum, Records of the Institute of Government.

13. George Esser to Albert Coates, October 29, 1959, Albert Coates Papers.

14. "When Ideas Become Institutions," *Greensboro Daily News*, February 24, 1959.

15. William B. Aycock to Albert Coates, December 16, 1959, Records of the Institute of Government.

16. Clyde Ball to Albert Coates, October 29, 1959, Records of the Institute of Government.

17. George Esser to Albert Coates, undated memorandum, Records of the Institute of Government.

18. J. Alexander McMahon, interview with author, May 7, 2008.

19. George Esser, interview with Fran Weaver, June–August 1990, Southern Oral History Program.

20. George Esser, interview with Montgomery Wolf, April 2, 2004, Southern Oral History Program.

21. Albert Coates, "The Great Reversal," unpublished manuscript, William McWhorter Cochrane Papers.

22. Albert Coates to Henry Brandis Jr., March 28, 1962, Records of the Institute of Government.

23. John L. Sanders to Albert Coates, October 15, 1959, Records of the Institute of Government.

24. Henry Brandis to Albert Coates, April 6, 1962, Records of the Institute of Government.

25. William Aycock, interview with Molly Matlock-Parsons, August 31, 2004, Southern Oral History Program.

26. William Aycock, interview with the author, January 9, 2008.

27. Ibid.

28. Aycock interview with Matlock-Parsons.

29. "Staff Tribute" and "Response," *Popular Government*, vol. 29, no. 1 (September 1962).

Chapter Thirteen

1. Albert Coates, "Report on the Beginning, Growth, Present Status and Future Needs of the Institute of Government," undated, Records of the Institute of Government.

2. "Coates Words and Music: How He Built the Institute," *Greensboro Daily News*, September 2, 1962.

3. Coates, *What the University of North Carolina Meant to Me*, p. 149.

4. Milton Heath Jr., interview with author, April 30, 2008.

5. Albert Coates, *What the University of North Carolina Meant to Me*, p. 154.

6. Gladys Coates, *Fifty Years with Albert Coates*.

7. Ibid.

8. Albert Coates, *What the University of North Carolina Meant to Me*, pp. 161–62.

9. Coates, *What the University of North Carolina Meant to Me*, p. 183.

10. "To Whom It May Concern: An Answering Letter from Albert Coates to Inquiring Friends," March 22, 1968, News Bureau, University of North Carolina at Chapel Hill.

11. Albert Coates, *The Story of the Institute of Government*, p. v.

12. Albert Coates, *By Her Own Bootstraps: A Saga of Women in North Carolina* (privately published, 1975), p vii.

13. Addendum, Exhibit A, Institute of Government History, Records of the Institute of Government.

14. William Friday, interview with author, May 30, 2008.

15. Donald Hayman, interview with author, May 2, 2008.

16. Albert Coates to Phillip Washburn, February 24, 1987, Albert Coates Papers, and Phillip Washburn, interview with author, April 20, 2009.

17. Douglass Hunt, "Script adapted from written and oral suggestions of Albert Coates, taking into account the several discussions he, Mrs. Coates and I have had about these proposed arrangements," February 5, 1989, Gladys Coates private collection.

18. "In Memoriam," Albert Coates Papers.

19. Nancy Winkle, "Memorial Celebration Honors Albert Coates," *Daily Tar Heel*, March 30, 1989.

20. Mark Schultz, "Albert Coates Remembered at UNC Memorial Service," *Chapel Hill Herald*, March 30, 1989.

21. Michael R. Smith, interview with author, March 16, 2009.

Bibliography

ARCHIVES AND MANUSCRIPT COLLECTIONS

Cambridge, Massachusetts

Harvard University, Harvard Law School Library Special Collections
- Roscoe Pound Papers

Chapel Hill, North Carolina

North Carolina Collection, Louis Round Wilson Library, University of North Carolina at Chapel Hill
- Thomas Wolfe Letters

Southern Historical Collection, Louis Round Wilson Library, University of North Carolina at Chapel Hill
- E. C. Branson Papers
- Albert Coates Papers
- William McWhorter Cochrane Papers
- John Ehle Papers
- George H. Esser Papers
- William C. Friday Papers
- Frank Porter Graham Papers
- Henry W. Lewis Papers
- Joseph L. Morrison Papers
- Elmer R. Oettinger Jr. Papers
- John L. Sanders Papers
- Susie Sharp Papers
- Richard Walser Papers
- Capus M. Waynick Papers
- Henry Horace Williams Papers
- Louis Round Wilson Papers

University Archives and Records Management Services

Office of the President of the University of North Carolina System: Frank Porter Graham Records, 1932–1949

Office of the President of the University of North Carolina System: Gordon Gray Records, 1950–1955

Office of the President of the University of North Carolina System: William Clyde Friday Records, 1957–1986

Chancellors Office Record Group, William B. Aycock Records

Records of the Institute of Government

Raleigh, North Carolina

North Carolina Division of Archives and History
- Official Papers of Governor O. Max Gardner
- Official Papers of Governor Clyde Hoey
- Official Papers of Governor Melville Broughton
- Official Papers of Governor William B. Umstead
- David S. Coltrane Papers
- Gertrude Weil Papers

Smithfield, North Carolina

Johnston County Heritage Center

INTERVIEWS BY AUTHOR

William B. Aycock
Jack Elam
William C. Friday
Donald Hayman
Milton Heath
J. Alexander McMahon
James C. N. Paul
John L. Sanders
Michael Smith
M. S. Van Hecke
Phillip Washburn

OTHER INTERVIEWS

Southern Oral History Program Collection, Southern Historical Collection, Louis Round Wilson Library, University of North Carolina at Chapel Hill
- Gladys Hall Coates, interviewed February 19, 1986, by Sarah Wilkerson-Freeman (L–29)
- George Esser, interviewed June–August 1990 by Fran Weaver (L–35)
- Albert Coates Project (L–8) (Interviews conducted by Montgomery Wolf and Molly Matlock Parsons)
  - Zebulon D. Alley (L–229)
  - William B. Aycock (L–230)

M. Alexander Biggs (L–231)
Robert G. Byrd (L–232)
B. J. Campbell (L–233)
Jack Elam (L–234)
George H. Esser (L–235)
William C. Friday (L–236)
Roy G. Hall (L–237)
Donald Hayman (L–238)
Charles Knox (L–239)
Henry Lewis (L–240)
Roddey M. Ligon Jr. (L–241)
Ernest W. Machen Jr. (L–242)
J. Alexander McMahon (L–243)
Fannie Memory Mitchell (L–244)
Richard A. Myren (L–245)
Elmer Oettinger (L–46)
Mary Oliver (L–246)
J. Dickson Phillips
John L. Sanders (L–247)
John Scarlett (L–248)
Basil L. Sherrill (L–249)
Robert Stipe
John Webb (L–250)

NEWSPAPERS AND OTHER PERIODICALS

Alumni Review (UNC)
Chapel Hill Herald
Chapel Hill Weekly
Charlotte Observer
Greensboro Daily News
News & Observer
Popular Government
Reader's Digest
Saturday Evening Post
Smithfield Herald
Social Forces
South Atlantic Quarterly
State Magazine: Down Home in North Carolina
Tar Heel, Daily Tar Heel
University News Letter
University of North Carolina Magazine
Winston-Salem Journal
Yackety Yack

BOOKS AND ARTICLES

Adams, Agatha Boyd, ed. *Paul Green of Chapel Hill.* Chapel Hill: University of North Carolina Press, 1951.

———. *Thomas Wolfe, Carolina Student: A Brief Biography.* Chapel Hill: University of North Carolina Library, 1950.

Aulis, Jack. *75 Years of Service: A History of the North Carolina League of Municipalities.* Raleigh: North Carolina League of Municipalities, 1983.

Avery, Laurence G., ed. *A Southern Life: Letters of Paul Green, 1916–1981.* Chapel Hill: University of North Carolina Press, 1994.

Bailyn, Bernard. *Glimpses of the Harvard Past.* Cambridge, MA: Harvard University Press, 1986.

Battle, Kemp Plummer. *Memories of an Old-Time Tar Heel.* Chapel Hill: University of North Carolina Press, 1945.

Bethell, John T., Richard M. Hunt, and Robert Shenton. *Harvard A to Z.* Cambridge, MA: Harvard University Press, 2004.

Coates, Albert. *The Beginning of Schools for Law Enforcing Officers in North Carolina.* Chapel Hill: University of North Carolina Professor Emeritus Fund, 1983.

———. *Bridging the Gap Between Government in Books and Government in Action.* Rev. ed. Chapel Hill: University of North Carolina Professor Emeritus Fund, 1976.

———. *By Her Own Bootstraps: A Saga of Women in North Carolina.* Privately published, 1975.

———. *Citizens in Action: Women's Clubs, Civic Clubs, Community Chests: Flying Buttresses to Governmental Units.* 1976. Held in the North Carolina Collection, Louis Round Wilson Library, University of North Carolina at Chapel Hill.

———. "The Codification of Criminal Procedure in North Carolina." *North Carolina Law Review* 9, no. 1 (1930).

———. Commencement Address, June 3, 1968. Chapel Hill: School of Law, University of North Carolina, 1968.

———. *Crime and Punishment.* Raleigh, NC: Edwards & Broughton, 1931.

———. "Crime Is Local." *North Carolina Law Review* 14, no. 4 (1936).

———. *Edward Kidder Graham, Harry Woodburn Chase, Frank Porter Graham: Three Men in the Transition of the University of North Carolina at Chapel Hill From a Small College to a Great University.* Privately published, 1988.

———. "Guide to Victory, Prepared for the North Carolina Office of Civilian Defense." *Popular Government* 9, no. 1–4 (1943).

———. *A History of the North Carolina State Highway Patrol As I Have Known It.* Chapel Hill: University of North Carolina Professor Emeritus Fund, 1983.

———. "In the Supreme Court of the Ames Competition: Emil Borah v. Nathaniel P. Banks Et Al; Brief for the Plaintiff-in-Error." Held in the North Carolina Collection, Louis Round Wilson Library, University of North Carolina at Chapel Hill.

———. *My Brother, Kenneth, 1904–1974.* Privately published, 1975.

———. "The Phi Beta Kappa Society in the University of North Carolina at Chapel Hill: A Talk by Albert Coates on its 75th Anniversary, December 6, 1979." Held in the North Carolina Collection, Louis Round Wilson Library, University of North Carolina at Chapel Hill.

———. *Preliminary Draft of a Plan for County, District and Statewide Schools of Law Enforcing Officers for the Continuous Study of the Problems of Crime and Criminal Law Administration*

in the Cities, the Counties and the State of North Carolina. Held in the North Carolina Collection, Louis Round Wilson Library, University of North Carolina at Chapel Hill.
———. *The Story of the Institute of Government.* Privately published, 1981.
———. "The Story of the Institute of Government, the University of North Carolina, Chapel Hill." The National University Extension Association. *Studies in University Extension Education*, no. 2 (July 1, 1944).
———. "The Story of the Law School at the University of North Carolina." *North Carolina Law Review* (1947), 109.
———. "The Task of Legal Education in the South." *American Bar Association Journal* 16, no. 7 (1930): 464–67.
———. "The Task of Popular Government." *The University of North Carolina News Letter,* vol. 18 (1932).
———. *The University of North Carolina at Chapel Hill: A Magic Gulf Stream in the Life of North Carolina.* Privately published, 1978.
———. "What Harvard Has Meant to Me." *Harvard Alumni Bulletin*, February 17, 1962, 380–83.
———. *What the University of North Carolina Meant to Me.* Privately published, 1968. Held in the North Carolina Collection, Louis Round Wilson Library, University of North Carolina at Chapel Hill .
———. *What the University of North Carolina Meant to Me: A Report to the Chancellors and Presidents and to the People With Whom I Have Lived and Worked From 1914 to 1969.* Richmond, VA: William Byrd Press, 1969.
———. *What the University of North Carolina Meant to Me From 1914 to 1918.* Privately published, 1968. Held in the North Carolina Collection, Louis Round Wilson Library, University of North Carolina at Chapel Hill.
———. "William Brantley Aycock. Chancellor of the University of North Carolina at Chapel Hill." *Popular Government* 25, no. 2S (1957): 18–21.
Coates, Albert, and Gladys Hall Coates. *The Story of Student Government in the University of North Carolina at Chapel Hill.* Chapel Hill: University of North Carolina Professor Emeritus Fund, 1985.
Coates, Gladys Hall. *The Albert Coates I Know.* North Caroliniana Society Imprints, no. 3. Chapel Hill: North Caroliniana Society, 1979.
Corbett, David Leroy, ed. *Public Papers and Letters of Governor Angus Wilton McLean of North Carolina 1925–1929.* Raleigh, NC: Council of State, 1931.
———, ed. *Public Papers and Letters of Governor O. Max Gardner.* Raleigh, NC: Council of State, 1937.
Covington, Howard E., Jr. *Once Upon A City: Greensboro North Carolina's Second Century*, Greensboro, NC: Greensboro Historical Museum, 2008.
Covington, Howard E., Jr., and Marion A. Ellis. *Terry Sanford: Politics, Progress, and Outrageous Ambitions.* Durham, NC: Duke University Press, 1999.
Donald, David Herbert. *Look Homeward: A Life of Thomas Wolfe.* New York: Ballantine Books, 1987.
Ehle, John. *Dr. Frank: Life with Frank Porter Graham.* Chapel Hill, NC: Franklin Street Books, 1993.
Griswold, Erwin N. *Ould Fields, New Corne: The Personal Memoirs of a Twentieth-Century Lawyer.* New York: West Publishing Co., 1982.

Henderson, Archibald. *The Campus of the First State University*. Chapel Hill: University of North Carolina Press, 1949.
Holman, C. Hugh, and Sue Fields Ross. *The Letters of Thomas Wolfe to His Mother*. Chapel Hill: University of North Carolina Press, 1968.
House, Robert B. *The Light That Shines*. Chapel Hill: University of North Carolina Press, 1964.
Johnson, Guy Benton, and Guion Griffis Johnson. *Research in Service to Society: The First Fifty Years of the Institute for Research in Social Science at the University of North Carolina*. Chapel Hill: University of North Carolina Press, 1980.
Little, M. Ruth. *The Town and Gown Architecture of Chapel Hill, North Carolina*. Chapel Hill, NC: Preservation Society of Chapel Hill, 2006.
Love, Cornelia Spencer. *When Chapel Hill Was a Village*. Chapel Hill, NC: Chapel Hill Historical Society, 1976.
McEvoy, Joseph Patrick. "Don't Shoot Your Sheriff: Teach Him!" *Reader's Digest*, October 1943, 21–25.
Morrison, Joseph L. *Governor O. Max Gardner: A Power in North Carolina and New Deal Washington*. Chapel Hill: University of North Carolina Press, 1971.
Olivier, Warner. "The Ugly Duckling at Chapel Hill." *The Saturday Evening Post*, February 24, 1945, 14–15, 72, 74.
Sanders, John L. "The Institute of Government at Fifty." *Popular Government* 46, no. 3 (1981).
Sanders, John L. "The Institute of Government in the University of North Carolina," *Popular Government* 59, no. 2 (1993).
Snider, William D. *Light on the Hill: A History of the University of North Carolina at Chapel Hill*. Chapel Hill: University of North Carolina Press, 1992.
Surratt, Reed. *The Ordeal of Desegregation*. New York: Harper & Row, 1966.
Sutherland, Arthur E. *The Law at Harvard: A History of Ideas and Men*. Cambridge, MA: Belknap Press of Harvard University Press, 1967.
Vickers, James. *Chapel Hill: An Illustrated History*. Chapel Hill, NC: Barclay Publishers, 1985.
Wager, Paul. *County Government in North Carolina*. Chapel Hill: University of North Carolina Press, 1928.
Walser, Richard G. *Thomas Wolfe Undergraduate*. Durham, NC: Duke University Press, 1977.
Wettach, Robert H., ed. *A Century of Legal Education*. Chapel Hill: University of North Carolina Press, 1947.
Wilson, Louis Round. *The University of North Carolina 1900–1930: The Making of a Modern University*. Chapel Hill: University of North Carolina Press, 1957.
———. *Louis Round Wilson's Historical Sketches*. Durham, NC: Moore Publishing Co., 1976.
Winston, Robert Watson. *Horace Williams: Gadfly of Chapel Hill*. Chapel Hill: University of North Carolina Press, 1942.

Acknowledgments

IT IS ALWAYS APPROPRIATE to recognize the founder of the feast and for that we must raise a toast to Gladys Hall Coates. Without her generous gift to the university, we would not have this book about her dear husband, Albert. Gladys and Albert were a complete and total package. Gladys's steadfast love and support carried Albert forward as she set aside her own comforts and desires in aid of his cause. She shared his vision, and believed so completely in him and his work, that, in the end, perhaps, it was not so much a sacrifice as a calling.

I learned of the great strength of their relationship through the letters that Ann Simpson of the School of Government rescued from the Coates home on Hooper Lane after both were gone. Thank goodness Ann recognized what she had and preserved personal memorabilia that made all the difference in the telling of this story. I found Albert's words aplenty in the books, correspondence, and newspaper clippings that accumulated over the years in the files that Albert left behind. But it was these forgotten boxes of letters, packets of photographs tied with faded ribbon, and materials glued in a family scrapbook moldy with age that brought Albert alive and became the complement to all the words that he put on paper.

Indeed, Albert's published works fill a library shelf. That is why I am grateful to Jason Tomberlin of the North Carolina Collection, who saved me hours of labor by chasing down all manner of publications that carry the Coates byline. Jason organized those works into a comprehensive bibliography that will be useful to scholars and researchers for years to come. He also helped find within the North Carolina Collection other essential materials that helped flesh out this story.

Among the important building blocks for *The Good Government Man* were the interviews of Coates's former colleagues at the Institute of Government that were conducted in 2004 and 2005 by Molly Parsons and Montgomery Wolf. Some of those interviewed had died by the time my work began early in 2008. Without the efforts of Molly and Montgomery, whom I never met, the accounts of men and women who knew Albert better than most would have been lost forever. The collection of these interviews was organized by Robert Anthony, curator of the North Carolina Collection, who has been a faithful shepherd of this entire project from those early days to the last signature required for publication.

Bob Anthony was available to help throughout the research and writing of this book. I am grateful for his support and the careful reading of the manuscript by him and his committee, the men and women who are carrying forward Gladys's desire for the publication of biographies of the university's presidents. Working with Anthony on this committee were Michael Hill of the state's Office of Archives and History; Janis Holder, university archivist emeritus; H.G. Jones, curator emeritus of the North Carolina Collection; and John L. Sanders, director emeritus of the Institute of Government. I am especially thankful to John Sanders for the unique perspective and wise counsel that comes from more than fifty years of extraordinary service to the Institute, the university, and the state. His careful reading of the manuscript, not once but several times, contributed to the accuracy of the finished book.

The photographic record that accompanies the text is the result of the determined efforts of Stephen Fletcher, the photographic archivist of the North Carolina Collection. Stephen successfully retrieved a generation of images of Coates and the campus of the university, along with pictures of those who orbited about both man and place.

I also acknowledge Albert Coates himself for a personal gift. The opportunity to research and write his story has given me a greater appreciation of University of North Carolina President Edward Kidder Graham and the men he inspired nearly a century ago to expand the university in service to the people of the state. Coates took Graham's words as gospel and was relentless in fulfilling the mission Graham laid out for him, usually against the longest of odds. But what adversity could ever prevail against a man whose credo was: “Oh, Lordy. It's a great life if you don't weaken, and not so bad if you do”?

Index